T0305607

Auditor Essentials

Internal Audit and IT Audit

Series Editor:

Dan Swanson

Dan Swanson and Associates, Ltd., Winnipeg, Manitoba, Canada

The *Internal Audit and IT Audit* series publishes leading-edge books on critical subjects facing audit executives as well as internal and IT audit practitioners. Key topics include Audit Leadership, Cybersecurity, Strategic Risk Management, Auditing Various IT Activities and Processes, Audit Management, and Operational Auditing.

Cognitive Hack: The New Battleground in Cybersecurity... the Human Mind
James Bone

Implementing Cybersecurity: A Guide to the National Institute of Standards and Technology Risk Management Framework
Anne Kohnke, Ken Sigler, and Dan Shoemaker

The CISO Journey: Life Lessons and Concepts to Accelerate Your Professional Development
Eugene M. Fredriksen

Data Analytics for Internal Auditors
Richard E. Cascarino

Practitioner's Guide to Business Impact Analysis
Priti Sikdar

Why CISOs Fail: The Missing Link in Security Management--and How to Fix It
Barak Engel

Supply Chain Risk Management: Applying Secure Acquisition Principles to Ensure a Trusted Technology Product
Ken Sigler, Dan Shoemaker, and Anne Kohnke

Project Management Capability Assessment: Performing ISO 33000-Based Capability Assessments of Project Management
Peter T. Davis and Barry D. Lewis

Operational Auditing: Principles and Techniques for a Changing World
Hernan Murdock

For more information about this series, please visit https://www.crcpress.com/Internal-Audit-and-IT-Audit/book-series/CRCINTAUDITA

Auditor Essentials
100 Concepts, Tools, and Techniques for Success

Dr. Hernan Murdock, CIA, CRMA

CRC Press
Taylor & Francis Group
Boca Raton London New York

CRC Press is an imprint of the
Taylor & Francis Group, an **informa** business

AN AUERBACH BOOK

CRC Press
Taylor & Francis Group
6000 Broken Sound Parkway NW, Suite 300
Boca Raton, FL 33487-2742

© 2019 by Taylor & Francis Group, LLC
CRC Press is an imprint of Taylor & Francis Group, an Informa business

No claim to original U.S. Government works

Printed on acid-free paper

International Standard Book Number-13: 978-1-138-03691-8 (Hardback)

**Visit the Taylor & Francis Web site at
http://www.taylorandfrancis.com**

**and the CRC Press Web site at
http://www.crcpress.com**

Contents

Author

Dr. Hernan Murdock, CIA, CRMA is vice president, audit division for MIS Training Institute. He has held positions as director of training for an international audit and consulting firm, and various audit positions while leading and performing audit and consulting projects for clients in the manufacturing, transportation, high tech, education, insurance, and power generation industries.

Dr. Murdock is a senior lecturer at Northeastern University where he teaches management, leadership, and ethics. He earned a DBA from Argosy University, Sarasota, Florida in 2007; a CSS from Harvard University, Cambridge, Massachusetts in 1996; and an MBA and BSBA from Suffolk University, Boston, Massachusetts in 1992 and 1990, respectively. He also holds the following certifications: CRMA Certification in Risk Management Assurance (IIA), 2013; QAR Accreditation in Internal Quality Assessment/Validation (IIA), 2008; AchieveGlobal Leadership and Customer Service: Deliver and Develop Levels, 2007; IDC Certified Instructor (IIA), 2006; and CIA Certified Internal Auditor (IIA), 2001. He is the author of *Operational Auditing: Principles and Techniques for a Changing World* (CRC Press, 2017), *10 Key Techniques to Improve Team Productivity* (The IIA Research Foundation, 2011), and *Using Surveys in Internal Audits* (The IIA Research Foundation, 2009). He has also written articles and book chapters on whistleblowing programs, international auditing, mentoring programs, fraud, deception, corporate social responsibility, and behavioral profiling.

Dr. Murdock has conducted audits and consulting projects, delivered seminars and invited talks, and made numerous presentations at internal audit, academic, and government functions in North America, Latin America, Europe, and Africa.

Dr. Murdock can be reached at Hernan.Murdock@gmail.com.

Introduction

As business processes become more complex, information more widely dispersed, and the risk environment more complicated, the need for internal auditors to adapt to this new environment becomes imperative. The internal auditing profession has undergone many changes over the past few decades. Consistent efforts have been exerted to rebrand the profession and change its image from the corporate cop to one of a trusted advisor that adds value to its clients in noticeable ways. This requires a change in mindset, focus, and approach. The work of internal auditors has evolved from transaction and regulations-based into a risk-based activity.

To be effective in this new and evolving environment, internal auditors must have familiarity, if not expertise, in a wide range of topics. They must develop technical and soft-skills, learn and know how to use various tools, and be able to apply all of this in their assurance and consulting engagements. But what are those skills, tools, and techniques? How should they be used and when? This guide answers those questions.

Auditor Essentials organizes an extensive list of topics alphabetically for easy reference. It provides key information in simple, practical, and realistic terms that new and current internal auditors can understand readily and apply immediately. Over the past 20 years working as an internal audit practitioner and instructor I've found myself either learning, using, or teaching about these topics. The list includes items that have been part of internal auditing for decades and that experienced auditors have mastered. New auditors should too. The list also includes new and emerging topics that internal auditors are grappling with as they find better ways to serve their clients in these rapidly changing times.

To improve the profession's image and be perceived as valuable to their organizations, internal auditors need to think beyond the technical requirements, typical checklists, and audit report templates used during their engagements; they must also think about the client's experience. How we interact with them is as important as what we audit. This guide provides insights on ways that I and many others have learned to interact with audit clients to ease the anxiety of being audited, build a

1

collaborative relationship, and leverage our independence and objectivity so we help them achieve their objectives.

Internal auditing is also an art. Many auditors believe, or at least behave, as if all that matters are numbers and documents. While the technical elements represent an indispensable aspect of the review process, creativity, visualization, style, and tone also matter. Since the art of internal auditing is so important, in this book I provide tips and techniques to enable that balanced approach.

The increasing demands on internal auditors make it imperative for them to have high levels of education and pursue relevant certifications. Having a diversity of skills makes it possible to effectively examine the programs and processes the organization depends on. Achieving certifications also demonstrates a commitment to the profession that facilitates career advancement. But internal auditors must go further and develop an ability to understand the context of their education and certifications as much as the content. This means balancing the theoretical with the practical, and making the confusing, simple.

Internal auditors must also know how to be persuasive. They must be able to articulate the value of each engagement, put risks and controls in the proper context, write memos and reports effectively and clearly, make productive presentations, and lead results-driven meetings. Every engagement should be conducted with a goal of supporting the achievement of business objectives.

Internal auditing is more than finding and listing problems. To be effective, internal auditors must also understand the factors causing the problems identified, and be sufficiently creative to brainstorm possible solutions, filter those alternatives, and select the most feasible option based on available resources and priorities. Best practices are not necessarily the best option for every organization. More facts, figures, and data may only confuse matters if they are not subject to critical thinking, business acumen, and an understanding of what the audit client is experiencing and needs. So instead of just telling you what you as the auditor should do (because situations vary, and it would be a disservice to give cookie-cutter answers), I provide suggestions throughout the book to make sure that you can think through your particular scenario, and understand the client's perspective before you proceed.

I worked in industry for 8 years before transitioning to internal audit, and over the years I've interacted with businesspeople in multiple industries around the world. This perspective is also reflected in the topics chosen, the information provided about them, and the summary following each entry. By combining multiple skills and tools covered in this book you will be better prepared to address diverse situations effectively.

Internal auditing has changed significantly over the past three decades and will continue to change in the future. Auditors must be agile, simultaneously looking into the past to understand what happened, looking deep into the present using data analytics and other tools to understand events as close to real time as possible, and looking into the future using trend analysis, extrapolation, correlation, and a keen awareness of emerging risks to tell management about forward-looking expectations. After all, how useful is it to tell management about problems that occurred months ago? Pointing things out long after they occurred is becoming less useful than ever before.

The internal auditor of the future is going to be deeply involved in the process of counseling, examining, and recommending to the board and management how to address significant strategic risks and initiatives, reduce costs, enhance operational excellence, strengthen the organizational culture, build an engaged workforce, address IT and cybersecurity concerns, protect data and physical facilities, and leverage the power of automation and artificial intelligence. The rate and speed of change is increasing, and internal auditors cannot shy away from it. Internal auditors must embrace change, promote its effective implementation, act with a sense of purpose and urgency, and help the organization do the same.

The list of essentials topics contained in this book will give you a solid footing as you face the winds of change swirling around us. I invite you to gain familiarity, and build your expertise, on as many of these topics as you can. My 20-year internal audit journey has exposed me to these topics and I'm constantly learning new ways to adopt them and enhance their applicability. Knowing and using them have made my journey a very exciting and productive one. I wish you an enjoyable, productive, and successful journey as well!

Chapter 1

Anonymous Polling/Voting

Internal auditors are increasingly performing reviews of qualitative subjects that require the collection of opinions and preferences. These include audits that enquire about the credibility of the organization's whistleblowing program, the ethical practices of the management team, the credibility of the leadership team, and the transparency of hiring practices, among others. These reviews often require the collection of qualitative data, organization of that information for analysis, and concluding on the implications for the organizational future. One very powerful tool is anonymous polling/voting. By collecting information from many individuals, internal auditors can get insights about the workforce's opinions and by transforming this into objective information, get critical insights about these very difficult topics.

Anonymous polling tools are often a combination of software and hardware. The software works like a surveying application, allowing participants to register their responses to questions, and rate or categorize the items presented. The hardware was traditionally handheld devices resembling remote controllers for TV or cable boxes, but recent technology now allows participants to use their smartphones, laptops, desktops, and tablets through Internet connections.

There are many benefits to this technology. For example, when collecting sensitive information, participants may prefer their answers be kept confidential. When collecting information during focus group meetings and other facilitated sessions, it can make the session more interactive. This enables the session leaders to collect and analyze the information real time and ask follow-up questions immediately.

Internal auditors can use anonymous polling during:

Risk Assessments: Use this tool to streamline a list of risks after brainstorming sessions, rating risks based on likelihood, impact, velocity and persistence, rating corrective actions (e.g., controls) in terms of their suitability, effectiveness; rate residual risk and whether that residual risk is considered acceptable.

Strategic Planning: Select from competing initiatives after brainstorming sessions, rating initiatives based on their impact, effort, and feasibility.

Surveys: Collect and evaluate participants' responses.

Testing: Training and development programs, orientation sessions, and onboarding events lend themselves for this tool since organizations may want to assess memory, comprehension, and understanding of concepts taught.

Summary

1. Anonymous polling/voting provides a versatile mechanism to collect information from participants while making the event more interactive.

2. Anonymous polling/voting can be used for a variety of internal audit projects, such as surveys, risk assessments, strategic planning, training and development programs, and auditing sensitive topics such as ethics, sexual harassment, safety in the workplace, management behavior, and the corporate culture.

3. Anonymous polling provides the option for real-time participant response, so internal auditors can adjust their presentation based on the needs of the audience.

Chapter 2

Association of Certified Fraud Examiners (ACFE)

The Association of Certified Fraud Examiners (ACFE) is the world's largest anti-fraud organization and a key provider of anti-fraud training and education. Its activities focus on reducing business fraud and inspiring public confidence in their institutions. It has created a wide base of common knowledge in the field of fraud examination and its mission is to reduce the incidence of fraud and white-collar crime, while assisting in the detection and deterrence of fraud. They do this by:

- Providing, administering, and promoting the Certified Fraud Examiner (CFE) examination and certification.
- Providing membership services to individuals in all job functions and industries, as well as students and educators.
- Publishing *Fraud Magazine* and *The Fraud Examiner* newsletter.
- Setting standards for admission and continuing education through mandatory continuing professional development.
- Mandating that CFEs adhere to a code of professional conduct and ethics.
- Advocating for the enhancement of the recognition of CFEs to business, government and academic institutions.

The CFE credential focuses on fraud deterrence, prevention, and detection. Recipients of the certification are trained to identify the red flags that indicate fraud risks or evidence of fraud. The goal is to protect institutions of all types, sizes, and industries by helping management implement processes to prevent fraud from occurring and uncovering it if it is occurring. This knowledge balances an understanding of methods, financial transactions and schemes, legal considerations, and investigative procedures. CFEs are expected to have the ability to:

■ Understand how fraud is committed and how it can be detected
■ Examine records and documents to trace and detect anomalies
■ Apply interviewing techniques to witnesses and suspects to obtain information and confessions
■ Analyze data, transactions, and financial statements
■ Write investigation reports, and provide advice and litigation support
■ Testify in court
■ Understand what motivates individuals to commit fraud
■ Locate and recover hidden assets
■ Conduct background checks
■ Reconstruct accounting records

Some of the industries with the highest concentration of CFEs are

■ Public accounting
■ Banking and other financial services institutions
■ Insurance companies, agents, and related services
■ Federal/national and state/provincial governments

Becoming a CFE

To become a CFE, applicants must be members of the ACFE, meet minimum academic and professional requirements, be of high moral character, and abide by the bylaws and Code of Professional Ethics of the ACFE. Academic requirements include a bachelor's degree, its equivalent or 2 years of fraud-related professional experience for each year of academic study. There is no specific field of study requirement for academic study. At the time of certification, applicants must have at least 2 years of professional experience in a field related to the detection or deterrence of fraud, such as Accounting, Auditing, Criminology, Sociology, Fraud Investigation, Loss Prevention, and Law.

Applicants must also pass the CFE Exam, which is computer-based and has four sections. This exam can be taken at any time and the questions are generated from a master database, so no two exams are alike. The total exam time is approximately eight hours and tests the applicants' knowledge of the four major areas of the body of knowledge:

1. Fraud Prevention and Deterrence
2. Financial Transactions and Fraud Schemes
3. Investigation
4. Law

Each section may be taken separately, but all four must be taken within 30 days. Results are available within 3–5 days due to review and processing.

The Report to the Nations on Occupational Fraud and Corruption (RTTN)

One of the most troublesome problems facing economies around the world is the blight of fraud and corruption. The ACFE is one of the most authoritative organization providing thought leadership, training, and certification for professionals dedicated to combating this problem. Every 2 years, the ACFE surveys its membership around the world and asks them if their organizations have been the victim of fraud during the previous 2 years. If so, it asks participants to share questions like the following:

■ The type of fraud that was committed, such as fraudulent financial reporting, misappropriation of assets, fraudulently obtaining revenues, and assets from employees or third parties
■ Demographics about the perpetrator, such as gender and role in the organization
■ How it was discovered
■ How long the fraud was carried out before it was detected
■ How much it cost the organization financially
■ In what part of the world the fraud occurred

The results, analysis, and summary are shared in the Report to the Nations on Occupational Fraud and Corruption. Some of the findings from recent reports include:

■ Fraud is estimated at between 5 and 7 percent of revenues.
■ Median loss is $130,000.
■ Affects all types of organizations: For-profit/non-profit, large/small, domestic/international.
■ More than one fifth of frauds involved losses of $1 million or more.
■ Median time to detection is 16 months.
■ High-level perpetrators (e.g., executives, owners) cause the greatest damage to organizations.
■ The main source of detection is whistleblowing/ethics hotlines at over 40 percent.[*]

---

[*] Additional information about the Association of Certified Fraud Examiners (ACFE) and their work, including the Certified Fraud Examiner (CFE) certification and the Report to the Nations on Occupational Fraud and Corruption (RTTN) is available at www.acfe.com.

These findings suggest there is more that can be done to reduce fraud and its corrosive effects on organizations. Internal auditors can play a key role keeping fraud at bay by helping management implement better programs to deter, prevent, detect, and investigate fraud.

Summary

1. The ACFE provides fraud-related information that all internal auditors should be familiarized with. This information can be applied during the creation of anti-fraud programs, during internal audit projects, and during fraud investigations.
2. The CFE certification is considered a valuable tool helping to enhance the credentials, marketability and personal brand of internal auditors.
3. The Report to the Nations on Fraud and Corruption is a bi-annual survey that provides valuable details about the prevalence of fraud, high-fraud countries and functions within organizations, and useful statistics. This information can be used to enhance the general knowledge of internal auditors, increase the quality of fraud risk assessments, and to raise awareness among non-auditors about the risk of fraud.

Chapter 3

Audit: Compliance

Compliance audits focus on verifying that the program or process being reviewed adheres with laws, regulations policies, procedures, contracts, and other applicable obligations, such as service level agreements (SLAs) and letters of understanding (LOU). These compliance requirements may be imposed internally (e.g., policies and procedures), externally (e.g., laws, regulations), or jointly (e.g., contracts).

Compliance audits have been a staple of internal auditing for decades and it is a constant element in the practice of internal auditing. Over the years, the emphasis on compliance has shown an ebb and flow; sometimes increasing, sometimes decreasing, as determined by political priorities, recent scandals, and economic events. After a major setback, such as an environmental, regulatory, or financial collapse, internal auditors have typically been expected to dedicate more time and effort into performing compliance reviews in an effort to promote adherence with established requirements and protect the interests of the stakeholders affected by the events.

Interestingly, when economic conditions improve, management and other stakeholders often pull back, encouraging or even demanding that internal auditors in particular, and all auditors in general, ease up on compliance reviews since these reviews are seen as unnecessary and a hindrance on business activities. This back-and-forth movement, sometimes also equated to the motion of a pendulum, makes compliance audits swing toward more compliance at times, and less compliance at others.

Unfortunately, as this lack of emphasis persists, the likelihood of a recurrence of breakdown increases, and when this happens, there is a reactionary response, swinging the pendulum in the direction of increased compliance again.

Examples

This dynamic is evident in the period before and after the dot.com, Enron, WorldCom, Tyco, Waste Management, and Adelphia years, when the Sarbanes–Oxley Act of 2002 and similar laws in Canada (C-SOX) and Japan (J-SOX) were enacted. During the 1990s, executive compensation and the number of earnings restatements increased significantly, as did the conflicts of interest between clients and their audit firms, whose efforts to become more client focused centered disproportionately on selling non-auditing services. The Sarbanes–Oxley Act of 2002 applies to companies whose stock trades in the US stock markets. Since many insurance companies are mutual firms and not publicly traded, but are exposed to substantial financial risk, they were required by their regulator, the National Association of Insurance Commissioners (NAIC), to comply with the self-imposed insurance industry Model Audit Rule (MAR). Similarly, the 2008 financial crisis caused primarily by loose lending practices and the bundling of collaterized debt obligations resulted in the passing of the Dodd–Frank Act in 2010.

Implications for Internal Auditors

Internal auditors have traditionally performed financial and compliance reviews and they protect the organization from malfeasance and other poor operational, financial, and compliance practices. Unfortunately, too many stakeholders consider compliance reviews a nuisance and obstructive to "real work getting done." Compliance reviews are essential to verify that the organization is meeting its performance expectations and failure to do so, can result in poor execution, fines, penalties, the loss of contracts, reputation fallout, and other negative financial and non-financial outcomes.

Internal auditors are well-positioned to assist the organization meet compliance requirements and avoid the negative consequences that noncompliance may cause. Furthermore, modern internal auditors recognize that it is not merely a matter of whether the organization meets its compliance requirements, but also *how* it does this. That's to say, organizations can comply by implementing burdensome, bureaucratic, paper and labor-intensive procedures to comply, or they can examine their practices to ensure compliance while acting with economy, efficiency, and speed in mind. Automation, less paperwork, clear expectations, effective training, and error-proofing are key to ensuring compliance at a lower cost.

Fines and Penalties

There is often the fear of fines and penalties for noncompliance. These can range from relatively minor sanctions and reprimands, to the loss of contracts, licenses, cease-and-desist orders, and large financial penalties. It is important to note that organizations shouldn't comply only to avoid fines and penalties, they should follow prevailing laws and regulations because it is the right thing to do. A common ethical debate for many is whether multinational corporations should follow local law (i.e., the laws of their host countries) or the laws of their home country. In general, organizations should follow both.

Another important question is "should we do compliance audits when nothing is found?" While this is an important question, the mere act of auditing a program or process is valuable in and of itself, because it will remind employees, contractors, and others that compliance is always expected. So, asking "how many errors or frauds did you find?" to undermine the contribution of compliance professionals is misplaced. The thought process ought to be "how many errors or frauds did we prevent by performing a compliance review?"

Notorious Cases to Date

There are many compliance requirements, but in general, the enforcement of laws and regulations varies by industry, location, and regulatory interest at a point in time. However, organizations ignore compliance requirements at their own peril. For example, in the payment card industry (PCI), there are many regulations designed to protect the use and storage of the cardholder data used to process transactions. PCI affects millions of businesses, banks, web hosts, merchants, distributors, hosts, terminals, service providers, banks, and credit card institutions. It affects transactions over the Internet, telephone, and point of sale (POS) terminals. With the increase in data breaches and the related losses in the millions of dollars, this topic has received widespread attention. According to IBM's 2017 Ponemon Cost of Data Breach study, the global average cost of a data breach is $3.62 million and the average cost for each lost or stolen record containing sensitive and confidential information is $141. Despite all the new and innovative tools and technologies data breaches still happen.[*] Globally the cost is estimated to rise to $2.1 trillion by 2019.[†]

Organizations who accept payment cards (credit or debit) over the Internet, telephone, or terminals as payment; stores card data, or processes card transactions, is responsible to be PCI compliant. These organizations must conduct an in-house annual audit of PCI systems and perform quarterly scans of PCI systems from the outside by approved scanning vendors.

In addition to the losses due to a breach, fines, and penalties can be costly too. According to Focus on PCI, the consequences of not being PCI compliant range

---

[*] To view the 2017 Ponemon Cost of Data Breach study, visit www.ibm.com/security/data-breach.

[†] See www.itgovernanceusa.com/blog/global-cost-of-data-breaches-will-rise-to-2-1-trillion-by-2019/.

from $5,000 to $500,000 every month until they address all compliance issues. Organizations that fail to resolve the problem satisfactorily could even have their ability to accept cards revoked. Even if a company is 100 percent PCI compliant and validated, a breach in cardholder data could still occur. Cardholder Breaches can result in the following losses for a merchant:

- $50–$90 fine per cardholder data compromised
- Suspension of credit card acceptance by a merchant's credit card account provider
- Loss of reputation with customers, suppliers, and partners
- Possible civil litigation from breached customers
- Loss of customer trust which affects future sales

Another example relates to the Occupational Safety and Health Administration (OSHA), a unit within the United States Department of Labor (DOL), which develops workplace health and safety standards. There are many regulations affecting organizations in the construction, maritime, agriculture, and other industries. It addresses imminent danger situations, severe injuries and illnesses, worker complaints, injury records, and the posting of notices.

Employers must comply with all applicable OSHA standards or be subject to fines and penalties as shown on Table 3.1.

The Employee Retirement Income Security Act of 1974 (ERISA) is a federal law that sets standards for most voluntarily established pension and health plans in private industry to provide protection to individuals in these plans. ERISA requires plans to provide participants with plan information including important information about plan features and funding. It sets minimum standards for participation, vesting, benefit accrual, and funding. It also defines the fiduciary responsibilities for those who manage and control plan assets.

ERISA does not cover retirement plans established or maintained by governmental entities, churches for their employees, or plans that are maintained for the sole purpose of complying with applicable workers compensation (WC), unemployment or disability laws (Table 3.2).

Table 3.1 Potential 2016 OSHA Penalties[a]

Violation Type	2016 Maximum Penalty
Other than serious violations	$12,600
Serious violation	$12,600
Willful violation	$ 126,000
Repeat violation	$ 126,000

[a] See www.oshaeducationcenter.com/articles/2016-osha-fine-increases.aspx.

Table 3.2   ERISA Penalties for Compliance Violations[a]

Civil Penalty/Monetary Penalty Description	Maximum Penalty Effective August 1, 2016
Failure to furnish statement of benefits to former retirement plan participants and beneficiaries or failure to maintain records for a retirement plan.	$28 per employee
Failure or refusal to file annual report.	$2,063/day
Failure or refusal to file annual report.	$2,063/day
Failure to notify single employer DB plan participants of certain benefit restrictions and/or limitations arising under Code Section 436.	$1,632/day
Failure to furnish certain multiemployer defined benefit plan financial and actuarial reports upon request by participant, beneficiary, or employee representative.	$1,632/day
Failure by plan sponsor or plan administrator of multiemployer DB plan to furnish estimate of withdrawal liability upon request to participating employer.	$1,632/day
Failure to furnish of automatic contribution arrangement notice to defined contribution (DC) plan participants.	$1,632/day
Failure of Multiple Employer Welfare Arrangement (MEWA) to file required report.	$1,502/day
Failure to furnish employee benefit plan documents to DOL upon request (including plan and trust documents, summary plan description, summary of material modifications collective bargaining agreement).	$147 per day but no greater than $1,472 per request
Failure to furnish blackout notice or notice of right to divest employer securities to participants and beneficiaries in DC plans.	$131 per day per required recipient

(Continued)

Table 3.2 (*Continued*)   ERISA Penalties for Compliance Violations[a]

Civil Penalty/Monetary Penalty Description	Maximum Penalty Effective August 1, 2016
Failure of multiemployer DB plan sponsor to adopt a funding improvement plan for plan in endangered status (or failure to adopt a rehabilitation plan for plan in critical status). Also applies to failure to meet benchmark by end of funding improvement period for endangered plans (that are not seriously endangered plans).	$1,296/day
Failure by employer to inform employees of Medicaid/CHIP coverage opportunities.	$110 per day per employee
Failure of group health plan's plan administrator to provide state with timely coverage coordination disclosure form for Medicaid/CHIP eligible individuals.	$110 per day per participant or beneficiary
Genetic Information Nondisclosure Act (GINA) violation by group health plan sponsor/health insurance issuer.	$110 per day per participant or beneficiary (if not corrected before notice of violation is received—subject to minimum of $2,745 per day per participant or beneficiary for de minimis violations or $16,473 per day per participant or beneficiary for violations that are not de minimis; maximum of $549,095 for unintentional failures
Failure of a Cooperative and Small Employer Charity Act (CSEC) DB plan sponsor to establish or update a funding restoration plan.	$100/day
	$15,909 per prohibited payment
Failure to provide Summary of Benefits Coverage to participant or beneficiary of group health plan.	$1,087 per participant or beneficiary

[a] See www.shrm.org/resourcesandtools/hr-topics/benefits/pages/erisa-penalties.aspx.

Scandals in Brazil, Malaysia, and Thailand, at Samsung, Volkswagen, Petrobras, and Siemens, at The Fédération Internationale de Football Association (FIFA) and at Walmart, show how pervasive and problematic corruption is. Some incidents are discovered through the release of documents, like the Panama Papers, others by whistleblowers, like at the Rio de Janeiro Olympics. The fact that corruption, money laundering and the funding of terrorism and other illicit ventures has been an ongoing problem for decades has resulted in the passage of Anti-Money Laundering and Countering the Financing of Terrorism (AML/CFT) provisions. Some of it is evident in the Know Your Customer (KYC) requirements, which stipulates that organizations should be able to identify and verify the identity of their clients. While most people tend to associate these provisions with organizations in the financial services industries (e.g., banking, insurance, money management), they apply to all organizations.

This is part of a global effort. The United States has the USA Patriot Act of 2001. Canada the Financial Transactions Reports Analysis Centre (FINTRAC). There is the Australian Transaction Reports and Analysis Centre (AUSTRAC) responsible for enforcing the Anti-Money Laundering and Counter-Terrorism Financing Act 2006, among many others.

Some typical characteristics are that all institutions should have a rigorous process in place to consistently screen clients, especially anyone who is a politically exposed person (PEP), properly train employees, and use data to identify risky transactions or activities that may indicate that the funds are the product of fraud and other dishonest acts, drug trafficking, smuggling, money laundering, or conducting business in countries deemed as being under sanction or on watch lists.

An AML/CFT program should include:

- Risk assessments to evaluate the organization's products, affiliations, and dynamics to identify concerning situations. The review may examine the type, volume, geographic source and destination, and beneficiary of transactions.
- Identification of suspicious transactions and activities.
- Verification that there is a culture conducive to reporting anomalies and suspicious transactions.
- Documentation to verify the source, destination, and beneficiary of all transactions, especially cross-border ones and those involving PEPs.
- Automation to verify that individuals and organizations that have been blacklisted are blocked. This includes the Specially Designated Nationals (SDNs) list provided by the U.S. Office of Foreign Assets Control (OFAC).
- Verification of the nature and activities of nonprofit organizations and their financial transactions.
- Assessment of high-risk countries as indicated by Transparency International's Corruption Perceptions Index (CPI).

There are many compliance requirements varying by country, industry, and some applicable only to organizations of certain sizes. It is essential for organizations to identify all of their compliance requirements, put in place mechanisms to ensure they remain compliant, and that changes are brought to the attention of those responsible for compliance. Organizations should also have a monitoring mechanism in place, including a remediation process.

Summary

1. Compliance audits represent a fundamental aspect of internal audit and a key expectation from stakeholders. Every organization is subject to a variety of requirements based on geographic location, industrial sector, size, enforcement tenor, and stakeholder expectations.
2. Compliance requirements are set internally (e.g., policies and procedures), externally (e.g., regulations), or a combination (e.g., contracts). The key for internal auditors is to understand the applicable requirements and the intent of those obligations (i.e., the spirit of the law).
3. Noncompliance can result in fines and penalties, reputational damage, customer abandonment, suspension of license to operate, criminal prosecution, and lawsuits, among others.

Chapter 4

Audit: Department

The internal audit department can be any division, department, team of consultants, or other practitioners that provide independent, objective assurance, and
consulting services. The unit's goal is to help an organization accomplish its objectives and improve the organization's operations. Adding value has long been considered a goal of internal auditors, and the audit department should aspire to do so
by developing and practicing the creed of a mission and values statement focused
on bringing a systematic, disciplined approach to evaluate and improve the effectiveness of governance, risk management and control processes (GRC) in the short
and long terms.

To ratify and preserve its independence, internal audit departments should be
"off-to-the-side" of their organization's organizational chart. This means that while
the CEO/President has direct reports aligned functionally (e.g., finance, production, IT, HR, manufacturing), by product or service, by geography, or otherwise,
the internal audit department should not report directly like them but should have
a dotted reporting line (administratively). If this is not possible, it should report to
someone with substantial authority and influence to remain connected and aware
of business dynamics, issues, priorities, and initiatives. The direct reporting line
should be to the Audit Committee of the Board of Directors. This arrangement also
provides protection, so the internal audit function can review any and everything
containing sufficient risk warranting review, yet immune from undue influence or
interference.

The scope of work is the entire organization, so all business operations are subject to review with the goal of analyzing and improving their operating practices.
This scope is increasingly also extending beyond the organization to include third-
party providers and business partners. Given this broad mandate, the internal audit
department must collectively have the knowledge, and the variety of skills and
competencies to perform its duties.

During the 1990s, large accounting firms (often referred to as CPA firms) developed and expanded their internal audit units and offered their services in the marketplace. Without any regulatory restrictions, they were often an organization's external auditor, internal auditor, tax advisor, and consulting services provider. Many thought that this practice offered significant advantages to the client organization and the accounting firms because the client organization would benefit by reducing internal audit costs and by accessing the CPA firm's broad expertise. Costs would be lowered by eliminating overlapping positions, audit effort, and by replacing employees with variable-cost contractors. Accounting firms gained significant outsourcing fees and could better balance workloads because they could shift from external to internal audit activities during the off-peak season. Lastly, the knowledge gained while performing internal audits would facilitate the performance of the annual financial statement audit.

Of course, this ignored the fact that there was a conflict of interest in this arrangement, which became apparent during the high-profile reporting frauds involving Enron, WorldCom, Waste Management, and Andersen. These scandals suggested that combining internal and external audit services was not as effective as having separate external and internal auditors. Furthermore, it also highlighted the fact that having an in-house internal audit department may be better at detecting and reporting fraudulent activity. As a result, Section 201: Services Outside the Scope of Practice of Auditors of the Sarbanes–Oxley Act of 2002 forbids "internal audit outsourcing services," so external auditors can no longer "wear both hats."

Many in-house internal audit departments experience difficulties obtaining sufficient, and appropriately qualified auditors to meet their annual plans. The shortage of internal auditors or the inability to recruit and retain needed talent has forced many organizations to either outsource the function, or co-source with a third party that can lend the number of auditors and the requisite skillset to audit complex topics like cybersecurity, derivatives, the global supply chain, and the IT infrastructure.

Oversight of the Internal Audit Department

Audit Committees must be actively engaged in directing the organization's internal audit function. They should approve:

- The internal audit charter.
- The risk-based audit plan.
- The budget and resource plan.
- The appointment and removal of the chief audit executive.
- The compensation of the chief audit executive.

The audit committee must also:

- Receive communications regarding the performance of the internal audit function.
- Determine the degree to which it is meeting its annual plan and any inappropriate scope or resource limitations.
- Designate a competent individual, preferably within senior management, to be responsible for the internal audit function.
- Determine the scope, risk, and frequency of internal audit activities.
- Evaluate the adequacy of the audit procedures performed and the adequacy of the findings.

All these activities strengthen the internal audit department and allow it to perform its duties with the needed resources and without interference. The specific scope, scale, and performance of the work may vary based on factors such as the organization's size, industry, complexity, geographic dispersion, risk and control maturity, legal and cultural environment, and regulatory requirements.

While the size of the internal audit department could consist "of a department of one" to hundreds of internal auditors, the mandate is similar: provide assurance and consulting services to help the organization improve its operations, achieve its objectives, and improve the effectiveness of risk management, control, and governance processes.

Summary

1. The internal audit department should be free of operational responsibilities to preserve its independence and objectivity.
2. The activities of the internal audit department may be supplemented and shared with a third-party provider (i.e., co-source) or completely performed by a third-party provider (i.e., outsourced). While third parties can sometimes provide the expertise, staff augmentation, and flexibility that a resident internal audit department cannot, care is warranted to ensure familiarity with the specific needs and nuances of the organization served.
3. The audit committee plays a pivotal role ensuring that the internal audit function has sufficient knowledge, competencies, access, recognition, and resources to perform its duties effectively.

Chapter 5

Audit: Environmental

Environmental auditing is the objective analysis, testing, and documentation of how well an organization, its management processes, and equipment are performing with the goal of helping to protect the environment and provide credible information to stakeholders. It generally involves a systematic and documented assessment of compliance with company policies, regulations, and stakeholder expectations. It tests performance against regulatory requirements, internal company standards, and good management and operating practices.

Environmental auditors measure the effects of activities on the environment against established criteria or standards. In general, this involves:

- Verifying compliance with environmental requirements
- Evaluating the effectiveness of the organization's environmental management systems (EMSs)
- Assessing risks from regulated and unregulated materials and practices.[*]

Organizations are increasingly recognizing the importance of environmental considerations and realize that their environmental performance will be questioned by a wide range of stakeholders. Environmental auditing is used to help manage and reduce the adverse effects of human activities on the environment.

These assessments are an important link to better compliance and improvements in other aspects of an organization's performance, such as identifying opportunities to prevent pollution that can significantly reduce operating costs. Environmental auditors identify and encourage management to correct violations,

---

[*] See the EPA's Environmental Audit Program Design Guidelines for Federal Agencies, which is available at www.epa.gov/sites/production/files/documents/envaudproguidemas.pdf.

prevent the recurrence of the issues identified, and correct instances of environmental harm.

According to SOAS University of London, environmental audits involve the following elements:

- Verification: Evaluate compliance with regulations or other criteria
- Systematic: Audits are performed in a planned and methodical manner
- Periodic: Reviews are conducted according to an established schedule
- Objective: Audit results are reported without unsubstantiated opinions
- Documented: Notes are taken during the audit and the findings are recorded
- Management tool: These audits can be integrated into the organization's management system, such as a quality or EMS[*]

An environmental audit should not be confused with an environmental impact assessment (EIA), which is an anticipatory review designed to predict the impact on the environment of a future action, and to inform those making a decision whether the project should be authorized or not. An EIA is a legally mandated tool for many projects in many countries. Environmental auditing is performed while a project or activity is already ongoing and is used to check on existing practices.

ISO 14001[†] is the international standard that specifies requirements for an effective EMS. It provides a framework that organizations can follow, but it does not establish environmental performance requirements. It is a voluntary standard that can be used by any organization regardless of size, location or industry wishing to establish, improve or maintain and EMS to meet its environmental policy and requirements. The requirements of the standard, and the characteristics of the EMS are determined by the organization's industry, location, environmental policy, and their products and services.

ISO 14001 covers the context of the organization, its leadership, planning, support, operation, performance evaluation, and improvement mechanism. Since environmental considerations are taken in the context of dynamic business environments, an environmental audit should also include in their scope the organization's interactions with external parties, an evaluation of the existence of consistent leadership engagement, the presence of a risk-based planning and controls approach, and review relevant documentation.

An environment audit might also include verifying that the organization has a policy statement and quantifiable objectives, up-to-date organizational charts

---

[*] For more details about environmental audits and its characteristics, see www.soas.ac.uk/cedep-demos/000_P508_EAEMS_K3736-Demo/unit1/page_14.htm.

[†] More information about ISO 14001 can be obtained at www.iso.org/iso-14001-environmental-management.html, https://www.iso.org/files/live/sites/isoorg/files/archive/pdf/en/environmental-labelling.pdf and http://asq.org/learn-about-quality/learn-about-standards/iso-14001/.

and job descriptions, that the environmental program has adequate resources, that documentation is controlled and sufficiently detailed, verifying there is a management representative, and sufficient and competent personnel to make sure the quality and environmental managements systems can function effectively. Other common areas reviewed include the proper labeling and declaration of products to verify the claims made (e.g., percentage of recycled content, biodegradable, reduced water, or energy consumption).

In addition to its flagship CIA (Certified Internal Auditor) certification, and other widely known credentials like the CFSA (Certified Financial Services Auditor), CGAP (Certified Government Auditor Professional), CRMA (Certification in Risk Management Assurance), and CCSA (Certification in Control Self-Assessment), the IIA also offers the CPEA (Certified Professional Environmental Auditor), and the CPSA (Certified Process Safety Auditor) certifications jointly with BEAC (the Board of Environmental Auditor Certifications). These credentials demonstrate the holder's understanding of current environmental, health and safety regulations, and an understanding of process safety elements including those that involve hazardous waste and explosive materials.*

Environmental auditors use many of the same tools and techniques traditional internal auditors use, such as checklists, questionnaires, walkthroughs, and observations. But while performing or in proximity to hazardous materials, they are required to wear protective clothing and other safety equipment to protect the audit team from exposure to hazardous materials. The EPA's Environmental Audit Program Design Guidelines for Federal Agencies indicates that such clothing may include hard hats, protective eye wear, steel toed boots, respirators, and chemical suits. Audit personnel should be trained in the proper use of this equipment.

An environmental audit may include the review of spill or release records, hazardous substance inventory records, assessment documents, remedial investigation documentation, soil sample and groundwater monitoring data, release discovery and notification protocols, and documents, engineering and cost evaluations, and sampling and analysis plans. It may also include the reference and use of maps to evaluate water direction flows, and potential surface and groundwater contamination of wetlands. This would be needed to evaluate a facility's stormwater management plan, for example. A wind rose may also be useful to assess prevailing wind direction and intensity for facilities with significant air emissions characteristics. As such, environmental auditors may be involved in preparing a baseline risk assessment, conduct interviews, perform observations, review documents, verify the existence and condition, and reproduce/recalculate figures to determine:

---

* For additional information about these certifications, see https://na.theiia.org/certification/BEAC/Pages/Get-Started.aspx.

- What hazardous materials* exist, and in which way they are stored, used, treated, transported, and disposed
- If any spills exceed reportable thresholds
- If required notifications were made (e.g., internally/externally, verbal/written, timeline requirements)
- Waste handling (e.g., timeline, manner, destination) procedures
- That MSDS (Material Safety Data Sheets), proper labeling, toxic substance, and disease registry notifications are in place
- Appropriate and timely training
- Appropriate and consistently used protective equipment
- Whether acceptable exposure levels have been established and if worksites are safe to use (e.g., ventilation, lighting)
- Whether required licenses and permits where obtained and remain up to date
- General reduction of toxicity, mobility, or volume of substances
- Complied with required public comment and notification periods, if applicable, and keeps related minutes and related documentation (e.g., transcripts)
- Verify that the organization has evaluated the threat of
  - Exposure to human populations, animals, waterways or the food chain
  - Storage of hazardous materials that may pose a threat of release and migration
  - Threat of fire, flood, explosion and adverse weather conditions†

Summary

1. Environmental auditing can improve an organization's resource utilization by increasing operating efficiency, reduce waste, lower costs, show that environmental impacts are being measured and managed effectively, meet legal requirements and stakeholder expectations, and make sure that environmental obligations are being managed and met consistently.

2. Environmental auditors, in collaboration with the organization's management, should focus on promoting appropriate attitudes and behaviors, including the voluntary disclosure of violations, cooperation, the institution of preventive measures and compliance programs, ensuring internal disciplinary action, performing periodic compliance audits, and making sure that schedules for remedial action to audit findings are adhered to.

---

* I use the term hazardous substances for simplicity, but more specific terms are sometimes used. For example, the EPA's Protocol for Conducting Environmental Compliance Audits refers to Extremely Hazardous Substances, Hazardous Substances, Toxic Chemicals, and Hazardous Wastes.

† For additional information about the EPA's Protocol for Conducting Environmental Compliance Audits, see www.epa.gov/sites/production/files/documents/apcol-cercla.pdf.

3. The increasing focus on climate change, healthy living and the protection of the environment is increasing the attention given to environmental audits. Pre-project EIAs are often required as anticipatory reviews and environmental audits are often performed to verify compliance with established standards and expectations.

Chapter 6

Audit: Financial

Financial Auditing is an independent and objective evaluation of an organization's financial reports and the processes that produce those reports. In general, it relates to the accounting (or recording) of transactions and how those activities flow into the different financial statements. It is primarily the work of external auditors, who are sometimes referred to as CPAs. The purpose of this work is to give investors, regulators, directors, and management reasonable assurance that financial statements are materially accurate and complete.

There are similarities and differences between internal and external auditors. Both are similar in that they are expected to be independent and objective, and they review processes to verify congruence between expectations and performance. But differences exist; some are nuanced, and others are substantial. Whereas external auditors are always contracted by the audit client, internal auditors can be employees of the organization or independently contracted. Organizations base their decision to outsource the function on the availability of qualified internal auditors. A very common middle ground is achieved by co-sourcing some projects but retaining a core group of internal auditors. The co-source providers are often hired to perform specialized reviews.

While external auditors always serve third parties (e.g., regulators, investors, creditors), internal auditor serve the organizations' directors, and management.

External auditors' work is always retrospective, except for the determination if the organization is a going concern. The concept, or assumption, of going concern is that the organization will be able to continue operating so it can to carry out its objectives, and meet its commitments and other obligations. In other words, the company will not be forced out of business or liquidate its assets in the foreseeable future.

The focus of external auditors is either annual (for year-end reviews) or quarterly. Internal auditors' focus and timeline are often different. It can focus on the past to determine past practices and results, and to gain a better understanding of historical events that produced today's outcomes. But this retrospective view can extend multiple years rather than just one. And it also has a forward-looking perspective that is increasingly strategic and risk-based, focusing on the dynamics that can create, protect, or erode stakeholder value years into the future.

There are three very important elements associated with financial reporting: Reasonable assurance, materiality, and the auditors' opinion.

Reasonable Assurance

Similar to internal auditors, external auditors provide reasonable assurance, but not an absolute guarantee. Financial auditors use many of the same techniques that internal auditors use (e.g., interviews, observations, walk-throughs, testing) to determine if the financial reporting process is working effectively and the controls needed to produce reliable financial statements are in place and working as intended. If the processes and internal controls over financial reporting are in place and working as intended, then they can conclude that the financial statements are accurate and reliable. However, auditors still cannot guarantee that there were no human errors, miscommunications, or deliberate actions, especially if perpetrated by colluding individuals, that may lead to incorrect financial reports.

This being the case, however, does not preclude the responsibility of external auditors to work diligently to identify anomalies. The Statement on Auditing Standards No. 99 (SAS 99): Consideration of Fraud in a Financial Statement Audit, which was issued by the Auditing Standards Board of the American Institute of Certified Public Accountants (AICPA), compels external auditors to conduct brainstorming sessions to determine how and where the entity's financial statements might be susceptible to material misstatement due to fraud. It also requires the auditor to evaluate the entity's programs and controls, gather information, and retain documentation related to their efforts to identify risks of material misstatement due to fraud.

Materiality

This is a concept related to the significance of a discrepancy in an amount used during the preparation of financial statements. An amount is considered material to the company if its omission or misstatement influences the decision of users (e.g., investors, creditors). Since the financial statements are prepared based on many transactions and amounts, an appropriate question is, could there be a misstatement in any of these many transactions? Quite often, yes, because there could the thousands of transactions. So, a related question is, how significant are the discrepancies between what those transactions and amounts are compared to what they should be? Are these discrepancies minor, so that a reader of the financial statements would still be comfortable that they are reasonably accurate and therefore reliable, or are these discrepancies large enough to make the reader uncomfortable relying on these reports?

For example, an expenditure of $200 on paper and office supplies could have been forgotten or recorded incorrectly. That amount is immaterial even for small organizations. But an expenditure of thousands of dollars is material to many organizations. Yet, the materiality threshold for multi-billion-dollar companies may be in the millions of dollars.

Recently, the concept of materiality has expanded and, in many respects, encompasses other activities that could put in question the future prospects of the organization and its impact on others. Since the long-term goal of an organizations, its investors, and many other stakeholders, is for the entity to be a viable entity into the foreseeable future, the Global Reporting Initiative states that materiality encompasses "issues that have a direct or indirect impact on an organization's ability to create, preserve or erode economic, environmental and social value for itself, its stakeholders and society at large."*

The calculation of the materiality threshold is not subject to a universal formula, but varies based on the size, nature, and risk associated with the discrepancy. There are, however, some common rules. Many organizations set materiality at 0.5 percent of revenues, between 0.5 and 2 percent of gross profit, 5 percent of pre-tax income, and 0.5–2 percent of assets.

Opinion

External auditors' goal is to be able to render an opinion on the quality of the financial statements and the processes and controls that were instrumental in their preparation. Ideally, this opinion is that in all material respects, the financial records and statements are presented fairly and appropriately, and in conformity with an identified financial reporting framework such as Generally Accepted Accounting Principles (GAAP). This opinion is referred to as an unqualified opinion—the external auditors have no reservations. A qualified opinion, on the other hand, indicates that the organization did not follow GAAP or provided limited information, so it is a cautionary note to the readers of the financial statements. The independent auditors found something in the financial statements, or their preparation and disclosures, that is a cause for concern.

* To read the full report Defining Materiality: What Matters to Reports and Investors, go to www.globalreporting.org/resourcelibrary/Defining-Materiality-What-Matters-to-Reporters-and-Investors.pdf.

Assertions

An assertion is a positive statement or declaration. The Merriam-Webster dictionary defines assertion as "a declaration that something is the case." In terms of financial statements, they are the positive statements and explanations that management makes to the report users about the recognition, quantification/measurement, presentation, and disclosures of the information contained in the financial statements. Essentially, when submitting those reports, management implies that they are a true representation of the activities that occurred and the value of items during the fiscal period (quarterly or annual) covered. During a financial statement audit, auditors obtain and review evidence to determine if these assertions are supported and met.

Standards for fieldwork require auditors to obtain sufficient and competent evidence to support the opinion given. This evidence is related to the management assertions contained in financial statement components. AU Section 326 of the AICPA Professional Standards lists the following management assertions:

Assertions about transactions and events
- Occurrence: Transactions and events that have been recorded have occurred and pertain to the entity
- Completeness: All transactions and events that should have been recorded have been recorded
- Accuracy: Amounts and other data relating to recorded transactions and events have been recorded appropriately
- Cutoff: Transactions and events have been recorded in the correct accounting period
- Classification: Transactions and events have been recorded in the proper accounts

Assertions about account balances at the period end
- Existence: Assets, liabilities, and equity interests exist
- Rights and obligations: The entity holds or controls the rights to assets, and liabilities are the obligations of the entity
- Completeness: All assets, liabilities, and equity interests that should have been recorded have been recorded
- Valuation and allocation: Assets, liabilities, and equity interests are included in the financial statements at appropriate amounts and any resulting valuation or allocation adjustments are appropriately recorded.

Assertions about presentation and disclosure
- Occurrence, rights, and obligations: Disclosed events and transactions have occurred and pertain to the entity
- Completeness: All disclosures that should have been included in the financial statements have been included

- Classification and understandability: Financial information is appropriately presented and described, and disclosures are clearly expressed
- Accuracy and valuation: Financial and other information are disclosed fairly and at appropriate amounts (Table 6.1).*

Financial Statements

Financial statements are reports about an organization's financial results, condition, and cash flows. They are useful to understand how the organization generates cash, the sources of that cash and how it is used; to determine if the organization has the ability to repay its debts; the amount of equity the organization has accumulated over time; and to understand the details regarding important transactions as outlined in the disclosures that accompany the financial statements.

There are three primary financial statements:

Balance sheet. It shows the organization's assets, liabilities, and stockholders' equity as of the report date (i.e., the last day of the fiscal year). It does not show information covering a span of time, so it is akin to a snapshot of the organization's condition on that date.

Table 6.1   Financial Statement Assertions

Transactions and events	Occurrence Completeness Accuracy Cutoff Classification
Account balances	Existence Rights and obligations Completeness Valuation and allocation
Presentation and disclosure	Occurrence Rights and obligations Completeness Classification/ understandability Accuracy Valuation

---

* For a more comprehensive review of financial statement assertions, and the documentation and testing requirements, see AU Section 326—Audit Evidence, available at www.aicpa.org/Research/Standards/AuditAttest/DownloadableDocuments/AU-00326.pdf.

Income statement. It shows the results of the organization's operations and financial activities for the reporting period (i.e., the entire fiscal year). Income Statements include revenues, expenses, gains, and losses.

Statement of cash flows. It shows changes in the organization's cash flows during the reporting period. It includes three types of cash flows: (1) Operating activities (these are the revenue-generating activities of the organization, like product sales, royalties, commissions, vendor invoices, and payroll). (2) Investing activities (these are the payments made to acquire long-term assets and cash received from their sale, like the purchase of fixed assets). (3) Financing activities (these are activities that affect the equity or borrowings, like the sale of company shares, the repurchase of shares, and dividend payments).

Note: The Income Statement and the Statement of Cash Flows may appear to be the same on the surface, but there can be significant differences between the two. There can be timing differences between the time a transaction is recorded and when the related cash is received or spent. If the organization receives large capital investments, those would not appear on the Income Statement. Lastly, there could be discrepancies if the organization recognizes revenue before cash is received. This last point of revenue recognition could become fraudulent if the conditions for revenue recognition are not followed. A discussion of the different methods used for revenue recognition is beyond the scope of this book, but in general, US GAAP has complex, detailed, and different revenue recognition requirements for specific transactions and industries varying, for example, between software and real estate. The result was that different industries use different accounting for similar transactions. In May 2014 the Financial Accounting Standards Board (FASB) and the International Accounting Standards Board (IASB) issued guidance to improve comparability across industries. The effective date for public companies is 2018.*

Supplementary notes. Includes explanations and additional detail of various activities and accounts, as mandated by the applicable accounting standard used (e.g., GAAP, IFRS).

Ratio Analysis

Another important aspect of financial auditing is the use of ratios. This is the quantitative analysis of information in a company's financial statements to evaluate the organization's financial and operating performance. The main aspects of evaluation

---

* For more information about the new revenue recognition standards, see www.fasb.org/jsp/FASB/ Page/ImageBridgePage&cid=1176169257359#section_7 and www.journalofaccountancy. com/news/2017/sep/revenue-recognition-changes-affecting-preparers-201717560.html and www.pwc.com/us/en/cfodirect/issues/revenue-recognition.html.

are efficiency, liquidity, profitability, and solvency. This analysis can shed valuable insights into the organization's strengths and weaknesses.

Ratios help to connect the three financial statements and provide information that makes it easier to compare companies within industries. Comparing companies across industries is not always valid. For example, liquidity needs vary from industry to industry as some are more cash-intensive than others. Food stores need more cash constantly to buy inventory compared to software firms, so the liquidity ratios of companies in these two industries are not comparable to each other.

The purpose is to compare a company's performance to determine if it is improving or deteriorating, compare a company's financial condition with the industry average or compare a company to one or more other companies in its sector to see how the company measures up.

Trend analysis of company ratios is also important as the results over multiple years may provide a more useful perspective than solely examining a single period's figures.

Efficiency Ratios: They are also called activity ratios and they evaluate how a company uses its assets and liabilities to generate sales and maximize profits. They show the overall operational performance of the company by presenting how many times per year inventory is replenished or receivables are collected. Key efficiency ratios are as follows:

$$\text{Asset turnover ratio} = \frac{\text{Sales}}{\text{Average total assets}}$$

$$\text{Inventory turnover} = \frac{\text{Cost of goods sold}}{\text{Average inventory}} \text{ or } \frac{\text{Sales}}{\text{Inventory}}.$$

$$\text{Days' sales in inventory} = \frac{\left(\text{Average inventory}\right)}{\text{Cost of goods sold}} \times 365$$

Liquidity Ratios: These ratios measure a company's ability to pay off its short-term debts using the company's current (or quick) assets. Liquidity ratios include:

$$\text{Current ratio} : \frac{\text{Current assets}}{\text{Current liabilities}}$$

$$\text{Quick ratio} : \frac{\text{Current assets} - \left(\text{inventory} + \text{prepaid expenses}\right)}{\text{Current liabilities}}$$

Profitability ratios. These ratios show how well a company can generate profits from its operations. They measure the company's ability to earn an adequate return. When analyzing a company's margins, it is highly recommended that they be compared against its competitors and those of other firms in the industry because margins vary among industries. Companies in industries where products are considered commodities (i.e., easily replicated by other companies) typically have low margins, and those in industries that offer unique products with high barriers to entry usually have high margins. Profitability ratios include:

$$\text{Profit margin} = \frac{\text{Net income}}{\text{Net sales}}$$

$$\text{Return on assets}\,(\text{ROA}) = \frac{\text{Net income}}{\text{Total assets}}$$

$$\text{Return on equity}\,(\text{ROE}) = \frac{\text{Net income}}{\text{Shareholders' equity}}.$$

$$\text{Return on capital employed} = \frac{\text{EBIT*}}{\text{Total assets–current liabilities}}.$$

$$\text{Gross margin ratio} = \frac{\text{Revenue–cost of goods sold}}{\text{Revenue}}$$

Solvency ratios. They are also called financial leverage ratios, and they compare a company's debt levels with its assets, equity, and earnings to evaluate whether a company can pay the principal and interest on its long-term debt. If a company does not have enough cash flows to cover its debt, bondholders, and other creditors may stop providing it new loans and under extreme circumstances, force it into default. Solvency ratios include:

$$\text{Debt to equity ratio} = \frac{\text{Total liabilities}}{\text{Shareholders' equity}}$$

$$\text{Debt to assets ratio} = \frac{\text{Total debt}}{\text{Total assets}}$$

$$\text{Interest coverage ratio} = \frac{\text{EBIT*}}{\text{Interest expense}}.$$

*EBIT=Earnings Before Interest and Taxes, also known as Net Operating Profit

Summary

1. While external auditors are primarily tasked with performing the financial audits for their client organizations, internal auditors routinely perform

financial audits as well. Key differences are that external auditors render an opinion with their year-end audits, use larger materiality thresholds, rely heavily on ratio analysis, and generally spend less time at their client organizations than internal auditors.

2. Ratio analysis links the three financial statements and provides useful figures to compare a company with others in terms of its operational performance, profitability, competitive position, and financial strength.

3. Internal auditors can add value by demonstrating their independence and competence so external auditors can rely on their work and thus reduce the amount of testing external auditors must perform. Also, by focusing on adjusted materiality thresholds considered meaningful to their organizations, evaluating the efficiency of the accounting closing and financial reporting processes to eliminate rework, delays, excessive transaction re-classification, and the overall effectiveness of internal controls over financial reporting, internal auditors can make a valuable contribution to their organizations.

Chapter 7

Audit: Integrated

Internal auditors historically performed their reviews in a somewhat compartmentalized manner. Financial reviews were common as the traditional offspring of the work performed by external auditors. This became so pervasive that the word "auditor" meant financial statement auditor to most people, and these professionals were CPAs. Compliance reviews were also common as part of the natural focus of auditors, who were instructed, and eventually widely embraced, the idea that their primary purpose was to verify compliance with the organization's internal and external compliance requirements. This second group was often compared to the work that regulators did. As operational reviews became more common, some auditors were labeled "business auditors" to encapsulate these three main types of reviews: Financial, Compliance, and Operational audits.

During the 1970s and especially during the 1980s, another development emerged. As computers became more pervasive, it became evident that IT auditors were needed to understand and review computer systems. These IT auditors examined technical subjects including data input, processing and output, interfaces, data reliability, and system development, among other topics. Over time, IT auditors became somewhat insulated in their work, focusing on hardware and software topics, while "traditional" internal auditors focused on accounting, financial, compliance, and operational matters.

During the 1990s, "business" auditors realized that their financial, compliance, and operational controls were increasingly being performed by computer systems. In fact, the organization depended on reports, access restrictions, and input/output configurations that impacted the quality of the work done. System issues resulted in operational errors, delays, and impacted customer and vendor relations. Capacity constraints limited employee productivity and the poor usage of computer applications could quickly result in unreliable reports and inconsistent service delivery.

In this environment, the concept of integrated auditing emerged linking business concerns with the systems that supported business activities.

It is no longer possible, feasible, or desirable to substantially separate operational activities from the systems where the information is captured, manipulated, and exported from. Virtually all organizations' success depends on the reliability, stability, capacity and consistency of the computer systems that support, and increasingly drive, business activities. In fact, the fast transition to online business activities means that computer systems must be in working order at all times.

Integrated auditing benefits everyone. For companies, covering IT processes within other audits helps to identify issues with system-generated reports, calculations, data feeds, access controls, data integrity, system processing speed, and some information security that impacts operations, compliance, strategic, and financial outcomes.

For the audit client, instead of performing one type of audit (e.g., compliance), then returning later to do another type of audit (e.g., financial), and yet again to conduct another type of audit (e.g., IT), the audit team can do one audit and address all these topics. This is less time-consuming, less costly, less disruptive for the audit client, and also more helpful because the report is comprehensive. The audit client may be just as eager to look at the full picture as well. A single report that corroborates all the specific risks across disciplines alleviates the guesswork for the client. For internal auditors, working on integrated audits is an opportunity to learn across disciplines and synthesize the risks found in IT and other disciplines to gain a complete view of risks and controls in the organization.

Can an individual acquire sufficient knowledge to audit these dynamics alone? Increasingly "no." Performing integrated audits is often done through team composition, where some of the team members focus on the business topics (e.g., financial, compliance, operational) and others focus on the IT aspects of the engagement, but together cover a wider scope without the audit silos typical in the past.

Planning and Fieldwork

During integrated audits, the audit programs include both "business" and systems dimensions. The objectives, risks, and controls should cover the business and IT-related items and provide a more comprehensive scope of work. During fieldwork, internal auditors should avoid testing separately during the same review. Rather, the internal auditors involved should coordinate their efforts, so system-related questions can be researched and answered promptly rather than waiting for a separate IT review. This synergy can provide a more comprehensive review, identify issues that may be overlooked by one-dimensional auditors, and provide more balanced recommendations. For example:

■ Are claims and beliefs related to access controls supported by system records?
■ Are activities being performed at unusual times, by unexpected individuals?

- Is data captured and processed, subsequently transmitted or reported completely and accurately?
- Are data stored and backed-up as expected?
- Is data retained as required, and destroyed at the end of the record-retention period?
- Are multiple copies of electronic records retained and escaping the document/data destruction guidelines?
- Do entries, reversals, and adjustments make sense?
- Are instructions for the use of the systems clear and are they being followed?
- Is the algorithm that generates report "x" correct? Is it complete and accurate?
- What are the access control parameters and do they align with business needs?

Reporting

At the end of the audit, it is very important for all internal auditors involved to coordinate their work and to write a report that is coherent. This is a common issue with integrated audits—that the format and language differ substantially, making it clear to the reader that there are very different authors involved and the report reads like two reports awkwardly and forcibly put together.

To minimize this problem, the documentation of any findings should follow a similar pattern and structure. While the details will differ and may include more technical terms and acronyms for the IT components, the technical language should be explained as they would be under any other circumstance. The elements of the findings should be similar, and the structure followed should be parallel. The person editing and proofreading the report should not merely copy and paste the work of the different auditors, but make sure the format, tense, and tone used are comparable, so readers navigate the document seamlessly.

It is important to remember that many operational issues are the result of mistakes made, not due to willful malice or fraud. Many of these issues occur at the point of data entry. So, while an auditor may identify a problem downstream, knowing that data entry is done manually and is performed by overworked and poorly trained employees is important because the human-to-machine interface is a key factor in the problem.

Similarly, if an algorithm pulls data from multiple databases, but is not retrieving certain product classification or location codes, having that knowledge of the databases and the algorithm used will help the auditor to identify the root cause of the problem.

Integrated auditing provides career advancement opportunities for all types of internal auditors too. By working side by side, business auditors will learn from their IT counterparts, and vice versa. In fact, going as far as possible into each other's territory would enhance the value of the corresponding auditors, broaden their skillset, help them identify root causes better, and help them provide more insightful findings and recommendations (Figure 7.1).

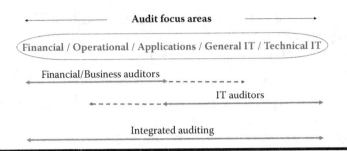

Figure 7.1   Integrated auditing.

The internal audit profession has come a long way from the days when audits were largely associated with gathering information about financial systems and the financial records of the organization. Today, internal auditors are expected to address in their annual plans non-financial subject areas, like safety, security, information systems performance, and environmental concerns. A similar dynamic is taking place in the nonprofit and government sectors, where there has been an increasing need for performance audits, examining their success in satisfying mission objectives and demonstrating that they are maximizing the value for money received. The result is that there are now internal auditors who specialize in security audits, information systems audits, and environmental audits as well.

Using a holistic approach produces a more effective outcome. Getting rid of what looks like silos and replacing those with an integrated approach that brings together these niche knowledge bases can result in an integrated review that yields dramatic results for the organization. To do this, internal auditors need to have a heightened awareness about the diversity of risks affecting organizations, so they have a broader perspective and think creatively and differently when preparing their audit programs.

Summary

1. Integrated audits represent a great opportunity to apply a broader scope to internal audits. With it, internal auditors can address operational, compliance, and strategic subjects, while seamlessly incorporating IT subjects as well.
2. Financial and operational risk and controls are intertwined with IT systems and processes, so internal auditors should join these subjects rather than perform separate audits. The deeper understanding gained from the IT component will increase the level of assurance that can be obtained from business topics alone. Similarly, recommendations will be more effective and encompassing if they address the business and IT-related elements affected.
3. Internal auditors can increase their personal brand and increase the quality of their recommendations by becoming more proficient in the IT systems the organization uses.

Chapter 8

Audit: Operational

Operational auditing is an evaluation of management's performance and the program or process' conformity with applicable policies and procedures. This evaluation includes, among other things, an appraisal of the structure, objectives, risks, controls, procedures, supporting systems, and human involvement. The result is the identification and promotion of good operating practices, the pursuit of high levels of efficiency, economy, and effectiveness in the achievement of relevant goals and objectives. This may be achieved by reducing waste, rework, delays, underutilization of resources, streamlining activities, maximizing the use of technology, and the optimal deployment of workers.

Constant pressures to increase profitability, relentless competition in most industries, and stakeholders' changing expectations are driving the need for operational audits. Internal auditors are also increasing the number of operational audits to provide higher value to their clients.

Some key questions helping to shape the objectives, scope and focus of operational reviews include:

- Is the structure conducive to achieving the organization's strategic and operational objectives?
- How is performance measured?
- What are the goals and metrics that measure success?
- Are financial and operational information reliable, useful, and distributed timely to those who need to know to make decisions and do their jobs effectively?
- Are operations guided by the principles of economy, efficiency, effectiveness, equity, ethics, ecology, and excellence?

- Are tangible and intangible assets safeguarded and the benefit from those assets maximized?
- Is the program or process complying with all prevailing laws, regulations contracts, and other requirements?

Implications for Internal Auditors

Internal auditors were historically trained in accounting, certified as accountants, and recruited from accounting firms. This is no longer the prevailing practice in most organizations as the profession has come to the realization that internal auditors do more than accounting-related work. As such, internal auditors today are trained in a variety of fields, business or not, and are sought more for their ability to "think risk," than their accounting or financial credentials.

This shift has created numerous opportunities for today's internal auditors, who are now free to think more like business managers and do what I was told to do early in my career: "When you start an audit, imagine you are the manager of the unit and ask yourself, how would you run this unit so it is successful?"

This paradigm shift requires technical (e.g., management, organizational behavior, operations management, regulatory/industry-specific, accounting, financial) and soft skills (e.g., communication, curiosity, discipline, assertiveness, leadership, resourcefulness).

Operational Risks

Internal auditors should remember, and remind their clients, that accounting and financial implications are often the result of operational failures. The problems begin in operations and are subsequently evident in the financial statements. If the organization is effective operationally and strategically, its success will be evident in the financial statements and ratios. If the organization is failing operationally, the problems will be evident in the financial results. This will hold true unless there is fraud or financial manipulation to hide the true conditions.

Notorious Cases to Date

Industrial organizations are known to invest heavily in environmental health and safety to ensure a safe workplace with minimal or no accidents or injuries. Investments in quality control are made to ensure the products and services produced and delivered meet customer expectations. Internal auditors can learn from this dynamic and focus on related risks as well.

A common criticism of government entities and some nonprofit organizations is that they are very bureaucratic, wasteful, slow, and often fail to achieve their objectives. This has often been compounded by the fact that many internal auditors have audited these entities for years. In fact, it is not even within scope or in the audit program for many internal auditors reviewing these entities; this should and is changing.

Increasingly, internal auditors are conducting value for money audits, which are similar to operational audits. These reviews include the 7Es: Efficiency, effectiveness, economy, ethics, ecology, equity, and excellence. When used in the form of a balanced scorecard, these elements form the basis for a well-rounded evaluation of any organization.

Another important area of focus when performing operational audits should be capacity.

- Can the program or process meet customer demands without a decrease in quality or speed?
- Do workers have the requisite knowledge and motivation to perform their duties, identify opportunities for improvement, and deliver what the customer wants?
- Are there bottlenecks or unnecessary delays affecting product or service delivery?

Organizations should review their structures, systems, and processes to identify and eliminate operational waste and inefficiency. Useful topics and areas of interest include:

- Producing and shipping parts that don't meet customer requirements or safety regulations
- Software bugs
- Incorrect data entry
- Wrong, poorly prepared, or unsafe product delivered to customers
- Misdiagnoses in healthcare, or misidentified sources of problems in other production and service environments
- Packages or luggage not delivered to their desired destination on time or not at all
- Moving merchandise, tools, or supplies among various locations unnecessarily
- Making customers wait in person, on the phone, online, or while waiting for transactions and documents to be processed
- Excessive searching for parts, tools, equipment, or material
- Disorganized workspaces
- Filing documents unnecessary and delays retrieving them when needed
- Multiple approvals for small spending requests

Summary

1. Operational audits present a formidable opportunity for internal auditors because they address subjects of great interest to the board and management. Topics like efficiency (e.g., productivity), effectiveness (e.g., goal attainment) and economy (e.g., cost containment and value maximization) are central to the success of all organizations.
2. Understanding the operational drivers of financial results will make the internal auditors familiar with these processes very valuable to their organizations and will likely open opportunities for career advancement within and outside internal audit.
3. Operational auditing is ideally positioned to evaluate day-to-day practices that impact workplace conditions that affect employee and customer satisfaction, differentiate the organization from its competitors, and makes it a socially responsible corporate citizen.

Chapter 9

Audit Committee

Organizations with a board of directors often have various committees to facility decision-making and address matters without the need for the entire board to get involved. The audit committee (AC) is one of these committees.

ACs are typically responsible for:

- Evaluating, selecting, and hiring the organization's internal and external auditors.
- Reviewing and ensuring financial statements are prepared according to all applicable accounting rules and regulations.
- Serving as the recipients and/or the arbiters of allegations of improprieties related to the preparation of the organizations' financial statements.
- Providing the budget for the internal and external auditors.

Since ACs assume such important and complex responsibilities, it is best if the members of the AC are independent and external to the organization. This can be defined in a variety of ways, but it generally means that members are not employed or engaged (e.g., consultants) by the organization.

Another important feature of effective ACs is that they contain at least one financial expert. Although this is required of companies subject to the Sarbanes Oxley Act of 2002 (Section 407), all organizations can benefit from this practice. A financial expert is an individual who through experience, training, or both, is familiar with Generally Accepted Accounting Principles (GAAP) and financial statements; can assess the general application of GAAP to accounting for estimates, accruals, and reserves; has experience preparing, auditing, analyzing, or evaluating financial statements with the complexity similar to the company's financial statements; understands internal controls over financial reporting (ICFR); and has an understanding of AC functions.

The organization's Chief Audit Executive (CAE) should report directly to the AC and discuss with its members any matters that are the cause of concern regarding the organization's compliance, financial, operational, strategic, IT, and other matters under the CAE's purview.

The AC should receive internal audit reports, especially those containing findings of high importance. These are often submitted at least quarterly. Other items in these reports include:

- The audits completed, in progress during the period, and forthcoming.
- Progress being made toward the completion of the internal audit department's audit plan, including budget, percent completion of the audit plan, and key vacancies.
- Need for co-sourcing or other resources to perform unique projects or investigations.
- Status of findings reported in previous audits and whether they were remediated as expected or still outstanding.
- Other matters pertaining to the oversight responsibility of the AC.

In many organizations it is commonplace for internal audit managers and even staff to accompany the CAE when making presentations to the AC. This provides the AC an opportunity to meet the staff performing these reviews, but also for the staff to become better acquainted with the AC, its areas of interest, and its communication style and expectations.

Standard 1300 indicates that the internal audit function should have in place a Quality Assurance and Improvement Program (QAIP) consisting of an internal and external review mechanism. The AC should select and approve the external reviewer, receive a report summarizing the results of such review and enforce the remediation of deficiencies noted. Other elements of the QAIP, like survey results, should be provided to the AC as well.

Summary

1. Internal auditors report to their AC, which is also responsible for the hiring, performance evaluation, budget and oversight of the CAE, and the internal and external audit functions.
2. Internal auditors submit reports to the AC at least quarterly, listing the audits and other projects closed, in progress, or to be initiated, and the status of previously reported findings.
3. AC members are ideally external to the organization and contain at least one financial expert.

Chapter 10

Audit Plan

The audit plan is the result of a process to identify the engagements the internal audit function will work on. It is the result of a combination of activities, mostly anchored on the organization's risk assessment. The risk assessment begins with the identification of the risk universe and important activities of the organization with the goal of deciding what and when they should be audited. The list may include general ledger (GL) accounts, geographic locations, systems, products, services, and compliance requirements the organization considers important to its success and as such should be examined by the internal audit function. Other inputs to the audit plan are:

- Recurring audits, such as those mandated by regulators. Others are recurring because they represent an essential and high-risk activity within the organization, such as branch, sales office, or store audits.
- Special initiatives and projects including new computer applications, mergers, acquisitions, joint ventures, and partnerships.
- Direct requests from the board of directors or due to management's specific concerns.

Audit plans should be diversified and include Operational, Financial, Compliance, and IT reviews, with a portion of available resources reserved for Special Projects and Fraud Investigations. The percentage allocated to each category varies by industry and organization, since some environments are heavily regulated and may require a larger percentage of the internal audit budget allocated to compliance. Organizations at a lower level of control maturity may also require more compliance audits. In general, however, there should be a balance based on the organization's current and future needs so areas of importance are not neglected.

The audit plan should be approved by the Audit Committee of the Board of Directors and shared with senior management annually.

Although a great deal of effort and care is spent preparing the audit plan, this is not a static document. As the fiscal year progresses, organizational imperatives may change requiring the re-allocation of audit resources to accommodate changing conditions. That said, a typical measure of internal audit effectiveness is the percentage of the audit plan completed at the end of the fiscal year.

The process of preparing the audit plan is a great opportunity to get the Audit Committee and Senior Management involved in the identification of auditable areas. By soliciting, considering, and when possible, including their requests, internal auditors can use this opportunity to engage business leaders and verify that the audit plan reflects the needs and concerns of the organization.

Some CAEs share the audit plan with the business at the beginning of the year as a way to alert the organization of impending audits. This early notification helps to ensure coordination with line management (e.g., vacation schedules) and that the timing of the audits won't interfere with critical business needs (e.g., system updates and rollouts, planned company shutdowns). Other CAEs notify audited units several weeks or a few months in advance about upcoming audits. This is often done through an Engagement Letter.

Multi-year audit plans are very useful to embed strategic planning into the process. Increasingly, organizations develop 5-year audit plans, which provide a mechanism to link hiring plans, rotation programs, and co-sourcing arrangements into the staffing and competency needs.

Summary

1. The audit plan should be risk-based and focus on the larger risks the organization is exposed to.
2. Some audits are mandated by regulators or other stakeholders and may be recurring regardless of the perceived risk rating.
3. Audit plans should strive to diversify the reviews performed so there is a balance between the different types of audits conducted. The goal is to address organizational needs.

Chapter 11

Audit Program

The audit program defines what the auditors are going to review. In many respects it serves as a roadmap, showing auditors how to navigate the engagement, and a fence, keeping auditors within the stated objectives. The image of the roadmap is important, so auditors move throughout the audit with a sense of purpose, examining relevant risks and controls. Conversely, the idea of a fence is equally important because without constraints auditors are likely to wander away from their intended purpose and suffer from scope creep.

When developing the audit programs, it is important that they be done based on risks. For that to happen effectively, the auditor must identify the relevant business, program, or process objectives first; identify and link the related risks; then determine which controls are present and connect them to the related risks. The audit program is the collection of audit steps that will be performed to verify the presence and performance of controls and other remediation procedures to mitigate risks within the defined risk appetite. The Risk-Control Matrix facilitates this alignment and is a tool frequently used by internal auditors.

After preparing the audit program, auditors should arrange the audit steps in descending order based on the risk and controls that mitigate them. Similarly, they should assign auditors to perform those tests and verification procedures, so the fieldwork is more effective. Failure to prioritize audit steps often leads to individuals auditing the easier items first causing project management problems. The primary issue is that if delays occur, or findings are found to be more complex than anticipated, auditors run out of time before they can perform an in-depth analysis of the situation and search for the issues' root cause.

The audit program should be reviewed and agreed upon before testing begins so a strategy can be prepared before fieldwork starts. When testing begins without such a review and strategy formulated, the team is likely to test inefficiently (e.g., selecting more samples than necessary when transactions could be subjected to multiple tests, interviewing clients and asking for documents multiple times and in poor sequence).

Although the audit program defines what will be tested, why, and in what sequence, it is not intended to be an inflexible document. After testing begins auditors may discover that risks are more significant than initially anticipated, that controls are under-performing, or that documents and data are not as readily available as anticipated. If these and similar situations emerge, auditors should revisit the audit program to determine if larger or additional samples must be selected, testing must be enhanced, procedures reduced, or other needed changes made to better evaluate prevailing conditions.

Status updates consist of a summary of activities performed, in progress, and upcoming. With that in mind, they relate back to the progress being made on the completion of the audit program. Consequently, making this connection explicit to the team's manager and team members, will serve as a valuable mechanism to keep everyone's attention focused during the engagement.

Summary

1. The audit program serves as a roadmap, showing the auditors how to navigate the testing requirements for the engagements, and a fence, keeping the auditors from wandering off topic and engaging in scope creep.
2. Audit steps should be arranged in descending order, addressing higher-risk items first, and lower-risk items as needed and time permits.
3. Audit programs should be risk-based and focused on examining the impact of risk on the achievement of business objectives.

Chapter 12

Audit Universe

The audit universe consists of the complete range of potential audit activities and auditable entities. It generally includes programs, initiatives, units, risks, and activities an organization is engaged in, exposed to, and that collectively contribute to the achievement of the organization's objectives.

The audit universe can be treated as a risk universe as well, as it constitutes the foundation for the risk assessment, whose elements are analyzed to prioritize the internal audit function's efforts. By focusing audit efforts on topics that warrant most attention, internal auditors can maximize the use of their resources and concentrate on what matters most to the organization.

The audit or risk universe identifies all risks that could be subject to audit. The result is a list of possible audit engagements that could be carried out. It should be aligned with the organization's strategic and operating plans. This document could be organized in various ways, including by business unit, product service lines, geographic location, programs, systems, controls, or risks.

Every organization is different in terms of its structure, processes, priorities, risks, geographic reach, market volatility, regulatory requirements, and maturity, so every organization's "universe" will look differently. The risk assessment, therefore, is a vital component into the preparation of an audit universe and the subsequent development of an audit plan.

Organizations are in a constant state of change, caused by internal and external factors, so the audit universe, risk assessment and audit plan, are also subject to change. While these dynamics create a constantly changing audit universe, it remains vitally important because it allows the internal audit activity to be clear about the extent of coverage of key risks and other risk areas annually. It allows the audit committee and senior management to better evaluate, and value, the priorities assigned to auditable activities. It also allows auditors to determine when to perform their reviews, and how rigorous those reviews should be.

Table 12.1 Audit Universe Planned Coverage

Tier 1	High risk High/full coverage
Tier 2	Medium risk Medium coverage
Tier 3	Low risk Low/no coverage

In general, an audit universe, aided by a risk assessment and an audit plan, makes sure that cyclical audit reviews result in auditing the oversight over significant risks rather than risks that have little or no significance to the organization. The result is that entities and programs with lower risk ratings would be audited at a different frequency than those with a higher risk rating. In fact, some areas could potentially never be audited, if they are adequately being reviewed by other assurance providers within the first and second lines of defense*.

The planned coverage can be arranged in tiers, showing the relative importance of each item in the audit universe. Board and senior management priorities and regulatory demands also influence each tier and each item's classification (Table 12.1).

Organizations generally align their audit universe to coincide with their multi-year audit plan, so that all items in the audit universe are reviewed at least once during the multi-year cycle.

Summary

1. The audit universe is an important element in the internal audit department's planning of its activities. All auditable entities should be reviewed within a reasonable amount of time to ensure coverage.
2. The audit universe may include programs, processes, information systems, geographic locations, products, services, and general ledger accounts.
3. The audit universe is subject to change as the organization's structure and activities change over time. Internal auditors should examine their audit universe at least annually to make sure their list is complete.

---

* For more details about the first and second lines of defense, please refer to the Three Lines of Defense Model.

Chapter 13

Balanced Scorecard

The balanced scorecard is a system used for planning and management to make sure business operations are aligned with the organization's vision, mission, and strategy. It is used to monitor performance against goals. It is also useful to improve communications because it standardizes measurements and facilitates the creation of a common performance-management language. Thirdly, it balances the goals pursued with the manner in which those goals are attained by using various measures to determine success.

The balanced scored is used by for-profit and nonprofit organizations alike as a performance measurement framework that adds strategic nonfinancial performance measures to traditional financial metrics to give managers and executives a more "balanced" view of organizational performance. While the phrase balanced scorecard has been widely used since the early 1990s, the roots of this type of approach began decades before. It has become a strategic planning and management system that enables organizations to transform their strategic plans from a lengthy, expensive, and passive document into the daily roadmap for the organization providing actionable feedback. It helps senior management turn strategies and plans into reality.

In terms of its contents, the balanced scorecard contains financial measures. But it is important to remember that financial measures are retrospective and focus on the past. To look forward, create value and succeed, organizations must also monitor metrics related to employees, customers, suppliers, processes, technology, and innovation.

Employees

The main resource for most organizations, especially those in knowledge-based industries, is their workforce because they are the most important asset and main value creators. So, when it comes to employees the balanced scorecard should measure training, engagement, and cultural attitudes at the individual and organizational levels. Some of the key questions are as follows:

- Do workers know what they need to know?
- Is that knowledge institutionalized and documented, or does it reside only in their heads?
- Is the organization taking action to prepare workers for future knowledge needs?
- Do employees embrace change and continuous learning given the changing nature of the world around us?
- How engaged is the workforce?

It is imperative that organizations implement metrics to guide the allocation of training funds where they can maximize their utility. Furthermore, training should also include coaching, mentoring, and other mechanisms workers can use to get help and answer questions when needed.

Customers

An organization cannot succeed without satisfying the needs and wants of its customers. Customer satisfaction is paramount—without customers there is no business. The concept of leading indicators is also useful here, because unhappy customers will buy less, recommend the company less, post negative reviews online, complain more, and eventually find other suppliers that meet their needs. So, tracking satisfaction levels, purchasing patterns, and retention figures is important. Customer segmentation is also important because customers should be analyzed in terms of the types of customers, and the kinds of processes that provide them the products and services each customer group is looking for.

Poor performance-involving customers is a leading indicator of future decline, even if current financial results are positive.

Suppliers

Many organizations depend heavily on third-party providers for needed supplies, or to handle activities that are not part of the organization's core activities (e.g., IT, payroll, warehousing, transportation). It is very important for organizations to monitor the performance of these external business relationships. Poor controls and service delivery by these entities can cause substantial security, continuity, compliance, and strategic damage.

When organizations outsource activities, they do not eliminate the related risks; they retain most or all of them, share some, and create new ones as well.

Processes

Process-focused metrics make it possible for managers to know how well the business is running, and whether its products and services conform to the organization's mission and customer requirements. These metrics must be designed carefully by those who know these processes most intimately because outside consultants will only have a limited understanding of its characteristics and aims.

Process metrics are increasingly also including environmental impacts affecting our planet. Some of the traditional metrics (e.g., scrap) can be linked to environmental impacts. Others related to the type of waste produced, the method of disposing of such waste, and the sourcing of materials (e.g., fair trade) are increasingly watched.

Technology

The balanced scorecard is not a piece of software. Unfortunately, many people believe that implementing some form of software is the same as implementing a balanced scorecard. The process and metrics must come first. Then after developing and implementing these, performance-management software can be used to obtain the appropriate performance information to the right people at the right time. Automation adds structure, discipline, and accuracy to a balanced scorecard system, helps transform disparate corporate data into information and knowledge, and helps communicate performance information.*

Innovation

Market disruption is occurring at a fast pace in most industries, so organizations must be careful not to succumb to complacency and believe that because a business model and operating practice was successful in the past, that it will remain so in the future. Innovation is key.

While metrics may be somewhat harder to come by than employee, process, and customer metrics, it is important for a mechanism to be in place that relates quality, idea generation, training, and research and development investments geared toward

---

* For more information, see www.balancedscorecard.org/Resources/About-the-Balanced- Scorecard.

the evaluation of existing products and services, and the introduction of improved and new ones.

Balanced scorecards help employees focus their attention on what matters most for the organization to be successful; it measures accomplishments (outcomes), not just work (output); provide a way to see if the organization's strategy is working; and provide a means to compare performance and gauge progress over time.

There will always be a need for financial information, but disproportionately focusing on monetary results often leads to unbalanced situations with regard to other perspectives. Organizations should consider the way results are obtained, and adopt a multidimensional approach that considers risks, tangible and intangible costs, reputation, satisfaction, and stakeholder relations.

Summary

1. Balanced scorecards should be designed aligning the organization's mission and vision, to the strategy, to objectives and specific actions that helps management gauge progress.
2. It allows organizations to measure success applied to multiple dimensions, mainly profit, people, process/planet, customer, technology, and innovation.
3. Metrics should be developed carefully, by those who know the organization well, and select those indicators that will provide hindsight, insight, and foresight.

Chapter 14

Benchmarking

Benchmarking is the process of searching for the best performance by comparing business operations, processes, activities, and metrics in a particular organization, with a competitor or in an entire industry. What is measured varies. It typically includes quality, quantity, time, and cost of activities. It may also include elements related to structure like span of control, which refers to the number of subordinates a supervisor has.

Benchmarking allows internal auditors to add value by going beyond verifying compliance with existing policies and procedures. Typical compliance testing confirms that the practice meets the minimum requirements of the criteria. Benchmarking, on the other hand, evaluates performance against its potential.

The process of benchmarking usually involves identifying the best organizations in the industry, or another industry with similar processes, and comparing the results to one's own. The goal is to learn how well those leading organizations perform and what they do that makes them successful. A plan can then be prepared to adopt or adapt those best practices to make changes and improve performance. While benchmarking can be done as an isolated event (i.e., one time only), it is best if treated as a continuous practice within an overall process of improving performance.

Some of the typical benchmarking metrics are as follows:

- Cost per unit
- Cycle time to produce product X or deliver service Y
- Number of units produced per measure of time
- Number of defects per unit of measure (e.g., volume, time) produced
- Number of accidents per unit of measure (e.g., volume, time)

A very important consideration during any type of benchmarking is the determination that the partners are comparable organizations. This avoids the problem of "comparing apples and oranges," which describes the error of comparing two or more items or groups that cannot, or should not, be compared because they are unrelated or dissimilar. Typical issues emerge when the organizations are in different industries, but even within an industry, care is warranted because the organizations could be of vastly different sizes or operate in different geographies that have different requirements. Another important observation is to make sure the units used are comparable, if not, that they are converted, as is the case between metric and the English system.

Benchmarking can be:

Internal: Comparing performance between different groups or teams within an organization

External: Comparing performance with companies in a specific industry or across industries. These can be difficult to conduct because organizations may treat their metrics as proprietary information. When shared, it is often made public to a limited cohort and subject to confidentiality restrictions, so joining a trade association or similar group may increase the chances of obtaining external benchmarking data. Some organizations that provide assistance and share benchmarking information include the American Productivity & Quality Center (APQC), the Benchmarking Exchange, and Best Practices & Global Benchmarking Council.*

Benchmarking can be done to identify and compare results related to costs, efficiencies, and productivity as a way to improve back-office operating areas and processes. This can enhance the design during reengineering (i.e., process redesign initiatives). It can also be done in complex functions like Human Resources, Accounting and Finance to assess timelines, and costs per transaction.

In the public sector, benchmarking is done to improve public administration and improve the efficiency, effectiveness, and overall quality of government services. This is closely related to value-for-money initiatives.

Summary

1. Benchmarking consists of making a comparison with other business operations or organizations. It typically includes quantitative, qualitative, time, and cost metrics.

---

* For additional information about these organizations, see www.apqc.org/, www.benchnet.com/, and www.best-in-class.com/.

2. It can be done internally or externally, and it is important to verify the methodology used to make sure the entities used in the analysis are comparable.
3. Internal auditors can use benchmarking to add additional value for their clients beyond verifying compliance with existing policies and procedures. By evaluating performance over time and in relation to other entities, internal auditors can assess the unit's performance against its potential, and not only against its requirements.

Chapter 15

Benford's Law

Benford's Law relates to the frequency distribution of leading digits in many sets of numerical data, including utility bills, stock prices, population numbers, lengths of rivers, and other types of large data sets. The Law states that in many naturally occurring collections of numbers, the number 1 appears as the leading digit about 30 percent of the time, while the number 9 appears as the most significant digit less than 5 percent of the time. On the other hand, if the digits were distributed uniformly, they would each occur about 11.1 percent of the time (100 percent divided by 9 possible digits). These 9 digits are 1 through 9 and exclude 0, because zero as a leading digit is negligible.

Simon Newcomb, an astronomer, shared his findings in the late 1880s after noticing that in logarithm tables, the earlier pages, which started with 1, were much more worn than subsequent pages.

The phenomenon was again noted in the 1930s by the physicist Frank Benford, who tested it and was credited for it. His data set included the surface areas of rivers, the population sizes of US communities, street addresses, molecular weights, and even the numbers contained in an issue of Reader's Digest. He provided thousands of observations to prove his findings.

Uses in Internal Auditing

Benford's Law can be used to detect possible fraud and data manipulation because people who make up figures tend to follow patterns and generally distribute their numbers uniformly. Also, people usually attempt to circumvent established authorization protocols and the data will show this manipulation. For example, an employee submitting false payment vouchers may follow a pattern to keep consistent or organized records in an attempt to conceal the abuse. Similarly, an employee subject to approval thresholds may split transactions just below such threshold to circumvent the approval limits. When this happens, there is a higher than expected number of transactions with the leading digits, which would be noticeable during a comparison of the first-digit frequency distribution from the data with the expected Benford's Law distribution. The result would indicate anomalous results.

Extensive work in this regard was conducted by Mark Nigrini, who showed that Benford's Law could be used in audit and forensic accounting as a fraud indicator. He has shown how it can be applied in forensic analytics to detect purchasing card fraud, errors, waste, and abuse. Other areas within organizations where Benford's Law is particularly suitable are as follows:

- Credit card transactions
- Purchase orders
- Loan data
- Customer balances
- Journal entries
- Stock prices
- Accounts payable transactions
- Inventory prices
- Customer refunds

Benford's Law also makes predictions about the distribution of second, third, and subsequent digits. IDEA, a software tool widely used by internal auditors,

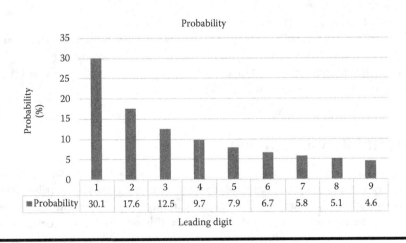

	1	2	3	4	5	6	7	8	9
■ Probability	30.1	17.6	12.5	9.7	7.9	6.7	5.8	5.1	4.6

Figure 15.1 First leading digit distribution using Benford's Law.

can perform tests up to the fourth digit. ACL can do the same up to six digits (Figure 15.1).*

Benford's Law is expected to apply to certain data sets and not others:

Expected to Comply	Not Expected to Comply
• Numbers that result from mathematical combination of numbers (e.g., quantity × price) • Transaction level data (e.g., disbursements, sales)	• Where numbers are assigned sequentially (e.g., check numbers, invoice numbers) • Where numbers are influenced by human thought (e.g., prices set by psychological thresholds such as $1.99) • Accounts containing firm-specific numbers (e.g., accounts set up to record $100 refunds) • Accounts with a built-in minimum or maximum • Airline passenger counts per plane • Telephone numbers • Data sets with 1,000 or fewer transactions • Data generated by formulas (e.g., YYMM#### as an insurance policy number) • Data restricted by a maximum or minimum number (e.g., hourly wage rate)[a]

[a] Additional information about Benford's Law and how it can be used by internal auditors is available at www.isaca.org/Journal/archives/2011/Volume-3/Pages/Understanding-and-Applying-Benfords-Law.aspx and http://faculty.usfsp.edu/gkearns/Articles_Fraud/Benford%20Analysis%20Article.pdf.

Summary

1. Benford's Law provides an analytical tool to identify anomalous transactions that internal auditors can investigate further.

---

* For more information about the capabilities of two leading internal audit analytics software, see IDEA features at https://www.casewareanalytics.com/blog/idea-tech-tip-using-benford%E2%80%99s-law and ACL at https://enablement.acl.com/helpdocs/analytics/13/user-guide/en-us/Content/da_analyzing_data/c_about_benford_analysis.htm.

2. It is a versatile tool applicable to a variety of transactions. Internal auditors may find it particularly useful when reviewing thresholds and cutoffs in large randomly-generated data sets.
3. Data analysis tools like ACL and IDEA have functions that calculate and display the distribution of the leading digits. The analysis can also be done with common tools like Microsoft Excel.

Chapter 16

Board of Directors

An organization's board of directors constitutes the highest authority after the owners/shareholders. In the case of for-profit, publicly-traded companies, they are selected by the shareholders during the organization's annual meeting. Nonprofit organizations sometimes have volunteer or appointed boards. Other names for similar bodies are board of trustees, board of regents, board of governors, and executive board, and they are responsible for, among other things:

1. Setting the overall direction, or strategy, of the organization
2. Setting and supporting the tone at the top
3. Evaluating the performance of the organization's most senior manager (e.g., CEO, President)
4. Reviewing the performance of the organization's Chief Audit Executive (i.e., CAE)
5. Evaluating and approving the organization's auditors' plan, and budget

For decades there has been a vibrant debate about the role of boards and the relationship between them and the organization's internal auditors. In general, boards are designed to provide oversight over the organization's highest executive (e.g., CEO, President) and to make sure that the interests of stakeholders are protected.

Corporate governance has gained a great deal of attention since the financial breakdowns involving Enron, WorldCom, Adelphia, Tyco, and many others between 2000 and 2002. A clear manifestation of this was the enactment of the Sarbanes–Oxley (SOX) Act of 2002. While compliance with SOX is required for companies trading their stock in United States equity markets, it is also required by some creditors and regulators who view its provisions as exemplars of best practices.

Within SOX, key provisions addressing the role of the board of directors (or its namesake), and the most senior executives, include:

Section 301: The establishment of audit committees that must be composed solely of independent directors.

Section 302: Certification by CEOs and CFOs of company financial reports.

Section 402: Prohibition of any form of personal loans to executives or board members.

Section 403: Disclosures of transactions involving management and principal stockholders.

Section 406: Required disclosure regarding codes of ethics for CEOs and senior financial officers.

Section 805 and 1102: Enhanced criminal penalties for any executive action to obscure, tamper, hide, or misreport financial statements or corporate tax returns.

But before 2002, the Blue-Ribbon Committee (BRC) on Improving the Effectiveness of Corporate Audit Committees examined the role of boards and recommended improvements. In August 1999 The CPA Journal reported on recommendations that the SEC Chair Arthur Levitt and the BRC made.* Among its recommendations was that board members be able to commit sufficient time and energy to meet their responsibilities and stressed the importance of ensuring proper disclosure and transparency in financial reporting. Another requirement was that listed companies have at least a two-member audit committee composed exclusively of independent directors and having financially-literate members. Audit committees should have a charter defining their mission, external auditors should be accountable to it, and there should be independent communications with auditors to discuss questionable accounting tactics by management.

The National Association of Corporate Directors (NACD) Blue-Ribbon Commission on Culture as a Corporate Asset reports that directors should treat corporate culture as an asset and a unifying force influencing stakeholder engagement, Enterprise Risk Management (ERM), business models, strategy, goals and targets, recognition and reward systems, and talent and leadership development. It recommends boards take action in six areas:

1. Board oversight responsibilities
2. Assessing boardroom culture
3. Embedding culture into discussions about strategy, risk, and performance
4. CEO selection and evaluation
5. Reward and recognition systems
6. Communication with shareholders and stakeholders

---

* See http://archives.cpajournal.com/1999/0899/features/F34899.HTM.

The NACD recommends looking beyond compliance when setting the scope of the organization's culture oversight. In addition, directors should not examine this topic from afar, but also get an "on the ground" view by interacting with employees at all levels of the organization.*

Trends

PwC conducts an annual Corporate Directors survey, and the top six findings from its 2017 report are as follows:

1. Membership: Forty-six percent believe that someone should be replaced, and twenty-one percent stated that two or more people should be replaced from the board. This finding shows the need for qualified and committed individuals on the board who can effectively fulfill their duties given changing business dynamics. Self-assessments are being used to identify areas for board improvement.
2. Diversity: Eighteen percent said that diversity has had no benefit on their board, and only 59 percent believe it enhances company performance even though several studies show a correlation between women on boards and strong company performance. Eighty percent of female directors say gender diversity is happening too slowly, but only 33 percent of male directors feel the same way.
3. Executive Pay: Seventy percent of directors say US executives are overpaid, which is interesting because boards of directors are responsible for setting the compensation of key company executives. Drivers of this situation include the race for top talent, peer group comparisons and a heavy emphasis on incentive pay that results in large payouts when the stock market and economic performance is strong.
4. Shareholder Engagement: Although investors expect to engage with directors more often and on more topics, only 42 percent of directors say someone on their board (other than the CEO) directly engaged with investors during the past year. Twenty-three percent say no director (other than the CEO) should directly engage under any circumstance.
5. Environmental Concerns: Forty two percent of directors say they won't need to change their company strategy in the next three years because of environmental concerns. Although institutional investors are increasingly focusing on environmental, social and governance (ESG) issues, 40 percent of directors say they don't think climate change should play a role, and 29 percent say the same about resource scarcity. This is contrary to reports showing that support for environment-focused shareholder proposals increased

---

* To view the NACD Blue-Ribbon Commission on Culture as a Corporate Asset report, visit www.nacdonline.org/Resources/Article.cfm?ItemNumber=48256.

from 24 percent in 2016 to 32 percent in the 2017 proxy season reflecting a shareholder realization that climate and other sustainable issues are linked to corporate strategy, can impact growth opportunities, and affect the ability to create long term value.

6. Technology: Ninety one percent of directors say they will need to modify their company's strategy in the next three years due to the speed of technological change. This includes cybersecurity and its impact on strategy and ERM, as 86 percent say technology is challenging to oversee and 25 percent state they have not identified who might attack the organization's digital assets.*

Boards are often comprised of multiple committees to facilitate their work and address many of the diverse objectives of today's boards. Typical committees include:

Executive: It is a group of directors appointed to act on behalf of the board of directors. They traditionally acted on behalf of the board between board meetings and follows up and acts on actions taken on board decisions. It typically consists of a chairperson, vice-chairperson, secretary, and treasurer (i.e., board officers) and committee chairs.

Audit: Selected members of a company's board of directors responsible for hiring internal and external auditors, helping auditors remain independent of management, and oversee the process of preparing the company's financial reports. Most audit committees consist of three to seven directors independent of the company's management

Nominating: It focuses on evaluating the board of directors of its company and examining the skills and characteristics that are needed in board candidates. It often identifies suitable candidates for various director positions, reviews, and changes corporate governance policies. They are often comprised by the chairman of the board, the deputy chairman, and the chief executive officer. This committee sometimes has Corporate Governance added to its title.

Compensation: It sets the compensation level of senior management, which may include salary, bonuses, stock options, and company stock. Members of the compensation committee should be independent directors

Strategic: It recommends to the board, for approval, major strategic, and policy initiatives that will impact the direction and the activities of the organization

Risk: It is an independent committee that has responsibility for the risk management policies of the organization and oversight over the governance, risk management, and compliance frameworks

Other: Some organizations have established Corporate Social Responsibility (CSR), public issues and diversity committees to promote a culture that

---

* To view the summary and download the full report, go to www.pwc.com/us/en/governance-insights-center/annual-corporate-directors-survey/top-6-findings.html.

Table 16.1 Typical Board of Directors Committees

Committee
Executive
Audit
Nominating
Compensation
Strategic
Risk

emphasizes these topics and reviews corporate performance against those standards. It considers the impact of the organization, its operations, and programs from a CSR, public issues, and diversity perspective, taking into account a multi-stakeholder perspective that includes shareholders, clients, employees, communities, and regulators.

While the exact number of members on each committee will vary by organization, they typically have three or more members (Table 16.1).

Duties

The duties of the boards of directors include:

- Establishing high-level general policies and setting strategic objectives
- Selecting, reviewing, and when necessary, terminating, the performance of the chief executive officer, president, executive director, or similarly titled officer
- Making sure sufficient financial resources are available
- Approving annual budgets
- Being accountable to the organization's stakeholders for its performance
- Setting the salaries, compensation, and benefits of senior management

One of the key responsibilities of boards, especially the audit committee of the board, is the review and sign-off of the organization's financial statements. The SOX Act stipulated in Section 407 that audit committees must have at least one member who is a financial expert. This individual should have, through education and experience as a public accountant, auditor, principal financial officer, comptroller, principal accounting officer of an organization, or from performing similar functions, an understanding of generally accepted accounting principles, financial statements, experience in the preparation or auditing of financial statements, the application of accounting principles, experience with internal controls; and an understanding of audit committee functions. In general, the financial expert must understand the preparation of financial statements and be able to question the appropriateness of financial transactions and their record-keeping. Having a financial expert on the audit committee is a practice that all boards should implement, whether the organization is required to comply with the SOX Act or not; whether it is for-profit or not.

Two important responsibilities of boards are to ensure they have the requisite expertise within their membership, and apply proper oversight over business activities and assets. Boards must look inward to make sure they have the appropriate skillset to discharge their duties and oversee the way the organization operates, how it is structured, how issues are communicated and remediated, and how assets are protected and enhanced. This bi-directional approach to board duties would then highlight the importance of ensuring proper governance, risk management, and compliance structures and processes are in place. Other areas of importance include assessing its own purpose, culture, leadership, information flows, accountability, and sustainability.

Summary

1. The board of directors is the highest authority in an organization and is responsible for setting the tone at the top, overseeing the strategy for the entity, providing funding, and overseeing the activities of the company's senior managers in pursuit of the organization's mission and strategy.
2. The board is comprised of several committees, including the audit committee, which internal and external auditors report to.
3. Boards must ensure they have the requisite skills to discharge their duties, including collectively having knowledge of corporate governance, risk management, compliance, and financial expertise.

Chapter 17

Cause and Effect Diagram

One of the challenges internal auditors encounter when analyzing a finding is identifying the root cause of the problem. What caused the problem? After all, unless that source is identified and corrected, it is likely the recommendation won't correct the problem and the issue will recur.

The Cause and Effect Diagram, also commonly known as the Fishbone Diagram (for the shape of the completed diagram) and Ishikawa Diagram (for the name of Kaoru Ishikawa, who invented it), serves as a very useful visual tool to identify the root cause of problems.

The following steps are followed when completing a Cause and Effect Diagram:

1. Draw the general shape of a fish, and place the problem statement (i.e., effect) at the head of the fish
2. Identify the four to six general categories of issues that contribute to the problem statement and place them around the periphery as arrows pointing to the backbone of the fish. For a list of common categories, see Table 17.1. These items only represent major categories that cause variation, but other categories can be used as well. When preparing the Cause and Effect Diagram, items can be chosen from either column. The list of typical categories can be longer than six items, and in some cases, it is categorized based on the type of organization or environment where the effect is being analyzed. As shown on Table 17.1, the list is slightly different when the exercise is performed in an industrial vs. a service organization.
3. Brainstorm related items and place them as smaller arrows connecting the sub-causes to the major causes in a drill-down manner. These smaller bones represent more detailed causes or sources of the problem.
4. Identify the top two or three items that have the biggest influence on the effect.
5. Explore two or three corrective actions to correct each of the items

Table 17.1 Typical Fishbone Diagram Causes

Service Environments	Industrial or Manufacturing Environments
• Policies	• Machinery/equipment/technology
• Procedures	• Methods/process
• Training	• Materials/money
• System (IT)	• Staffing/manpower
• Technology	• Measurement/inspection
• Environment	• Environment/mother nature
• Plant and equipment	• Maintenance
• Processes	• Suppliers
• Customer	
• Budget/funding/money	
• Management	
• Skills	

When done drawing the diagram, it should become clearer why the issue exists, which items are most influential in causing the problem, and some ideas to correct the problem itself. I have found this tool, and especially Steps 4 and 5 very useful moving the analysis beyond problem identification and into solution mode.

The Fishbone Diagram is a great tool and serves as a very useful supplement to the CCCER (Criteria, Condition, Cause, Effect, and Recommendation) Model used by many internal auditors to document internal audit findings. The Condition is placed as the head of the fish, and the bones represent the Causes. This information makes recommendations more valuable, precise, and useful to audit clients.

Fishbone Diagrams are ideal for participative exercises, where auditors can engage the rest of the team or client employees to identify the root cause of issues and brainstorm solutions. By collecting and evaluating the ideas of several people, internal auditors can obtain better information and involve those affected in remedying the issues identified (Figure 17.1).

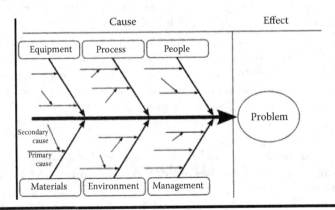

Figure 17.1 Fishbone Diagram.

Summary

1. The Fishbone Diagram is a versatile and useful tool to identify the root cause of audit findings and generate ideas to correct them.
2. These diagrams help to promote collaborative auditing practices within the audit team, and between auditors and their clients.
3. Since Fishbone Diagrams are visual, they are easy to understand, construct, discuss, and use.

Chapter 18

CCCER/5C

CCCER and 5C are the acronyms used to document the main components of internal audit findings and observations.

C: Criteria: Refers to the expectations set by relevant stakeholders. It can consist of accounting or financial standards, laws, regulations, contractual terms, policies and procedures, best practices, or other performance standards. When the criteria are not clearly defined, the internal auditor may rely on the organization's mission or vision statements, organizational values, or prevailing best practices as the basis for the criteria used to evaluate the program or process. It denotes what should exist.

C: Condition: This consists of what the auditor discovered as a result of applying auditing procedures. It can include verbal and corroborated testimony, written documents, testing procedures, observations, and calculations. Condition is what exists; the current state.

C: Cause: The cause is the reason the condition exists, and it explains why the problem occurs. It should identify the source or root cause of the problem, and not merely the symptoms or manifestation of the problem.

E: Effect: It indicates the impact the condition has on the organization, program, or process. This could be financial loss, reputational damage, bodily injury or death, or other impacts. There could be other effects, such as customer or employee dissatisfaction, delays, rework, waste, and inconsistent performance, which may eventually result in financial loss or reputational damage.

R: Recommendation: This is the action, or collection of actions, that corrects the cause, stops the effect, and returns the condition so it equals or exceeds the criteria. Although internal auditors typically develop recommendations to address the anomaly noted, they are encouraged to work collaboratively with their clients to formula the best corrective action. By using a participative style, they may generate more suitable recommendations and build stronger relationships with their clients.

When auditors and business managers work together, managers get to see the issues from their perspective, and they can draw the same conclusions because they are looking at the same evidence. This will likely result in the manager being less defensive and instead wanting to correct the issue more readily than if merely told about it.

Note: By replacing Effect with Consequence, and Recommendation with Corrective Action, the CCCER becomes 5C: Criteria, Condition, Cause, Consequence, and Corrective Action.

Quantification

Quantifying the Condition and the Effect is a good practice because it provides more precision to the magnitude and characteristics of the observation. By quantifying as much as possible, the internal auditor would be able to pinpoint when, where, who, and how often, the observation occurs, the impact of the issue, and the value and benefit of the recommendation. Due to the diversity of business conditions and dynamics, quantifying the finding is not always something that can be done easily or accurately. Under no circumstances should internal auditors communicate impact figures that cannot be supported to a reasonable degree.

Summary

1. The CCCER/5C Model is widely used by internal auditors to document internal audit findings. It consists of Criteria, Condition, Cause, Effect (Consequence), and Recommendations (Corrective Action).
2. Robust audit evidence collection and evaluation, adding a rating or risk element (e.g., High, Medium, Low), adding as many quantitative elements as possible, and working with process owners to develop recommendation/corrective actions help to make the CCCER/5C Model more effective.
3. Under Cause, internal auditors are highly encouraged to research the root cause of problems and avoid listing symptoms.

Chapter 19

Certifications

"Internal auditors must possess the knowledge, skills and other competencies needed to perform their individual responsibilities" (Standard 1210). This proficiency can be obtained and maintained through training. Additionally, obtaining a relevant certification also demonstrates the internal auditors' commitment to learning and that they have acquired sufficient knowledge to pass a certification exam.

Multiple certifications are available and often pursued by internal auditors. They are offered by different organizations dedicated to providing skills internal auditors need to perform their duties. Table 19.1 lists some of the most common certifications.

Some questions participants in my seminars often ask me include:

Question. Which certification is appropriate for me?

Answer. It depends on the individual's career track and ambitions. Some internal auditors may choose to stay in the operational realm and focus on the CIA certification, which is a general, industry-neutral certification that has become widely recognized as the premier certification for internal auditors. For many, the CIA has matched the recognition previously afforded to the Chartered Accountant (CA) and the Certified Public Accountant (CPA) credential, which focuses on accounting and tax topics. Others may want to obtain a certification that is more focused on their industry of choice, such as the CFSA (financial services) or CGAP (government). Some internal auditors may choose to follow an IT track and obtain the CISA certification. Other auditors may want to focus on information security and pursue the CISM or CISSP. So, it depends, but there are many options to choose from.

Question. How many certifications can I obtain?

Answer. There is no limit to how many you can obtain. Some internal auditors want to make a lateral move in their careers, broadening their skillset and

Table 19.1 Common Certifications Pursued by Internal Auditors

Organization	Certification	Description
Institute of internal auditors (IIA)	CIA	Certified internal auditor
	CFSA	Certified financial services auditor
	CGAP	Certified government audit professional
	CCSA	Certification in control self-assessment
	CRMA	Certification in risk management assurance
The Board of environmental health and safety auditor certifications (BEAC) in partnership with the IIA	CPEA	Certified professional environmental auditor
	CPSA	Certified process safety auditor
Information systems audit and control association (ISACA)	CISA	Certified information systems auditor
	CISM	Certified information systems auditor
	CGEIT	Certified in the governance of enterprise IT
	CRISC	Certified in risk and information systems control
Association of certified fraud examiners (ACFE)	CFE	Certified fraud examiner
(ISC)[2]	CISSP	Certified information systems security professional
	SSCP	Systems security certified practitioner
	CCSP	Certified cloud security professional

(Continued)

Table 19.1 (*Continued*)   Common Certifications Pursued by Internal Auditors

Organization	Certification	Description
	CAP	Certified authorization professional
	CSSLP	Certified secure software lifecycle professional
	HCISPP	Healthcare information security and privacy practitioner
	ISSAP	Information systems security architecture professional
	ISSEP	Information systems security engineering professional
	Associate of (ISC)^2	Associate of (ISC)^2
Project management institute (PMI)	PMP	Project management professional
	PgMP	Program management professional
	PfMP	Portfolio management professional
	CAPM	Certified associate in project management
	PMI-PBA	PMI professional in business analysis
	PMI-ACP	PMI agile certified practitioner
	PMI-RMP	PMI risk management professional
	PMI-SP	PMI scheduling professional
The open group architecture forum (TOGAF)	TOGAF 9	TOGAF Open enterprise architecture standard
	Open CA	The open group certified architect
	Open CTS	The open group certified technology specialist

credentials to encompass additional focus areas. This way they are more competitive during their job search and can better differentiate themselves from the competition by having multiple certifications, including the ones that will open doors for them in the direction of their career ambitions.

Question. How many certifications should an internal auditor obtain?

Answer. It depends on your time availability, skills, and career interests. There is no maximum. In fact, over the years I've met internal auditors with five or more certifications.

Question. Is having a certification required for upward mobility?

Answer. I've noticed an interesting trend during the past three decades—organizations are increasingly requiring candidates for hire and promotion to have at least one certification. When I started in the profession it was common for organizations to state in their vacancy listings that a CPA was required. Later it was common to see job postings that read "CPA or CIA" required. More recently, it is common to see CPA, CIA, CISA, or similar certifications listed as either highly desirable or required. So, the types of certifications sought after is expanding, at the same time, it is more common to see the job requirements state "highly desired" or "required." This transition shows the broadening of the qualification expectations for internal auditors beyond the CPA, and the expectation that as internal auditors advance in their careers that they have at least one certification. This is increasingly also evident in the requirement to have a certification before promotion into internal audit management positions.

Many organizations will pay for the exam's registration fee, study guides, provide paid time off to study, and paid leave to take the exam the first time. If the candidate fails to pass the exam the first or subsequent times, the candidate is typically expected to pay personally for the expenses of retaking the exam. Some organizations also pay a bonus or give a raise to candidates who pass certification exams. Given the many short and long-term benefits, monetary and otherwise, it behooves internal auditors to take the time to pursue at least one certification in their careers.

Question. Is continuing education required?

Answer. Yes, for most certifications the requirement is 40h of continuing professional education (CPE) per year.

Question. So, if I have multiple certifications, would I need to double or triple the CPE hours?

Answer. No, CPE hours can be used for multiple certifications. You should look closely at the type of training, however, because some unique requirements may apply. For example, the IIA requires 2 CPE hours in the subject matter of ethics per year for its certifications.

Summary

1. Having at least one certification is becoming increasingly common among internal auditors and is also highly expected for job qualification and promotion.

2. There are many options for internal auditors to choose from. It depends on the industry and what specialty is best aligned with the auditors' career ambitions.

3. Organizations are increasingly paying for test preparatory materials, registration and provide paid time off to sit for certification exams. Internal auditors should consider pursuing certifications as the cost is typically borne fully by their employers, and the benefits are in the form of monetary and career advancement.

Chapter 20

Charter

A charter is a document that outlines the goals, expectations, resources, and mandate of an organization or endeavor. Internal audit departments and internal audit committees of the board of directors/trustees/regents should have a charter in place that is reviewed and re-certified annually. Charters should indicate, among other things:

- The mission, vision, scope, and purpose
- Authority
- Independence and objectivity of the function
- Composition/membership
- Functions
- Resourcing/funding
- Access to information, data, records, and individuals

The charter is an essential document to establish the mandate internal audit has within the organization, and the protections afforded this function to perform its duties undeterred. It should also clarify who has the authority to hire, reward, discipline, and terminate the chief audit executive. Best practices and regulatory guidelines recommend that only the audit committee have this authority.

The internal audit charter should also provide information regarding the types of audits internal auditors are authorized to perform. Typically, the list includes compliance, financial, operational, forensic, information technology and information security audits. Special projects, such as consulting and advisory services, should be part of the list too. By defining the types of audits, it makes it clearer for everyone in the organization what internal audit does and how they can best partner with them. Listing the diversity of projects that internal audit performs could be a valuable enhancement for some organizations lacking a history of internal auditing and whose board and employees may be unaware of the variety of engagements internal auditors perform. For those organizations where the internal auditors have focused disproportionately on one type of reviews (e.g., compliance), it provides a mechanism to broaden the scope of work and the opportunities for internal auditors to add value in additional ways.

It is a good idea to post the internal audit department charter within the organization's intranet where it is available for review by interested parties. The charter should be reviewed and re-certified annually by the board of directors.

Project Charters

Similarly defined as mentioned above, a project charter defines and authorizes a project's scope and objectives, and other key elements such as the timeline and budget. The charter should be created at the Initiation phase*, before significant resources are assigned and spent. An early project charter can be as short as a single or a few pages long.

The Project Management Institute (PMI) and best practices recommend that projects, especially medium and large ones, have a project charter developed, ratified by senior management, and implemented before the project begins. Having a project charter in place will avoid, or at least minimize, issues later.

The charter documents the relationships between the project and the organizational strategy. Although scheduling, funding, scoping and communication have generated a great deal of attention, not enough attention is given to the charter in effective project management. A project charter should be precise and comprehensive. The PMI's PMBOK Guide, third edition defines a project charter as "a document issued by the project initiator or sponsor that formally authorizes the existence of a project, and provides the project manager with the authority to apply organizational resources to project activities." A key word in this definition is "authority." It authorizes both the project and the project manager. The PMBOK Guide also states that the charter should provide information regarding:

- Requirements
- Business needs
- Summary schedule
- Assumptions and constraints
- Business case, including return on investment, if feasible and possible

The formality of the document may vary, and it could be as simple as an e-mail or memo. It doesn't even have to be in one document, although it would be best if it

---

* The Project Management Institute (PMI) defines project phases as: Initiating, Planning, Execution, Monitoring and Controlling, and Closing.

were. In general, there are some key questions that characterize a charter and the key components and practices it seeks:

- Authorization for its existence: Is there a sponsor, does the sponsor know the project exists, and does the sponsor agree that it should exist?
- Authorization of the project manager: Does the sponsor know who the project manager is? Does the sponsor support the PM's leadership role in the project?
- Authorization to provide resources: Did the sponsor give the PM authority over money, people, and other needed resources to complete the project?
- How has the sponsor indicated agreement with the questions above?
- How and where was that indication made? Is it in writing? Was it documented in meeting minutes? Who was in attendance if it was done verbally?

Note that throughout, the theme is "authorization." I have witnessed project managers struggle on several occasions because their authorization, or authority, was limited and the effects were felt in the form of limited or late funding, limited cooperation and time commitment by business partners, and limited enforcement powers to remediate issues.

Informal Formats

In addition to an e-mail or meeting minutes, many of the contents and spirit of a charter could be defined in a work order since it gives specific people authority over resources and provides an overview of the scope. The accompanying signatures or electronic approvals also give this document the legitimacy from the parties involved.

While not ideal, verbal instructions from a manager, followed by supporting documents about the desired results, business needs, and progress updates, can also be treated as providing the elements of a charter.

The details contained in a project could be limited at first; just enough to begin the needed research, gather business requirement or define the final deliverables. Then subsequently, the charter can be revised to provide more details regarding the requirements, schedule and budget needed.

Charters can be instrumental in giving projects a good start. They provide an opportunity to improve organizational maturity by defining the scope, budget, timeline and purpose of these initiatives and the rationale for the investment that they inevitably require. All of these items can be linked to risks and controls. In addition, charters help to decide whether the project should proceed or continue, connect to organizational goals and strategies, and provide controls over the authorization/accountabilities involved and the allocation of organizational assets.

Summary

1. A charter provides the authorization, and outlines the goals, expectations, resources and mandate of an organization or endeavor. As such, the audit committee and the internal audit function should have their own charter, which should be ratified annually.
2. Audit charters should outline the different activities that internal auditors perform, or could perform, making it clear that modern internal auditing goes beyond compliance and financial reviews.
3. Projects generally represent a high-risk activity in organizations and a key success factor is having a charter during its initiation, and subsequent adjustments as the project advances, defining its authority, purpose, scope, resource requirements, and timeline.

Chapter 21

Check Sheet

Check sheets are one of the most common tools used by internal auditors, even though it is rarely called by that name. A more common name is tally sheet. Check sheets are a structured form used to collect and analyze data, often obtained real time or tabulated from previous sources. Data are recorded by making check marks on it.

Check sheets make it easier to count and track the number of instances of an attribute examined during an engagement, like transaction testing. These sheets are useful to document the frequency of problems, defects, defect causes, events, or other phenomena.

To prepare a check sheet:

1. Identify and document the criteria that will be used during the evaluation of the transactions chosen
2. Decide what event, condition, or problem will be examined and documented
3. Decide when and for how long the data will be collected
4. Design the check sheet so data can be recorded simply and clearly. Documentation may include tick marks or numbers
5. Place headers to label all columns and rows
6. Select the transactions (e.g., sample items) that will be examined
7. Record on the check sheet the results of the examination

Figure 21.1 shows a sample check sheet of the number of errors made while paying invoices.

Check sheets should indicate who filled out the form, what was collected, what each tickmark represents, demographic information for each item tested (e.g., an identifying batch, source or lot number), where the collection occurred, when

	Mon	Tues	Wed	Thurs	Fri	Total
Processed without Approval	4	3	1	2	2	12
No PO created for invoice	3	1	5	3	1	13
No PO Referenced on Invoice	2	3	3	1	0	9
Charged to Wrong Cost Center	3	2	1	0	2	8
Goods Not Received	2	3	1	0	3	9
Calculation Error	0	0	1	1	0	2
Total:	14	12	12	7	8	53

Figure 21.1 Simple check sheet.

the collection occurred (e.g., hour, shift, day of the week), and why the data were collected.

By listing each suspected defect cause, the period when the output was generated, and the operator or machine used, internal auditors can determine the root cause of errors. During the testing, and especially at its conclusion, the types of errors, their sources, and characteristics should be noted. Internal auditors can then prepare a Pareto Diagram or a Cause and Effect Diagram to help them identify the root cause of the issues.

Summary

1. Internal auditors can use check sheets to quantify the number of defects by type, location, or cause (e.g., operator, system) during testing.
2. By including critical attributes for each transaction in the design of the check sheet, internal auditors can identify the source or root cause of problems identified.
3. Since check sheets often represent the main document prepared during transaction testing, internal auditors should make tickmarks simple to use and the check sheets self-explanatory.

Chapter 22

COBIT

COBIT is one of the most widely recognized and used internal control frameworks for documenting internal controls in the Information Technology (IT) environment. The name is an acronym for Control Objectives for Information and related Technology. It was created by the Information Systems Audit and Control Association (ISACA) as an alternative to other internal control frameworks, such as COSO's IC-IF, that provided a very comprehensive focus on financial and operational risks and controls, but was short on details on IT risks, controls, and related topics. In fact, beyond risks and controls, COBIT has become a highly regarded control framework for generally accepted standards for IT control practices, IT management and staff, and IT audit.

The Framework was initially released in 1996 and has undergone several revisions and upgrades over the years. The most recent release was version 5.0 released in 2012. This version provides guidance on two domains: IT Governance and IT Management. In addition, ISACA linked each enabling process to internationally recognized standards and frameworks, such as COSO IC-IF and COSO ERM, ISO 9000, 31000, 27000, and 38500, TOGAF, Project Management Body of Knowledge (PMBOK) and Information Technology Information Library (ITIL).

IT Governance

Evaluate, Direct, and Monitor

There is a single segment for this topic with multiple enabling processes defining it. IT Governance delineates the responsibilities of the board and senior management over governance and engages these parties in their role defining, overseeing, and promoting IT strategy for the organization. It states there must be transparency with stakeholders, that IT benefits are delivered, and that risks to the IT infrastructure are optimized. This segment of the framework is labeled Evaluate, Direct, and Monitor (EDM).

There are five enabling processes in this segment:

EDM01—Ensure governance and framework setting and maintenance
EDM02—Ensure benefits delivery
EDM03—Ensure risk optimization
EDM04—Ensure resource optimization
EDM05—Ensure stakeholder transparency

IT Management

Align, Plan, and Organize

This domain has four underlying subcomponents. The first identifies the ways the organization's IT function covers strategy, and identifies the ways IT can best contribute to the achievement of the organization's objectives. COBIT argues that the strategic vision should be planned, communicated, and managed. To be successful in this regard, a proper organizational and technological infrastructure needs to be in place.

There are several key skills, activities, and outputs needed for the organization to successfully align its IT infrastructure, plan for the short and long terms, and organize itself effectively for success. These include the development and deployment of IT policies, a clear and comprehensive IT strategy, the identification and management of its IT architecture, constant pursuit of innovation, and sound financial and portfolio management.

This component has thirteen enabling processes and is labeled Align, Plan, and Organize (APO).

APO01—Manage the IT management framework
APO02—Manage strategy
APO03—Manage enterprise architecture
APO04—Manage innovation
APO05—Manage portfolio
APO06—Manage budgets and costs
APO07—Manage human resources
APO08—Manage relationships
APO09—Manage service agreements
APO10—Manage suppliers
APO11—Manage quality

APO12—Manage risk
APO13—Manage security

Build, Acquire, and Implement

The second subcomponent posits that to realize the organization's IT strategy, IT solutions, and actions must be identified, developed, or purchased, implemented, and subsequently integrated into the business processes. While making changes and maintaining existing systems, it is imperative that these actions be properly controlled.

Essential skills, outputs, and activities include business analysis, definition of business requirements, project management, systems programming, usability evaluation, capacity management, and hardware and software decommissioning.

This segment is labeled Build, Acquire, and Implement (BAI) and has ten enabling processes.

BAI01—Manage programs and projects
BAI02—Manage requirements definition
BAI03—Manage solutions identification and build
BAI04—Manage availability and capacity
BAI05—Manage organizational change enablement
BAI06—Manage changes
BAI07—Manage change acceptance and transitioning
BAI08—Manage knowledge
BAI09—Manage assets
BAI10—Manage configuration

Deliver, Service, and Support

The third subcomponent focuses on the delivery of required services ranging from traditional operations, security, business continuity, and training. In essence, to deliver needed services, the necessary support processes must be established. The Deliver, Service, and Support (DSS) segment has six enabling processes.

Essential skills and outputs include availability and problem management, incident and service desk management, security administration, IT operations, and database administration.

This segment is labeled DSS and has six enabling processes.

DSS01—Manage operations
DSS02—Manage service requests and incidents
DSS03—Manage problems
DSS04—Manage continuity
DSS05—Manage security services
DSS06—Manage business process controls

Monitor, Evaluate, and Assess

The fourth subcomponent focuses on supervision and argues that all IT processes need to be regularly assessed over time to make sure they are of high quality and ensure they comply with internal control requirements. Performance management, monitoring of internal controls, and regulatory compliance are included, because they are essential for the provision of IT governance.

Essential skills, competencies, and outputs include compliance reviews, performance monitoring, and auditing controls.

This segment is labeled Monitor, Evaluate, and Assess (MEA) and has three enabling processes.

MEA01—Monitor, evaluate, and assess performance and conformance
MEA02—Monitor, evaluate, and assess the system of internal control
MEA03—Monitor, evaluate, and assess compliance with external requirements

In addition to the domains explained above, COBIT has Five Principles:

1. Meeting Stakeholder Needs to highlight the imperative that organizations exist to create value for their stakeholders through benefits realization, risk optimization, and resource optimization.
2. Covering the Enterprise End-to-end, which means the organization must recognize the linkages, roles, activities, and relationships that exist between the enterprise's owners and stakeholders, who delegate to the governing board the setting of strategy and value enhancement. The governing board in turn sets the direction for the organization's management, who then instructs, aligns, and mobilizes the organization's operations, activities, and workers, for execution on behalf of owners and other stakeholders. These operations and activities must report on the results achieved, issues encountered, and related matters to management, who must be appropriately monitored by the Governing Body that is accountable to the Owners and other stakeholders. These linkages form a chain, that if interrupted is sure to affect the success of the organization and potentially hinder its value creation and sustainability. In fact, it has been my experience that most organizations' issues can be pinned to a point in this continuum. Conversely, organizational strength is enhanced by making this chain stronger (Figure 22.1).

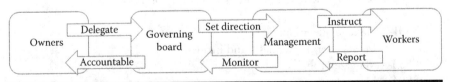

Figure 22.1 Key stakeholder roles, responsibilities, alignment, and relationships. (Adapted from COBIT 5 Introduction.)

3. Applying a Single Integrated Framework by aligning COBIT 5 with other relevant and highly regarded standards and frameworks used by organizations, such as:
   a. COSO Internal Controls-Integrated Framework (IC-IF)
   b. COSO Enterprise Risk Management (ERM)
   c. ISO 9000
   d. ISO 31000
   e. ISO 27000
   f. ISO 38500
   g. ITIL: Information Technology Information Library
   h. TOGAF: The Open Group Architecture Forum
   i. PMBOK: Project Management Body of Knowledge
   j. CMMI: Capability Maturity Model Integration
4. Enabling a Holistic Approach that integrates multiple enabler categories so their needs, interests and characteristics are addressed effectively:
   a. Principles, Policies and Frameworks: This relates to the role that behaviors influence practical guidance for daily management
   b. Processes: They are the activities performed to achieve objectives and generate outputs that support IT goals
   c. Organizational Structures: Consist of the key decision-making entities in an organization
   d. Culture, Ethics and Behaviors: This relates to the individuals and the organization. Unfortunately, this topic is very often underestimated as a success factor in governance and management activities.
   e. Information: It must be pervasive throughout any organization, and deal with all information produced and used by the enterprise. Information is required for the organization to be governed appropriately, and for keeping it running effectively. At the operational level, information is often the key product of the enterprise itself.
   f. Services, Infrastructure and Applications: This includes the infrastructure and applications that provide the organization with IT processing and services.
   g. People, Skills and Competencies: The organization's IT infrastructure is closely linked to people, what they do and how they do it. Individuals are required for successful completion of all activities, for making correct decisions and taking corrective actions when required.
5. Makes a Clear Distinction and Separates Governance from Management. Each comprises different types of activities, requires different organizational structures, and serve different purposes. While governance makes sure that stakeholder needs are met, sets direction by prioritizing initiatives, making decisions and monitoring performance, management plans, builds, runs, and monitors activities to make sure they are aligned with the direction set by the governing board.

Summary

1. COBIT* is ISACA's governance, management, and internal control framework for enterprise IT.
2. The framework consists of five principles, seven enablers, and 37 processes.
3. It covers technical, and not so technical subjects, including cost and budget management, training and human resource management, project management, risk management, change management, asset management, continuity management, knowledge management, information security, and monitoring activities.

---

* For more information about COBIT 5, Enabler Guides and Professional Guides, see www.isaca.org/COBIT/Pages/Product-Family.aspx.

Chapter 23

Code of Ethics

Organizations function within a complex web of stakeholders, and their interests range from profit maximization, brand and market share protection and expansion, and compliance with laws and regulations. Adherence to ethical practices is a common expectation. However, individuals gain an awareness of what is ethical and what is unethical based on their background and upbringing, and is subject to the influence of their families, communities, religious teachings, and legal practices.

This diversity of backgrounds can create some complications, especially as organizations hire, contract, and do business with ever-more-diverse individuals and organizations around the world. Without some guidance and clear expectations regarding what is right and what is wrong, the potential for inappropriate behavior increases. To address this situation and breach the gap in knowledge and practice, organizations are highly encouraged, and increasingly mandated, to have a Code of Ethics (COE).

The COE should be as comprehensive as feasible, providing guidance and examples of acceptable and unacceptable behaviors. In addition, the COE should go beyond a rules-based approach and provide guidance from a values-based perspective.

- Rules-Based—These documents and the related culture it aims to promote focuses on prescribing what is acceptable and what is not. It often provides a list of acceptable, unacceptable, and questionable practices. While this provides a great deal of clarity, it results in very lengthy documents. Another key limitation is that in the end it is impossible to anticipate every business scenario and its appropriateness. Also, rules-based COEs can create a culture of pushing the envelope where "if the policy doesn't say I can't do it, it means I can do it." However, that may not be a true or effective decision-making formula. Additionally, rules-based approaches can promote a culture of looking for loopholes. In general, they focus on the word of the law and outlining acceptable and unacceptable practices.

■ Values-Based—These documents focus on the spirit of the law and rely less on lists of acceptable/unacceptable practices, but rather on the organization's values and how to act according to them. They focus on the spirit of the law and emphasize guidance, training, values, and principles of conduct. By focusing on building the capacity to navigate real life scenarios, individuals develop a better ability to respond appropriately without extensive yes/no scenarios.

■ Combination—These documents combine rules and values-based elements, explaining the organization's values and intent, and listing acceptable and unacceptable practices not with a goal to provide an all-inclusive list, but rather as illustrations.

Regardless of the perspective employed, organizations should also include a mechanism for individuals to escalate questions and concerns to someone who can help them make the best decision. This could be an ethics hotline, Human Resources, Legal Counsel, an Ombudsperson or similar.

The COE should be presented to newly hired employees during the onboarding process upon hire, and opportunities to ask questions should be available so new employees understand its applicability and intent. The COE should be easily available as a resource if questions arise later during the individual's tenure.

Since contractors and consultants are spending ever increasingly higher amounts of time on company facilities, it is a good idea to provide the COE to these individuals as well, and require adherence with its instructions. Similarly, requiring vendors/suppliers to follow the COE is a good practice to encourage ethical behavior and values alignment. This is important as many organizations have encountered difficulties because their contractors or suppliers have engaged in activities that puts the organization in disrepute and causes various forms of liability.

The COE should be reviewed periodically to make sure it is meeting the organization's needs and is updated as conditions change. It is also advisable for organizations to have employees recertify annually that they agree and will comply with it.

COE documents should include guidance related to:

■ The organization's values, rights, and obligations
■ Engagement in outside business activities, obtaining employment and consulting
■ Disclosing personal or relative's interests with employees, customers, competitors, lenders, and suppliers
■ Use and purchase of company assets
■ Serving as a director or officer of other organizations
■ Political involvement and contributions
■ Illegal and unethical acts

- Falsifying or concealing internal or external information
- Giving and receiving gifts, loans, and business entertainment
- How the organization competes
- Fraud, bribery, and facilitation payments
- Conflicts of interest
- Safeguarding important information
- The application of human rights standards in the business
- Environmental responsibilities

The COE represents a very valuable instrument to define company expectations and serves as a guiding tool when questions emerge regarding what appropriate and inappropriate conduct is. It should be readily available for employee, contractor, vendor, and customer review. It should also provide clarity when finding the ethical course is unclear.

Summary

1. The COE outlines the mission and values of the organization, how those affiliated with it are supposed to behave, make decisions, and approach problems.
2. New employees should receive a copy upon hire and all employees should recertify their agreement to abide by its principles annually.
3. The COE is an important component of an organization's governance infrastructure and should be included in an audit of the corporate culture.

Chapter 24

Communications Matrix

Auditors in-charge must make sure that team members have the information they need to do their jobs. They must also manage the expectations of audit management and audit clients by communicating how things are progressing, and seeking assistance as needed to keep the audit moving forward. This can be as simple as talking to the audit team members about how they are doing on their assigned work or holding regularly-scheduled status meetings. Regardless of the approach used, communication goes a long way toward ensuring the audit or consulting engagement is successful.

On smaller audits, communication is generally simple and does not require much effort. But maintaining effective communication becomes more complex the larger a project gets, the more people are involved, and the more dispersed team members and other stakeholders are. Larger projects require communication to be planned early on, taking into consideration the needs of everyone involved.

Effective communications are an important aspect of effective internal auditing. It has been identified as a key skill of internal auditors and the *Standards* indicate that internal audit must be free from interference when communicating resulting (Standard 1110.A1), the chief audit executive must communicate and interact directly with the board (Standard 1111), the results of the quality assurance and improvement program must be communicated (Standard 1320), the internal audit activity's plans, resource requirements, and the impact of resource limitations must be communicated (Standard 2020), and internal auditors must communicate risk and control information to appropriate areas of the organization (Standard 2110). Given the importance of communication, is there a tool to facilitate their management?

The Communications Matrix is used to summarize, facilitate, and manage communications by defining the details regarding communication activities. It can be used during the team or department's activities, and during the course of a project.

Table 24.1 Communications Matrix

Communication Type	Description and Purpose	Delivery Method	Frequency	Participants	Responsible	Deliverables
Opening meeting	Introduce the team, review the audit scope, objectives and approach.	Face-to face	Once	Audit team, process owners	In-Charge	Agenda, presentation, minutes
Audit team meeting	Review status of the audit	Face to face, or conference call	Weekly	Audit team	In-charge	Agenda, minutes
Status report	Report the status of the audit, including activities, progress and issues encountered	E-mail	Every 2 weeks	Audit team, audit sponsor, division V.P.	In-charge	Project status report
Team morale	Morale and team building exercises	Event (preferably offsite)	Quarterly	Audit team	Manager	Team event

The key components of a communications matrix are the communication type, description, delivery method, frequency, documents, participants, and those responsible for making sure each communication event takes place according to the plan. Table 24.1 shows a sample communications matrix for an audit.

How to Create a Communications Matrix

The first step is to identify the relevant stakeholders that should receive communications. For an audit, this typically include the audit team, internal audit management, the key contact during the audit and the audit sponsor.

The next step is to define the types and purpose of each communication type, followed by a decision about the method that will be used. This can include face-to-face, e-mail, formal report, team meeting, conference call, or video conference.

The next step is to determine the frequency of the communication. For some stakeholders, this could mean a weekly communication. For others, like members of senior management, it could be every 2 weeks while others are as needed. Be careful about communications that don't have a frequency indicator (i.e., as needed) because they are often neglected and ignored. Also, it is a good idea to avoid having large time intervals between communications. For most audits, the largest communication interval is probably monthly. Within the internal audit function, status reports are submitted to the audit committee quarterly.

Identify who the participants are for each communication type, as these are the individuals who will receive the communication. This is usually the distribution list, or the list of attendees for meetings.

Next, determine how communication will be provided. Some stakeholders may tell you, or you may know from experience, but this typically includes written, face-to-face, phone, and video conference. I prefer communicating face-to-face whenever possible, but audit communication can take many shapes and forms. In this step, brainstorm how you will fulfill the communication needs for each stakeholder given the time availability of those involved and what is practical. When possible, look for types of communication that can cover more than one stakeholder's needs.

Another important step is to identify the person responsible for preparing and distributing the communication. Without an owner, there is a possibility that the activity won't be performed.

If there is a deliverable, such as a report, memo, meeting agenda, or presentation, add that to the matrix as well. It is often useful to have a template for recurring items so there is consistency at every defined interval. Also, using templates where appropriate throughout the department will make reports and communications comparable.

Some Communication Matrices include a column to indicate if the activity is Mandatory, Informational, or Optional. This is useful, but I am always cautious about entries marked less than mandatory because they are sometimes forgotten or ignored even though they are important.

Another interesting item I believe is useful is an estimate of the cost involved. This will likely take the form of time: How long will the communication medium take? How long is the event? For example, a status report could be estimated at taking one hour to prepare and the related meeting taking one hour a week. If a communication activity takes a lot of time to prepare and deliver, but provides little communication value, it should be evaluated or discarded. If a communication activity takes little effort and provides a lot of value, it should be included in the final Communication Matrix. Mandatory communications should be retained regardless of the cost, but opportunities for efficiency gains should be searched. If such an activity is very time consuming, you may want to negotiate with the stakeholders involved to find a less-intensive alternative.

When preparing status updates and reports, if they take much longer than estimated, the situation should be examined to determine why this is occupying more administrative time. Could it be the lack of, or a poorly structured, template? The absence of easily available data? Is it the lack of cooperation by those providing input into the report?

In general, a Communication Matrix captures the who, what, when, where, how, and why of audit communications. With this tool, transparency, accountability, consistency, and timeliness should increase, No one with an interest in the success of an audit should feel left out of important communications or find out too late that problems remain unsolved due to communication problems. By being proactive and using a Communications Matrix, internal auditors can avoid these issues and minimize the disruption that poor communications can create.

Summary

1. Effectively communicating means more than producing voluminous status update reports; it also requires providing relevant stakeholders the information they need, on time, in a useful format.
2. A Communications Matrix improves communications within the audit team, the internal audit function, and with relevant stakeholders.
3. A Communication Matrix documents the who, what, when, where, how, and why of engagement communications.

Chapter 25

Computer-Assisted Audit Tools and Techniques (CAATTs)

Internal auditing historically consisted primarily of interviews, the sampling and inspection of paper documents, verification of approvals, recalculations, and other manual procedures to verify the accuracy, completeness, appropriateness, and timeliness of business activities. These generally focused on compliance and financial reviews and workpapers were maintained, as the name implies, in paper form.

Starting in the 1980s, and rapidly accelerating since the 1990s, internal auditors have consistently increased their use and dependence on computers to perform their work. This shift coincided with the increasing use of computer systems in organizations, so as transactions were executed on computers, and as records were retained in digital form, internal auditors found it useful and appropriate, if not required, to review electronic records. So, the data explosion was met with a proliferation of software tools to collect and analyze this data, and significant increases in computing power through faster processors and more memory to hold and analyze it.

The rapid increase in electronic transactions created another problem; population sizes increased substantially raising some key questions, like how large should the sample be to produce reliable results? Are there issues that escape detection due to the sheer size of the population? How pervasive is the problem identified if the procedure did not involve statistical sampling? In general, persuasiveness of evidence became a troublesome issue because the volume of data could not be reviewed manually.

With CAATTs, which is the use of computers to automate internal auditing procedures, internal auditors can audit the entire population. This practice typically includes using basic office productivity software like spreadsheets, word processors and text editing software, but more advanced software packages that use statistical analysis and business intelligence tools are increasingly becoming available. What is often considered basic spreadsheet software, like Microsoft Excel, today can process a million records and has multiple data analytics plug-ins giving it enough features to perform complex analyses and examine most populations.

More advanced software applications, like ACL and IDEA, have no file size limitations, can manipulate files with different formats, keeps a record of all queries performed on the data, allow for the writing of scripts (i.e., mini-programs similar to spreadsheet macros) that allow the repetition of queries, automated reporting, and many other advanced features. The result is that today internal auditors can examine 100 percent of transactions with relative ease, increasing the persuasiveness of evidence, identifying anomalies that in the past escaped detection, and can more accurately quantify the scale and value of irregularities (Table 25.1).

In addition to the variety of tools, their features have also improved over time. I remember using ACL in the 1990s when a bright yellow parallel-port plug-in contained the corresponding license to enable the software to work on my desktop or laptop. Later, the license was captured within the software itself during the installation and the user interface became more user-friendly. Subsequently, server versions enhanced capacity, flexibility and speed by being able to work directly with the databases rather than having to download the data. Other than the increase in capacity, speed, and power, the improved ease of use has eliminated most excuses that prevented internal auditors from using data analytics in the past.

Table 25.1   Commonly Used Data Analytics Software

Microsoft Access
Arbutus
IDEA
IBM Business Analytics
IBM Cognos
IBM SPSS
Lavastorm
Picalo
SAP Business Objects (BOBJ)
SAS
SQL
Tableau
WizSoft (e.g., WizRule, WizWhy)

Benefits and Examples

In terms of the benefits, it is important to underscore the improvements to the persuasiveness that CAATTs produce. Rather than rely on sampling, which presents its own limitations in the internal auditors' ability to extrapolate the results from the sample to the population, CAATTs allow the internal auditor to test all transactions, making discussions about sample size and extrapolation mute. It also allows the internal auditor to evaluate erstwhile risks that were virtually impossible to evaluate. For example, splitting transactions to circumvent approval thresholds is a problem in many organizations and sampling is unlikely to result in matching transactions being selected during the sampling process. A singular transaction tested would fall within the approval threshold, but it would have at least another matching transaction, which when added together, would total more than the approval limit.

Another example is payments made after a termination date. With thousands or even millions of transactions processed, the likelihood that any of the 30–50 transactions tested in a sample was paid past the termination date is unlikely. Furthermore, even if one was detected, it would be very difficult to extrapolate that occurrence to the entire population, determine why it occurred, how pervasive the problem might be, and the monetary impact to the organization.

Consider another example: cycle-time analysis. Many organizations have been audited by internal auditors whose focus has been on completeness, accuracy, authorization and proper cutoff (e.g., posting to the general ledger in the period when the transaction occurred). However, these auditors have never scrutinized why transactions and processes take as long as they do. In many cases, customers and employees are well aware of the slow processing and delays, and have learned to live with those unfortunate realities. The question is, why haven't' internal auditors reviewed these cycle times, opined on them, and provided recommendations for improvement? The common answer is that they haven't examined that subject or even considered slow processing a risk to the organization's reputation. In many companies, speed has not been treated as an operational objective with impacts on customer service, customer retention, sales, and rework, which is a common root cause of delays, has not been examined from a cost and efficiency perspective. With CAATTs, all transactions can be examined, and a comprehensive cycle-time analysis can be prepared to identify the source, extent, and root cause of the problem. With this information, internal auditors can make recommendations to correct the problems.

Key Considerations

During audit planning it is important to take time to identify the necessary data. This can be difficult if the internal auditors don't know what is available, where it

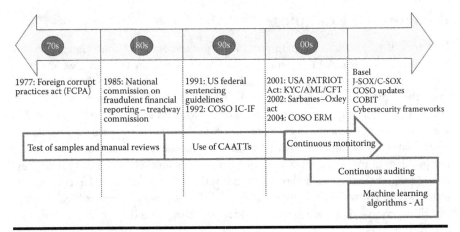

Figure 25.1 The evolution of automation in internal auditing.

is stored and in what format. Consultations with process owners and IT will help, but having a data inventory should be on the internal auditors' to-do list for the future so they know what is available and can either request it, or better yet, extract the data themselves.

When you get data, do you have all of it and is it correct? Internal auditors should verify the completeness of the data by comparing the results with another authoritative source. This reconciliation will help you avoid going down the wrong path. For example, quarterly published sales financial results on the Income Statement with the total shown for the sales data received. Remember that inaccurate data analysis resulting in invalid findings and misplaced control recommendations will have a very negative impact on the audit department's reputation.

The result is that internal auditors are applying CAATTs more frequently and successfully during the course of their work. They are gaining greater insights into operational, compliance and other aspects of the organization to perform more comprehensive reviews and gain a better understanding of what and where things are truly happening. By using CAATTS internal auditors can gain a more intimate understanding of the organization and its processes, perform more comprehensive reviews, identify root causes, and develop more precise recommendations.

The direction of CAATTs and data analytics in general suggests more automation (Figure 25.1). The introduction of more sophisticated continuous auditing mechanisms through the use of artificial intelligence (AI) allows computers to do "smart" things to help internal auditors, like identifying outliers and patterns, and issuing a notice for the auditors to research further. It has become quite apparent that writing queries and scripts to address every conceivable scenario yields good, but limited results, because conditions keep changing and fraudsters concoct new schemes.

Machine learning (ML) may be able to help. By using AI applications and gaining access to reams of data, computers will be able to sift through it, and learn on its own using systems like neural networks what is acceptable and what isn't. So rather than teaching computers how to do everything, it is more efficient to code them to think like humans. For example, if the computer could go through the data, classify it, use probabilities and patterns to identify what is acceptable, use trends and probabilities to make decisions and predict outcomes, it could "see" more than an auditor could. Then if a feedback loop is created that enables learning by telling the system whether the decisions were correct or incorrect, it would modify its approach in the future. This will be a formidable help to detect fraud, identify changes in processing patterns, recognize outliers, and other issues. We are getting closer to AI using ML-enabled CAATTs, but we are not there yet.

Summary

1. CAATTs allow internal auditors to test 100 percent of the transactions in a population, rather than having to rely on sampling techniques. Testing the entire population increases the persuasiveness of internal audit findings and recommendations.
2. By using CAATTs internal auditors can test risks that in the past could not be tested efficiently or cost-effectively. It also makes it possible to determine how pervasive issues are and assess the impacts to the organization better.
3. The availability and sophistication of CAATTs continues to increase and internal auditors should embrace these advances whenever possible.

Chapter 26

Conflict of Interest

A conflict of interest (COI) is created when the parties involved in an activity or transaction fail to meet the fiduciary responsibilities that they were initially tasked with. When an employee who was hired to pursue the organization's interests and exercise all reasonable efforts to purchase supplies economically for the organization's operating activities is otherwise engaged in making private deals that further his own interests while lowering the interests of the employer, this person is in the midst of a COI.

Conflicts of interest are a common concern of internal auditors because they can result in massive instances of abuse for personal financial gain through fraud. Since protecting the organization is one of internal auditors' main objectives, they must examine the organization's structure, practices, expectations, and monitoring mechanisms to minimize the possibility of conflicts of interest.

Conflicts of Interest represent a risk because they can corrode the organization's ethical fabric. As such, organizations typically issue policies and statements that forbid conflicts of interest in:

- Fact: Where conflicts of interest are clearly evident and for all practical purposes, undisputed.
- Appearance: Where it may not be clear that a COI occurred, or the parties involved sought and addressed the COI appropriately by disclosing the condition, recusing themselves from the related activities, or similar acts.

The appearance of conflicts of interest are a concern because although those involved may have made the proper disclosures and taken appropriate action, others may not be privy to the arrangements made and interpret the events as a sign of corruption, favoritism, nepotism, and self-dealing granting others an implied permission to engage in similar practices. Over time this corrodes the ethical environment and others may conclude that it is acceptable behavior. It may reach the point where individuals conclude that *"managers* are doing it so I should be able to do it too" or even worse, *"everyone* is doing it, so I should too."

To address this condition, organizations are highly encouraged to develop a COI policy, an annual certification statement, and provide mandatory training. These documents should contain, at a minimum:

- Definition and examples
- Prohibition to engage in activities that may constitute, in fact or appearance, by anyone, a COI
- Required action tó avoid, disclose, and correct conflicts of interest
- Guidance when operating in foreign countries given diverging viewpoints, expectations, and practices

These statements should be presented to newly hired employees promptly upon hire and instruct them to disclose, in writing, any present COI in fact or in appearance. Annual re-certification should be obtained from all employees and there should also be a requirement that if a COI emerges between re-certifications, that it be disclosed immediately. If universal coverage is not possible or feasible, then at the very least key high-risk and prominent employees should complete and sign a COI statement annually.

Auditing Conflicts of Interest

Auditing COI can be difficult because this topic typically involves parties outside the organization. Key audit steps include:

1. Verify that a COI policy is in place, that it was ratified within the past two years, and that it is readily available to employees (e.g., on the company's intranet, the employee handbook)
2. Confirm that a COI statement was signed by all employees, and key contractors, within the past year.
3. Determine if COI is covered in onboarding, ethics, or similar training, and how often it is provided to employees.
4. Verify that all conflicts disclosed in the COI statements were appropriately addressed by the assigned party (often either the Legal Department or Human Resources).
5. Review public records for key vendors and search public databases for affiliations by high-risk individuals, such as purchasing agents and contract managers. This step is increasingly becoming easier as vendors, contractors, and other third-party stakeholders file ownership statements, which are available as public records. Individuals making vendor selections should have

written documentation stating that no conflicts exist during their vendor selection process. If there is a suspicion of impropriety, the review of the vendor and employee demographics would naturally become more exhaustive.

6. If possible, compare personnel records to vendor master data to determine if there is matching information. For example, names, initials, addresses, phone numbers, bank routing and account numbers, tax, and other identification information.

Summary

1. COIs degrade the judgment of the person involved and enable fraud, corruption, nepotism, favoritism, self-dealing, and other inappropriate actions within the organization.
2. A COI policy should be in place, annual statements should be filed by all employees disclosing any conflicts, and training should be available. There should also be clear administrative sanctions in place in the event a COI was not disclosed, and the individual involved acted upon it for the benefit of someone other than the organization.
3. Internal auditors can test this topic as a separate review, or as part of an overall ethics audit.

Chapter 27

Consulting

The Institute of Internal Auditors (IIA) defines the internal audit activity in its *Standards* as "a department, division, team of consultants, or other practitioner(s) that provides independent, objective assurance and consulting activity designed to add value and improve an organization's operations." While the main task of internal auditors is to evaluate the degree to which the organization is adhering to applicable compliance expectations (i.e., assurance), the definition adds "... and consulting." This has been an interesting and challenging, if not controversial item on the definition because on the surface it appears to contradict the requirement that internal auditors remain independent and objective in their work. But this duality of purpose is required, expected and advantageous to the internal auditor and the client alike as it provides many opportunities to demonstrate the value that internal auditors can add to their organizations.

Consulting relates to advisory and client service activities that are agreed with the client and intended to add value, and improve an organization's governance, risk management, and control processes without the internal auditor assuming management responsibility. Examples include counsel, advise, facilitation, and training. It also means giving information, recommendations, and warnings. Internal — auditors are consulting every time they give advice to someone who is in a position to make the ultimate choice or decision.

While there is a gray area between these two elements, they are certainly not mutually exclusive. Internal auditors can, and should, try to meet both aspects of the definition because they complement each other and enhance the opportunities to add value to their organizations.

The Merriam Webster Dictionary defines consulting as "providing professional or expert advice."* There are two very important elements to this definition. First,

---

* See www.merriam-webster.com/dictionary/consulting.

it supports the mandate that auditors be proficient and competent in their work (Standard 1210). Second, internal auditors give "advice," which the Merriam Webster Dictionary defines as providing "recommendations regarding a decision or course of conduct."*

Most, if not all, practicing internal auditors have experienced at one point or another the apathy or outright pushback from clients who fail to see the value in the compliance work that internal auditors perform. While auditors know that they are adding value for their clients, helping them avoid mistakes, theft, and other forms of abuse, some business leaders don't. In fact, many audit clients narrowly view internal auditors as being obstructionists and overly conservative. This negative perception is exacerbated when internal auditors focus exclusively on providing lists of problems without helpful recommendations or even the root cause of the problems shown.

I believe that "consulting" can be viewed from a dual perspective: First, in the form of advisory services and special projects as the definition states. Beyond that, however, I also consider "consulting" as an approach. Consultants typically work collaboratively with their clients. They take a deep interest in understanding the objectives and challenges of their clients, and search for ways to help them operate more efficiently, effectively, and economically. Their communications are balanced in that they present issues, but also provide ample coverage of recommendations and how to improve practices. Since consultants know they are hired or fired based on the results of their work, they thrive to delight the client, demonstrate that the price paid was worth the services received, and try to cross-sell services by constantly looking for additional business opportunities.

Internal auditors should incorporate a similar mindset while conducting their reviews, whether they are advisory services or otherwise, and without compromising their independence (during implementation and operation of recommendations) or objectivity (by remembering that they ultimately report to the board of directors and are the advocates for other stakeholders too).

When conducting consulting or advisor services, internal auditors should make sure there is clarity regarding the role the internal auditors and the clients will play. The process of clarifying expectations begins with making sure these services are explained to the board and senior management. Standard 1000.C1 states "The nature of consulting services must be defined in the internal audit charter."

A common concern is whether internal auditors would lose their independence and objectivity by performing consulting services if they need to perform assurance services later. The *Standards* provide some clarity in that regard by stating "the internal audit activity may provide assurance services where it had previously performed consulting services, provided the nature of the consulting did not impair objectivity and provided individual objectivity is managed when assigning resources to the engagement" (Standard 1130.A3). The overarching rule is that "If internal auditors have potential impairments to independence or objectivity

---

* See www.merriam-webster.com/dictionary/advice.

relating to proposed consulting services, disclosure must be made to the engagement client prior to accepting the engagement" (Standard 1130.C2).

There are many benefits to consulting, including:

- Offsetting costs that would otherwise go to outside consultants
- Continued and enhanced relationships with auditees
- Makes internal auditors available to provide assistance before, during, and after the engagement
- Availability to help business whenever necessary
- Provides an in-depth knowledge of the organization
- Creates an ability to leverage and expand audit knowledge
- Use of internal and external benchmarking

There are different types of consultants:

- Advisory Consultants: Analyze problems and give recommendations to the client. They do not implement.
- Operational Consultants: Advise and help the client during implementation or handle implementation on their own.
- Process Consultants: Skills-oriented generalists with expertise in one or more technical areas.
- Functional Consultants: Apply their skills to a particular environment. For example, a hospital facilities expert would concentrate on consulting to hospitals.

When advising clients, internal auditors should remember that an important part of the job is to help the client move from what they know and believe in, to a position where they understand, come to the realization, and agree that improvements are needed. To do this a step-by-step process is very effective; it is usually called the Socratic Method based on asking and answering questions to stimulate critical thinking, and it may be applied as follows:

- Why do you think this problem exists?
- What alternatives or options are there to do things differently?
- What are some of the advantages of the different options?
- How do you think others, who have a say or are impacted by this change, will react?
- How do you suggest we address the consequences of their actions?
- Others have encountered these difficulties when they tried that. What can we do to prevent those things from occurring?
- What are the benefits if we tried the following approach?

While it is easy to succumb to the temptation to just tell the client what to do, it is best to be patient and work with the client in a collaborative manner when giving advice.

IT Consulting

A very interesting dynamic has developed over the years. Many years ago, internal auditors reviewed system development initiatives after the systems were released to the business and were in production. The problem with that approach was that any issues identified requiring code changes were very expensive and disruptive when found at this point in the development cycle. In fact, the National Institute of Standards and Technology (NIST) report The Economic Impacts of Inadequate Infrastructure for Software Testing reports that it costs 30 times more to fix defects post product release, but the costs are much lower the sooner they are identified (See Figure 27.1).

Therefore, internal auditors started reviewing system development initiatives while the application was under construction.

This was much better, because missing or poorly-designed controls could be identified, reported, and corrected while under construction. Additionally, common issues like making payments for unnecessary expenses (e.g., overbilling, pay rate errors, wasted supplies) could be identified and addressed before the work was completed. After work completion, trying to recover over-payments made can be a troublesome problem because vendors are not inclined to make reimbursements. But finding problems during construction has its limitations too, because contracts have already been signed, hardware and software decisions have been made, and vendors have been selected. So internal auditors shifted their attention even earlier in the project life cycle—they started reviewing system development initiatives while the system development initiative was in its conceptual stages.

This has proven to be far better because internal auditors can advise management about:

- Contracting: Making sure that details about the right to audit and provisions regarding sub-contracting, to name a couple, are included.
- Progress Reporting: Making sure there is a process for submitting timely progress reports that address scope, schedule, budget, quality, remediation, and escalation matters appropriately.
- Vendor Selection: Ensuring that vendors are technically qualified, financially solvent, and risk-control aware.
- Documentation: Verifying that a process is in place to make sure that client and user requirements will be documented fully, and that adequate system

Design and architecture	Implementation	Integration testing	Customer beta test	Post product release
1×	5×	10×	15×	30×

Note: "X" is a normalized unit of cost and can be expressed in terms of person-hours, dollars, etc.

Figure 27.1 Relative cost to fix software defects when found at different stages of system development.

code and user documentation will be delivered before those who built the system move onto other projects.

■ Testing: Verifying that a robust process exists to make sure the system delivers what the business requirements stipulate, and that software bugs will be corrected appropriately, timely, and economically.

The lesson learned was that by acting like consultants and catching defects early in the development cycle, organizations can significantly reduce their development costs.

Summary

1. Consulting and assurance work are not mutually exclusive, but for internal auditors to do both without losing their independence and objectivity, they must set clear roles, work in a support capacity, not accept operational responsibilities, and leave the final decision-making on consulting matters to their clients.
2. Today's internal auditors must possess a diversity of technical and soft skills. In addition to communication and critical thinking skills, auditor-consultants should embrace a participative style, and partner with their clients to find opportunities to add value.
3. Consulting is the label for special projects, but also a mindset and a work style. Consultants thrive on inquisitiveness, problem-solving, and customer service. Internal auditors should consider embracing both definitions of the term.

Chapter 28

Continuous Monitoring/ Continuous Auditing (CM/CA)

Internal auditors have traditionally selected samples of transactions and examined those sampling units during their reviews. The results were then used to determine if risks have negatively impacted programs and processes, and if controls are present and operating as expected. Unfortunately, sampling has some limitations:

1. Sampling error: How different is the population from what the sample shows?
2. Extrapolation: Can we use the information obtained from the sample and predict what will happen in the entire population?

To address the statistical gaps between a sample and the population it was extracted from, internal auditors started using software to help them examine larger number of transactions. They used typical tools such as Excel, Access, SQL, ACL, IDEA, SAS, Tableau, and Minitab, among many others. By examining hundred, thousands or even millions of records, in other words, by reviewing an ever-larger number of transactions and thus approximating the size of the entire population, internal auditors hoped to get a better understanding of underlying problems, pinpoint the source of the anomalies found, quantify issues better, determine how pervasive and costly issues might be, and address the shortcoming of sampling.

After an issue is identified, internal auditors and management often want to repeat procedures to monitor the problem and verify that the problem is not recurring. This is also done as part of regular monitoring and ongoing activities so that a problem can be identified as early as possible. When management performs this activity, it is referred to as continuous monitoring (CM). If it is performed by internal auditors, we refer to it as continuous auditing (CA).

CM: Management is responsible for the establishment and monitoring of objectives, risks, and controls. They should not wait for auditors and regulators to find and communicate issues. By implementing a CM mechanism, they can get in front of issues and preemptively, or shortly after its occurrence, intervene to correct the problem. Examples might include transaction monitoring, manual overrides, errors, defects, cost statistics, late shipments, and delays.

CA: Internal auditors are responsible for reviewing programs and processes, but should not co-manage business operations. They should remain independent to protect their objectivity (Standard 1100) and when internal auditors are responsible for an operational responsibility that the internal audit activity might audit, the internal auditor's independence and objectivity may be impaired (Practice Advisory 1130.A2-1). However, some risks may be significant enough, that internal auditors may want to know promptly if an issue has occurred. CA provides information that relates to compliance with policies, procedures, regulations, and other topics that support financial and operational reporting activities and goals. The following examples illustrate CA:

- Split transactions to circumvent approval limits
- Reviewing payroll demographics against vendor demographics
- Payments to specially designated nationals (SDNs), or transaction amounts that should generate a suspicious transaction report (STR)
- Suspicious vendor activity (e.g., round numbers, unexplainable frequency, or intervals)
- Employees with bogus Tax IDs

Developing a Continuous Auditing Program

Both CM and CA typically rely on IT-enabled tools to monitor processes, transactions, and accounts to improve the effectiveness of internal auditors and management. CA can augment internal audit's efficiency by honing into questionable activities for further research, rather than spending a great deal of time sampling transactions wondering if anything will be identified.

After identifying known risks, understanding the related controls, selecting the appropriate data set, and writing the algorithm to probe the corresponding transactions, internal auditors can develop reduced and more focused audit programs. With CA, procedures are scheduled to run automatically so as the company's systems perform periodic jobs, they also performs analytics to determine if risks have occurred, KPIs and KRIs are acting erratically, and controls have failed. Notifications can be made via e-mail, queued reports, dashboard displays, or other notifications for management or internal audit to act on and review further.

With CA and the produced results, internal auditors can perform short yet high-impact audits that focus on seeking answers to identified anomalies. For example, an audit could consist of *three days* reviewing the abnormal payments sent to a vendor, rather than *4 months* reviewing vendor payments. The result would be more efficient, better targeted, and less intrusive risk-based audit.

There is a gray line between CM and CA, and internal auditors should avoid intervening so much in management activities that they appear to co-manage or act as the control point themselves. But waiting two years to identify anomalous payments that were made to a bogus vendor, or a series of payments to an advertising agency that acted as a front for bribery payments in a foreign location is not acceptable either. When developing CA routines, internal auditors should allow controls to work, and consider the underlying risk at all times.

CM vs. CA Examples

Scenario One

A customer payment collection process has a control (e.g., reconciliation) in place so that unknown cash receipts from unidentified customers or missing invoice numbers go through review and clearance within 5 business days. This way funds are not left in an unapplied cash account, which would make the paying customer appear delinquent resulting in mistaken invoices, late fees, and delinquency notices.

CM might trigger a notice to management after 7 business days showing that the control failed since it was supposed to clear the payment in 5 days. Also, escalation notices in tracking reports should be produced in set intervals to make sure the misapplied payments are researched and the funds credited to the corresponding customer and outstanding invoice.

Internal auditors don't need a CA notification after 7 days. They may not need a notification after 10 or even 15 days. Given the risk involved in this scenario, 25 days may be a reasonable window because at 30 days a new invoice will be generated, and the new invoice will show the arrears, prompting a call, e-mail, letter, visit, or silent indignation by the customer who knows that the payment was made, but is receiving an unpleasant notice and fined late fees. Effectively, the initial control breakdown triggers other negative events for the organization.

Scenario Two

An organization has segregation of duties procedures in place so that employee A working in Accounts Payable processing payments to vendors is unable to create new vendor records. Due to carelessness or disregard for company policy, employee B with new vendor creation access rights provides employee A the login information. Management is unaware of this situation.

Employee A creates a bogus vendor record, uses his home address and phone number as the vendor address, and processes two payments that month.

CM generates a report at month end showing the names of new vendors created, but it does not indicate the address and phone number of the new vendor created, and it does not go through the process of searching through the human resources information system (HRIS) to search for address matches. Since the new vendor was created with the login credentials of the appropriately assigned employee, this does not raise any concerns.

Internal audit's CA procedure runs quarterly and gathers new vendor, and vendor master file changes, and compares those to HRIS demographics: name, initials, address, phone numbers, tax ID, name of contact at vendor, initials of contact at vendor, and any instances where the only address is a P.O. Box number but no physical address. Since this procedure runs quarterly, it shows matching addresses and phone numbers and also indicates that the two payments made the first month were followed by weekly payments thereafter.

Identifying the problem within 3 months of the control breakdown allows internal audit to intervene and stop the fraud, rather than 1 or 2 years later when an Accounts Payable, Vendor Master File, or Order-to-Pay audit is performed.

Summary

1. CM is done by management and CA is done by internal auditors, whose mandates overlap in their oversight role over risks and controls.
2. While internal auditors should retain their independence and objectivity, long time intervals between reviews can allow control breakdowns to grow and cause significant damages to the organization; CA can help narrow those time intervals by automating the review of transactions and identifying risky situations that warrant immediate intervention.
3. CM and CA require usable data, a risk-mindset, coordination with control owners and timely remediation. These continuous procedures can improve governance, risk management, and compliance while reducing costs.

Chapter 29

Controls

Controls are actions taken by the board, management, employees, and other personnel to mitigate the likelihood and/or impact of risks. They are an essential ingredient in typical internal audit reviews, as most reviews involve the identification and assessment of the presence and effectiveness of internal controls.

It is also important to remember the purpose of internal controls: mitigate risks that stand in the way of the achievement of business objectives. With this in mind, it is critical that the number and type of internal controls be commensurate with the risks they are supposedly mitigating. Too few controls, and the program or process is exposed to risks materializing that could result in financial loss, reputational damage, and legal liability, among other impacts. Too many controls, and the program or process becomes bureaucratic with longer-than-necessary cycle times, excessive operating costs, waste, and inefficiency (Table 29.1).

Review, Decision, Action (RDA)

Controls are dynamic and often require a review, a decision, and an action. For example, when logging into a computer system, an indispensable control is the authentication of the identity and credentials of the individual; this typically consists of the requester's ID and password. The ID submitted is compared to the table showing all acceptable IDs and the same occurs with the submitted password. If both agree, a decision is made to grant access. If one or both are incorrect, the computer system will deny access. Review, Decision, Action.

A similar process is followed when performing reviews and approvals. The operator must compare the relevant items and upon satisfactory inspection, sign-off on the transaction for execution (e.g., authorize a purchase, authorize a payment). Review, Decision, Action.

Table 29.1   Risk-Control Imbalance

Excessive Risks	Excessive Controls
Loss of assets	Bureaucracy
Loss of grants	Reduced productivity
Poor business decisions	Increased complexity
Noncompliance	Increased cycle time
Increased regulations Public scandals Inability to achieve objectives	Increase in no-value activities

Table 29.2   Review–Decision–Action

R	A review is performed comparing two or more elements as part of a processing rule. This review produces a result or output.
D	The preceding result or output is used to make a decision based on established parameters, which can often be expressed in If:Then terms.
A	The preceding decision produces an action based on processing rules. Possible actions include grant or allow, refuse or decline, delay, or re-route.

The same occurs during bank reconciliations. The operator will review the balance as indicated in the corresponding GL account, compare it to the balance as indicated in the bank statement, perform appropriate additions and subtractions to account for deposits and payments subsequent to the statement cut-off date and verify that all transactions are properly accounted for resulting in no variance. Items (e.g., payments, deposits) outstanding for an extended amount of time require further review and clearance so all monies are accounted for before the operator signs off on the bank reconciliations. Review, Decision, Action (Table 29.2).

Some mistakenly believe that checklists and forms are tantamount to controls, when in fact they are merely instruments for the performance of the underlying control. Forms are ineffective if the operator doesn't use them effectively.

A Holistic Approach

When using the COSO IC-IF Framework, many auditors emphasized the internal control component at the expense of the other components. An emphasis on internal controls in the absence of the other components is likely futile because weaknesses in other components can undermine the quality and performance of internal controls. For example, if the unit suffers from a lack of accountability and consequences when there is poor work performance (i.e., poor control environment), bank reconciliations (i.e., control) may not be performed as expected during the monthly oversight procedures (i.e., monitoring).

If documentation is incomplete (i.e., information and communication) when submitted for review before payments are authorized (i.e., control), and are ignored by the manager (i.e., monitoring) the risk of fraud (i.e., risk assessment) will likely increase.

Preventive and Detective Controls

There are several ways of categorizing internal controls. The most common one is Preventive vs. Detective. Preventive controls, as the name implies, prevent the occurrence of errors, omissions, and other undesirable outcomes, stopping them before they occur. Detective controls identify errors after they occur (Table 29.3).

The concept of segregation of duties involves the separation of incompatible duties, for example, separating the approval of a transaction and the related payment. A typical requirement is that an employee who is authorized to initiate a payment to a vendor is not also authorized to sign vendor payment checks. This control is designed to reduce the risk of unauthorized payments.

Approval limits and authorizations involve the assignment of restricted approval thresholds to assigned individuals, often based on role and title. In general, individuals within an organization will receive higher approval limits as they progress higher within the organization's ranks.

Passwords limit access to IT systems. By controlling access to software programs related to accounting, payment, and other systems through the use of passwords and access codes, the organization lowers the risk of errors, omissions, and unauthorized transactions.

Other important controls in the IT environment require that only the minimal staff required to implement IT production changes have access to the production environment. Authorization processes should involve stakeholders to assess and mitigate risks associated with proposed or required changes. Also, supervisory processes should encourage IT management and staff to perform their duties responsibly and be able to detect unacceptable performance.

Table 29.3 Examples of Preventive and Detective Controls

Type	Description
Preventive	Segregation of duties, approval limits, authorizations, locks, passwords
Detective	Physical inventory and fixed assets counts, cycle inventory counts, reconciliations, confirmations

Inventory is the quantification and valuation of merchandise, fixed assets, and other goods. These items could be used for resale (e.g., finished goods, merchandise), production (e.g., raw materials, subassemblies, work in process, consumables, spare parts), or support activities (e.g., tools, repair equipment). Since its value is substantial it must be counted and valued accurately at the end of each accounting period. A full physical count could be done every quarter and at year-end during the preparation of financial statements, but due to concerns of substantial adjustments, especially downward, many organizations implement cycle counting.

Cycle counting involves counting a subset of inventory items daily or weekly. This can be done by setting groups: A for most commonly used or historically inaccurate items, B for less so, and C for the least commonly used items. The items to be counted are system generated and the organization can identify anomalies, improve the process, and correct the accounting discrepancies. Another approach is to use the Pareto method, whereby items are counted based on percentage of inventory value, so the items with the highest value are counted more often, while those with lower value are counted less often.

Ultimately, the ideal scenario is for organizations to maintain a perpetual inventory system, so they can keep a daily record of changes in inventory. This can be accomplished through barcoding and using scanners that transmit data automatically, thus reducing the risk of errors. Beyond the obvious financial statement repercussions of over or under-stating inventory and fixed asset balances, there are significant operational risks too, as not having the items needed where it is supposed to be can impact their availability to meet customer requests, manufacturing needs, and service delivery requirements.

Reconciliations consist of comparing two sets of records that relate to the same transaction and analyzing any differences. For example, reconciling the cash account balance on the company's accounting records to its bank records could identify whether any payments recorded by the company were not received by the bank, or whether any withdrawals reported by the bank were not accounted for by the company.

Budgeting and monitoring by comparing operating and financial results to budgets or forecasts, or to the results in prior periods, could be a way of identifying unusual activities. Investigating deviations could uncover errors in the records showing operating result variation or unanticipated changes in business activities.

A confirmation is a notice or letter sent to a client or client organization requesting information. There are two types of confirmations: positive and negative. A positive confirmation occurs when the client or client organization is asked to return a document, either confirming or disputing, the account information sent to it by the auditor. A negative confirmation asks the client or client organization to respond to the auditor only if they find a discrepancy between their records and the information provided by the auditor. For example, a confirmation letter informs the bank that at year-end the bank balance was $10 million. If this is a negative confirmation, and the bank agrees with this figure, it does not have to contact the auditor to confirm the supplied information. Conversely, if this is a positive confirmation, the bank is expected to respond in the affirmative, confirming the accuracy of the figures provided.

Although negative confirmations do not require as much follow-up work by auditors as positive confirmations, they are not considered as high-quality evidence as positive confirmations because some clients may not have received the request or bothered to respond to the request even if they detected a discrepancy. If no response is received, the auditor will assume that the customer agrees with the information presented to it in the confirmation. For this reason, most auditors prefer to use positive confirmations over negative confirmations, despite the additional cost.

Negative confirmations are best used in situations where the organization's internal controls are already considered to be strong, in which case the confirmation process is used as a secondary audit procedure for the accounts under review.

Confirmations are typically used to verify bank balances, loan amounts, inventory, accounts receivable, and accounts payable. These should not be confused with trade confirmations, which are sent electronically or by mail when a broker executes a buy or sell order.

Compensating Controls

Another category is compensating controls, which are put in place when requirements cannot be met explicitly as stated or expected. They satisfy the requirement when the preferred or desirable measure is too difficult or impractical to implement. They may also be called alternative controls. For example, processes should have a separation of duties between authorization, custody and record-keeping. In a situation involving the lack of segregation of duties, the best corrective action typically involves hiring additional staff, but that is often impractical. Another option then, is to reengineer the process so the work assignments are apportioned differently. A third option is to implement a compensating control in the form of supervisory review, whereby another individual reviews the work of the individual performing these incompatible duties to verify their appropriateness.

Internal Controls and Efficiency

The publication of the organization's financial statements can be summarized as the timely and accurate publication of the organization's Balance Sheet, Income Statement, Statement of Cash Flows, and any other schedule and accompanying notes. As a result, it does not matter much how many adjustments, reversing entries, reclassification of transactions or other corrections must be made as long as the financial statements are published accurately by the due date. Consequently, correcting all mistakes is paramount and rework is not a great concern.

When performing other types of reviews, such as operational, strategic, and value-for-money reviews, rework is clearly the manifestation of a weak or broken process that is costlier than it should be, is error prone, and triggers required corrections. With this in mind, it is clear that Preventive controls are preferable to Detective controls.

I believe that failure to understand this dynamic is a key reason so many internal auditors have neglected over the years to report process inefficiencies, delays, rework, and excessive cycle time; the auditors followed a financial audit practice legacy. Over the years I have witnesses many processes that are very inefficient, even though internal auditors have audited that program or process multiple times, but never reported on this dynamic as a finding.

Automated vs. Manual Controls

Another classification is automated vs. manual. Automated controls are performed by computer systems and other types of machines. Manual controls are performed by individuals (Table 29.4).

Manual controls, because they are dependent on and performed by individuals, are less dependable than automated controls. Computer systems, for example, will consistently perform the same action every time if the inputs meet the established criteria. Humans, on the other hand, may perform an action inconsistently, partially, or not at all due to lack of concentration, fatigue, apathy, personal interest, sabotage, fraud, or a lack of competency. This constitutes the concept of human frailty.

Given these limitations, and the fact that automated controls are less expensive per transaction than manual controls, it is surprising that so many programs and processes today still contain and depend so heavily on manual controls.

Another categorization of internal controls is Hard vs. Soft controls. Hard controls are regarded as traditional controls, are easier to observe in action, and evaluate. They are formal, objective, and quantitatively measurable. Soft controls tend to be informal, subjective, intangible, and often focus on workplace environmental characteristics and practices. Soft controls are "an internal control based on intangible factors like honesty and ethical standards (Table 29.5)."*

Table 29.4 Examples of Automated and Manual Controls

Automated	Batch checks, exception reports, access authentication, payroll/benefit calculations, automated cancellation of login rights after 90 days of no use
Manual	Supervisory review and approval, bank reconciliation, signed conflict of interest (COI) or code of ethics (COE) statement

---

* *The Auditor's Dictionary* by David O'Reagan, Wiley & Sons, 2004.

Table 29.5   Examples of Hard vs. Soft Controls

Hard	Policy/procedures Organizational structure Reconciliations Locks Validations Exception reports Segregation of duties Reviews Authorizations Passwords Confirmations
Soft	Supervision Code of ethics/conduct Stakeholder perception Empowerment Competence Motivation Management philosophy Strong leadership Openness

As internal auditors gain a deeper understanding of business dynamics, it has become evident that organizational dynamics, culture, work environmental factors, workplace philosophy, and general tone play a crucial role in the quality of internal controls. The massive corporate scandals like the ones that destroyed Enron, WorldCom, Adelphia, and to some degree the Wells Fargo scandal, were exacerbated by the poor leadership, neglect of internal controls, lack of employee empowerment, and pervasive reluctance to talk truth to power.

Let's consider an example that I often use in my seminars. A corporate executive returns from a business trip and submits an expense report. An employee in the Accounts Payable (or other processing unit within the organization) notices upon inspection of the submitted expense report that the executive is requesting reimbursement for:

- A car, whose size is larger than corporate policy allows
- A hotel rating and room, of a larger size (e.g., suite) than is allowed under corporate policy
- Multiple diners on the meal receipts based on the number of appetizers, entrees, desserts, and drinks claimed without evidence that these were business meals

The question then becomes, would the lower ranking employee, who by now would suspect that the executive traveled with his family, question and return the expense report, or process it as submitted since an executive has submitted it?

Another example involves a CFO or Corporate Controller who instructs an employee in Accounting to recognize a sale as realized even though the signed contract has not been received yet because it is the end of the accounting period and recognizing the sale a consummated would increase reported revenues. Would the lower ranking employee, who knows that prevailing revenue recognition standards prohibit the recognition of that outstanding transaction as being recognized as earned revenue still process it?

This demonstrates the importance of empowerment; if the employee who is responsible for performing a control activity is not empowered to do the job, what then is the expected quality of the internal controls?

Contingency Plans: Business Continuity and Disaster Recovery

While controls play an essential role protecting the organization's assets and keeping risks at bay, it is also important to note the vital role that disaster recovery plans play. These plans should be part of the organization's overall business continuity plans and provide an additional layer of protection if controls cannot provide sufficient protection. After all, natural and man-made disasters occur unexpectedly, and their effects can be catastrophic.

Internal auditors can help their organizations avoid merely having ad hoc or reactive plans and develop more robust plans to improve preparedness. Improvements can often be made in terms of comprehensive operational prioritization risk assessment of various scenarios, cost-effective response planning and making sure the plan is tested periodically to avoid significant gaps. These should be working documents that are updated as changes occur, such as the implementation of new technologies, the deployment of new products and services, the acquisition of new businesses, or entry into new markets.

Although controls are central to the role of internal auditors, they should be careful that in the zeal to deploy an abundance of controls to mitigate risks appropriately, they don't unwittingly create bureaucracy. That imbalance is costly to organizations resulting in reduced productivity, increased complexity, increased cycle time, delays, higher costs per transaction, and an increase in no-value activities. Furthermore, the well-intentioned frameworks, programs, policies, and procedures can become so routine that they stifle the creativity, resiliency, and flexibility that are supposed to complement these items and help organizations thrive in today's competitive environment.

Summary

1. Internal controls play a key role in helping organizations achieve their objectives by mitigating the risks that threaten the achievement of objectives. Controls should not be regarded as obstacles, but as enablers. However, too many controls create bureaucracy, inefficiency, and increase the cost structure of programs and processes.
2. There are many ways of categorizing controls. It is important for internal auditors to work with management to make sure the mix of types and their placement in programs and processes maximize their contribution.
3. In addition to controls, internal auditors should examine the need for contingency plans to protect company assets in the event that unexpected events occur.

Chapter 30

Control Charts

Control charts are used to study how a process changes over time. Similar to a line chart, data are plotted in time order. These charts contain a central line showing the average, and two additional lines showing the upper control limit (UCL) and the lower control limit (LCL) determined by historical data or by the maximum and minimum allowable values set by performance specifications. By comparing the current data to these three historical lines, it is possible to extract conclusions about the process. For example, is any variation noted consistent and predictable (i.e., the process is in control)? Or is variation inconsistent and unpredictable (i.e., the process is out of control)?

Control charts can be used to:

- Control ongoing processes by finding and correcting problems as they occur.
- Predict the expected range of outcomes from a process.
- Determine whether a process is stable (in statistical control).
- Analyze patterns of process variation from special causes (non-routine events) or common causes (built into the process).
- Determine whether a quality improvement project should aim to prevent specific problems or to make fundamental changes to the process.

Controls, like risks, must be monitored and the tracking of their performance will provide management with valuable information about their strengths and weaknesses. With this information management can proceed to take action to strengthen them. Control charts are a very effective tool to identify errors, anomalies, and variation requiring intervention and correction.

Control charts are one of the Seven Basic Tools of Quality and although it is widely used by quality control specialists, it is seldom known, and even less frequently used, by internal auditors. This is unfortunate, because control charts can help auditors determine if the process is stable and under control. Furthermore, these charts can be used to predict the future performance of the process and if the process is not in control, an analysis of the chart can help to identify the source of the problem.

While the sophistication level can vary, they typically consist of the following:

1. Points representing the mean (i.e., average), ranges or expected value of measurements of a characteristic in samples taken from the process at different times are identified. These data points are similar and related to the sample units internal auditors select for testing during audits.
2. The mean using all the samples is calculated (e.g., the mean of the means, mean of the ranges) and a center line is drawn at the value of the mean.
3. The standard deviation for the mean of the values is calculated using all the samples
4. Upper and lower control limits, typically set at three standard deviations of the center line, are drawn to indicate the thresholds at which the output is considered statistically 'unlikely' and out of bounds. The UCL and LCL can be set by process performance limits as well.
5. Additional lines may be drawn at one and two standard deviations above and below of the center line, creating bands around the mean to assess the frequency of observations or transactions in each zone. This division into zones provides a mechanism to formulate rules that can be translated into risk triggers or concern points.

If the process is in control, more than 99 percent of the transactions will fall within the control limits (i.e., three standard deviations of the mean). If there are observations outside these thresholds, or if there are patterns as explained below, this suggests there are sources of variation that will increase costs due to errors, omissions, or other process anomalies.

There are several rules that are applied to control charts to identify anomalies. Table 30.1 describes the most common rules and the explanation.

The rules and the statistical analysis involved can be substantially more complex, but in practical terms, most internal auditors don't need to go to that level of detail. It is enough to say that by setting upper and lower control limits, and by observing the patterns as shown Table 30.1, internal auditors can substantially increase the sophistication of their data analytics and support their findings with measurable data. They can identify patterns, trends, and relate those to actual, suspicious anomalies and research them before problems compound. This in and of itself can enable better data analytics and continued controls auditing for high-risk activities.

Examples

EXAMPLE 1—RULE 1

Internal auditors are familiar with Rule 1; the characteristics of an item are outside acceptable limits. If the graph is plotting processing times, it would be a payment

Table 30.1 Common Control Chart Rules and Explanation

Rule	Explanation	
A single point outside 3 SD limit above or below the center line.	Since the data point is outside the upper or lower control limits, this indicates the threshold has been breached and the item is outside the acceptable limits. The process is out of control.	**Rule 1:** One point is more than 3 standard deviations from the mean UCL ··· 3σ ··· 2σ ··· 1σ ··· $\bar{x}$ ··· LCL
Two out of Three consecutive points on the same side of the mean fall in Zone A or beyond.	Zone A is the outermost band around the centerline and having two points there signal a near miss. Near misses should be analyzed to determine what happened to prevent a future point from being outside the upper or lower control limits.	**Rule 5:** Two (or three) out of three points in a row are more than 2 standard deviations from the mean in the same direction UCL ··· 3σ ··· 2σ ··· 1σ ··· $\bar{x}$ ··· LCL
Four out of five consecutive points on the same side of the mean fall in Zone B or beyond.	This indicates a shift in the process and a need to examine the reason for the drift.	**Rule 3:** Four out of five consecutive points fall zone B or beyond UCL — A — B — C — $\bar{x}$ — C — B — A — LCL

(Continued)

Table 30.1 (*Continued*) Common Control Chart Rules and Explanation

Rule	Explanation	
Six or more consecutive points increasing or decreasing	This indicates a trend.	**Rule 3**: Six (or more) points in a row are continually increasing (or decreasing)
Eight points in a row in Zone B, A, or beyond, on either side of the center line (without points in Zone C)	This indicates oscillation and may indicate there are sub processes within the process being reviewed.	**Rule 8**: Eight points in a row exist with none within 1 standard deviation of the mean and the points are in both directions from the mean
Nine consecutive points on the same side of mean fall in zone C or beyond	May denote a shift or drift in the process. For example, the machine is out of calibration or the department or operator is slowing down.	**Rule 2**: Nine (or more) points in a row are on the same side of the mean

Source: Operational Auditing: Principles and Techniques for a Changing World, p. 146–148.

made late (i.e., longer time than the UCL allows). If the graph is plotting monetary amounts, it could be a payment for an amount higher than allowed (e.g., T&E expense for an expensive meal or airline ticket). If the graph is plotting the dimension of a ball bearing, it would indicate the diameter is larger than allowed (i.e., it won't fit the assembly).

EXAMPLE 2—RULE 2

This is what is often referred to as "a near miss". Consider an ambulance service where the response time should be within 20 minutes, and in two of the last three emergency calls, the ambulance barely made it to the victim in time. Will the medical first responders get to the next call too late to save the person's life?

EXAMPLE 3—RULE 4

A claims processing unit has a requirement that claim payments be disbursed within 3 business days. Processing times in the unit have been increasing, consistent with Rule 4, but no payment has been made past the 3 business days (otherwise it would trigger Rule 1). Typically, internal auditors would not consider this a finding because processing times are within the policy requirements, but an important question is, what is happening that payment processing times are getting longer? How long before Rule 1, an outright breach, occurs and a payment is late?

EXAMPLE 3—RULE 5

Cycle time data are plotted with longer processing times above the center line and shorter processing times are noted below the center line—Rule 5 is noted. Upon closer examination, the auditors determine that all points above the center line correspond to one operator, while those below correspond to another. The data shows that one operator is performing his duties consistently, but differently from the other operator. The operator whose data is shown on the top side of the graph is following procedures as required and it takes the times plotted to review and process the transactions. The other operator, whose data is shown on the lower side of the graph, is skipping certain review steps, hence processing times are shorter.

The auditors have identified a processing problem that if left to continue may not be identified for months or even years, when a review of transactions shows multiple errors due to the skipped processing steps.

Control charts indicate dynamics and possible patterns highlighting anomalies. These events must be researched. When the source of the variability suggests a better practice than the one currently in place, it possibly should become the new way of performing the work. When the source of the variability is unacceptable, it should be identified and removed.

Summary

1. Control charts provide valuable information about the dynamics in a process that can help internal auditors identify problems beyond the traditional pass/fail approach.

2. These charts are a great supplement to any work done developing Key Performance Indicators (KPIs), Key Risk Indicators (KRIs), Continuous Monitoring (CM), and Continuous Auditing (CA).
3. As internal auditors move beyond providing hindsight, control charts can help them provide deeper insight and foresight.

Chapter 31

Control Self-Assessment (CSA)

Management is responsible for the organization's programs and processes, and their related objectives, risks, and controls. This is a widely espoused axiom by internal auditors. Yet when managers are asked about risks and controls, a troublingly high number are unaware of these responsibilities. Given this condition, it should not come as a surprise that too many organizations have poor risk assessment and management mechanisms, or that their controls receive scant attention. Managers don't know what controls mean or what they should do about them. Instead, they leave it up to the internal and external auditors to look after. Control self-assessments (CSAs) are a great tool to correct this deficiency.

CSAs consist of templates, questionnaires, and other forms that ask process owners, managers, and business leaders to document:

- The nature of the process under their responsibility
- Key parameters and demographics of these programs and processes, such as volumes, key inputs and outputs, and systems depended upon
- Key actors participating in the performance of the related work and whose knowledge and diligence are key for success
- Key risks threatening or affecting the success of the program or process
- Key controls protecting the program or process
- Monitoring mechanisms and reports in place that are depended upon
- Which key indicators would alert management of anomalies

The CSA documents are distributed at least annually to process owners for completion and are collected in internal audit as documentary evidence for review and discussion. This information is very valuable during the preparation of internal audit's risk assessment and when preparing audit programs.

A main concern of CSAs is the lack of objectivity on the part of the document preparers. Since they own, oversee or work within the program or process, the preparer is not independent and may be motivated to present a more favorable picture of prevailing conditions than is true. Their lack of knowledge or sophistication could also compromise the completeness and quality of these documents. Given these potential shortcomings, internal auditors should apply appropriate levels of professional skepticism to these documents. Trust, but verify.

To improve the quality and use of the CSA process, internal auditors should:

- Help management by providing orientation and training sessions on why these documents are important and how to complete them appropriately.
- Use these documents during the risk assessment process and audit planning phase to calibrate the rating of related risks.
- Re-visit CSA documents after completing internal audits to determine how accurate the contents were and provide feedback to management to improve their future quality and reliability.

The third bullet is particularly important and often neglected. This is what I refer to as "the feedback loop." After CSA forms are completed, and an audit is performed, the results of both should be compared. Sometimes the CSAs indicate that conditions and practices are in order, therefore, there is little residual risk to be concerned about. If the audit indicates that conditions are not that favorable, this discrepancy should be communicated to management and as necessary supplemented with appropriate training so the next time the CSAs are completed they are more accurate.

If the CSAs indicate that conditions are deficient, but the audit returns satisfactory results, that should also be communicated to the corresponding management. While the discrepancy could be due to being overly conservative, it may also indicate they are not as familiar with the operational results as they should be and they can benefit from the positive feedback.

Ideally, both the CSA and audit results will be similar, showing there is a great deal of reliability in the process.

Either way, this feedback loop provides a way to calibrate the CSA process and make sure that it provides management with a reliable source of information to manage their programs and processes better, identify weaknesses early, and serve as an input for the performance evaluation process.

Summary

1. CSAs provide a mechanism for managers to demonstrate their ownership of the objectives, risks, and controls they are responsible for.

2. The information contained in CSAs can be used to better understand a process while planning an audit, and as a key element during risk assessments.
3. CSAs should have a feedback loop, so the information provided by process owners is compared to audit results, and the results used to calibrate the process. Deviations can indicate a lack of knowledge about risks, controls, and prevailing practices, a desire to distract and conceal, or a misplaced reliance on existing controls.

Chapter 32

Corporate Governance

Corporate governance has gained a great deal of attention as a result of devastating discoveries, like the Volkswagen scandal precipitated by the revelation that the company had installed software designed to cheat nitrous oxide (NOx) emissions[*], the GapKids manufacturing plants that employed child labor in India[†], the mining dam burst and devastating mudflow in Brazil involving Vale, BHP Billiton and Samarco[‡], and Toshiba's inflation of net profits over several years[§]. There is a growing awareness that corporate governance, and the structures and culture that it creates, play a pivotal role in the quality of internal controls. From a definitional perspective, corporate governance refers to the structures, policies, accountability parameters, and regulations, both internal and external, that establish the standards of performance within an organization.

Corporate governance is heavily influenced by an organization's stakeholders, who communicate their expectations for proper conduct, especially as it relates to the pursuit of profitability, ecological responsibility, and fair and respectful treatment of those people impacted by its activities. This concept is often associated with the Three Ps: Profits, Planet, and People, also referred to as the Triple Bottom Line.

Corporate governance is about the relationships between the organization's stakeholders and the accountabilities that lie among them, especially as it relates to owners, the board, and management. The *Standards* define governance as "the combination of processes and structures implemented by the board to inform, direct,

---

[*] See www.bbc.com/news/business-34324772.
[†] See www.nytimes.com/2007/11/15/business/worldbusiness/15iht-gap.1.8349422.html.
[‡] See www.theguardian.com/sustainable-business/2015/nov/25/brazils-mining-tragedy-dam-preventable-disaster-samarco-vale-bhp-billiton.
[§] See www.wsj.com/articles/toshiba-accounting-scandal-draws-record-fine-from-regulators-1449472485.

manage, and monitor the activities of the organization toward the achievement of its objectives." In the IT environment, IT governance consists of the leadership, organizational structures, and processes that ensure that the enterprise's information technology supports the organization's strategies and objectives.

Internal auditors are required by the *Standards* to help improve the governance of their organizations by making recommendations. Standard 2100 states "The internal audit activity must evaluate and contribute to the improvement of the organization's governance, risk management, and control processes using a systematic, disciplined, and risk-based approach. Internal audit credibility and value are enhanced when auditors are proactive, and their evaluations offer new insights and consider future impact."

The goal of corporate governance, and the purpose of the structures and expectations established, is to ensure that management is accountable to the board, which is in turn accountable to the owners (Figure 32.1).

Internal auditors play a key role by providing independent and objective assurance regarding the quality of risk management, internal controls, operating practices, reliability of reporting mechanisms, and the effectiveness and efficiency of the use of available resources. Sometimes management forgets the purpose of compliance, which is to ensure accountability to the owners and other key stakeholders of the organization. Compliance is not important in a vacuum. It is not important in and of itself. Compliance is a means to ensure accountability.

A common approach is to combine governance with risk management and compliance to create a comprehensive framework within organizations. This is often referred to as GRC. Compliance has been the focus of attention for internal auditors for decades, yet massive compliance failures continued to occur. In 2002 the Sarbanes–Oxley Act put a heavy emphasis on internal controls and governance as the failures of once celebrated companies was associated with corrupt leadership, misguided incentives, and poor corporate cultures. In 2004, COSO ERM was released and it was updated in 2017, putting a spotlight on risk management

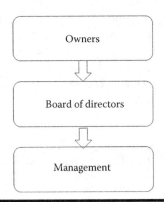

Figure 32.1   The cascading accountability link.

as a means to identify and manage the risks that cause compliance, financial, and operational failures.

Governance clarifies the expectations for proper behavior within organizations and appropriately reward or punish those entities whose practices are deemed unacceptable. Frustration with corporate corruption, insider trading, bribery payments, nepotism, long work hours without breaks, exposure to high noises, extreme temperatures, stifling humidity, child labor and hostile work environments have drawn attention to this subject from its early incarnation in the 1970s to date.

Corporate Governance and Investor Behavior

The greater attention being placed on corporate governance is often evidenced in traditional and social media, as well as in the substantial increase in the amount of money invested in organizations deemed socially responsible. In fact, many mutual funds have emerged since the 1980s whose investment philosophy is to invest in companies considered having a strong governance and being ethical in their conduct. Research tools have also emerged helping investors find such companies. Examples include Standard and Poor's GAMMA (Governance, Accountability, Management, Metrics, and Analysis), Institutional Shareholder Services (ISS), the Investor Responsibility Research Center, Governance Metrics International (GMI), The Conference on Sustainable, Responsible, Impact Investing (SRI), Parnassus, TIAA-CREF, Domini, and PAX, among many others.

Socially responsible investing is increasing, and the amounts involved are presently in the trillions of dollars. Shareholder activist groups are very engaged, and their influence can be felt in boycotts, votes for or against certain board members, some significant strategic decisions, and resolutions during shareholder meetings. In general, corporate governance is important because the behavior of organizations is being rewarded or punished by institutional and individual investors whose purchases and sales make company stocks rise or fall. Internal auditors can help their clients protect the value of their organizations (Table 32.1).

Corporate Social Responsibility and Corporate Governance

The impact of corporate social responsibility and especially its impact on the planet is still in its reporting infancy. KPMG's Survey of Corporate Responsibility Reporting 2017 shows that only 28 percent of large and mid-cap companies globally, and 49 percent of the top 75 US companies based on revenue, acknowledge the financial risks of climate change in their annual financial statements. Although disclosed by some, none of these companies quantify these risks in financial terms or use scenario analysis to estimate and model the potential financial impact.

Table 32.1 Important Components of Corporate Governance

Item	Desirable Characteristics
Board of directors	Staggered board member elections Responsible for oversight of internal and external auditors Board reviews
Audit committees	Presence of a financial expert Independent audit committee members
Ethics hotline	Existence of a credible and responsive anonymous mechanism for the capture of allegations of inappropriate activities within the organization
Corporate culture	Transparency, openness, honesty, equality, fairness
Competence	Learning organization Training, coaching, and mentoring
Other	Independence of the compensation committee members Disclosure of related party transactions Timely and accurate disclosures in the financial statements

This report was based on a study of 4,900 annual financial and corporate social responsibility reports from the top 100 companies by revenue in 49 countries. While more comprehensive reporting is still evolving, most of the climate-related financial risks is evident in the financial reports from Canada, France, South Africa, Taiwan, and the United States. Major drivers of this reporting are stakeholder and investor interest, US SEC requirement to include climate change-related disclosures, the Sustainability Accounting Standard Board's industry -specific Sustainability Accounting Standards and the UN's Sustainable Development Goals (SDGs). As such, 43 percent of the largest 250 global companies by revenue are linking corporate responsibility activities to the SDGs, and 39 percent of the top 100 companies by revenue are doing so as well.**

Transparency in organizations is enhanced when there is openness and disclosure of anything that doesn't jeopardize privacy, security, or legal requirements. Organizations should have a process to ensure that anything disclosed is accurate and reliable, deliver the information people want, put information in the proper context so it can be understood, compared or benchmarked, and provide information to those who need to know so they can make decisions effectively and timely. This stakeholder-driven approach will enhance communication practices

---

** For more details and to read the entire KPMG Survey of Corporate Responsibility Reporting 2017, see https://home.kpmg.com/xx/en/home/campaigns/2017/10/survey-of-corporate-responsibility-reporting-2017.html.

and satisfy a larger number of stakeholders. Enhanced transparency is more than a nice thing to do, it is rapidly becoming a key expectation and strategic imperative for healthy public and employee relations.

Key Questions to Improve Transparency

What message do we want to give?
Who is the target audience?
Where is this audience located?
When do we want to reach our audience?
How do we want to reach our audience?
What are the legal issues and concerns?

Corporate Governance and Third Parties

An increasingly important mechanism to enhance corporate governance beyond corporate walls is the expectations that third parties will abide by the organization's code of ethics and avoid engaging in activities that will bring disrepute to the contracting organization. This can be done by making sure that contracts include the requisite language and the expectations are written clearly, including proper monitoring activities to verify compliance with these expectations and mitigate risks. A key provision is the right-to-audit clause in contracts.

The right-to-audit clause should be clear, specific about what information is accessible, advance notification periods, time allowed for reviews, who can perform the audit, and how deficiencies will be resolved.

Compliance plays a key role supporting the structures, policies, and procedures that enhance corporate governance. It provides the mechanism to verify that accountabilities are clear, that practices are aligned with those accountabilities, and that activities enhance the best interests of as many stakeholders as possible.

Internal auditors can play a key role helping organizations strengthen their corporate governance processes. They can monitor the infrastructure, processes, media, and contents to make sure that actions are consistent with good practices. The result will be fewer information gaps, an improved image, more trust among stakeholders and business partners, and a healthier corporate reputation.*

Summary

1. Corporate governance has received a great deal of attention due to a large number of significant corporate failures, many caused by poor leadership, defective cultures, and weak oversight.

---

* For more information, see The Transparent Organization, Internal Auditor, June 2011, p. 24–25.

2. Corporate governance affects the valuation of companies and may attract supporters and detractors. Due to the impact on value creation, internal auditors are encouraged to evaluate governance related topics and recommend improvement where necessary.

3. GRC is the aggregation of corporate governance, risk management, and compliance under one umbrella. Internal auditors are involved in promoting strong GRC programs and incorporating its elements in the audit plan.

Chapter 33

COSO IC-IF

The Committee of Sponsoring Organizations (COSO) of the Treadway Commission issued its original internal control framework (Internal Control-Integrated Framework) in 1992 as a result of its study of the financial reporting scandals and failures that occurred in the 1980s. This framework was issued with the intent of providing a standardized mechanism to evaluate internal controls, but beyond that, to also help organizations gain reasonable assurance that they will be able to achieve their objectives.

The COSO IC-IF framework consists of five components that affect the organization along three main categories of objectives and risks: Compliance, Reporting, and Operations. The five components are as follows:

1. Control Environment

    It refers to the organizational culture, as exemplified in its open or closed-door nature, organizational structure, assignment of accountabilities, competence, oversight by the board of directors, leadership, and expectations for adherence with applicable rules, regulations, policies, procedures, and other performance standards.

2. Risk Assessment

    Involves the identification, quantification, measurement, and decision on the best manner to treat risks affecting the organization's ability to achieve its objectives. The identification of risks is primarily the result of a risk assessment. Risk measurement is typically done along two dimensions:

    – Impact: The significance of the risk as an impact to the business if the risk were to occur.

    – Probability: The likelihood that the risk identified occurs

Additional dimensions noted by COSO but not as widely used by organizations yet are:

- Velocity: The speed at which the risk may affect the organization. Some risks are slower to occur, such as demographic changes; others faster, such as technological change and cybersecurity attacks.
- Persistence: The length of time over which the risk's impacts may linger if the risk were to occur after the cause of it stops. Some risks' impacts are short-lived, like a trucking company accidentally spilling milk, while others may last a long time, such as the same company spilling gasoline or pesticides due to the environmental and reputational damage.

3. Control Activities

These are the most widely used actions to mitigate risks. Control activities can be categorized as preventive, detective, compensating, automated, manual, hard, soft, or entity-level controls.

4. Information and Communication

This component refers to the flow of information within the organization. Ideally, information will flow in multiple directions:

- From the Top Down: These communications consist of plans, instructions, guidance, and expectations for performance.
- From the Bottom Up: These consist of reports, concerns, requests, and other communications of the results of the organizations' activities.
- Laterally: This refers to the coordination and communication that should exist in organizations.

5. Monitoring

Monitoring involves the review and supervision that should exist whereby business activities are examined continuously or periodically to verify that actions are consistent with expectations, that concerns are addressed, and corrective actions take place. Monitors consist of the operating units themselves, reviewing units such as Corporate Compliance and Loss Prevention, internal and external auditors, regulators, and other inspectors.

COSO IC-IF as a Management Framework

The COSO IC-IF is a management framework, but it was adopted, used and enforced primarily by compliance professionals who used it to evaluate the quality and condition of the organization's internal control structures and practices. As this happened, it became more of a compliance tool and less of a management enabler. Furthermore, compliance authorities and auditors focused primarily on the third component of the framework: Control Activities.

At the time of the 2013 COSO IC-IF release, Dr. Larry Rittenberg stated in his book COSO Internal Control-Integrated Framework: Turning Principles into Positive Action:

Internal audit needs to understand - and consider - the link between objectives, risks and controls. If objectives are not properly articulated (including a risk appetite and risk tolerances), then there is a deficiency in the control environment that should be brought to the attention of senior management and the board. There is another important lesson here: It is difficult to overcome a breakdown between senior management and board oversight. Focusing more on control activities cannot compensate for such a deficiency. (p. 28)

The COSO Internal Control-Integrated Framework includes 17 principles that further define and expand the five components (see Table 33.1). In addition, there are 81 points of focus that add even further detail regarding these principles. Covering those points of focus in detail is beyond the scope of this book.

As its name suggests, the COSO IC-IF Framework is integrated. As such, internal auditors should consider all components working together, rather than in isolation. For example, a healthy control environment will promote a culture of transparency, accountability and competence. This control environment will enable the identification of relevant risks and the identification, implementation and support for appropriate control activities. The chosen control activities will be communicated to those operators and managers who need to know about this, and over time, the monitoring activities, performed by a designated reviewer, will verify that all of these elements are functioning as expected.

Table 33.1 COSO IC-IF Components and Principles

Component	Principles
1. Control environment	1. Commitment to integrity and ethical values 2. Board of Directors exercises oversight responsibility 3. Establish structure, authority and responsibility 4. Commitment to competence 5. Enforce accountability
2. Risk assessment	6. Set suitable objectives 7. Identify and analyzes risks 8. Assess risk of fraud 9. Identify and analyze significant change
3. Control activities	10. Select and develop control activities 11. Select and develop IT GCCs 12. Mobilize through policies and procedures
4. Information and communication	13. Use relevant information 14. Communicate internally 15. Communicate externally
5. Monitoring	16. Conduct ongoing/separate evaluations 17. Evaluate and communicate deficiencies

Conversely, a deficient control environment could result in a workplace where nepotism, favoritism and poor management results in the hiring and placement of unqualified workers within the organization. The lack of knowledge and engagement by these workers could result in not identifying important risks that threaten the achievement of business objectives. Since the risks have not been identified, or misunderstood, control activities could be deficient or nonexistent. Poor communication and collaboration in the workplace will result in control activities not performed effectively (where they exist) and when deficiencies are known, these deficiencies are not communicated to those who need to know to bring about the needed changes. Poor monitoring and supervision would further intensify the issues, prolonging their presence and the cumulative impact.*

Summary

1. The COSO IC-IF Framework is the most widely recognized and used internal control framework globally. As such, it constitutes a centerpiece in the methodology of internal auditors.
2. It has five components, 17 principles, and 81 principles.
3. The COSO IC-IF Framework is widely used by external auditors and is the internal control framework most companies use in the US to comply with the Sarbanes–Oxley Act.

---

* The COSO Internal Control-Integrated Framework Executive Summary and additional material can be obtained at www.coso.org/Pages/default.aspx.

Chapter 34

Creativity

Creativity is the use of the imagination or original ideas. In internal auditing it is sometimes viewed as not such an indispensable skill; after all, the main thing auditors have to do is know the rules that set the criteria for review, check transactions and business activities to see if people and systems are doing what the criteria requires, and document discrepancies. Since the criteria are set by management, they are indisputable. Compliance is nonnegotiable. Accounting and financial reporting rules are nonnegotiable. Internal auditors don't write the rules, they make sure the rules are enforced. Right? Wrong!

Business dynamics are changing rapidly, and internal auditors must realize that the criteria (i.e., what constitutes "the expected practice") is often changing, how audits are performed, how the results are communicated, what recommendations are appropriate, and the timeline for remediation, are often changing too. Internal auditors must change. But how?

Creativity (or artistry) and auditing have been seen for too long as mutually exclusive. An artistic auditor, accountant, or compliance officer—an oxymoron. That is no longer the case.

Creativity in internal audit can be applied in every phase of the internal audit cycle:

1. Planning

   Defining the scope. Historically auditing was done one fiscal year at a time. That was the legacy of external audit who signs off on financial statements at year-end. Some reviews were even shorter; only one quarter worth of transactions to verify some financial controls were operating as expected. In internal audit it is becoming increasingly apparent that operational and strategic risks are not limited to three or 12-month cycles. For example:
   a. The increase in nonperforming loans may have a 6-month lag since the date when the bank started lending to higher-risk borrowers. But the

increase in accidents at the factory could be due to lax training that originated when the company trainer retired 18 months ago and new hires since then have not received adequate workplace safety training.

b. The higher employee turnover started 2 years ago when new managers stopped getting supervisory training, and performance evaluations were no longer reviewed by anyone in Human Resources—just filed away.

c. Construction projects and IT development initiatives started running into significant cost overruns, delivering late and being prone to shoddy workmanship 4 years ago when progress reports became optional, project managers were assigned based on availability rather than fitness for the project, and budgets were assigned based on political clout, not documented need.

d. Moving away from checklist auditing. Instead of downloading a checklist from the internal audit department's database, prior internal audit workpapers, or an online database subscribed to, internal auditors should brainstorm what procedures would help answer the two fundamental questions:

- What are the objectives of the area being audited and are they being achieved efficiently, effectively, and economically?
- How do we know if all the relevant risks, including fraud, IT and security-related, have been identified and mitigated appropriately by the related controls?

2. Fieldwork

a. Sampling or 100 percent testing: Internal auditors customarily chose samples to review transactions, but in an increasingly digitized world, why not look at the entire population? Are the tests performed checking to see if objectives are being achieved and verify the risks are not materializing (including the risk of fraud), or is it just to perform a control-based audit that confirms the control is being performed regularly? Testing the entire population can provide deeper insights than a sample can, especially if the sample is not statistical.

b. When there is a problem in a sample, identifying what is unique to all those items and examining that triggering event. It may also be helpful to pull all transactions with that same characteristic, time of day, shift, operator, vendor, or customer, to see how big the problem is. This quantification is also helpful to make the finding more persuasive and build a business case that is more compelling for action.

c. Internal auditors should avail themselves of the many tools available for root cause analysis, so they avoid the "this is broken, fix it" approach to writing audit findings. The 5 Whys, Fishbone/Cause and Effect

Diagram, Is–Is Not Method, Affinity Diagrams, are all effective tools for root cause analysis that promote creativity and can be used individually or as a group.

3. Reporting

    a. Is the department still writing text-heavy, jargon-laden, clumsy-sounding reports? When was the last time internal audit asked the audit committee if the reports meet their needs, or showed the audit committee different formats, including some with charts, graphs, and figures?

Internal auditors can no longer approach situations from a binary perspective. The following are some binary-type questions and the limitation of such an approach:

- Did the document have a signature showing approval? Yes/No. Well, lots of documents are signed without a review. It is called rubber-stamping.
- Did they do a reconciliation? Yes/No. Many reconciliations are mathematically incorrect, but they look fine because "a plug" is made so it ties out.
- Did employees have an exit interview upon departure? Yes/No. Also important is asking why these individuals left. Would the departing employee consider returning? Did the person leave under duress? Notes are not always reviewed either, so sexual harassment and other workplace dysfunctions persist because it was not asked about, or it was not acted upon even though it was disclosed.
- Is the amount accurate? Yes/No. Yes, but the purchases are sometimes unnecessary, and the purchased items were delivered to a noncompany address anyway.
- Was it posted in the correct period? Yes/No. But was the amount reversed in the next or a subsequent period because the merchandise was defective, not requested or the contract was rescinded indicating revenue manipulation?

These are just some examples of how internal auditors, using creativity, would ask different questions because as shown, the Yes/No answers could provide a false sense of security. Internal auditors can use creativity to audit better, learn "what is really going on," look more expertly at patterns, dynamics, motivations, and explanations, rather than just what is on the surface.

Identifying present and emerging risks requires imagination. Finding innovative ways to examine risks within thousands or millions of transactions requires creativity. Looking for anomalous transactions that could indicate abuse or fraud by someone who knows the controls requires "thinking like a fraudster." Envisioning patterns that correlate one event with another, and a decision with its effects, requires visioning. Writing reports that convey the appropriate tone, and captures the attention of the audit committee and senior management is an art.

Summary

1. Creativity is essential for modern internal auditing. It is no longer enough to re-use checklists and perform controls-based auditing.
2. Creative auditors are able to plan better, handle fieldwork dynamics with resilience and ingenuity, and write more engaging reports.
3. As business conditions continue to evolve, internal auditors need creativity to anticipate risks, develop better procedures to evaluate them, and leverage technology for better data analytics and continuous auditing.

Chapter 35

Critical Thinking

Critical thinking is a process to raise awareness about our thoughts, beliefs, and opinions, and how to direct them rationally. It is essential for making clear, reasoned judgments. A great deal of casual thinking, if left to itself, could be uninformed and become biased, distorted, or prejudiced. What critical thinking does is enable people to think with an open mind by recognizing and assessing their assumptions, implications, and the related practical consequences. Critical thinking is essential for effective internal auditing.

To be a critical thinker, one must be willing to explore, question, evaluate, and search diligently. It involves a great deal of problem solving and reasoning to understand the facts and decide what to do with that information. This entails raising vital questions, and formulating them clearly and precisely. One must be careful about assumptions and cannot be afraid to be wrong. It involves gathering and assessing relevant information, interpreting it effectively, and coming to well-reasoned conclusions and solutions.

In addition to gaining deep insights into situations, critical thinkers should also work collaboratively and communicate effectively with others in figuring out solutions to complex problems. Critical thinking enables internal auditors to amplify their contributions to their clients. This is done by:

- Making thoughtful observations that address important points of interest.
- Listening attentively to others for what is said, how it is said, and what is not said
- Recognizing and defining problems
- Being curious, asking relevant questions, and using multiple sources to find facts
- Challenging and examining beliefs, assumptions, and opinions
- Assessing the validity of statements and arguments

- Knowing the difference between logical and illogical arguments
- Making wise decisions and judgments
- Finding valid solutions

Bloom's Taxonomy

Bloom's Taxonomy is a very important element of critical thinking, because it shows the enrichment of the thought process through levels of complexity. There are three domains: Cognitive (related to knowledge and its application), Emotional (related to the way people react emotionally and their ability to feel others' pain or joy), and Psychomotor/action-based (related to the ability to physically manipulate a tool or instrument). We will only focus on the first domain here, as the second is discussed in Chapter 42: Emotional Intelligence, and the third is beyond the scope of this book.

The levels of thinking framework are quite instructive about the progression, and goal, that every internal auditor should pursue. At the initial level, individuals are able to *remember* facts and figures so through memorization, they can recall or repeat facts and events. Next is the ability to *understand* the meaning of material and state an issue in one's own words. This makes it possible to describe and discuss issues. By using the concepts gained, individuals arrive at the next level where they can *apply* those concepts to interpret their meaning. The *analysis* phase involves the ability to break down material into its components so that its structure and ingredients can be understood. In the case of internal audit, the individual is able to distinguish fact from inference, can compare and contrast facts, and can examine situations critically, all of which are valuable attributes to effective testing. The penultimate level relates to an ability to *synthesize* information and understand structures and patterns effectively. This is important to develop new plans through derivation and creative thought, in addition to producing effective communications. At the highest level is the ability to *evaluate*, formulate, present, and defend judgments and opinions about information, the value of ideas, integrate information and knowledge using evidence, and sound criteria.*

These levels appear in descending order in Table 35.1.

Errors in Reasoning

Internal auditors must be able to draw accurate conclusions from the observations made, the information reviewed, and the tests performed. Reasoning is the process of thinking in a logical and sensible way. There are two primary ways of reasoning:

---

* For a more detailed examination of Bloom's Taxonomy, refer to www.bloomstaxonomy.org/Blooms%20Taxonomy%20questions.pdf.

Table 35.1 Bloom's Taxonomy: Levels of Thinking

Level	Description	Ability to
Evaluation	Related to making judgments about the value of ideas/ materials for given purpose.	Assess, weigh, argue, formulate, develop new ideas, and concepts.
Synthesis	Building structure/pattern from diverse elements, putting parts together to form a coherent new whole.	Organize, integrate, group.
Analysis	Separating or breaking down material or concepts into component parts so that its structure can be better understood. Able to distinguish between facts and inference.	Appraise, compare, contrast, differentiate, examine, test.
Application	Using learned information and implementing material or concepts in a new situation.	Demonstrate, employ, illustrate, interpret, solve.
Comprehension	Understand or grasp the meaning from material. Able to state a problem or concept in one's own words.	Classify, describe, discuss, explain, paraphrase.
Remembering	Remembering, recalling, or retrieving previously learned information.	Define, list, memorize, recall, repeat.

Inductive: This type of reasoning is built on common sense and past experience moving from specific facts or occurrences to general principles, theories, rules, or conclusions. Experience lets you predict what you think might happen the next time there is a similar situation. Because it is heavily influenced by past experience, it could be accurate and correct, but it could also lead to hasty generalizations or confusing correlation with causation (i.e., events happen together, but one does not cause the other). So, individuals should be careful when making comparisons and attempting to draw conclusions in their arguments about what causes an event.

Deductive: This type of reasoning follows a logical process whereby a conclusion is based on the agreement of multiple premises that are generally assumed to be true. It is a top-down logic process because it moves from generalizations to specific conclusions. An argument or conclusion is based on two facts or premises. If both are true, then the conclusion must also be true. If one or both is invalid, then the conclusion or argument is invalid. The conclusion must follow logically and not go beyond or make assumptions about the premises. Some of the errors that can be made are what's referred to as slippery slope, where the assumption is that one event will undoubtedly lead to another, likely worse, outcome. A false dilemma is where two scenarios are presented as the only two possible outcomes or solutions, when in fact there could be other reasons or solutions. Circular reasoning is another error in deductive reasoning, characterized by the rephrasing of the problem or the solution, in effect, starting where you want to conclude, and vice versa. For example, why were those inventory items recorded as obsolete? Because I labeled them obsolete!

Distraction

Internal auditors should be careful when interacting with audit clients not to succumb to distracting techniques. These are designed to shift the focus from the real issues, whether it relates to a problem, its root cause, or the potential solutions to those issues.

A common distracting technique is called red herring, where an unrelated topic is used to divert attention from the subject at hand. An example might be a conversation like this:

Auditor: Weekly cycle counting at the stores is very important and required by the procedures manual.
Audit client: You know what is also important? Stopping shoplifters. They steal groceries and clothes all the time.

Another example:

Auditor: We reviewed the daily sales report for March and noticed that incorrect amounts were entered 12 times.
Audit client: You shouldn't write me up for entering the wrong amount on the daily sales report. Auditors should be focusing on the managers that make forecasting mistakes and cause stock-outs that frustrate customers.

Another distracting technique is called ad hominem, which consists of attacking the person rather than the argument. This is similar to the expression "don't shoot the messenger." For example:

1. She complained about that? You can't believe her, she doesn't have a college degree.

2. His idea won't work. He was just hired last year.
3. Why should I do bank reconciliations? You don't!

Straw man is yet another distracting technique. While the technique's name is peculiar, it is based on creating a false contradiction—one that is not really there. It pretends to refute an argument that was presented, when in fact it is refuting an argument that was not presented at all. For example:

- You want me to work late to finish the review on time? I can't spend my entire life working, you know.
- Management decided to reduce the store renovation budget. What do they want us to do, organize a bake sale to keep the stores from looking like abandoned warehouses?
- The District Manager asked us to keep the stores clean. She expects us to work all night sweeping, scrubbing, and polishing floors?

Reasons vs. Excuses

When reviewing documents like budget analyses and reconciliations, an auditor may notice a comments section supposedly explaining variances. A review of those comments may indicate the repetition, rephrasing, or minimization of the issue, rather than explaining what caused the problem. Where a corrective action is warranted, sometimes what is entered is a request for further investigation or a delayed deadline for its correction. Instead of a reason and explanation for the discrepancy, what is recorded is an excuse.

A reason is an explanation for why something is the way it is, and everyone involved should take responsibility for their part in the situation. An excuse, on the other hand, is an explanation to supposedly explain why something is the way it is, but it always involves blaming someone or something that isn't involved in the matter or the conversation. If another person is mentioned, that individual is usually unable to share their side of the story. The difference is generally the lack of accountability and an absence of direct mention of what those involved did or failed to do.

The following are some examples of excuses that may be given when controls fail and risks materialize:

- Our employees stole from us. What really happened? We didn't have a reliable system of controls for screening candidates, for effectively supervising them as we should have, or for monitoring their actions, so we lost a lot of money due to theft.
- Our vendors cheated us. What really happened? We didn't do enough price research or know enough about negotiation techniques, so we ended up paying too much.

■ The customer was unreasonable. What really happened? We didn't manage customer expectations or communicate timely and in sufficient detail to understand what the customer really wanted, so the client is no longer buying from us.

A common issue is that some people don't recognize a problem because they want to avoid taking responsibility or corrective action.

Groupthink

Internal auditors should apply critical thinking to their review of evidence as well. For example, some individuals assign credibility to information based on the source. While this is not necessarily wrong, we must be careful not to blindly accept it because "if he said so, it must be true." Testimony often requires corroboration because overreliance on someone's competence and authority without corroboration or a verifiable track record can result in unfavorable results. This condition is sometimes observed where there is groupthink.

Internal auditors are valued for their ability to analyze complex situations and formulate accurate conclusions (insight), and for their ability to use their knowledge and analytical skills to anticipate issues and the future outcome of present decisions and actions (foresight). Groupthink is therefore unacceptable because groupthink occurs within a group when the desire for harmony or conformity in the group results in irrational or dysfunctional decision-making. Individuals try to minimize conflict without critically evaluating alternative viewpoints. Instead, they suppress dissenting viewpoints and isolate themselves from outside influences, ideas, or information.

Today's internal auditors cannot afford groupthink in their units. Everyone needs to think critically about the topics at hand, and together produce the best product.

Root-Cause Analysis

The ability to identify the root cause of issues is a common skill sought in internal auditors. Root-cause analysis (RCA) requires critical thinking. The following are some essential steps in this process:

1. To develop an effective solution, we must first identify the real problem. To avoid treating symptoms or consequences it is important to get information.
2. Don't get overwhelmed and break down the problem:
   a. What do we know?
   b. What don't we know?

   c. When did the issue start?

   d. Who is contributing to the issue?

   e. Have we spoken with the people who know this situation best?

3. Manage assumptions

   a. Have some assumptions been made? If so, what are they?

   b. Who made those assumptions and based on what?

   c. Were any of those ideas based on insufficient or faulty information?

   d. Are there some pre-conceived notions that are potentially clouding or distorting the thought process?

   e. Is there supporting or corroborating evidence?

Critical thinking is disciplined, rational, informed, and open-minded. Our goal is not just to describe events, but also to solve problems and identify effective action items. Today's internal auditors must enhance their ability to understand the past, explain the present, and predict the future using rational thought. A key expectation is that internal auditors will become change agents without compromising their independence.

Critical thinking is a purposeful process. That means that it should lead to action. Internal auditors do not engage in critical thinking from a philosophical or conceptual standpoint only; they use critical thinking as a way to give valuable insight and foresight to their clients, and to become effective agents for positive change.

Summary

1. Critical thinking is a key skill of effective internal auditors. It enables clear thinking to identify important facts and make informed decisions.

2. It helps to avoid faulty evidence and poorly derived conclusions. It also helps to protect internal auditors from errors in reasoning, succumbing to distracting techniques and groupthink.

3. RCA depends on critical thinking.

Chapter 36

Corporate Culture

Internal auditors have traditionally audited topics related to compliance, financial, accounting, information systems, fraud, and similar topics. The focus has not been too prominent with regards to the organization's corporate culture. However, conditions are changing as a result of the collective realization that the organization's corporate culture plays a key role in the quality, volume, consistency, and sustainability of business results and internal controls.

Corporate culture refers to the shared system, values, beliefs, and traditions that influence and govern how individuals behave within organizations. It impacts how employees dress, act, do their jobs, communicate, and interact with colleagues, vendors, suppliers, customers, and other stakeholders. The soft controls in an organization form the basis for the corporate culture, which is arguably the most powerful control in an organization. It influences employee behavior every moment, every day, in ways that they may not be aware of.[*]

Corporate culture is seldom defined expressly, but rather implied. It develops over time based on the words and leadership style, the hiring practices and treatment of others, and the individuals who are hired and assimilated into the organization. Hence, it is generally organic, social, and cumulative. In addition to the actions of employees, it can be evidenced in the language used, what is encouraged, discouraged, rewarded, and enforced through administrative disciplinary measures.

Managers are the lens through which employees view the company. They search for cues on what is acceptable or not, and what is rewarded or punished. Since senior executives are unable to interact with all employees all the time, managers become the filter through which senior executives view employees. This multi-directional

---

[*] Best Practices: Evaluating the Corporate Culture by James Roth, IIA Research Foundation, 2010, p.6.

dynamic underscores the importance of transparency and healthy communication channels up, down, and across the organization.

If an organization's corporate culture deteriorates, it can concurrently pull down the quality of internal controls, the organization's discipline, its focus on customer service, and other elements with it. When employees are not customer-focused, they will generally not pursue matters to completion, search for necessary resources, research anomalies, act with a sense of urgency, or communicate fully or often, which are required for effective internal controls and a healthy control environment. These weaknesses will jeopardize any organization's ability to achieve its objectives.

To employees, managers are the company, and if managers behave poorly, or are unable to manage the basics of their role well, it will be extremely difficult to inspire employees to meet organizational goals or live organizational values. Employees are strongly influenced by the conduct of management, and managers build and reinforce organizational culture with everything they say and do. This is an essential concept all managers must recognize and why it is so important they understand how they are viewed by employees. Everyone is continually affecting others with their words and actions. Therefore, managers and employees alike must always set a good example.

Employee Engagement

There are several drivers of employee engagement.

Onboarding and Messaging: New employees should go through a well-developed and delivered employee orientation program that provides an in-depth description of the organization, how it functions, how employee compensation is managed, and expectations of all employees. To make sure new and existing employees receive timely communications and are equally clear about the organization's vision, a high-ranking executive (e.g., CEO) should send periodic notifications like e-mails, robo-calls, voice-mail messages, social media posts recapping recent events in the organization and in the industry. The focus on transparency can help employees feel more engaged.

Involvement: A mechanism similar to the suggestion box of yesteryear should be re-introduced. There should be a way for employees to share workplace improvement ideas. Suggestions can be for their department or another area of the organization. Once the idea is submitted, it can go to the appropriate manager who is expected to reply to the person who submitted the idea. Another initiative could be a "Coffee with the Boss," "Lunch with the CEO," or similar monthly casual open forum where any employee can meet with the CEO (or other designated executive) to ask questions, share concerns, and feel connected. Another idea is to create workgroups within each department for more shared decision-making, especially if employees feel that decisions are being made without their input. This would be similar to quality circles, where a group of workers who do similar work meet regularly to identify, analyze, and solve work-related issues. Organizational cultures improve when everyone shares relevant and timely information.

Rewards and Recognition: People do what is measured and repeat what is rewarded. A recognition program from managers to employees, and for employees to reward one another promotes desirable behaviors and encourages employees to recognize one another for their good work. Having awards presented at an annual meeting accompanied by financial rewards is also helpful.

Employee Engagement and the Workplace

There are three discernible stages of employee engagement.

Engaged: At this stage, employees are passionate and enthusiastic, feel profoundly connected to their organization and it is often also evident in the fact that they drive innovation. Employees who are actively engaged usually show lower turnover and absenteeism, higher customer loyalty, and fewer accidents. When examined in relation to internal controls, engaged employees do their jobs well, research discrepancies, communicate issues, follow-up as needed, and feel it is their responsibility to protect the organization since they identify with it.

Not Engaged: At this level, employees are similar to sleepwalking, because they have no passion for the work even though they go to work and put in their time, but don't do much more. They generally just want to get through the work day, but do so without energy or excitement. The impact on internal controls is the apathy, groupthink, and indifference that keeps them from researching anomalies, asking questions when they don't understand something or are witnesses to issues. The feeling that "it is not my job" allows issues to continue unresolved.

Actively Disengaged: At this point, employees may sabotage company initiatives and employee goodwill. They may commit fraud, show disrespect for the company and its customers, and undermine others. Their selfish attitude can sometimes be described as "I don't get paid enough for this" or worse, "get yours while you can."

COSO and the Corporate Culture

COSO Internal Control-Integrated Framework (IC-IF) refers to the control environment as its first component and emphasizes the importance of soft and entity-level controls. Some of the techniques used to assess the control environment, soft and entity-level controls include surveys, structured interviews, and audit techniques that identify and assess tangible and intangible elements of the organization. For example, there are entity-level control questions for management and employees that could potentially highlight areas of concern. But these procedures are not fail-proof because asking these questions could make some individuals uncomfortable and if unethical individuals involved in the scheme keep their agreement, this exercise may not succeed, and they could continue the fraud.

But this should not deter internal auditors. They should ask anyway because others not involved, or those involved may cave in, and provide the information needed to begin an investigation.

COSO IC-IF identifies seven factors that make up the control environment:

1. Integrity and ethical values
2. Commitment to competence
3. Board of directors and audit committee
4. Management's philosophy and operating style
5. Organizational structure
6. Assignment of authority and responsibility
7. Human resources policies and practices

There are five principles that underline the control environment and provides additional clarity regarding the expectations for a strong, healthy, and effective workplace. They are as follows:

1. Commitment to integrity and ethical values
2. The exercise of oversight responsibility by the board of directors
3. Establishment of the structure, authority, and responsibility throughout the organization
4. Having a commitment to competence
5. Enforcement of accountability

Changing the Culture

It likely took the organization a long time to create the current culture, so changing it will also take some time and lots of effort. It is important to remember that attitudes shape people's behaviors, and these behaviors, performed collectively and with little thought, then define the culture. So, to change an organization's culture we should work through the sequence: Reshape the attitudes of those involved, which will then change their collective and repeated behaviors. Then these natural actions will define the new culture. You can't go straight to changing the culture, especially through policy changes like some organizations do. This is generally a recipe for frustration and eventually, disappointing failure.

Some organizations make fast movements toward cultural transformation by removing parts or all their leadership team to make the cultural shift. This can work, but again, what the new team will need to do is define the new expectations, new rewards, sanctions for not getting on board, leading by example (i.e., demonstrating the behavior they wish to see in others) and giving those affected hope that the new behavior will give them the results they hope for. All of this then improves the attitudes of those involved leading them to modify their behavior to be in line with the expectations and new policies set by the new leaders, thus resulting in the desired culture. The sequence is followed. So, whether this is done gradually by the existing leadership team, or drastically by extricating the old guard and brining in new leaders, all three elements must be present.

Another important element in preserving, or appropriately changing, the organization's culture is the proper onboarding of new hires and providing reminders through training and sharing stories.

Too many organizations pay insufficient attention to onboarding. Other than putting new hires through the process of signing many documents on their first day of work, some organizations fail to provide enough orientation in those crucial days immediately after hire, to indoctrinate new employees on the organization's values, expectations, and work practices. When large numbers of employees join the organization with insufficient indoctrination, they will likely behave in accordance with their own personal histories, rather than those of their new organization, thus gradually, but assuredly, changing the culture.

Organizations with strong cultures also perpetuate and share the stories that characterize their cultures. Stories about the organization's founders, their values and behavior, the display of the actions of managers and other employees that demonstrate these values is also important, as it gives these ideas real life context.

Auditing the Culture

Evaluating the corporate culture is an internal audit best practice. Many of the major business frauds and failures are due to weaknesses, or the outright breakdown, of the organization's culture. This is an area that is gaining increasing attention due to the realization that culture plays a key role in the quality of internal controls. The willingness to take ownership, transparency, accountability, discipline, and teamwork are desirable characteristics of successful organizations, yet lacking these attributes will likely reduce the reliability of internal controls as control breakdowns will likely follow.

Auditing the corporate culture is challenging because it is difficult to measure. However, there are focus areas or themes that can be used for guidance, and ways to transform subjective information into objective data.

Areas of focus should include:

Retaliation: One of the highest indicators of workplace misconduct is fear by workers that if they raise issues, they will suffer retaliation. Fear of retaliation is not only significant in and of itself, but may be a proxy for other problematic cultural factors such as distrust of management. Data (e.g., from surveys) on employee willingness to address matters with their immediate supervisor or to use the compliance hotline, as well as their views on what would happen if they reported misconduct, can be meaningful. Internal auditors can be instrumental examining the measures on how issues are reported and ultimately addressed.

Rewards and Incentives: Recognition, reward, and incentive programs can demonstrate positive cultural messages and reinforce the desired cultural characteristics. Do executives who don't meet compliance objectives risk having their annual bonuses reduced? A measure to develop, assess, and enforce ethical practices and measure follow-through in executive performance evaluations and compensation criteria is important.

Management Style: Internal auditors should analyze information related to the organization's employee turnover and retention, especially when turnover is excessive. Through employee interviews, auditors can determine whether the turnover rate is due to organizational changes, stress caused by management's philosophy, or operating practices, like unreasonable sales goals, or inappropriate compensation packages.

Talent Management: Organizations can actively recruit new hires based on culturally consistent, desired behaviors and reinforce these attributes during the onboarding process. Internal auditors should examine the records of employees who have had poor performance evaluations in the past years and determine whether those employees were appropriately qualified in relation to the job description. Also, review whether the company's hiring practices appropriately match employee qualifications, skill sets, and experience to the position and job description to identify possible nepotism, favoritism, or discrimination.

Survey employees: Examine what their opinions are about the work environment, the leadership style of their managers, the credibility that their managers have, and their feeling of belonging and working toward a common goal.

Employee Manual: Determine if the organization's values and operating principles are embedded in these crucial documents:

- Training: This segment should include reviewing the topics covered in training related to the company's values and operating practices, when these classes are offered, and who attends.
- Messaging: Review notifications sent by the organization's leadership that encourages adherence with the organizations' values and policies. This could include e-mails, voice mail messages, town hall meetings, and guidance for staff meetings.

Disciplinary Measures: This involves a review of performance evaluations to verify that behaviors unbecoming of company employees result in consistent, timely, and commensurate disciplinary action to rectify deviations.

Performance Evaluations: Verify that performance evaluations include consideration of the company's values, and that it rewards behaviors that demonstrate
adherence with these values.

Auditing culture involves a combination of tangible and intangible items. While
some items, like verification that all employees acknowledged receipt of the
organization's values statement and that performance evaluations make reference to these values, are tangible, others are intangible. In most cases, these
intangible questions can be converted to tangible and quantifiable ones by conducting surveys and focus groups. For example, an important question related to
the organization's culture than has a significant impact on subsequent employee
behavior is whether or not employees believe that their managers' actions are
consistent with the organization's values. If there is a lack of symmetry between
the two (e.g., employees believe that managers are hypocritical because they
act as if they are above the law—"do as I say but don't do as I do"), it is likely
that a toxic work environment is present or will emerge soon. By conducting
an anonymous survey and collecting employee responses showing that this is
a pervasive belief, an otherwise intangible topic is now numerical and can be
addressed objectively.

Another important consideration is whether the organization wants to do a
single audit of culture across the organization or build elements of auditing corporate
culture into existing audit programs. The answer lies within each organization's
preferences, capabilities, and maturity level. It may be easier to incorporate some
elements into individual audits (i.e., tactical approach), but if results are unsatis-
factory, or benchmarking suggests that problems are pervasive, an enterprise-wide
review may be more effective (Table 36.1).

Table 36.1   Ten Key Tests of the Ethical Climate

What (Objective/ Risk/Control)	How
Indicators of a healthy ethical climate	
1. Managers remind employees frequently of ethical considerations related to their work	Manager interviews
2. Employee perception of departmental commitment to enforcing high ethical standards	Workforce survey
3. Employee agreement that managers set good ethical example.	Workforce survey

(Continued)

Table 36.1 (*Continued*)   Ten Key Tests of the Ethical Climate

What (Objective/ Risk/Control)	How
Indicators of problematic ethical climate	
4. Managers express fatalistic attitudes toward unethical behavior	Manager interviews
5. Integrity investigations performed effectively	Review of investigative unit database
6. Employee agreement that they are personally aware of unethical or illegal behavior by company employees	Workforce survey
Indicators of the financial and administrative impact of differences in ethical climate	
7. Number and cost of successful claims filed by customers for damage caused by employees, or of employees for damage caused by managers	Legal department database
8. Injuries to employees involving time lost from work	Worker's compensation claims data
9. Complaints made by customers	Complaints database
10. Employee assessment of the value their department provides to customers	Workforce survey

Source: Adapted from *Best Practices: Evaluating the Corporate Culture* by James Roth.

Summary

1. Internal auditors are increasingly recognizing the importance of auditing the organization's corporate culture because it is a very powerful influence on the quality of internal control. It is a key ingredient in the COSO IC-IF control environment component.
2. While cultural data is predominantly subjective, tangible data can be obtained by conducting interviews, focus groups, and surveys.
3. There are elements of the corporate culture that are auditable at all phases of an employee's work life-cycle within the organization: Recruitment, Hiring, Training, Management, Performance Evaluation, Promotion, Disciplinary Actions, and Termination.

Chapter 37

Data Analytics

Organizations are collecting, analyzing, and using more data today than ever before. These data can be instrumental in getting deeper insights into customer preferences, vendor practices, and business dynamics to increase effectiveness, efficiency, and overall value. At the same time, these companies need individuals who can analyze and interpret these data, transform these into information, use these to understand business dynamics for continued improvement and value creation, and protect these from loss or abuse.

Internal auditors have relied on interviews, observations, document reviews, and recalculations for decades as they review business practices to identify opportunities for improvement. For many years the work was done by relying on paper (i.e., hardcopy) records and the results and conclusions were predominantly based on the examination of samples. With the widespread adoption and use of computer systems in the 1980s, a mass digitization began that has resulted in the accumulation of massive amounts of data available for auditor examination today. While I don't believe we will eliminate the need to examine paper records in the foreseeable future, I believe it is imperative that internal auditors move aggressively toward the widespread adoption of data analytics as a key activity in their planning and fieldwork activities.

In general, data analytics has been an under-utilized technology in the internal audit profession. It is one of the best ways for auditors to work smarter, not just harder.

Data analytics consist of a wide variety of quantitative and qualitative techniques to better understand the business. It requires the extraction and analysis of the data to glean insights regarding the behaviors and practices of individuals and organizations. When it comes to risk, the threats to the achievement of business objectives, behaviors, practices, and errors determine success or failure: the very key focus points of internal audit reviews.

Big data, and the analysis of the large data sets involved to identify patterns, trends, and relationships is important in all industries. Today there are more tools to perform the required extraction and analysis than ever before. The result is that internal auditors can gain a deeper understanding of the processes they review, gain more comprehensive insights into the business dynamics, and can recommend changes to automate processes and their related controls. All of this has the potential for auditors to be instrumental in helping management reduce costs and improve overall performance. Data analytics can be applied to virtually every function in an organization, including human resources, marketing, accounting, finance, and operations.

Internal auditors must learn to use data analytics to verify controls are working as intended, determine if risks are materializing and to what extent, and find out if objectives are being achieved. This requires an inquisitive mind that views business dynamics from different angles. With this attitude, internal auditors are free to investigate and find solutions to business concerns.

Risks vs Controls Testing

When internal auditors select and examine a sample of transactions, they typically, not always, do it to verify that the controls they believe are in place are actually in place and working effectively. If not careful, however, the internal auditor could make one of several mistakes:

1. Test controls that have no related risks.
2. Test controls for which the related risk is of low impact or likelihood. In other words, test non-key controls.

Some controls may even appear to be working when in fact they have been manipulated, as is the case with split-transactions. Consider a scenario where a Purchasing department has approval limits as shown on Table 37.1.

A requisition is submitted to Buyer A to buy items valued at $75,000. Instead of escalating the requisition to Buyer B, Buyer A convinces the vendor to process the transaction and submit two invoices, one for $50,000 and a second for $25,000.

Table 37.1 Sample Approval Limits in Purchasing Department

Purchaser	Limit
Buyer A	Up to $50,000
Buyer B	Up to $100,000
Manager	Up to $250,000

This way both transactions fall within Buyer A's approval range. The buyer has now successfully circumvented the control over approval limits. Subsequently, when the internal auditor selects a sample and reviews transactions, this action would likely escape detection because the odds of both transactions being selected in the sample for the test is very low. However, this anomaly is fairly easy to detect using data analytics, where sorting purchases by date, vendor, item number, and purchasing agent should result in the identification of matches. When that occurs, the next step is to add the corresponding monetary amounts to determine if the approval thresholds have been circumvented, confirming the split-purchase action.

Key Steps for Successful Data Analytics

Determine what data are needed. Internal auditors can waste large amounts of time in the "sea of data" most organizations have. To avoid this problem, internal auditors should first consider the objective of the review, and the objectives and risks of the program or process being examined. Then ask the following four questions:

1. What data would tell me if the objective is being achieved?
2. What data would tell me if the risks are happening or not? Remember to consider all relevant risks based on the objective of the review.
3. What data would tell me if the controls are working as expected?
4. What data would tell me if the controls are being manipulated?

Determine what data are available. If the organization has conducted a comprehensive data inventory and an up-to-date data library is available, that would be the go-to resource. Otherwise, the internal auditor should review prior year workpapers, talk to other internal auditors who may have knowledge about the area under review, or talk to subject matter experts in the operating unit or IT.

Determine where the data are located. The data may be stored in mainframes, client/servers or be kept by end users so data extraction must be considered as well. The format of the data may be a significant determinant of the ability to use the data as these could be stored in a format that is unworkable, but this is becoming a less worrisome issue because manual formatting procedures or automated data conversion features in software applications are becoming increasingly common.

In some cases, the internal auditor can skip data extraction and directly access the files and databases. This may occur because the files/data are too large, or due to privacy restrictions that limit the movement of data from one geographic jurisdiction to another, like the Data Protection Act restricting the transfer of personal data outside Europe unless substantial safeguards are applied. The reverse scenario may also occur, where the analysis is done outside the database where the data are stored because there is a weak or slow connection, or if the work will degrade performance of live systems.

Internal auditors should make it clear to data owners and custodians that there will be no modification of the data, and access is limited to view only.

In the longer term, internal audit should learn and have the ability to do its own data extraction. Asking IT for data may take longer than necessary and as long as someone else provides the data, the question remains whether all the data needed were provided.

Inaccurate data analysis will result in invalid control recommendations and will have a very negative impact on the audit department's reputation. So, upon receipt of the data, internal auditors should verify its accuracy to official records (e.g., summary reports or financial records) to make sure there is an accurate and complete data set. Some examples of data reconciliation:

■ Customer order information to reported sales
■ Payroll information to human resources master data
■ Payable information to financial statements
■ Credit files to accounts receivables information
■ Fixed asset records to asset accounts
■ Pricing information to master data files

Internal auditors must use data to find out what happened, understand what is happening and why (i.e., root cause analysis) and look forward to predicting as best as reasonably possible, what is likely to occur. Being able to identify trends, correlations, and predict future behaviors and outcomes would provide a very valuable service to their organizations. This ability to use data as a tool to look forward will greatly enhance the contributions of internal audit, provide greater assurance, add value to organizations, contribute in meaningful ways to risk management, and help the organization achieve its objectives (Figure 37.1).

Data analytics programs and continuous auditing algorithms can be built to provide e-mailed notifications automatically to alert the appropriate individuals about red flags, which can turn large amounts of data into actionable information. The timely identification, exposure, and treatment of operational breakdowns or wrongdoing can substantially reduce monetary loss.

Data analytics makes it possible to efficiently analyze large volumes of data, identify outliers within an entire population, present the results in a variety of visual and tabular format, and provide a process to repeat and verify these actions. This allows internal auditors to test 100 percent of transactions (Table 37.2).

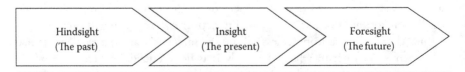

Hindsight (The past) → Insight (The present) → Foresight (The future)

Figure 37.1　The evolution of internal audit contributions.

Table 37.2   Key Steps for Successful Data Analytics

1. Assess risk
2. Inventory the data
3. Examine data access and protection
4. Determine data integrity
5. Analyze data
6. Report results

Successful Data Analytics

1. Assess risk: By conducting a risk assessment, the internal auditor would have a better understanding of where the risks are. For example: AR, AP, Payroll, Purchasing, Cash. It is also important to determine the threshold for fraud detection because fraudsters typically operate below the radar.
2. Inventory the data: Determine how and where data are produced, and where it resides. This inventory should include laptops, desktops, hand-held devices, mainframes, servers, global positioning systems (GPS) in company vehicles and other assets, time-card systems, telephone systems, and visitor check-in logs.
3. Examine data access and protection: Determine who has read and write access to the data, and how they can access the data. Remember that in addition to employees, data can sometimes be accessed by customers, vendors, business partners, and sometimes even competitors.
4. Determine data integrity: Ascertain if the data received are complete and valid. Also examine the format of the data, as lack of uniformity can create problems. Common issues occur with regards to dates, times, and amounts.
5. Analyze data: This step begins with the definition of expectations. It is important to know what to expect to see or not see, and what exceptions to look for before conducting the tests. All analysis should be documented thoroughly.
6. Report results: The results can be presented as charts, tables, narratives, or lists. The visual representation is increasingly preferred, but eventually depends on who the recipients are, what contents and level of detail they want, and how best to convey the results of the analysis. A combination of methods may be best.

Artificial Intelligence

Artificial intelligence (AI) is gaining a lot of attention lately. Machines appear to be learning, automation is becoming more pervasive, and humanoid devices approximating androids are in the news and for sale. The fact is that some aspects of AI are no longer the matter of sci-fi. It is already around us in the form of commuting assistance (e.g., Waze), dynamic pricing (e.g., Uber, Lyft), self-driving cars (e.g., Google), spam filters (e.g., Gmail), plagiarism checkers (e.g., Turnitin), reviewing payment card merchant transactions for potential fraud before authorization (e.g., FICO), online purchase suggestions (e.g., Amazon), grammar check (e.g., Microsoft Word), and facial recognition on smart phones (e.g., Apple). It can be described as computer systems that can predict human behavior.

When we consider IT and its activities ensuring system functionality, AI plays a role in hands-off infrastructure management. This is the remote, automated administration of server, storage, and network resources with minimal human assistance. For example, cloud providers are using this term when, for the most part, a system can run by itself. Some cloud services have AI capabilities built in and use machine learning algorithms to correlate events in the IT infrastructure with problems in application and business environments. Dashboards collect relevant data and issue alerts that allow operators to respond to events without having to physically touch infrastructure components; they can remotely reboot, shutdown, troubleshoot, patch, and re-install operating systems from a tablet or smartphone.

For internal auditors, AI can be a very useful tool to analyze data with greater accuracy. With data and statistical tools, internal auditors can even predict risk and the potential impacts to programs and processes.

Data analytics has become more feasible for large and small internal audit departments because there are many user-friendly software packages at a variety of prices. With these tools, auditors can test how transactions were generated, whether they were accurately recorded, if algorithms are working effectively as they process data, and assess the accuracy of reports by recalculating figures or comparing one set of figures with another to make sure they meet expectations. The automation of queries (e.g., scripts, macros), makes data analytics easier to repeat and reproduce, covering more transactions, from multiple sources, at more locations, more often. The result is that internal auditors can provide greater assurance by examining the populations, multiple time periods, and identify anomalies that in the past may have escaped detection using sampling or manual techniques. By employing the concept of AI into the data analytics realm, internal auditors can enhance their programs, scripts and macros by paying attention to false positives and making sure they use that information to calibrate their analytical procedures. By scrubbing the entire population for outliers, blanks, non-sensical data, internal auditors can reduce the amount of excess information they have to examine before they can assess and draw conclusions.

Internal audit is still early in the process of using AI in its work. A key requirement is that there be an abundance of reliable data, so some of it will need to be generated near or real time with the ability to access, store, and analyze it. Anomalies will need to be addressed through data cleansing to examine and transform the data, so they don't distort results. Complex algorithms and substantial computing power needs to be available to perform what-if and other forms of scenario analysis quickly.

As AI becomes a reality for organizations and for the internal auditors serving them, they will be able to collect the needed data real-time data, organize these, clean, and test these, then allow sophisticated algorithms through machine learning and AI to provide risk and control solutions. For example, AI could identify fluctuations in processing times indicating that an employee is missing important steps or not taking enough time to review transactions before approving them. In another scenario, delays in the servicing of key equipment or unusual pressure readings could indicate the possibility that the machine will malfunction harming operators and stopping production.

Regardless of what machines do, there will always be a need for a human to interpret results, research anomalies found and make sure that the right judgment is applied because decisions always have to be made to assess the risks, their levels, and the best way to mitigate them. For now, internal auditors should learn how to maximize the potential of their data analytics software (e.g., ACL, IDEA, SAS, Minitab), think about the risks to the organization's programs and processes, and try to obtain higher-quality and more abundant data that can help them analyze those risks. There is quite a lot that can be done with today's capabilities while machines become more adept at modifying their code to adapt to and anticipate changing conditions (Figure 37.2).

Example: Using AI to Evaluate Segregation of Duties

As companies reduce staffing levels and become leaner, fewer employees do more tasks so the risk of fraud increases. With data analytics, internal auditors can verify that no single employee can perform the three transaction components:

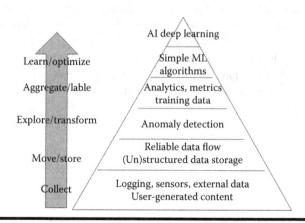

Figure 37.2 The Data Science Hierarchy of Needs. (Adapted from *The Financial Brand* by Monica Rogati.*)

* See Artificial Intelligence Needs a Strong Data Foundation at *The Financial Brand* by Monica Rogati, retrieved from https://thefinancialbrand.com/67039/ai-hierarchy-of-data-needs/ January 28, 2018.

authorization, custody and record-keeping. For example, when it comes to making vendor payments, a different person should be responsible for each of the related steps: Adding a new vendor, inputting the invoices, verifying the purchase order (PO) numbers, cutting the checks, and finally, mailing the checks. In electronic payment environments, the last two steps would be replaced by queuing the payment and releasing the payment.

Smaller organizations, due to their limited staff levels, often require more management oversight and diligence but data analytics can help ease the monitoring burden by using predetermined criteria to focus on high-risk transactions. If a process requires multiple users to successfully execute a transaction, and these typically require two or more days, it would be anomalous if data analytics revealed that these transactions (e.g., payments, refunds, customer credits) were processed the same day. The unusual nature of these transactions could indicate a breach of segregation of duties, fraud, or the sharing of passwords.

Summary

1. Internal auditors should increase their use of data analytics to identify risks, control breakdowns, and fraud during internal audits.
2. Successful data analytics require: risk assessment, data inventory, examination of data access, determination of data integrity, data analysis, and reporting of results.
3. Although many internal auditors look at data analytics as a detection tool, it is important to expand the expectations and usage of this powerful methodology, and consider its broader capabilities. While hindsight (detection—the past) has been the standard focus of data analytics, greater insight (understanding—the present) is needed to provide more comprehensive information to clients. However, the direction and objective should broaden even further, so internal auditors provide foresight (prediction—the future).

Chapter 38

Deficiencies—Design and Operating

There are several names given to the "issues" internal auditors identify during their reviews. The traditional label is *Finding*, but over the years other labels have emerged, such as Observation, Opportunity for Improvement, Weakness, and Deficiency. Since the enactment of the Sarbanes–Oxley (SOX) Act of 2002, the word Deficiency has taken a more specific meaning. According to Auditing Standard No. 5,* a Deficiency is defined as follows:

A deficiency in internal control over financial reporting (ICFR) exists when the design or operation of a control does not allow management or employees, in the normal course of performing their assigned functions, to prevent or detect misstatements on a timely basis.

Of these, there are two types: Design and Operating.

- Design: A deficiency in *design* exists when (a) a control necessary to meet the control objective is missing or (b) an existing control is not properly designed so that, even if the control operates as designed, the control objective would not be met.†
- Operating: A deficiency in operation exists when a properly designed control does not operate as designed, or when the person performing the control does not possess the necessary authority or competence to perform the control effectively.‡

It is important to define a control objective as well, since the definition of a design deficiency makes reference to it. A control objective for ICFR generally relates to a

---

* See https://pcaobus.org/Standards/Auditing/Pages/Auditing_Standard_5_Appendix_A.aspx.
† Ibid.
‡ Ibid.

relevant assertion and states a criterion for evaluating whether the company's control procedures in a specific area provide reasonable assurance that a misstatement or omission in that relevant assertion is prevented or detected by controls on a timely basis*.

These are essential definitions for anyone performing SOX Section 404 related reviews. What about the rest of internal auditors who do not perform these reviews? What can we learn from SOX that may be applicable to traditional internal auditors? Quite a lot.

Let's examine the control objective definition. As stated above it relates to providing reasonable assurance that the financial statement assertions can be achieved because the related controls prevent or detect possible misstatements or omissions. In operational programs and processes within organizations (i.e., everything else), a similar objective can be pursued. Namely, the related controls support the achievement of programmatic or operational business objectives by preventing or detecting risks that hinder the achievement of those objectives.

In terms of deficiencies, then, we can ask the following question about Design Deficiencies: Are there gaps in the design of the program or process, so that controls are missing where they should be and as a result, create a situation where a risk could materialize jeopardizing the achievement of objectives?

Consider the following conditions related to the program or process under review:

Condition	Reason
Too many controls given the related risks	This occurs because the risks have not been assessed appropriately and controls are increasingly accumulated around low impact or likelihood risks. This can also be caused by bureaucratic procedures.
No control to mitigate a risk	This occurs due to the oversight of management or previous internal auditors who have not identified relevant risks.
Operators performing incompatible duties	This can be caused for a variety of reasons, including transferred employees whose access rights have not been adjusted, reductions in workforce resulting in too-few operators, poorly designed and assigned system access rights.
Too many, and overreliance on manual controls	A legacy condition carried forward due to insufficient automation.
Too many, and overreliance on detective controls	Often due to general oversight and the assumption that all controls are equal.

---

* Ibid.

There is a great deal of opportunity to add value to our clients' organizations by examining how programs and processes are designed.

Similarly, we can relate Operating Deficiencies as follows: Are properly designed controls not performing as expected thus allowing the risk to materialize jeopardizing the achievement of objectives? As internal auditors we have traditionally focused on Operating Deficiencies, testing transactions and communicating them as Findings. But there is more that we can do by adapting our testing procedures to be:

1. Risk-based
2. Using data analytics more extensively to identify anomalies that sampling may not identify (e.g., split transactions, outliers, trends, bottlenecks, rework)
3. Quantifying the Condition and Effect of the finding more extensively

Internal auditors can, and should, leverage the lessons learned from the SOX Act of 2002. While it is a US-based law applicable to publicly-traded companies, the definition of control objectives and deficiencies is applicable to all types of internal audits with slight modifications. This adaptation creates opportunities to add value to our clients in many ways, thus enhancing our contributions in new and innovative ways.

Summary

1. Internal auditors' testing procedures have focused primarily on operating deficiencies, but many opportunities exist to add value by examining the design of programs and processes. Design weaknesses can result in longer cycle times, redundancies, and underutilization of the existing operating capacity.
2. Testing the operating integrity of internal controls is a form of inspection. Prevention is cheaper.
3. Walkthroughs, flowcharts, and narratives can identify design deficiencies. Data analytics provide a good opportunity to identify anomalies by testing 100 percent of transactions, rather than relying on sampling alone.

Chapter 39

E's

Internal auditors focus on a variety of subjects during their work and it is helpful to leverage acronyms and mnemonics to make sure that important coverage areas are not neglected. The Es represent a series of seven topic areas that are very useful, especially when performing operational audits. The seven Es are as follows:

1. Economy: This refers to the cost incurred while obtaining the inputs the organization, program or process needs to perform its activities. Two important questions to ask are: Is the organization paying a fair price for the inputs obtained? Is the organization getting the best value? Economy is important because waste, in any way, is against the interests of the organization's stakeholders. Overpaying can occur when buying inventory, fixed assets, supplies, and even when borrowing funds or paying for electricity, water, and waste disposal. Overpaying reduces the organization's profitability and lowers the amount of resources available for other needs.

2. Efficiency: This relates to the ratio of production (e.g., outputs) in relation to costs or inputs. Efficiency can be measured in terms of money, time, or energy. Everyone working within, or on behalf of, an organization has a responsibility to maximize the value and use of available resources. Like the lack of economy, inefficiency reduces the organization's profitability as it consumes more resources than necessary.

3. Effectiveness: It refers to the degree to which a program or process is successful achieving its goals and objectives. It focuses on whether the area being reviewed is successful or not. An inability to achieve relevant goals and objectives puts into question the follow-through on the responsibility of the organization as an agent of stakeholders, and the achievement of objectives as the reason resources were committed and used in the first place. The absence of clearly defined goals and objectives is an issue too.

4. Ethics: It is defined as the moral principles that govern a person's behavior. It also applies to organizations to the extent that the individuals managing, leading, and working within or for the organization make decisions that contain moral elements. Internal auditors are tasked with assessing and making appropriate recommendations to improve the organization's governance processes and for promoting appropriate ethics and values (Standard 2110). Ethics are a fundamental ingredient in well-functioning organizations and ethical breakdowns can be very costly, as exemplified in the scandals at Wells Fargo, Volkswagen, Theranos, Enron, WorldCom, Adelphia, and Parmalat, among others. Internal auditors cannot examine business transactions in a vacuum, because an unethical employee could falsify company records or engage in other inappropriate actions harming the company, colleagues, vendors, investors, customers, and the public.

5. Ecology: Concern for the environment has been on the rise for decades. Organizations today must adhere to environmental rules, laws, and regulations such as the Clean Air Act, Clean Water Act, and many others. Furthermore, the public has become less tolerant of organizations that pollute the air, water, and soil. Organizations cannot ignore the importance of environmental stewardship and acting like responsible corporate citizens. Volkswagen was embroiled in a very damaging scandal when software was detected underreporting the true emission levels of 11 million diesel-vehicles. The company agreed to pay $2.8 billion criminal fine in the United States[*] and set a provision of $23.9 billion to address the damages associated with the recall[†]. Other impacts include the resignation of the company's CEO and other senior executives and a substantial drop in stock price after the incident became public. At this time the impact on future sales of diesel-powered vehicles, and more specifically, the reduction in VW market share is still unknown.

6. Equity: This applies to the idea of treating everyone fairly. While many instinctively relate this concept to compliance with fair labor laws (e.g., hiring, termination, pay), the concept is much broader. Organizations should examine its practices to verify that they adhere to the principles of equity when promoting employees, when dealing with customers and suppliers, and in their interactions with the communities where they operate. United Airlines experienced a great deal of pushback when it removed a paying customer from an airplane because the airline needed seats to move flight crew members from one city to another. The unfairness of the practice, and the

---

[*] See www.wsj.com/articles/judge-slaps-vw-with-2-8-billion-criminal-fine-in-emissions-fraud-1492789096.

[†] See www.bloomberg.com/news/articles/2017-02-24/vw-s-profit-boost-clouded-by-6-8-billion-diesel-crisis-charge.

way this was done, reverberated in social media, damaging the company's reputation and costing millions of dollars.

7. Excellence: This concept relates to the performance of company work with high quality. Every internal audit should include in its review process an examination of the degree to which the work performed is of high quality, and all interactions are characterized by an element of superior customer service toward others. Poor workmanship, lack of reliability, and similar poor features carry a risk to the organization often reflected in higher-than-necessary returns, warranty claims, complaints, customer turnover, and reputation. Poor quality and workmanship is frowned upon in developed and developing countries alike, and has become a key differentiator in many industries.

The seven Es are a very useful tool when applied as themes during the development of audit programs or subsequently during fieldwork and reporting. Include the seven Es when developing interview questions, when providing status updates to the client, when conducting exit meetings and even when writing audit reports. Business leader-managers are focused on these themes, their organizations thrive or fail based on their ability to operate according to these principles. Internal auditors should too.

Summary

1. The seven Es provide a simple, yet very powerful tool to make sure that seven essential themes for organizational success are addressed during audit engagements.
2. They contain quantitative and qualitative elements, and provide a broad coverage of objective, risk, and controls topics.
3. While value-for-money audits generally focus on the Primary Three of economy, efficiency, and effectiveness, expanding the list to seven provides a more expansive coverage and value proposition.

Chapter 40

Eight Areas of Waste

An important action by internal auditors to add value to their clients is to identify waste and inefficiency. In fact, the Institute of Internal Auditors (IIA) states in the *Standards* that acting with due professional care means identifying areas of waste:

> Due professional care calls for the application of the care and skill expected of a reasonably prudent and competent internal auditor in the same or similar circumstances. Due professional care is therefore appropriate to the complexities of the engagement being performed. Exercising due professional care involves internal auditors being alert to the possibility of fraud, intentional wrongdoing, errors and omissions, inefficiency, waste, ineffectiveness, and conflicts of interest, as well as being alert to those conditions and activities where irregularities are most likely to occur. This also involves internal auditors identifying inadequate controls and recommending improvements to promote conformance with acceptable procedures and practices. Practice Advisory 1220-1 Due Professional Care

A key component of the lean business methodology is eliminating waste. The focus in organizations should be to spend more time and resources creating value for customers by eliminating, or at least, reducing, everything else. A common methodology is the Eight Areas of Waste, which identifies:

1. Mistakes/Errors: This involves the time and materials spent doing something that has to be scrapped or fixed due to poor quality. Examples include:
   - Making parts that don't meet customer requirements or safety regulations
   - Software bugs
   - Incorrect data entry
   - Misdiagnoses in healthcare

- Wrong product being shipped
- Setting product or service features different from what the customer requested

2. Transportation: This is related to the movement of people, inventory, tools, and other items more frequently or over longer distances than necessary. Examples include:
   - Moving parts, products, or tools from one location to another
   - Moving software from one server or database to another
   - Returning overstock inventory to another warehouse
   - Transporting produce across long distances instead of sourcing what is available locally

3. Waiting: This source of waste involves customers, associates, or parts sitting idle until they are needed or can be serviced. This occurs when the receiver is ready for the next step, but the process is not prepared. Examples include:
   - Customers waiting (e.g., in person, on the phone, online)
   - System downtime, software ready for QA, or for migration from development to production
   - Manufacturing processes waiting for the delivery or arrival of raw materials, semi-finished goods, or subassemblies
   - Customers forced to wait due to errors, equipment malfunction, or missing items

4. Motion: This involves the unnecessary movement of people or items within a work area. For example:
   - Workers searching for parts, materials, tools, or equipment
   - Excessive data entry or clicks on a system to perform a small task
   - Poorly structured or disorganized workspaces
   - Requiring users to re-enter the same information on company forms

5. Overproduction: This occurs when more is produced than consumed. This also occurs when items are produced too early. This waste type often triggers other types of waste, such as transportation, inventory, and motion. For example:
   - Producing items before the next stage in the process is ready to receive and use them
   - Producing items without a committed and ready buyer
   - Printing and filing unnecessary documents
   - Holding more items in inventory (e.g., warehouses or consignment locations) than will be needed and sold within a reasonable amount of time

6. Overprocessing: This relates to doing work that does not add value to the customer and can be resolved through simplification. It is important to remember that sometimes the best course of action is stop doing something rather than trying to do it better. For example:
   - Multiple approvals for a small spending request

- Making copies of a document when the same item can be viewed electronically
- Requesting unnecessary tests in a healthcare environment
- Entering the same data in multiple places in a paper or software form

7. Excess Inventory: This involves storing products or materials that are not needed within a reasonable amount of time. This condition is even more significant when the items involved are perishable. For example:
   - Buying, producing, or storing more product than historical or forecasted demand indicates
   - Excessive promotional materials
   - Storing unused or rarely used machines or tools
   - Having cabinets full of office supplies

8. Underutilized Personnel: This involves the waste of human potential. For example:
   - Employees placed and kept in positions that under-utilize their potential
   - Limited or absent career planning and development
   - Ignoring improvement ideas
   - Employees performing tasks that do not add value

Over the years, this list of Eight Areas of Waste has served me well as a roadmap while performing audit and consulting projects. Waste Number 2—Transporting was instrumental in making significant improvements at client locations. While performing an audit at a large warehouse we noticed the large number of forklifts moving about and wondered if there were opportunities to minimize the amount of travel required to stock and retrieve items. We asked for a report showing inventory part movements over the past 3 years to assess seasonality variations and gain a better understanding of activity patterns. With this information we identified the most commonly used items. We then prepared a chart of the warehouse and mapped the location of these high-demand items. The results indicated that these high-demand items were located throughout the facility, which explained why forklifts were moving all over the warehouse. We shared the results with management and after some discussions developed a plan to rearrange the warehouse. By clustering the most commonly used items (and creating wider path lanes to facilitate movement and avoid collisions) and moving the less frequently used items to the periphery and rear of the facility, the amount of time and fuel was reduced.

Waste Number 2: Transportation; Waste Number 3: Waiting; Waste Number 6: Overprocessing were instrumental in making substantial gains at a government agency that processed specialty visa applications. It was struggling under the weight of customer complaints, a decreasing reputation and the increasing attention of politicians whose constituents were demanding some remediation from the lengthy processing times. A review of the process using flowcharts showed that an application moved through various departments, buildings, and sections of the city as it was processed. There were numerous handoffs, an inability to identify the exact whereabout of items-in-process and delays due to time spent in-transit. After some discussions with the various offices involved in processing the requests and related documents, it was determined that treating each application like a case, and clustering the various processors, could accelerate the process. The forms were simplified, information was requested earlier to reduce waiting time, and several offices were relocated so rather than moving from building to building and from one section of the city to another, most of the work consisted of moving from one floor to another within the same building. The results were dramatic and processing times were reduced substantially.

Waste Number 7: Excess Inventory is often associated with traditional inventory kept on hand by manufacturing or retail organizations. That is not necessarily the case as was discovered during a review at a financial services organization. This company handled financial products, whose rates of return and fees changed quarterly. The organization's sales and marketing unit had a contract with a printer that gave them large-volume discounts. The prevailing practice was to print large quantities of brochures to secure the discount. After interviewing several of the sales and marketing personnel, looking at their invoices and the number of items discarded as unused, it was determined that it was cheaper to print a smaller number of brochures based on actual usage and pay the higher price, than place a larger order and obtain the volume discount. The number of discarded items was so large!

Internal auditors can make searching for waste a part of their routine audit activities. While some areas of waste may be obvious, others may be more subtle and harder to find. Either way, when waste is identified and corrected, internal auditors will help their organizations become more efficient, effective, and economical. It will also get them closer to being recognized as problem-solvers and trusted advisors.

Summary

1. Internal auditors add value by looking at what work is done and the results of those activities (outputs and outcomes). A great deal of opportunity exists to add value by also examining how work is done.
2. Eight areas of waste exist in many organizations. It consists of mistakes/errors, transportation, waiting, motion, overproduction, overprocessing, excess inventory, and underutilized personnel.
3. When internal auditors highlight operating deficiencies and recommend improvements that make operating units function better, they will transform their image from that of the corporate police and into an efficiency expert, whose insights are valuable for business success.

Chapter 41

Electronic Workpapers

Internal auditors are required to document what they did, why they did it, how it was done, and who did it. The general term used to describe these records is workpapers. So, workpapers are the documents created, collected, analyzed, and stored during the course of internal audit work, regardless of the type of work performed (e.g., compliance, operational, financial, IT). Since workpapers refer to the entire collection of documents, they consist of more than fieldwork documents. They refer to any and everything produced by the internal auditor, by the audit client, and relevant third parties during the engagement.

Standard 2300—Performing the Engagement states that "Internal auditors must identify, analyze, evaluate, and document sufficient information to achieve the engagement's objectives." And the information obtained must be sufficient, reliable, relevant, and useful to achieve the engagement's objectives, and to support the engagement results and conclusions. (Standard 2330—Documenting Information)

Workpapers constitute the evidentiary material internal auditors produce and rely on to show:

- What was done: This includes Planning, Fieldwork, Reporting, and the Administrative activities performed during the engagement.
- Why it was done: Every document created or reviewed should have a reason for its existence. This is typically related to the verification that objectives are being pursued and achieved, that risks have been identified and considered in decision-making, and that controls and contingencies are present and functioning as expected.
- Who did it: Documenting authorship is very important as accountability and an audit trail are essential for effective internal auditing.

- Who reviewed it: Evidence of supervision is required for effective internal auditing to demonstrate compliance with the Internal Standards for the Professional Practice of Internal Auditing (the *Standards)*, ensure quality control, and help develop internal auditors.

Workpapers can consist of any of the following:

- Narratives: Written description of activities within a program or process
- Flowcharts: Visual representation of the flow of activities within a program or process
- Walkthroughs: Step-by-step tests of all the procedures for a program, process, or plan
- Pictures: Photography or drawing of an area of interest
- Reports: Documents containing information organized in tabular, graphic, or narrative form
- Interview Notes: Narrative describing what was discussed during meetings with audit clients
- Presentations: Visual representations prepared with or for the client

Workpapers should "stand alone" so their contents are self-explanatory. This can be difficult for some internal auditors who "know what they mean" in their documentation, but this knowledge is not clearly evident in their documentation. The question, however, should be: Does a reasonably informed, but independent, reader know:

1. What was done
2. Why it was done
3. What information was examined
4. The source of that information
5. What the results were
6. Who did the work

Readers should not have to guess or assume they know what was done, or how the auditor arrived at the conclusions. Furthermore, readers should not have to contact the preparer for clarification. The documents should speak for themselves. In general, working papers should contain sufficient information to enable an experienced auditor without any previous connection with the audit to determine from them what was done, why it was done, and the evidence that supports the results, conclusions, and opinions.

There are two additional elements that are also very important:

Reproducibility: It is the ability of another individual, independent of the original person, to reproduce the work done using the raw data, records, computer programs or procedures, and arrive at similar results. There should be a high degree of agreement between initial and subsequent testers. A key question is: If someone else needed to reproduce the work done, would they have the needed details in the workpapers to know how to collect and examine the related information?

Repeatability: This refers to the consistency in obtaining similar results if the same procedures were performed subsequently. Internal auditors should strive for small variation. A key question is: If you needed to repeat the work done in the future, are the information and procedures sufficiently clear so you can repeat the procedures without having to rely on memory?

One of the rules of thumb I like to apply to the quality of workpapers and procedures followed is: Would someone else not involved in the audit understand the what, who, why, when and where of the procedures performed, and the related results and conclusions, without having to contact you? If they must contact you to get answers to any of these questions, your workpaper was not completed well enough to stand alone.

Another important consideration is that workpapers should be professionally prepared because they can be viewed by parties beyond the internal auditors in the department. Some of these other parties may include: regulators, external auditors, consultants, and lawyers who may request these documents for a variety of reasons, including Quality Assurance reviews and legal claims.

Since workpapers may be examined by others outside the internal audit department, preparers should not include language that is unprofessional, or opinions not based on facts and informed information. Similarly, assumptions and conclusions should be documented and verified for appropriateness based on the facts available.

Following is a list of typical documents arranged by phase:

Planning
- Audit program
- Information, document, and data requests
- Engagement letter
- Internal controls questionnaire (ICQ)
- Pre-Audit self-assessment questionnaire
- Risk evaluation/assessment
- Planning memo
- Interview template and notes
- Budget
- Prior audit reports

Fieldwork
- Testing documentation
- Interview notes

- Findings/observation form/template/audit point sheet
- Exit meeting notes and presentation

Reporting
- Draft report
- Management responses
- Final report
- Stakeholder template

Administration
- Status reports
- Findings monitoring/tracker
- Task assignments and Management
- Time tracking

Many internal audit units capture, store, and manage their workpapers in traditional server folders by project, using the sections: Planning, Fieldwork, Reporting, and Administration. Electronic workpapers may facilitate the document-management process, and provide a centralized repository for them. They also provide more detailed access controls, so read and write access can be assigned at various levels to team members working on an engagement and to other personnel within the internal audit department as needed.

The number of software packages providing electronic workpaper functionality has increased over the last few years and are widely used by auditors to facilitate the preparation, review, and archiving of workpapers. However, only 38 percent of chief audit executives (CAEs) say their organizations are using technology at an "appropriate" level or higher, according to the Global Internal Audit Common Body of Knowledge survey report from The Institute of Internal Auditors Research Foundation (IIARF). Twenty three percent of CAEs said their organizations rely primarily on manual systems and processes in internal audit. Electronic workpapers are internal audit's most commonly used IT tool worldwide, with 72 percent of respondents reporting at least moderate use.

Having an electronic workpaper application is not required, but highly recommended. A very important reason is that these software applications generally reference the documents automatically, so internal auditors can prepare documents directly into the software application or upload files. If internal auditors are using traditional server folders to document their workpapers, they should have a structure defining where documents are stored for easier filing and retrieval.

The following list shows some of the most popular workpaper software packages and is not meant as an endorsement:

Name	Additional Information
TeamMate	www.teammatesolutions.com/teamewp.aspx
MKinsight	www.mkinsight.com/functionality.aspx?id=15
CaseWare	www.caseware.com/us/products/working-papers
Workiva	www.workiva.com/solutions/audit-management
BWise	www.bwise.com/solutions/internal-audit/ bwise-internal-audit
AutoAudit	https://risk.thomsonreuters.com/en/products/ autoaudit-software.html
Open Pages	www.ibm.com/us-en/marketplace/ openpages-internal-audit-management
Auditor Assistant	http://rsmus.com/what-we-do/services/risk-advisory/ internal-audit/auditor-assistant.html
Galileo	http://magiquegalileo.com/

Summary

1. Electronic workpaper software facilitates the creation, review, archiving, and retrieval of audit documents.
2. The functionality is generally similar between applications, but internal auditors planning to purchase an electronic workpaper package should examine the stability, speed, user-friendliness, and reporting capabilities.
3. The internal audit methodology should be examined from a process-improvement perspective before purchasing an electronic workpaper package. No one should expect a new computer system to resolve process weaknesses.

Chapter 42

Emotional Intelligence

Intelligence Quotient (IQ) measures have been considered a key indicator of an individual's potential for success. It generally predicts how well an individual can handle the cognitive challenges of a demanding job. Career advancement requires intellect and expertise, key ingredients of IQ, but it also requires other attributes that differentiates the great from the good.

Over the years, IQ has found a worthy compliment: Emotional Intelligence (EI). *Psychology Today* defines EI as "the ability to identify and manage your own emotions and the emotions of others. It is generally said to include three skills: emotional awareness; the ability to harness emotions and apply them to tasks like thinking and problem solving; and the ability to manage emotions, which includes regulating your own emotions and cheering up or calming down other people." * It generally refers to the ability to identify, assess, and control one's emotions and manage relationships with others effectively.

Daniel Goleman stated in his book *Emotional Intelligence: Why It Can Matter More than IQ* that "EI abilities rather than IQ or technical skills emerge as the "discriminating" competency that best predicts who among a group of very smart people will lead most ably. If you scan the competencies that organizations around the world have independently determined identify their star leaders, you discover that indicators of IQ and technical skills drop toward the bottom of the list the higher the position. (IQ and technical expertise are much stronger predictors of excellence in lower-rung jobs.)" †

EI is a key requirement to effectively identify, interpret, and respond to every-day situations. Internal auditors must be aware of their emotions and moods, work effectively with audit clients, motivate themselves and colleagues, be steadfast when

---

* www.psychologytoday.com/basics/emotional-intelligence.
† This quote is also available at www.danielgoleman.info/how-emotional-intelligence-matters/.

confronted with roadblocks and disappointments, control their impulses, and not allow workplace pressure, deadlines or changing conditions to cause undue stress. Poorly managing one's emotions will limit the ability to think critically about engagement or departmental dynamics. While supervising others, emotionally intelligent managers must be able to manage themselves, team members, the audit client and other stakeholders so the engagement can be successful.

EI has two focus areas and four components as shown in Table 42.1.

Table 42.1 Emotional Intelligence

Major Focus Area	Components	Characteristics
Personal competence: How we manage ourselves.	Self-awareness	Recognizing one's own emotions and their impact. Using your gut to guide decisions. Knowing one's strengths and limits, and possessing a healthy sense of self-worth and capabilities.
	Self-management	Keeping disruptive emotions under control, showing honesty and integrity, being flexible when dealing with changing situations or overcoming obstacles. A strong drive to improve performance, readiness to act and take advantage of opportunities, and being optimistic.
Social competence: How we manage relationships.	Social awareness	Showing empathy by recognizing others' emotions, understanding their perspective and taking interest in their concerns, and meeting staff, client or customer needs.
	Relationship management	Being an inspirational leader through a compelling vision, be persuasive, provide feedback and guidance to others, initiate and manage change, display effective conflict management skills to resolve disagreements, build strong relationships and show teamwork and collaboration through cooperation and team building.

Source: Adapted from *Organizational Behavior* by Robert Kreitner and Angelo Kinicki.

Daniel Goleman, author of the book Emotional Intelligence, states that intelligence, determination, and toughness are important for success, but they are not enough. Also important are self-awareness, self-regulation, motivation, empathy and social skill. These attributes are characteristics of emotionally intelligent and effective leaders, and also crucial for success. Goleman argues that too many managers wrongly believe that compassion, empathy and understanding their staff's emotions impair the performance of business tasks so they ignore these topics. The opposite is true.

Team Emotional Intelligence

EI is not only an individual competency, but also an important attribute of highly productive teams. Trust among team members, a group identity shared by everyone on the team, and a sense of group efficacy lead to superior performance. Without these qualities team members fail to get truly engaged, cooperate or participate fully in the work.

If there is a disagreement in the team, emotionally intelligent teams will not immediately move to overpower those with different views or organize the majority against the lone dissenter. Instead, the team will hear the contrarian point of view and work collaboratively to clarify misunderstandings and solve the conflict. When a team member is struggling to keep up, the team will search for ways to help the person become more capable. When members are experiencing personal difficulties, the team will show empathy and cover for them. Emotionally intelligent groups show concern and compassion while holding each other up to high quality and performance standards. These dynamics increase friendship, cooperation, caring and high productivity.*

Audit managers should try to identify, understand and learn to respond appropriately to other people's needs, emotions, and behaviors when handling stress, change, tight deadlines or complicated tasks. They should be attuned to their colleagues' and clients' emotional changes so they can intervene and positively influence the appropriate reaction. By applying EI the internal audit function will be able to think critically and creatively, find better ways to perform the work and build strong and lasting relationships with their clients.

Summary

1. Professional and career effectiveness is considered as much about IQ as it is about EI. EI highlights and validates the importance of behaviors that support relationships, communication, empathy, collaboration, and perceptiveness.

---

* For a more detailed discussion of group emotional intelligence, see Building the Emotional Intelligence of Groups by Vanessa Urch Druskat and Steven B. Wolff in *Harvard Business Review on Teams That Succeed*, Harvard Business School Publishing Corporation, 2004.

2. Managing emotions is a key competency for effective management and leadership. Effective leaders are aware of their emotions, manage them appropriately, show social awareness, and manage relationships.
3. When internal auditors use EI they can build stronger, more productive teams, and improve the relationship within internal audit and with their audit clients and other stakeholders.

Chapter 43

Engagement Memo and Letter

The Engagement Memo is a document prepared by the internal audit team primarily for the internal audit team. It shows for the corresponding audit:

- Objective(s)
- Scope
- Budget
- Timeline
- Team leader
- Team membership
- Work program

This is a very useful document because it summarizes what the audit is about, it provides clarity about goals and objectives, resources, and the audit program. It is very important for the auditors working on the audit to familiarize themselves with its contents. Since auditors sometimes join an audit team after the project has commenced, either to augment its resources or because another auditor was pulled from the project to address other pressing matters, this document provides a useful guide to onboard the new arrival.

The contents of the Engagement Letter are very similar to the Engagement Memo, but the former is sent to the audit client. An important component of the Engagement Letter is that it also outlines the responsibilities and obligations of both parties (i.e., the internal auditors and the auditee), so it helps to clarify each other's roles.

206 ■ *Auditor Essentials*

The engagement letter is sent at the beginning of an audit or consulting engagement and constitutes the start of the audit, beginning the planning phase.

Summary

1. The engagement memo serves as a guide for the audit team, outlining the key aspects of the engagement like the scope, timeline, team membership, and engagement logistics.
2. The engagement letter serves as the announcement for the project and communicates officially to the client what the event will cover, what to expect during the engagement and reporting protocols.
3. Internal auditors should prepare a comprehensive engagement memo to make sure that all members of the audit team are aware of the purpose of the audit and to facilitate the onboarding of new auditors if needed.

Chapter 44

Enterprise Risk Assessment and Management (ERM)

Risk management is the identification, analysis, and control of risks that can jeopardize the achievement of objectives. Risk management should also involve harnessing opportunities since the inability to capitalize on positive events can also jeopardize, or at least limit, the organization's future success potential. In responding to risk, an organization may use acceptance, avoidance, transfer/sharing, minimization/mitigation, or any other strategy (or combination of strategies) to properly manage future events.

Internal auditors should review management's plan to verify that risk management processes and activities are adequate, risks are identified and managed effectively, and that there are status reports produced regarding key risks. Internal auditors can facilitate the identification and evaluation of risks, coach management on effective ways to respond to risks, champion and promote the establishment of a risk management function, and help to develop the organization's risk management strategy for board approval. In some cases, internal auditors can also coordinate risk management activities, consolidate the reporting of risks, develop and maintain the risk management framework, and help to develop the risk management strategy for board approval.

Although internal auditors are encouraged to help the organization implement and run an effective risk management function, they should abstain from setting the risk appetite and what is to be considered acceptable risk levels; establish, perform, or take responsibility for risk management activities; make decisions on risk responses; implement risk responses on management's behalf; and holding accountability for risk management. These are management responsibilities that if performed will interfere with internal auditors' independence.*

There are various frameworks and methodologies that provide guidance on how to manage organizational risks. The Committee of Sponsoring Organizations (COSO) Enterprise Risk Management (ERM) framework is highly regarded and widely used. It states that every organization exists to provide value for its stakeholders, and due to the inherent uncertainty facing all entities, management must decide how much risk to undertake as it grows stakeholder value. Risk presents both risks and opportunities, and ERM facilitates the alignment of risk appetite and organizational strategy, enhances the quality and speed of risk response decisions, it reduces operational losses, it improves the deployment of company resources, reduces performance variability, and enhances corporate resilience by being able to anticipate and respond to change.

ERM is a dynamic and ongoing process that is performed by people at every level of the organization, which should take a portfolio view of risk to provide reasonable assurance that the entity's strategy and objectives will be managed within the risk appetite. Objectives can be categorized in four main categories: Strategic, operations, reporting, and compliance.

The board of directors plays a key role in risk oversight, including proposing the strategy and risk appetite, aligning the business strategy and objectives with the entity's mission and core values, making significant decisions (e.g., mergers and acquisitions, capital allocation), approving management incentives and compensation, and participating in investor and stakeholder relations.

The framework focuses on:

Governance: The ERM Framework states that governance and culture set the organization's tone, reinforcing the importance of oversight. This risk oversight, setting of operating structures, also influences the ethical values, desired behaviors, and the establishment of the desired culture, attracting and retaining capable individuals, and promoting an understanding of risk in the organization.

Strategy and Objectives: ERM aligns and ensures that strategy, objectives, and risk management work together by analyzing and understanding the business context defining the risk appetite, evaluating alternative strategies, and formulating business objectives.

Performance: ERM is designed to identify, assess, prioritize, and respond appropriately to risk. It also includes the review of organizational performance to determine how effectively ERM is operating over time using a portfolio view of risk.

---

* For a more detailed review of these limitations, see *The Role of Internal Auditing in Enterprisewide Risk Management*, published by the Institute of Internal Auditors.

Review and Revision: To be successful today and in the future, organizations must assess change, align risk and performance, and continually pursue improvement to the ERM program.

Information, Communication, and Reporting: All of this requires continually obtaining and sharing information from external and internal sources leveraging technology and making sure that this information flows down (from the board and senior management in the form of guidance and instructions), up (from operating areas in the form of results) and across (among units to ensure coordination). Reporting also entails communicating risk information and reporting on the risk, culture and performance of the organization in general, and the program in particular.

The International Organization for Standardization (ISO) 31000:2009—Risk Management is also highly regarded and widely used. It provides principles, framework, and a process for managing risk. It can be used by any organization regardless of its size, activity, or sector. Using ISO 31000:2009 can help organizations increase the likelihood of achieving objectives, improve the identification of opportunities and threats, and effectively allocate and use resources for risk treatment. The ISO 31000:2009 global standard contains principles for effective risk management, stating that risk management should:

- Create and protect value
- Be an integral part of organizational processes
- Be part of organizational decision-making
- Explicitly address uncertainty
- Be based on the best available information
- Be dynamic, iterative, and responsive to change
- Be tailored to the organization's needs and circumstances
- Facilitate continuous improvement and the advancement of the organization*

Risk management is a process to proactively work with relevant stakeholders, internal, and external to the organization, to minimize negative outcomes and maximize or capitalize on opportunities. By taking this "defense" (i.e., protection from negative outcomes) and "offense" (i.e., harnessing opportunities), risk management becomes a more valuable tool for organizations. In addition, risk management doesn't have to be expensive. As stated in the ISO 31000:2009 framework, and COSO ERM, the program should be tailored to the organization's circumstances and resources, thus the level of formality, staffing, automation, and complexity of tools and techniques, should be adapted to the organization.

---

* For more information about ISO 31000:2009, see www.iso.org/iso-31000-risk-management.html.

Table 44.1 Risk Management Maturity Model

Level	Characteristics
5—Optimized	Risk discussion is built into the strategic planning, capital allocation, project management, and other processes as part of daily decision-making. A mechanism is in place that provides an early warning system to alert the board and management if risks rise above predetermined thresholds.
4—Integrated	Risk management activities are coordinated throughout the enterprise and across business areas. Risk management processes and tools are used where appropriate with metrics for risk measurement, monitoring, and reporting.
3—Defined	A common risk management and response framework is in place. The organization has a common view of risk and action plans are implemented to respond to high priority risks.
2—Initial	Risk is defined differently and managed separately throughout the organization. Limited rigor and discipline characterize the program and related processes.
1—Ad Hoc	Risk management is undocumented, in a state of change that depends on individual prerogatives and isolated actions, rather than a defined program and process.
0—Non Existent	

Source: Adapted from *Navigating Risk Management* by Norman Marks, Internal Auditor, June 2011, p. 31.

Regardless of the size and complexity of the risk management program, internal auditors may want to consider using a maturity model when evaluating the organization's risk management program. A five-tier model, like the one shown on Table 44.1, may be useful.

Many of its elements found in COSO ERM parallel those found in COSO's Internal Control—Integrated Framework (IC-IF), but the focus is on risk management, and its linkages to an organization's strategy and objective-attainment. The following outline shows the COSO ERM Components and the twenty Principles that define the framework.

Governance and Culture

1. Exercises Board Risk Oversight—The board of directors provides oversight of the strategy and carries out governance responsibilities to support management in achieving strategy and business objectives.

2. Establishes Operating Structures—The organization establishes operating structures in the pursuit of strategy and business objectives.
3. Defines Desired Culture—The organization defines the desired behaviors that characterize the entity's desired culture.
4. Demonstrates Commitment to Core Values—The organization demonstrates a commitment to the entity's core values.
5. Attracts, Develops, and Retains Capable Individuals—The organization is committed to building human capital in alignment with the strategy and business objectives.

Strategy and Objective Setting

6. Analyzes Business Context—The organization considers potential effects of business context on risk profile.
7. Defines Risk Appetite—The organization defines risk appetite in the context of creating, preserving, and realizing value.
8. Evaluates Alternative Strategies—The organization evaluates alternative strategies and potential impact on risk profile.
9. Formulates Business Objectives—The organization considers risk while establishing the business objectives at various levels that align and support strategy.

Performance

10. Identifies Risk—The organization identifies risk that impacts the performance of strategy and business objectives.
11. Assesses Severity of Risk—The organization assesses the severity of risk.
12. Prioritizes Risks—The organization prioritizes risks as a basis for selecting responses to risks.
13. Implements Risk Responses—The organization identifies and selects risk responses.
14. Develops Portfolio View—The organization develops and evaluates a portfolio view of risk.

Review and Revision

15. Assesses Substantial Change—The organization identifies and assesses changes that may substantially affect strategy and business objectives.
16. Reviews Risk and Performance—The organization reviews entity performance and considers risk.
17. Pursues Improvement in ERM—The organization pursues improvement of ERM.

Information, Communication, and Reporting

18. Leverages Information Systems—The organization leverages the entity's information and technology systems to support ERM.
19. Communicates Risk Information—The organization uses communication channels to support ERM.
20. Reports on Risk, Culture, and Performance—The organization reports on risk, culture, and performance at multiple levels and across the entity.

Summary

1. ERM involves the identification, analysis, and control of events that have an impact on the achievement of objectives. It is a dynamic process that involves people, processes and tools to collect, analyze, interpret, and respond to risks and opportunities. A key aspect of risk assessment and risk management is the ability to predict, prepare, and recover from adverse events.
2. ERM impacts corporate governance, culture, strategy, objective-setting, performance, and the communication and reporting of information.
3. Since the risk management function within the organization is part of the Second Line of Defense, internal auditors may audit this function, collaborate with it, and support its efforts to promote effective risk management within the entity.

Chapter 45

Ethics

The Merriam-Webster dictionary defines ethics as the discipline dealing with what is good and bad and with moral duty and obligation. Ethics are also defined as the theory or system of moral values and the principles of conduct governing an individual or a group. In a business context, ethics relate to the moral standards that apply to business policies, and behaviors. As internal auditors, we are concerned with what should be done during the course of business activities, but also with the structures, motivation, organizational accountability, and relationships that support or hinder ethical conduct.

The interest in ethics is more than philosophical. Business ethics, especially as pertains to the role of internal auditors, must be practical. This pragmatic perspective makes it applied and is concerned with behaviors—the product of ethical decision-making. But there is no quick and simple solution to ethical decision-making. It is a process that is best handled holistically and should be taught from an early age. Unfortunately, many would argue that education is not happening to all children/adolescents early enough and as such, bad tendencies, habits, and poorly-defined priorities are left to mature in these individuals. Managers and leaders must then oversee organizations where these employees and contractors make decisions that may be contrary to the principles of care, good judgment, healthy virtues, and empathy. Left to run their course unchecked, organizations run the risk of many stakeholders getting hurt financially and otherwise in the short and long term.

The IIA Standards state that internal auditors must assess and make appropriate recommendations to improve the organization's governance processes for promoting appropriate ethics and values within the organization (Standard 2110). The following is a brief look back showing how damaging ethical breakdowns can be:

- 1970s: The Ford Pinto scandal, where Ford performed a cost-benefit analysis and determined that it was cheaper to pay the claims resulting from a poorly designed vehicle that burst into flames when rear-ended even at slow speeds, than it was to modify the vehicle to make it safer. Beatrice Foods and W.R. Grace were sued for dumping chemical wastes and contaminating the drinking water of Woburn, MA.

■ 1980s: The Ponzi scheme involving ZZZZ Best Carpet Cleaning company that cost investors millions of dollars, and the insider trading scandals involving Ivan Boesky and Michael Milken (aka Junk Bond King).

■ 1990s: Jordan Belfort, portrayed in the movie *The Wolf of Wall Street*, cost investors approximately $200 million, and Jeff Skilling, the CEO of Enron, convicted of using accounting loopholes that eventually resulted in the company's $63.4 billion bankruptcy.

■ 2000s: Bernie Madoff, a former stockbroker and investment advisor defrauded his customers of an estimated $65 billion, and Allen Stanford was charged with fraud for crimes involving around $7 billion at his Stanford Financial Group.

The focus is typically ethics within the audit client's organization, but that scope is limited. Since organizations operate within a web of relationships, ethics must also extend beyond the organization's walls and consider the role that customers, vendors, and other business partners play in the setting and promotion of ethical values and conduct. Some well-known organizations like The Gap, Levi Strauss and Apple learned the hard way that what vendors and contractors do can also have an impact on their own ethical landscape.

■ The Gap: Scandal involving child labor in India
■ Levi's, Calvin Klein, Guess: Water pollution caused by manufacturing contractors in Mexico
■ Apple: Exploitation of workers by manufacturing contractor Foxconn in China

Auditing Ethics

Assessing an organization's ethical environment represents an atypical review for most internal auditors, who are accustomed to examining transactions and documents. Auditing ethics can be different. An audit of ethics often involves reviewing the organization's corporate culture. This generally involves examining the organization's values, employee opinions, the setting of expectations for moral conduct, and the response to unethical developments within the organization.

The following is a list of some of the key steps for conducting an ethics audit:

- Surveys: Enquire about the opinions of employees and other stakeholders as it relates to the fair treatment of employees, customers, and vendors; their belief that rules are applicable and followed by employees and managers alike; that infractions result in punishments to both employees and managers; that retaliation is forbidden, and the workplace does not have a hostile environment.
- Hotline: Verify that the ethics hotline is independent, is available to individuals within, as well as outside the organization, that qualified individuals respond to allegations of impropriety, and that all allegations are handled promptly.
- Code of Ethics (COE): Verify that the COE is reviewed and re-certified annually, that it is distributed to all employees, that contractors/consultants are expected to abide by its tenets, and that it includes at a minimum guidance on the following:
  - Treatment of Employees, Customers, Vendors
  - Corporate Social Responsibility and good Corporate Citizenship
  - Adherence with all applicable rules, regulations, and expectations
  - Handling of gifts and requests from government officials
- Conflict of Interest (COI): Verify that the COI is distributed annually and all employees and contractors sign off on the document stating that they have no conflicts of interest in fact or appearance, and if any were to emerge, they agree to disclose those immediately.
- Ethics Training: Verify that it is mandatory for all employees upon hire, and annually after that. It addresses topic that:
  - Underscore the expectations for ethical behavior, always, by everyone, everywhere
  - Provide examples of ethical, questionable, and unethical behavior
  - Answer questions and mentions the avenues available if difficult questions arise later
  - Explains the organization's anti-retaliation policy
  - Is provided in a language participants are comfortable communicating in.
  - It includes examples all employees can relate to.
  - Examples and exercises are refreshed periodically. If employees see the same examples year after year, they will lose their interest in the training
  - Logic should be built into the CBT program to limit participants' ability to fast forward through the material without reading and assimilating the information provided
  - An avenue is available for employees to ask questions after the class
  - It may be useful to require consultants and contractors to also take the ethics class. Some contracts put that burden on the contractor's hiring organization. When that is the case, it should be verified.

Summary

1. Auditing ethics is increasingly being added to organizations audit plans.
2. These audits include reviewing practices and documents like the COE, COI, ethics training, and allegations of wrongdoing. It also includes surveying employees to get their opinions about the ethical environment, leadership style, and workplace dynamics like harassment and retaliation.
3. In addition to employees of the organization, internal auditors should also check vendor, contractor, and consultant practices.

Chapter 46

Evidence

Internal auditors act like scientists in that they work from established objectives to prove or disprove one or more questions. Most audits can be reduced to asking, "Are the controls present and working as expected?" or "Have suspected risks materialized affecting the organization?" or "Why do we have this continuing problem with inventory shortages?"

With this in mind, internal auditors must collect information to answer the questions that the audit is supposed to answer. The answer doesn't have to be exhaustive, but internal auditors must do enough work to reach a point where they are reasonably confident about the answer. As internal auditors we need to apply our professional judgment, rely on testing, realize there are inherent limitations of internal control, and often have to rely on estimates when reviewing accounting matters, so audit evidence is generally persuasive rather than conclusive.

This is what we refer to as providing "reasonable assurance."

Evidence is "something that furnishes proof,"* or "that which tends to prove or disprove something; ground for belief. In a legal context it is "data presented as proof of the facts at issue and which may include the testimony of witnesses, records, documents, or objects."†

Evidence has many forms:

Testimonial

This type of evidence consists of verbal or written statements made by others, especially those who perform the work being audited. While others, such as managers and business executives may have a great deal of knowledge, they may not always know enough about the details of the program or process

---

* See www.merriam-webster.com/dictionary/evidence.
† See www.dictionary.com/browse/evidence

Table 46.1   Examples of Internal and External Evidentiary Matter

Internal	External
Policies and procedures Purchase orders Purchase requisitions Exception reports Inventory counts Reconciliations	Invoices Packing slips Bank statements Confirmations

being addressed, so it is best for internal auditors to give enough thought to whom they are interviewing.

Documents

This type of evidence consists of reviewing already existing information such as letters, contracts, records, invoices, and reports. These are internal or external documents that provide relevant information related to the process or program being audited. Table 46.1 shows examples of internal and external documents typically used as evidence.

An important attribute of documentation is recency: Is the evidentiary information recent or old? In general, recent or contemporaneous information is preferable to old or outdated information. However, some evidence is best if it is older but close timewise to the time when the event actually occurred. For example: An older picture documenting the condition of a warehouse or a fixed asset is preferable than the recent verbal testimony of the warehouse manager who describes the condition of the warehouse a long time ago.

The quality of evidence is also subject to the level of authoritativeness of the source. Evidence is more persuasive if it is produced or provided by someone who wields a great degree of authority, prestige or expertise on the subject. Authoritativeness is not always synonymous with the person's hierarchical position because a high-ranking individual may have an important title, but that same individual may not have a detailed knowledge, expertise or overall competence on the subject.

Observation/Physical

Internal auditors are encouraged to go and see for themselves the conditions, practices, properties, and events relevant to the audit being performed. By witnessing these dynamics themselves, internal auditors acquire more conclusive evidence than that obtained merely by verbal testimony, especially if these are obtained remotely.

A type of observation internal auditors often perform during planning or fieldwork is called walkthroughs. These are step-by-step tests of all the procedures for a program, process or plan that are generally performed with the knowledge of audit clients who explain their procedures by using a "live" document or transaction. As this item navigates the process, the steps are documented so the auditor gains a better understanding of the process and to verify congruence with official procedures documentation.

The quality of observation and inspection may be dependent on whether or not those being observed know or don't know this is happening. In social science research, socially desirability bias occurs when survey participants respond to questions in a way that will be viewed favorably by others, such as researchers or fellow participants. This contaminates the information collected. A similar dynamic may occur during audit observations. If those being observed know the auditor is observing their behavior they may change their actions so the auditor sees them favorably. The problem with this adaptation and behavioral change is that the auditor will have an inaccurate reading on workplace conditions and how the work is being performed. Consequently, internal auditors should consider whether it is more beneficial to perform their observations without the knowledge of those being observed. When doing so, however, internal auditors should also weigh the risk they may be considered duplicitous or devious.

This can be an important consideration while performing construction and environmental health and safety (EHS) audits. While touring the facilities is a standard procedure, it is often done while accompanied by the safety or plant manager who explains conditions, procedures, answers questions and introduces auditors to key employees. During these walks "everyone is usually in their best behavior." Internal auditors may even notice that the tour given is following a well-selected and predetermined course, so asking to go off course may be a good idea to see other places, or stop occasionally to see someone do something as a way to inspect for hazards that could lead to employee injury or illness. This makes the process more risk-based.

Later on during the audit, it may also be useful to observe the work being done from the observation platform, where a panoramic view of the facility sometimes reveals different behaviors and conditions related to the use of protective equipment, material storage, and vehicle movement. After familiarizing oneself with the safety protocol and while wearing protective gear, internal auditors should consider talking to workers at their work area rather than asking them to come to the administrative office or trailer area where auditors are usually stationed. By walking around internal auditors can observe dynamics in their natural setting and gain a better appreciation for the work being done.

Among the many lessons I learned over the years, one of my first was to never underestimate the knowledge of the administrative assistant. I've since even seen coffee mugs with the inscription: "Do you want to speak to the boss or to someone who knows what's going on?" This is similar to another axiom in internal audit: "In this profession you will meet and work with everyone from the board room to the mail room." At first I thought this was just a great career opportunity given the exposure and diversity of experiences this afforded, but it went much farther. In a risk-based auditing environment, anyone can have the knowledge about the process and conditions to help us identify areas for improvement. Similarly, anyone could have the knowledge about the diversity of topics we cover. Over the years I have spoken to messengers, receptionists, secretaries, drivers, junior staff, and of course many higher-ranking individuals, but authoritativeness has been had along the entire hierarchical chain. So, try to talk to the person with the deepest knowledge on the subject being examined and as much as needed and possible, corroborate verbal testimony to make that evidence more authoritative.

Relying on the Work of Others

When relying on the work of others, these parties must be objective and competent for their work to be considered. The internal auditor should consider the other assurance provider's quality and depth of work to have reasonable assurance the information received, and the findings derived from them, are based on sufficient, reliable, relevant, and useful information, as required by Standard 2310: Identifying Information.

The work of these other assurance providers must be appropriately planned, supervised, documented, and reviewed. The auditor should consider whether the audit evidence collected and used is appropriate and sufficient to determine the extent to which it can be relied upon. With this information, the internal auditor may decide if additional work or test procedures are needed to gain appropriate and sufficient audit evidence. Auditors should be satisfied, based on their knowledge of the business, work environment, operating procedures, techniques and information used by the assurance provider that the findings are reasonable. To increase the level of reliance on the results, the organization's internal auditors may need to retest results of the other assurance provider.

Summary

1. Internal auditors collect evidence to convincingly answer the audit questions. This evidence must be sufficient (to be convincing), reliable (to be credible), relevant (to the audit being performed) and useful (to the audit client).
2. There are different types of audit evidence, including verbal and written testimony, observation and inspection of conditions and activities, documents, and the (re)calculation of figures to verify their accuracy. This may be documented as summary memos, narratives, photographs, videos, drawings, charts, and worksheets.
3. Internal auditors may need to collect multiple items, at different times, to achieve a satisfactory level of persuasiveness and to gain reasonable assurance that the objectives are achievable, that risks are managed appropriately, and that controls are present and working as intended.

Chapter 47

Fieldwork

Fieldwork is the second of three phases of internal audits. During this phase internal auditors focus primarily on testing, but there are in fact two main activities that take place:

a. Verification that the controls reviewers were told were in place, are in fact in place. This is often accomplished by examining relevant policies and procedures documents, organizational charts and through interviews, flowcharting, and walkthroughs.
b. Verification that the controls in place are working as intended. This is often accomplished by testing these controls, which can be done through the testimony of knowledgeable individuals, observation of workplace activities, the inspection of relevant documents, the recalculation of key figures and the analysis of relevant data.

Internal auditors may test transactions by selecting a sample and examining those items to verify conditions and practices. With this knowledge, auditors extrapolate the results (within certain levels of confidence) and apply them to the population. Another approach is to test all relevant transactions (i.e., the entire population) through data analytics, which have become more prevalent as organizations have digitized their activities and the quality of query software has become more powerful and easier to use.

The work performed during fieldwork can be construed as an experiment, where the internal auditor is testing a hypothesis. Generally, Are the controls present and functioning? and Are the risks we are concerned about occurring to the detriment of stakeholders? While internal auditors do not refer to their work in such terms, especially the use of hypothesis, they establish objectives for their work. These objectives are twofold:

1. Business Objectives: The objectives the program or process under review has established for itself, and are they making satisfactory progress toward their achievement
2. Audit Objectives: The objectives the audit aims to achieve

Many auditors use Microsoft Excel to perform data analytics, while others use tools such as SQL, ACL, IDEA, and Tableau, among many others. By testing a larger data set, or even the entire population, internal auditors can gain greater certainty about prevailing dynamics and avoid having to extrapolate from the sample to the population when deriving their conclusions.

Discussing Findings with Audit Clients

It is very important that internal auditors discuss findings with audit clients during fieldwork to verify the accuracy of the auditors' results and confirm management's agreement. By bringing findings and concerns to the client's attention, internal auditors can get timely feedback, discuss the methodology followed to arrive at the issue, and begin the process of preparing a corrective action. This provides an opportunity to make corrections if the auditors misunderstood any aspect of the process or the related controls. Also, if the internal auditor misunderstood business expectations, practices, or if the data, documents, or information used was defective, those issues can be corrected promptly.

Early notification will give the client a chance to understand the nature of the issue, ask all pertinent questions regarding it and discuss the matter with those concerned up the chain of command. By getting agreement during Fieldwork, the Exit Meeting, and the Draft Report should receive greater acceptance, rather than the audit team getting bogged down in debates and discussions at that point. The Exit Meeting should not become a workshop. If concerns are discussed during fieldwork, there is agreement about the facts and the nature of the issue, and those who need to know about this are informed promptly about any concerns. The Exit Meeting should only be one to two-hours long, and proceed smoothly; there should be no need to engage in detailed discussion about transactions or activities noted, procedures followed, review documents or argue over details.

Status Updates

The fieldwork phase is also characterized by status updates to the client. The type and frequency of these status updates vary based on the needs of the client, but in general, internal auditors should err on the side of more communication than less. This means in most cases at least a weekly meeting to inform the client how the audit is progressing. Due to time constraints, some audit clients may not want, or be able, to participate in a weekly meeting. In those cases, a status update report or e-mail is recommended.

Typical topics to include in a Status Update Meeting include:

- Activities Performed: What the auditors reviewed and the results
- Activities in Progress: What is ongoing
- Activities Planned: What procedures are planned in the near future and any support needed to avoid delays
- Findings: Discuss new observations to confirm agreement with management

Auditing Outsourced Activities

Most of the discussion regarding fieldwork focuses on the work of auditors within their clients' organizations. However, outsourcing processes to third parties has become commonplace and while it gives organizations the opportunity to lower costs and gain efficiencies by focusing on their core competencies, it also introduces risks that should be examined. Outsourced activities include IT services, transaction processing, customer service, help desk services, accounting and financial duties, and human resources (e.g., background checks, employee assistance programs, health care benefits administration, payroll administration, recruitment and retirement benefits administration), among many others. Auditing these relationships can be a complex endeavor and involves more than visiting these providers' physical locations.

Due diligence should be performed before the outsourcing relationship starts, and performance monitoring should occur while the work is being done. Planning, such as setting clear expectations, and setting the guidelines for timely communications and frequent reporting are key. Internal auditors should remind management, if they don't already know this, that the organization can outsource the process, but the contracting organization retains the risks. In many cases, outsourcing activities are invisible to the hiring company's customers, but even when the outsourcing is known to customers, if problems occur these customers will put the responsibility on the organization, not the outsourced company.

The Statement on Standards for Attestation Engagements no. 18 (SSAE 18) is an auditing standard for service organizations that replaced the Statement on Auditing Standards no. 70 (SAS 70). This procedure is designed to provide insights into the controls at service organizations and is provided in a Service Organization Controls (SOC) report. Some service organizations use the SSAE 18 report status to show they are more capable and qualified during new vendor selection criteria.

SOC Type 1 are used during reviews related to the Sarbanes–Oxley Act of 2002 to show effective internal controls over financial reporting. SOC Type 2 are used for other outsourced activities and it focuses on controls relevant to security, availability, processing integrity, confidentiality, and privacy.

Internal auditors should consider requesting a Report on the Service Organization Controls (SOC 2). These reports are helpful to gain an understanding of the oversight of the organization, vendor management programs, internal corporate governance and risk management processes, regulatory oversight.

These SSAE-18 reports also enquire about sub-contracting activities to make sure third parties have a vendor management program and that a formal risk assessment process is in place to address the risks of sub-contracting, contracted activities.*

Companies should educate their outsource service providers on regulations and expectations related to operating procedures, while also performing ongoing performance monitoring to verify compliance. The terms of the relationship, and the right to audit records and facilities, should be included in the contract with the provider. The contract should also be clear about sub-contracting expectations and restrictions, compliance with laws and regulations (e.g., Foreign Corrupt Practices Act, UK Bribery Act), compliance with a Code of Ethics, liability and insurance, performance standards, supervision of the work, compensation and reimbursement of expenses, confidentiality and non-compete provisions, ownership of intellectual property, breach of contract, and provisions for conflict resolution.

Key risk areas include reputation damage; strategy and operational failure; lack of compliance with applicable laws, regulations and expectations; and security breaches. Language barriers, differing cultural norms, unexpected costs, higher inflation, capital restrictions, civil unrest, crime, legal constraints, and corruption may exacerbate outsourcing activities when the vendors used operate offshore. While outsourcing carries certain risks, there are opportunities to benefit from the services of third party that specialize in certain activities. The potential advantages include faster turnaround times, higher profitability, and improved customer service. So when internal auditors are auditing these relationships, they should assess whether risks and opportunities are managed effectively.

Summary

1. Discussing and clearing items during fieldwork makes the exit meeting more efficient and effective, and often expedites the publication of the draft and final reports.
2. Status updates should be provided to the client and management within the internal audit department.

---

* See www.ssae-16.com/soc-1-report/the-ssae-18-audit-standard/.

3. Fieldwork may extend outside the client's organization if there are outsourced activities. The terms and extent of this review will likely be defined by the right to audit clause contained in the contract. Another useful resource is the Service Organization Control (SOC 1 and SOC 2) reports based on SSAE-18 guidelines, and performance management reports.

Chapter 48

Findings

Internal auditors primarily add value to their organizations by identifying issues of importance and for making recommendations; issues hinder and recommendations enable, the achievement of objectives.

Issues are often referred to as findings. The word "finding" is commonly used to describe an audit observation, deficiency, weakness, or opportunity for improvement. These are the main building blocks of audit reports, which are exception-based. This latter term refers to the fact that internal auditors primarily communicate in their reports the concerns, or exceptions, identified during the review.

According to Practice Advisory 2410-A1, Communication Criteria, "communications must include the engagement's objectives and scope as well as applicable conclusions, recommendations, and action plans." Observations are the result of comparing criteria (what is expected) with condition (the current state). A common approach used to document audit findings is the CCCER/5C Model.

One of the most important elements related to audit findings that doesn't receive as much attention as it should, is the fact that findings are supposed to be persuasive. First, persuasive to the auditor who determines if a risk has materialized or not, or if a control is present and working, or not. To make this determination, it is very important for the information to be quantified and documented. Secondly, persuasive to the audit client, who should be convinced about the severity of the issue, the importance in relation to the achievement of objectives, and the future implications if not corrected. Here again, it is very important for the information to be quantified, well-documented, and credible.

Audit findings should be significant enough to deserve being reported because as management and the board wrestles with important matters and in some cases multi-million dollar financial concerns, internal auditors should be careful not to

Criteria	The expected performance as defined by rules, regulations, policies, procedures, contracts, or stakeholders. The criteria define what should be in place.
Condition	What the auditor identified during the course of the audit itself. It constitutes the description of the anomaly.
Cause	The source of the issue. The reason "why" the issue exists.
Effect	The impact that this condition has or could have. Asking the question "so what?" helps to define the implications of the issue and why it should matter to others. An inability to answer the "so what?" question with specifics could indicate there is no real issue, it is not substantial, or the internal auditor has not done enough research to understand the consequences of the issue.
Recommendation	The corrective action that if implemented successfully, and sustainably, will correct the Cause, prevent or stop the Effect, and stop the Condition so practices mirror the Criteria expected.

include matters of low significance in their communications. It will make them appear petty.

Audit findings should be well-documented by facts and evidence that is sufficient, reliable, relevant, and useful.

Sufficient: Sufficient information is factual, adequate, and convincing so that a prudent, informed person would reach the same conclusions as the auditor. This also means that there should be enough evidence to convince a reasonable and prudent individual that enough information was examined, enough people were interviewed, or enough testing was done to make the results sufficiently compelling.

Reliable: Reliable information is the best attainable information through the use of appropriate engagement techniques. Reliable information supports engagement observations and recommendations and is consistent with the objectives for the engagement.

Useful: Useful information helps the organization meet its goals.

Relevant: Relevant information is related to the objective of the audit and help it meet its goals.

The findings should be developed objectively, which is consistent with the expectation that internal auditors are objective in their work. In general, internal auditors should be driven by the facts surrounding the case and have no other objective, but to find and communicate truthful information. Findings should not be inflated, or minimized; only qualified sufficiently to ensure the tone is appropriate.

Findings should be presented in their totality in such a way that they compel management to take corrective action. This is often achieved by fully capturing the details of the findings as encapsulated in the CCCER/5C Model, quantifying elements as much as possible, relating the finding to the business objective that is threatened by the issue and a productive tone that argues the benefits of improving conditions and practices.

Findings Corrected during Fieldwork

Sometimes audit clients fix the finding during fieldwork. Sometimes they fix the finding after fieldwork but before the draft report is distributed. Sometimes the audit client fixes the finding after the draft report is sent, but before the final report is published. At any of these times, the audit client may request that the finding not be communicated in the audit report. The convention is to report the issue anyway because had the auditor not identified the problem, the issue would have continued. However, internal auditors must be fair in their presentation of the matter, so they should present the finding and give proper credit in their report stating that the issue was addressed and has been remediated.

However, it is also important to be careful that the client is not merely fixing the manifestation of the problem (e.g., the abnormal transactions). If that is all that is fixed, the problem will recur. Instead, they should fix the manifestation, as well as the root cause of the problem.

Summary

1. The CCCER/5C Model is widely used and provides a simple, yet very effective, way to document audit findings.
2. When documenting findings, internal auditors should remember that the objective is not merely to communicate issues, but to make this communication persuasive so it compels management to take corrective action.
3. If findings are corrected before the writing of the audit reports, the items should still be reported. However, the auditor should indicate that the item was addressed.

Chapter 49

Five Whys

Internal auditors often struggle with the need to identify the source of issues and recommend corrective actions that solve problems at the source. Otherwise, audit clients run the risk of making the mistake many people make: Trying to fix symptoms only to discover that the problem occurs again and again. Internal auditors need to dig beneath the surface and probe deeper when they encounter an issue.

The Five Whys is one of the simplest tools for root-cause analysis. It is easy to use, and the approach consists of asking "why" multiple items, each of which probes further into the source of the problem. Edward Hodnett was correct when he stated: "If you do not ask the right questions, you do not get the right answers. A question asked in the right way often points to its own answer. Asking questions is the A-B-C of diagnosis. Only the inquiring mind solves problems."*

In general, "root cause analysis is defined as the identification of why an issue occurred as opposed to only identifying or reporting on the issue itself. In this context, an issue is defined as a problem, error, instance of noncompliance, or missed opportunity" (Practice Adv 2320–2). Internal auditors should deliver insight to their clients, and this means they must avoid superficial findings and recommendations, identifying instead the drivers causing operational issues.

The five Whys method is an iterative technique used to explore the cause-and-effect relationships underlying a problem. The primary goal of the technique is to determine the root cause of a defect or problem by repeating the question "Why?" The process is sequential, and each question forms the basis of the next question. The "5" refers to the typical number of iterations needed to resolve the problem, but identifying the root cause may take fewer or more times than five.

---

* See https://allauthor.com/quotes/73876/.

To illustrate the process, consider a scenario where there is water on what should otherwise be a dry floor.

Problem statement: There is water on the floor.

Why 1: Why is there water on the floor?

Answer: Because water leaked from the ceiling.

Solution: Mop up the floor to dry the water.

Consequence: Water may continue to fall on the floor, thus mopping the water is an inadequate solution to the problem. Therefore, we should ask "why?" again.

Why 2: Why did the water leak from the ceiling?

Answer: Because the pipe overhead has poor fittings and that is causing the water to leak.

Solution: We can stop there and repair the pipe, but we should probably ask "why?" again.

Why 3: Why does the pipe overhead have poor fittings?

Answer: Because the pipe was not installed properly.

Why 4: Why wasn't the pipe installed properly?

Answer: Because the plumbing work was done by an unqualified plumber.

Why 5: Why did we use an unqualified plumber?

Answer: Due to poor vendor screening practices. The plumbing work was granted to the plumber through favoritism rather than skill and a proven history of good workmanship.

So, now we know what caused the water on the floor!

With this knowledge, we can now move forward to address the vendor contracting process to eliminate favoritism and not allow this plumber to do any additional work for the organization. If we stop at any of the preceding steps, we would continue to experience water leakage because that was merely a symptom of inadequate vendor selection and poor workmanship.

Let's examine another example where the auditor notes that the Service Department is making mistakes when responding to customer requests.

Why 1: Why are these mistakes occurring?

Answer: Because instructions are given verbally.

Why 2: Why are instructions given verbally?

Answer: Because Customer Service employees are not using a service form and they want to dispatch the service employees quickly.

Why 3: Why aren't Customer Service employees using a service form?

Answer: There is no service form in use to record the customer information. Employees take notes based on the phone call with the customer and proceed from there.

At this point, with three Whys we can see that the absence of a consistent method of capturing orders and communicating them to the Service Department is causing the problem. The problem can be fixed in several ways. If there are sufficient financial resources, a new order taking system can be bought and implemented. That would be ideal, especially if it interfaces with the inventory (for parts) and invoicing (for billing) systems. If that is not feasible or possible, then having a standardized form that is filled out while the Customer Service employee is in communication with the customer should help inform the service personnel what needs to be done.

Another example demonstrating the applicability during an audit when exceptions are noted:

Why 1: Why did these exceptions occur?
Answer: The cycle counts were not performed consistently as required.
Why 2: Why weren't the cycle counts performed consistently?
Answer: Employees didn't think they were important.
Why 3: Why didn't employees think the cycle counts were important?
Answer: Their manager never explained the purpose.
Why 4: Why didn't their manager explain the purpose?
Answer: The manager spends all her time performing her own tasks rather than properly supervising the warehouse staff.
Why 5: Why does she spend her time like this?
Answer: The manager was promoted to this role because she was an excellent individual contributor, but did not receive manager training.

It is now apparent that the manager did not receive supervisory training, delegation techniques, time management, and/or is under an excessive work load that limits her ability to properly supervise the staff and oversee what they are doing.

The benefit of the exercise is that by getting to the root cause internal auditors can prevent future instances of the exceptions and avoid other problems as well. Otherwise, this and possibly other control exceptions are likely to occur.

To avoid treating symptoms, the best auditors go beyond identifying exceptions solely. They don't stop when they see a control failure. They continue to probe until they find the source of the problem. With each answer, they ask "why did that happen?" multiple times until they can go no further.

The source of the problem could be related to people (e.g., their training, competence, comprehension or motivation), the process (e.g., unclear instructions or poor communications) or system related (e.g., data feed, algorithm). While the search for the root cause may take the auditor to other units of the organizations, it is important to follow those leads because doing otherwise often results in substandard outcomes. Granted, internal auditors don't have an infinite budget and conducting root-cause analysis takes time and effort, but merely mentioning problems superficially, or providing vague recommendations that address symptoms, will provide substandard results.

Summary

1. The Five Whys is an effective technique to find the root cause of problems.
2. Treating symptoms alone is not enough to sustainably eliminate a finding; auditors should probe for the root cause. This can be done by themselves or by working in partnership with the audit client.
3. The root cause could be isolated to one item, or it could be the combination of several items that together precipitate the issue.

Chapter 50

Flowcharts

Drawing flowcharts can be time consuming, but internal auditors can gain a wealth of information during and after preparing them. Flowcharts can contain up to three dimensions of data and by layering information, each dimension adds new details that provides deeper insights into how a process operates and where opportunities for improvement lie.

A flowchart is a type of diagram that represents a workflow or process. It shows the two most common items in a flow: Processing steps (as boxes) and Decisions (as diamonds). The order, or sequence, of the various activities is shown by arrows and they are used to design, analyze, document, and manage processes. These flowcharts answer the question: What Happens?

A flowchart can also be cross-functional by dividing the diagram into swimming lanes. Each lane represents an individual or organizational unit performing the activities within that lane. This approach allows internal auditors to identify responsibilities because it shows who performs an activity or makes a decision. These flowcharts answer two questions: What Happens? and Who Does It?

Flowcharts can also add a third dimension by showing the cycle times involved. This includes the amount of time the entire process takes from beginning to end, how much time each step takes (i.e., "the time in the boxes"), and the amount of time waiting or in transition between steps (i.e., "the time between the boxes"). By understanding the time element, internal auditors can better understand the speed, bottlenecks, and delays in the process. When all of the time "inside the boxes" is added, it represents the value-add time during the process since this time is spent processing transactions and performing activities. When all of the time "outside the boxes" is added, it generally represents the non-value-add time because it is the time spent waiting and transporting. These flowcharts answer three questions: What happens? Who does it? and How long does it take?

While waiting is often seen as a negative condition, that is not necessarily so. Manufacturing and industrial examples include letting cement cure, paint dry, or dough rise before subsequent steps are performed or transitioning to another phase. In service environments examples are harder to come by, because waiting usually means that someone or something is not available or ready, and the question should be, why?

This third dimension also raises the question: How do I get the time information? There are three approaches:

1. The traditional stopwatch approach can be used to record start and stop times. While it is arguably easier to use a stopwatch in industrial environments, it can be used to obtain readings during process observations and walkthroughs in a service operation too.
2. If the process uses document management software, there may be user and date/time stamps at each step of the process. That information can be downloaded and examined using data analytics to connect the flowchart with the various steps.
3. Takt time is the rate at which the operation produces output. The formula calculates the average amount of time, or pace, of activities, and it can be used to determine the pace to keep a process flowing without backlogs. It provides average times for all transactions during a period of time, so per-transaction information would need to be obtained through other means.

How to Draw an Effective Flowchart

- Define the process boundaries and identify the starting and ending points. These are usually depicted with an ellipse symbol.
- Agree on standard flowchart symbols to use. It is important to agree on a standard as this can become a source of wasted time debating which symbols to use. The rectangular box, for activities, and the diamond, for decisions, are the two most widely used and versatile symbols.
- Complete the big picture before filling in the details.
- Clearly define each step in the process. It is important of ask about non-traditional transactions, unusual pathways due to special circumstances, preferred customers, and other exceptions to the rule. The flowchart should be realistic, not only a reflection of what happens under ideal circumstances.
- Indicate who performs the activity or makes the decisions.
- Identify time lags and non-value-adding steps.
- Circulate the flowchart to others involved in the process to get their feedback.

Flowcharts don't work if they're inaccurate or if those providing the information are not directly involved in the process itself. The best information comes from team members that are true participants in the process and describe what really happens.

Getting Deeper Insights

If there are multiple pathways within the process (e.g., due to rule exceptions, rush-orders, preferred customers, favored vendors), showing on the flowchart the number and percentage of transactions that flow through each pathway can be eye-opening. Especially since in many cases management is unaware of these dynamics. Also, employees may know about the different pathways, but are unaware of the numbers flowing variously. These alternate pathways often become risk-aggregators because they tend to be repositories of management override and policy exceptions.

Enquire about transactions that are returned. Sometimes transactions don't flow smoothly from start to finish, but are returned because they lack key information, contain errors, are missing attachments or supporting documentation. These as backflows. Find out what are the common reasons transactions are returned because eliminating them can improve the process significantly.

Carefully compare the activities performed with the identity of the other participants in the process, and who reviews and approves transactions. This can indicate concerns about the segregation of duties. Other issues include over-burdening some individuals while others carry too light a load. This imbalance can cause errors and delays.

Review the flow of activities and the hand-offs that occur. Excessive handoffs can be problematic because with every exchange there is an increased risk of delays and things "falling through the cracks."

Examine the time "inside the box" and the time "between the boxes." Do any steps appear to take too long? This could indicate a lack of training, too much complexity, or that the individual is also responsible for other activities and the typical day is spent multi-tasking. Maybe a review of job responsibilities or priority-setting practices can help.

Ask about bottlenecks where transactions sit for a long time waiting for the next step to be performed. Is this acceptable or the result of someone struggling to keep up? Is there a need to assign a backup operator or decision-maker so transactions don't sit in a queue until someone returns?

Flowcharts depict certain aspects of processes and they are usually complemented by other types of diagram. For instance, Kaoru Ishikawa defined the flowchart as one of the seven basic tools of quality control, next to the histogram, Pareto chart, check sheet, control chart, cause-and-effect diagram, and the scatter diagram. Other common names include: flowchart, process flowchart, functional flowchart, process map, process chart, functional process chart, business process model, process model, process flow diagram, work flow diagram, and business flow diagram.

Where boxes cannot be directly connected with lines, or the diagram runs into multiple pages, it is useful to use connectors. But using too many can make the flowchart difficult to understand, so the drawer should balance the amount of detail and the size with each drawing.

Asking targeted questions and using a collaborative approach involving process owners will allow internal auditors to get more information from their flowcharts and provide value-adding recommendations for improvement.

EXAMPLE ONE

While discussing operational issues at a government agency, we identified a large number of transaction being returned, sometimes to previous processors because the transactions were missing something, but in many cases the items were returned to the customer. As we examined the situation, management was alarmed to find out that there were times when the returns occurred in the step immediately preceding the closeout of the request. So instead of customers receiving a letter with a resolution of the request—approval or denial, many were getting a letter several weeks and sometimes months after the item began the process informing the applicant that additional information was needed. The amount of effort put into processing the request to then return it was a waste and had created a poor reputation due to the deficient customer service provided. In some of the most surprising cases, the supporting documentation was submitted with the original application, but had expired due to the extreme bureaucratic procedures causing delays. So the customer was being asked to submit updated items due to the agency's own broken processes.

After some data analytics validated the information we learned during the flowcharting and walk-through processing, we determined that a simple solution would provide a quick improvement: prepare a checklist with all the requirements shown on it and implement it at the point of entry so a decision would be made to not begin the process unless all the information was presented.

This brought up another glaring anomaly in the agency: No one knew what all the requirements were to successfully process the forms because each group worked in a silo. Upstream processors were unaware what other groups downstream needed. So we conducted some interviews and assembled some workgroups with representatives from each unit to collect the information and prepare a consolidated list of requirements. At the same time, the group obtained data to quantify the nature and magnitude of the problem.

The process of documenting the requirements for the checklist was highly appreciated by the units involved who learned a lot from the experience. After preparing the checklist and identifying the top reasons why applications were returned, the application form was redesigned. Then we examined the process itself to reduce or eliminate unnecessary steps, consolidate some activities rather than have items go back-and-forth and the result was that the number of delays decreased substantially and customer satisfaction increased.

EXAMPLE TWO

Internal auditors at a small retail organization identified a bottleneck at an approval point within the process and wondered why that was occurring. After consultation with others in the process and the manager performing the approvals, they were informed that the delays were caused because the manager was responsible for several stores in the district and spent most of her time on the road visiting the different stores. Transactions were often delayed, some in an electronic queue, others in her e-mail inbox, and the rest in paper forms at her inbox back at the office. As the internal auditors examined the transactions requiring approval it was promptly discovered that the process would benefit from the requirement that all transactions be processed and approved electronically (eliminating the paper forms left in an inbox at the office). With all forms now being submitted electronically, a backup approver was assigned so an alternate was available during heavy travel times. This reduced the burden on the manager, eliminated the bottleneck and accelerated the review and approval of the requisitions.

Summary

1. Flowcharts represent a great tool to understand processes. They show the flow of documents and information, the role the relevant stakeholders play in the process, and the responsibilities for each step.
2. By identifying the various pathways in the process, the presence of delays, bottlenecks, rework and handoffs, internal auditors can better understand the dysfunctions in the processes reviewed and make helpful recommendations for improvement.
3. The time and effort invested in preparing flowcharts will result in substantial benefits through the deeper insights gained.

Chapter 51

Focus Groups

A focus group is a relatively small, diverse group of people who share a common knowledge or experience, and whose experience is considered valuable as an indicator of the reactions or views of a larger population. Through interviews and facilitated meetings, these groups can provide qualitative information for internal auditors because their opinions, beliefs, attitudes, and feedback can provide valuable insights, especially when evaluating subjective topics.

While focus groups are typically assembled for marketing research, they can be very helpful when auditing:

- Corporate culture
- Ethics
- The whistleblower hotline
- Management's leadership style and example-setting

Focus groups work best with groups of four to twelve individuals, when those participating have sufficient knowledge, experience and willingness to share freely, and sessions are interactive. Internal auditors must take notes as they would during traditional interviews.

Advisor councils and steering committees are similar and can also provide trends, share priorities, concerns and primarily differ from focus groups in that they focus on strategic subjects, rather than tactical ones.

Summary

1. Focus groups are a resource internal auditor should consider using, especially when the topic involves delicate subject.

2. Focus groups are well suited for audits of the organization's corporate culture, ethics, and the opinions of workers.
3. When working with focus groups, ground rules should be established regarding openness, transparency, freedom from the fear of retaliation, and confidentiality.

Chapter 52

Follow-Up Audits

A typical internal audit consists of a great deal of planning to understand the conditions, structures, and expectations of the area that will be reviewed. This is followed by the fieldwork phase where tests are performed, findings are documented, recommendations are researched and presented, and exit meetings conducted to verify that all relevant stakeholders agree with the results of the review. Most auditors consider the reporting phase to be the final phase of an audit. At this point a report is written explaining the scope, objectives, and findings of the review, sometimes accompanied by a conclusion, opinion, and rating.

The entire process can be very tedious and stressful for internal auditors who must achieve proficiency in the topic reviewed without working in that area, interview and examine the work of process owners who sometimes have decades of experience working in that functional area while the auditor may only have weeks of exposure to the subject. This is followed by a report that must present the results fairly, reflect the proper tone while containing sufficient, reliable, useful, and relevant information. If all goes well, management will agree with the findings and this agreement will be included as a formal response consisting of the plan of action and implementation deadline for each recommendation in the report. No wonder then that when the final report is published showing management's agreement with the findings, many auditors consider the audit done and closed. That is not so.

The findings contained in the final report must be monitored as indicated in Standard 2500—Monitoring. The internal audit function must have and maintain a system to monitor the disposition of results communicated to management. The objective of this process is to make sure that management actions have been implemented effectively to resolve the issues noted in audit reports. Note that management can conversely choose to accept the risk of not taking action, but this is often the exception to the rule.

If management chooses to accept the risk, internal auditors are expected to examine that decision considering prudent risk management provisions and the organization's risk appetite to make sure that excessive risks are not being accepted within the organization above and beyond what senior management and the board consider prudent. In some cases, management may accept, or want to accept a risk without understanding the implications or the precedent that this could set for the organization. This is a valuable contribution that internal auditors can make. For example, explaining that by not enforcing a policy it sends a signal to employees that the practice can continue with impunity, or that by allowing a certain amount of waste or errors, that it promotes a permissive culture that tolerates sloppy work and poor customer service.

In most cases, however, the findings will be entered into a database for their follow-up subsequent to the issuance of the final audit report. This follow-up, defined as the appropriate retesting, evaluation, and verification that the actions taken were adequate, effective, and timely to correct the audit finding. During this follow-up, internal audit verifies the completion of agreed-upon management actions and determine the status of open recommendations.

Internal audit uses the implementation deadline provided by management to determine when follow-up procedures should be conducted. Sometimes internal audit needs to wait for an appropriate amount of time beyond the implementation deadline to have enough data on which to perform follow-up procedures.

If the finding is of high financial impact, regulatory compliance, or could result in health and safety impacts, the resolution may be required with a relatively short turnaround time. For these items, there may be a one to 3-month deadline.

If the finding is of moderate impact, it may have a deadline of 6–12 months. If the item is of relatively low, but still sufficient importance that it is included in the audit report, the deadline could be 12–18 months. So the nature, timing, and extent of the follow-up are dependent on the type of audit and extent of the finding. In some cases, such as system implementations, audit findings require a substantial timeline for resolution. In those cases, since the follow-up could be 2 or more years away management should provide milestone deadlines so progress can be verified. In the case of a system implementation, milestones could be the dates for:

1. The Request for Proposals (RFP) to be released
2. The vendor to be selected
3. Project reaches 25 percent completion
4. Project reaches 50 percent completion
5. Project reaches 75 percent
6. Project is completed and released into production

Progress toward completion should also be monitored and verified, otherwise, there is a possibility that the deadline will arrive, and the remediation will be lacking. Although this follow-up process could make internal auditors look like the company's policeman, it is an indispensable role because audit findings must be taken seriously and remediated.

Follow-up is a process by which internal auditors evaluate the adequacy, effectiveness, and timeliness of actions taken by management on reported observations and recommendations, including those made by other assurance providers. This also applies to instances where the findings or recommendations are made by other assurance providers, internal or external to the organization. When reviewing management actions to address findings and recommendations, the internal auditor should determine whether management has implemented the recommendations or assumed the risk of not implementing them.

If management has decided to assume a risk that may be unacceptable to the organization, the situation must be discussed with senior management. The identification of risk accepted by management may be noted through a compliance or consulting engagement, monitoring activities on actions taken by management as a result of prior engagements, or by other means.

Overall, it is not the responsibility of the CAE to resolve the risk. But if the CAE concludes that the matter has not been resolved appropriately (e.g., more risk is assumed than is prudent, creates a precedent that is unacceptable, contravenes the organization's values or sound practices), the CAE must communicate the matter to the board for resolution (Standard 2600—Communicating the Acceptance of Risks.

If internal audit is satisfied with the actions taken, the item is closed in the database and the relevant stakeholders are notified. If the issues are not addressed sufficiently, the relevant stakeholders are notified, the item is identified as still open, recurring, or repeat finding, and often the rating is raised from its original rating.

Summary

1. The audit is not truly completed until the follow-up is performed and there is verification that the findings noted, and corrective actions agreed upon, have been implemented.
2. The due date for audit findings depends on the risk associated with the finding. Higher risk items should have a shorter implementation date.
3. For transaction-based findings, retesting may require a delay after the corrective action's implementation date to allow a reasonable number of transactions to be processed showing that the remediation action is working as expected.

Chapter 53

Force Field Analysis

A Force Field Analysis is a tool used to strategize the forces for and against a decision. It can be very useful when applied to an internal audit recommendation to understand the pros and cons of the action, make sure it is a well-reasoned course of action and demonstrate the results to audit clients. Many people struggle when trying to make a decision, sometimes due to limited resources, conflicting priorities, insufficient know-how, and other reasons. At the same time, many people have prepared simple pros-and-cons analysis, either formally or informally, when deciding where to go on vacation, what restaurant to go to for dinner, what car to buy or which elective to choose at school. So, it is useful and effective when making personal decisions, and it is also useful and effective when making important business decisions, because it provides a structured decision-making technique.

A Force Field Analysis helps to compare and evaluate the forces that promote change and those that resist change; the pros and cons; the arguments for and against. For change to occur, the forces "for" must be strengthened and the forces "against" must be weakened. This tool helps us analyze these opposite forces and communicate the reasoning behind the decision made.

The analysis can be done on a simple piece of paper, computer screen, flipchart, or whiteboard. The diagram can be either a large T (Figure 53.1) or as shown in Figure 53.2.

Step 1. The first step is to choose the desired format, using Figure 53.1 or Figure 53.2.

Step 2. Define the goal, objective or recommendation and write it at the top of the diagram (if using Figure 53.1), or in the middle of the diagram (if using Figure 53.2).

Step 3. Think about the forces that are driving change and write them on the left side of the diagram. Brainstorming can be particularly useful to identify as many forces as possible. Involving others, such as team members, audit clients, and

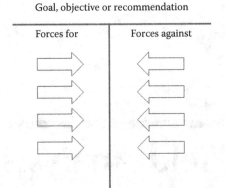

Figure 53.1 T-Shaped force field analysis.

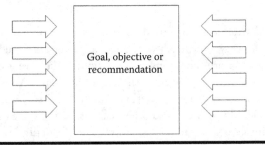

Figure 53.2 Alternate shape for force field analysis.

subject matter experts, is also recommended. These forces for change can be internal or external and could include:

Internal drivers: Poor morale, inadequate equipment, excessive costs, regulatory requirements.
External drivers: Regulatory requirements, competition, disruptive technologies, changing demographics

Step 4. Following an approach as described in Step 3, now think about the forces against change and write them on the right side of the diagram. These are the forces that hinder, are unfavorable, and in general, resist the goal, objective, or recommendation. These forces against change can also be internal or external and could include:

Internal drivers: Fear of change, existing organizational structure, negative attitudes
External drivers: Regulations and other commitments to customers and suppliers

Step 5. Assign a score to each driving and opposing factor. The rating scale can vary. You could use High, Medium, Low, or a Likert scale from 1: Weak to 5: Strong, based on the amount of influence each force has on the plan. When done, add up the scores for each of the sides (i.e., for and against). You can also do this graphically by making the length of each arrow (for or against) proportional to the strength of the force it represents. This is a step that is often skipped, but it is very important because it allows us to move on to Step 6.

Step 6. Analyze and apply the results. Based on the results obtained, it is now easier to determine which side: for or against, has a higher score. With this information you can decide whether or not to go ahead with the decision, recommendation, or change initiative. You can also strategize about ways to support and strengthen the forces for, and weaken or counteract the forces against. These actions will help to make the presentation of the idea, and its implementation, more successful. Strategies may include training staff, sharing samples and templates, providing payback or ROI calculation results, and offering to provide consulting support.*

EXAMPLE

When internal auditors present a recommendation, they are naturally on the side arguing in favor of the corrective action. Sometimes the client has objections and "pushes back" against it. The natural tendency is to reiterate the arguments for, provide supporting evidence for its importance and relevance, and if this is still unsuccessful, some individuals may speak more forcibly, faster, and louder until they force the client to agree by suggesting it is mandatory or threatening with having the matter reported to the CEO and the board for resolution. This approach is not effective as a way to build cooperative relationships with audit clients.

Instead, internal auditors can examine the arguments against and when presenting the matter to audit clients, they can address the objections and provide pragmatic, realistic, cost-effective arguments to address those objections. If the client has other objections, the meeting has already taken a collaborative tone and the internal auditors have demonstrated their desire to examine both sides of the situation and a willingness to discuss the situation openly. This demonstrates fairness, an unbiased disposition, a pragmatic mindset, and respect for the client's situation.

Summary

1. Force Field Analysis is useful to examine both sides of an initiative or course of action, like the corrective action to remedy a finding. It places arguments side-by-side.

---

* For additional information of Force Field Analysis, see www.mindtools.com/pages/article/newTED_06.htm and an illustration of its application in the healthcare industry at http://asq.org/healthcare-use/why-quality/force-field.html.

2. Internal auditors can use the analysis to improve their understanding of the dynamics supporting or hindering the course of action. By addressing objections proactively, it provides a useful negotiation and conflict resolution technique that goes beyond relying exclusively on the auditors' desired course of action.

3. It helps internal auditors demonstrate their understanding of both sides of an argument, show their balanced viewpoint of a subject and improve the interaction with audit clients.

Chapter 54

Foreign Corrupt Practices Act (FCPA)

The Foreign Corrupt Practices Act (FCPA) was enacted in 1977 in the wake of Watergate and amidst bribery scandals by large U.S. defense contractors. Upon passing the FCPA, Congress declared its policy that American companies should act ethically in bidding for foreign contracts and encourage the development of democratic institutions and honest, transparent, business practices. The FCPA required both issuers covered under the Securities Exchange Act of 1934 and all other U.S. nationals and companies (defined as "domestic concerns") to refrain from making any unlawful payments to public officials, political parties, party officials, or candidates for public office for the purpose of causing that person to make a decision or take an action, or refrain from taking an action, for the purpose of obtaining or retaining business. The FCPA also required issuers to maintain transparent books and records.

Enforcement of the FCPA continues to be a high priority for the SEC. This law prohibits companies based or managed by US managers, from bribing foreign government officials for contracts or other types of business.

The SEC has a list of companies charged with violating the FCPA going back to 1978, and the list shows companies in all industries, of various sizes, for profit and not-for-profit, showing that all organizations should take active measures to comply with the law. A sample of companies penalized for failure to comply with the FCPA appear on Table 54.1.*

---

* See www.sec.gov/spotlight/fcpa/fcpa-cases.shtml.

Table 54.1 Sample FCPA Fines and Penalties

Organization	Year	Description	Amount
BNP Paribas	2015	Violated sanctions against Sudan, Cuba, and Iran.	$8.9 billion[a]
Telia	2017	Bribes paid to gain business in Uzbekistan	$965 million[b]
Halliburton	2017	Bribes to gain oilfield contracts in Angola	$ 29.2 million[c]
Cadbury	2017	Bribes to obtain licenses for a chocolate factory in India	$ 13 million[d]
General Cable	2016	Bribes to win business in Angola, Bangladesh, China, Egypt, Indonesia, and Thailand	$ 75 million[e]
Teva Pharmaceuticals	2016	Bribes to government officials in Russia, Ukraine, and Mexico	$ 519 million[f]
Embraer	2016	Bribes to win business in the Dominican Republic, Saudi Arabia, Mozambique, and India.	$ 205 million[g]
Siemens	2008	Paying bribes to government officials to obtain business.	$1.6 billion
Volkswagen	2017	Used software to misrepresented the greenhouse gas emissions produced by its diesel engines.	$2.8 billion[h]
Wells Fargo	2016	Secretly issued credit cards without customers' consent.	$185 million[i]

[a] www.reuters.com/article/us-bnp-paribas-settlement-sentencing/bnp-paribas-sentenced-in-8-9-billion-accord-over-sanctions-violations-idUSKBN0NM41K20150501.

[b] www.sec.gov/news/press-release/2017-171.

[c] www.sec.gov/news/press-release/2017-133.

[d] www.sec.gov/litigation/admin/2017/34-79753-s.pdf.

[e] www.sec.gov/news/pressrelease/2016-283.html.

[f] www.fcpablog.com/blog/2017/9/21/telia-disgorges-457-million-to-sec-agrees-to-965-million-in.html.

[g] www.sec.gov/news/pressrelease/2016-224.html.

[h] www.usatoday.com/story/money/cars/2017/04/21/volkswagen-diesel-scandal-hearing/100739290/.

[i] www.nytimes.com/2016/09/09/business/dealbook/wells-fargo-fined-for-years-of-harm-to-customers.html.

Auditing for FCPA Compliance

Organizations with international operations should conduct FCPA reviews to verify compliance with the law. The decision to perform the audit, its scope, locations and frequency will be determined by a risk assessment that includes factors like Transparency International's Corruption Perceptions Index (CPI)* country rating, the complexity of the business, its size (e.g., based on revenue), the nature of the work performed, the industry involved (e.g., high risk industries like extractive, construction, manufacturing), volume of work done with state-owned businesses, and the use of third parties. The following are some suggested steps:

- Verify there is a comprehensive, up to date, and clearly articulated FCPA policy for employees, directors and agents/intermediaries in multiple languages as needed to provide clear guidance
- Make sure annual awareness training is mandated, delivered, and documented for employees, directors, agents/intermediaries, business partners, sales agents, and compliance personnel (e.g., internal audit, corporate compliance, legal, accounting)
- Confirm the whistleblower/ethics hotline is available 24 hours a day, 7 days a week accessible via phone, e-mail, Internet, fax, and mail box and with operators that speak the major languages employees communicate in
- Verify the assignment of FCPA awareness, compliance, and overall responsibility to a senior executive
- Verify the Code of Ethics makes specific mention of the requirement for compliance with anti-corruption policies
- Determine if there are clear disciplinary procedures to address violations of the FCPA policy
- Review transactions involving customers, vendors, distributors, freight forwarders, shipping/logistics providers, customs agents, advertising agencies, sales representatives, lobbyists, miscellaneous payments, and consultants to examine the absence of unspecified services, the lack of deliveries, and incomplete descriptions
- Examine commissions, bonuses, and finders' fees paid to make sure they are reasonable, and expected
- Review contracts with government agencies, business activities with politically exposed persons and verify there are no activities involving individuals or business on the OFAC list of specially designated nationals
- Review donations, political contributions, gifts, sponsorships, permits, rebates, refunds, travel, entertainment, and credit card advances

---

* The 2016 Transparency International Corruption Perceptions Index (CPI) is available at www.transparency.org/news/feature/corruption_perceptions_index_2016.

- Review credit terms, contracted prices, duties, fees, taxes, or charges for excessively favorable or abnormal arrangements
- Search for round-value payments, and payments to foreign locations, especially where the organization does not operate
- Examine legal entities, partnerships, and joint ventures to verify their purpose and activities
- Review bank reconciliations and processes related to cash advances, petty cash, cash payments, and employee reimbursements
- Verify a risk assessment is conduced that incorporates country-specific analysis, including information like the Corruption Perception Index (CPI) by Transparency International or the Bribery Risk Matrix by Trace International.*

Audit procedures include interviews, walkthroughs, the review of financial data and legal documents, sampling and data analytics to examine transactions, observation of business operating locations (e.g., to identify shell or front companies) and the review of training and policy documents.

Summary

1. Companies with international operations must comply with the Foreign Corrupt Practices Act (FCPA) and internal auditors frequently review transactions and documents, perform walkthroughs and conduct interviews.
2. Fines and penalties levied against companies found not complying with the FCPA have increased in frequency and amount over the past decade.
3. Data analytics are an important tool to help identify red-flag transactions.

---

* See www.traceinternational.org/trace-matrix.

Chapter 55

Fraud

The Merriam-Webster Dictionary defines fraud as the "intentional perversion of truth in order to induce another to part with something of value or to surrender a legal right," and also as "an act of deceiving or misrepresenting." As such, it is important first of all to differentiate fraud from an error or mistake. Fraud is intentional and often followed by concerted efforts to conceal the act.

The IIA Standards define fraud as "any illegal act characterized by deceit, concealment, or violation of trust. These acts are not dependent upon the threat of violence or physical force. Frauds are perpetrated by parties and organizations to obtain money, property, or services; to avoid payment or loss of services; or to secure personal or business advantage." In terms of our responsibility, the Standards also state that internal auditors must exercise due professional care by considering the probability of significant errors, fraud, and noncompliance. (Standard 1220. A1) and "evaluate the potential for the occurrence of fraud and how the organization manages fraud risk." (Standard 2120.A2), however, internal auditors "are not expected to have the expertise of a person whose primary responsibility is detecting and investigating fraud" (Standard 1210.A2).

It was widely agreed for years that internal auditors reviewed the quality of internal control and did not audit *for* fraud. They were frequently summoned to investigate fraud suspicions and incidents, but this was often handled *post factum* (after the fact). A significant limitation of this approach is that after fraud occurs, it is very expensive and difficult to research and recover amounts lost. A common characteristic of fraudsters is that they either spend the money stolen, or they hide their ill gains. As a result, it is often nearly impossible to fully recover the amount lost.

Fraudsters often know how to perpetrate and conceal their crimes because they know the internal controls in place and the limitations of these internal controls. This makes it very difficult to detect fraud and requires care and keen attention to this problem. Internal auditors should consider fraud prevention practices by management and the board when reviewing risk assessment and risk management activities. Similarly, internal auditors should include fraud detection procedures when developing audit programs.

Developing audit programs that include fraud detection techniques makes it necessary for internal auditors to "think like a fraudster," which means anticipating fraudulent schemes and imagining how an individual, alone or in collusion with others, could perpetrate a fraud and conceal it from detection. To do this, internal auditors should:

1. Brainstorm scenarios: This is done by imagining how someone could perpetrate the act. Creativity and gathering imaginative individuals who can think freely and liberally about scenarios is essential for this approach to work.
2. Leverage accumulated knowledge: This is done by leveraging existing fraud scenarios either from available resources (e.g., fraud experts, published information), industry or organizational databases.

When applying steps 1 and 2 above, internal auditors should then develop testing procedures to determine if these scenarios are occurring. For example:

Scenario 1

Check employee access rights to determine if a user has access to create a vendor in the computer system, and pay a vendor for purchases made. There are two primary locations where this can be investigated: 1. A list of access rights from IT that may show the ability to perform both tasks and 2. A list of purchases showing who created/approved the Purchase Order and who processed/approved the payment of the purchase made. It is a good idea to perform both tests because while the first test shows the potential to engage in such activities, the second shows if the action has occurred.

In terms of the number of transactions tested, both should be done at 100 percent of the population.

Scenario 2

Issuing payments for personal benefit: This would involve obtaining a list of payments processed and reviewing who the beneficiaries of the payments are with employee information from the human resources records. Fields of interest include payee names, addresses, bank routing information, tax IDs, and phone numbers.

This scenario should be tested at 100 percent of the population.

There are numerous scenarios that can be envisioned and tested, but the premise is fairly consistent—don't merely test that the control was performed or failed, but whether malice could underlie the transaction. In the case of Scenario 1, the user would be authorized in the system to transact the purchase and the payment because the user would be on the corresponding user tables. This is a segregation of duties problem, but the fraud would be the intentional use of this control issue for personal gain. In Scenario 2, the amount of the purchase may be budgeted for and the individual may have the authority to make purchases, but is the abuse of this authority that the internal auditor should search for.

Summary

1. Fraud is intentional and often accompanied by deliberate efforts to conceal the act. Internal auditors should conduct a fraud risk assessment to identify areas where fraud could occur and perform tests based on known or suspected fraud schemes.
2. Segregating incompatible duties is highly recommended to limit the potential for fraud. An additional concern is that beyond having an ability to engage in fraudulent behavior, an individual could act on this control weakness alone or collude with one or more people to commit fraud.
3. Data analytics and testing the entire population are highly recommended to identify anomalous transactions.

Chapter 56

Fraud Red Flags

Since a typical organization executes thousands, or millions, of transactions a year, it is extremely difficult, or nearly impossible, for internal auditors to thoroughly examine every transaction and activity exhaustibly. Instead, internal auditors must learn about anomalies and search for them during the course of their work. This involves paying close attention to irregularities while interviewing auditees, observing business activities, reviewing documents, and analyzing data and records. Some of these anomalies will indicate the potential for fraud, and hence they are regarded as fraud red flags. For example:

1. No vacations, periodic rotations, or transfer of employees. Fraudsters often do not take vacation out of concern that someone else filling in for them may discover their actions. As a result, many organizations have instituted 2-week mandatory vacation requirements for high-risk employees where another person performs the duties of the worker on vacation and has access to the computer records and physical workspace. This practice is also a regulatory requirement for financial services organizations like banks. Many frauds are concealed by an individual for a long time because no one else has access to the fraudster's workspace. It is important that the work not accumulate during the person's absence, and that the person not log into the company's computer systems while away from the office.

2. Familiarity or very long tenure in position. This is often considered a positive condition because individuals should gain more knowledge and become more competent performing their jobs the longer their tenure in their position. The problem originates, however, when managers reduce the amount of supervision and monitoring on long-tenure employees and treat trust as a substitute for effective controls. I believe a long tenure is generally a good environmental condition, but managers should not become complacent over time.

3. Conflict of interest with suppliers, customers, or other business partners. By becoming too familiar and cozying up with suppliers, employees could replace their fiduciary responsibility toward their employer and lower the rigor of their oversight responsibility. Furthermore, with increased familiarity, they may become susceptible to kickbacks, bribes, and inappropriate gifts. Organizations should consider periodically rotating employee assignments, providing annual ethics training, requiring the signature of conflict of interest and code of ethics statements, and reiterating the organization's zero-tolerance policy.

4. Inadequate pre-employment screening for high-risk positions. The pre-employment screening of employees is done to identify backgrounds and activities that are incompatible with the organization's values and could portend similarly problematic behavior in the future. Organizations should consult with their labor law counsel to make sure applicable laws are complied with. In addition to performing pre-employment screening through background and other checks, some organizations perform periodic reviews because while all reviewed parameters could meet expectations when hired, conditions could change over time.

5. Reluctance to provide data, or access to people. Restricting access to employees, records, and facilities could be indicative of a manager that wants to hide inappropriate activities. Internal auditors must have unfettered access to any individual, location, or record, whether electronic or hardcopy.

6. Limited communication of penalties for fraud. By not having, or enforcing the organization's zero-tolerance policy, management is indirectly tolerating fraudulent behavior.

7. Rapid turnover of key employees. Turnover dynamics should be studied to determine whether this is due to natural causes (e.g., retirement) or driven by managers who place inappropriate demands on employees. For example, an employee who is told by a manager to record a sale before it is allowed, to make inappropriate journal entries, or to make unauthorized payments may choose to leave the organization rather than compromise her ethical standards or risk losing professional certification credentials by being involved in such actions.

8. Inadequate training. Ethics training is often mandatory in organizations, but if it is of poor quality, discouraged, or disparaged, it will not be effective. In fact, not providing and resisting to invest sufficiently in ethics, fraud, and corruption training may indicate a careless, permissive, or complicit management.

9. Ineffective internal audit function. If the internal audit function is understaffed, under-resourced, under-qualified, or disrespected, it will be unable to properly perform its duties verifying the effectiveness of business structures and practices.

10. Poor accounting records. The lack of supporting documentation showing the rationale for a decision, or the action taken regarding accounting matters,

may be indicative of sloppy administrative practices, an effort to conceal inappropriate activities, or evidence of an environment where a fraudster could operate with limited likelihood of detection.

11. Unusually large number of banking relationships. It is common for organizations to have multiple bank accounts and banking relationships. This is often done to properly segregate funds and manage incoming, outgoing and held (e.g., escrow, reserve) funds. Some banks have local reach and due to favorable rates and fees, or to demonstrate positive community relations, organizations may choose to establish and maintain a relationship with them. Other banks have broader geographic reach and can provide international banking services that more complex and international organizations require. But if the number of banking relationships and bank accounts exceeds what appears reasonable and necessary, the internal auditor should question the need for the excess. Is this done as a way to hide funds? Is this done so funds can be moved around clouding the audit trail? Does this create an environment where funds could be parked without frequent oversight and allow an individual to embezzle them without timely detection?

12. Overly complex business structure. Similar to having multiple bank accounts, organizations may have multiple legal entities for legal protection, accounting organization, tax benefits or to preserve valuable brand value that could be lost by eliminating or consolidating business entities. However, an overly complex business structure that results in the movement of monies, the ownership of assets, or the assignment of liabilities between them without reasonable purposes, could indicate efforts to conceal fraudulent behavior.

13. Dishonest or overly dominant management: If managers are dishonest, employees may conclude that they can also engage in similar activities. If management is overly domineering, employees may not feel comfortable sharing their disagreement with decisions or actions they find objectionable.

14. Excessive reliance on computers and automation without adequate managerial oversight. The movement toward automation has generally resulted in increased efficiencies, lower per-transaction costs, lower cycle times due to higher speeds, and reduced errors. However, the absence of proper built-in controls and oversight could result in unscrupulous individuals who use these computer systems to engage in inappropriate activities without detection. The absence of paper documents and other visible files, the quick speed of execution, and the potential to delete records could result in computer fraud.

15. High stress, crisis, or overly competitive environment. Better organizations set and pursue diverse and aggressive goals and objectives. These motivate, establish direction, aide in the allocation of available resources and ensure that tactics support strategies. These goals and accompanying operating practices should demand hard work and purposeful actions. However, when these goals and objectives are excessive and unrealistic, employees will likely suffer from excess stress and when sustained, will create a crisis-type

work environment. This can also result in employees feeling an obligation to go to extreme ends to achieve, or pretend to achieve, these impossible goals. The pressure to achieve what is considered impossible actions is akin to what was discovered at Wells Fargo with the fraudulent account creation scandal, and to a certain extent at Volkswagen with the emissions testing defeat software.

16. Limited attention paid to details. Details matter and in environments where data is only examined at summary levels, unscrupulous employees could attempt to use this lack of detail to hide their fraudulent actions. The proliferation of digitized information, and the availability of tools to extract and analyze these large volumes of information begs for follow-through so management and internal auditors can drill down into the data to fully understand dynamics surrounding business activities, search for outliers, identify trends, gaps, and other patterns that may indicate the inclusion of inappropriate activities or the manipulation of business data hoping that the act will not be noticed among the large number of transactions.

17. Poor compensation. Employees should be compensated fairly for their efforts and contributions. When employees feel underpaid, the likelihood of them pursuing actions to "correct their grievances" increases. While this doesn't justify their actions, it may effectively explain them. In many developing countries this is a dynamic that has become a widely accepted justification for soliciting, or outright demanding, bribes, kickbacks, grease and facilitation payments, or the theft and personal use of company assets.

18. Unusual or large period-end transactions. As reporting periods reach their end, an incentive exists for individuals to record transactions that will improve the financial and operational results of the organization. While an increase in period-end activity is to be expected, as is the case of sales people who increase their efforts to close pending deals, or shipping departments to move merchandise out and get them on their way to the clients, care is warranted to make sure that all activities recorded are legitimate. Unusual activities also include reversing transactions past the period-end close, often indicating the manipulation of the initial transactions (e.g., sales or shipments) and the related transaction after the period-end reversing the entry.

19. Changing audit firms often. External and internal auditors are required to act with honesty, diligence and due professional care to ensure stakeholder interests are protected and advanced, and that rules, regulations, and other performance standards are followed. Audit firms, whether performing internal or external audit services, may decide to terminate their relationship with a client if it appears the client is being disingenuous in their dealings, refuses to follow guidance to correct deficiencies, and pressures the audit firm to allow questionable or outright inappropriate activities. When this happens, external audit firms may choose to sever the relationship rather than compromise their standards and reputation.

20. Overly liberal accounting practices. While most accounting standards are precise and clearly define expected recording standards, some are subject to judgment and interpretation. However, organizations are expected to be generally conservative in their decision-making when these conditions present themselves and abstain from being overly liberal. The taking of excessive licenses could eventually result in unjustified or fraudulent accounting practices.

21. Inadequate documentation or unexplainable transactions and activities: All business transactions should be accompanied by adequate supporting documentation, explaining their business purpose and rationale. When transactions are recorded without supporting documentation it raises the specter of manipulation and abuse. Company policies and procedures should establish the expectation for proper documentation and management practices should ensure compliance.

22. Increases in Accounts Receivable aging and write-offs. Unless sales are made in cash and collected immediately, they are recorded as Accounts Receivable (AR). These sales are reported in AR aging reports from the point of sale to collection. If the sale is recorded fraudulently (e.g., there is no customer who will pay for the so-called sale) the sale will enter the collection cycle and AR aging reports will show sales pending collection that move from Current (i.e., Zero to 29 days outstanding), then in 30-day increments (i.e., 30, 60, 90, 120, 150, and 150+ days outstanding) only to be written off as uncollectable balances when the transaction exceeds 150 days or so delinquent.

23. Excessive overtime. While hourly (i.e., non-exempt) employees are entitled to overtime pay when they work more than the weekly workweek hours, internal auditors should search for instances when the overtime charges are excessive, unusual, or continuous without it being justified.

24. Excessive employee or customer complaints. It depends on the exact nature of the complaints. For example: "wrong billing" where a future bill shows the account in arrears even though the customer states payment was made. This is indicative of payments being intercepted. Another example involves substitution, where a customer complains that the order was not filled as requested, such as fewer items than requested, items substituted, or damaged merchandise received instead.

25. Inadequate or poorly trained staff: Poorly trained staff performing control activities can allow frauds to be committed. For example, an employee performing bank reconciliations who does not know how to research unusual transactions and allows them to continue without the alarm they should engender, or a warehouse manager who is witness to missing merchandise but attributes it to being misplaced, damaged, or shoplifted when in fact it is being stolen by employees.

26. Living beyond means and financial difficulties. This red flag is difficult to identify, especially if the internal auditor is not privy to changes in lifestyle of

company employees. Research on committed frauds often show that the perpetrators' lifestyles change as they spend their ill-gotten gains on cars, houses, jewelry, trips, and entertainment. Information about questionable lifestyle changes can be obtained from co-workers and when allowed, background and credit checks.

27. Unusually close association with vendors or customers. Employees are encouraged to foster strong relationships with business associates, but the relationship with a third-party provider should always balance the business being exchanged with the performance and oversight required. Overly-friendly relationships can deteriorate into complacency, or the acceptance of inappropriate gratuities, kickbacks, and bribes.

Summary

1. Fraud red flags are high-risk dynamics that could indicate the presence of fraud.
2. When fraud red flags are present, internal auditors should exert additional care, and review related transactions and conditions to determine if there is additional cause for concern and investigation.
3. The list of fraud red flag is ever-growing, so internal auditors must remain vigilant and look for unusual transactions that warrant additional research.

Chapter 57

Fraud Triangle and Hexagon

Fraud is defined as the intentional misrepresentation or concealment of information to deceive others with the objective of gaining unfair or unlawful gains. It is a global problem affecting organizations of all types and sizes in all industries. Fraud is costly. The Association of Certified Fraud Examiners' (ACFE) 2016 Report to the Nations reports that organizations lose an estimated 7 percent of annual revenues to fraud. Fraud is difficult to identify, investigate, and prosecute. Attempts are made continuously to identify fraudsters' motives and modus operandi so that antifraud programs can be designed to prevent, detect, and effectively investigate fraudulent activities.

To varying degrees all organizations are subject to the risk of fraudulent activities being committed against them. Constant fraud risk management is called for to identify vulnerabilities, proactively reduce the likelihood of fraud and monitor the drivers of fraudulent activities. The Fraud Triangle, developed by Dr. Donald Cressey, has been used for many years to assess the three drivers of fraud: Need, Opportunity, and Justification.

Need

It is typically caused by circumstances that increase financial pressures. In this case, the individual has a financial problem that cannot be solved through legitimate means so inappropriate activities are seen as a way to remedy the situation. Examples include housing expenses, a child's tuition payments, elder care, and unexpected medical bills. Other needs are created by the lack of personal discipline or other weaknesses, such as a gambling habit, drug addiction, sustaining extra-marital relationships, a fancy for expensive jewelry, the need to acquire status symbols, or sustain a lavish lifestyle. In some cases, organizations' and investors' expectations for unreasonably high financial returns create pressures that lead employees to consider committing financial statement fraud. Other pressures are political and social, where individuals feel they cannot appear to fail due to their reputation, community involvement, or high-ranking position within the organization.

Since need can be a precursor of fraudulent activities, auditors should search for conditions that point to significant changes in employee needs and wants. Internal control questionnaires (ICQs), interviews with managers, surveys, and interaction with department staff will encourage conversations about lifestyle changes that may be early warning signals of future issues. Taking a proactive approach to identify risk factors early on can yield huge dividends through early intervention and counseling.

Opportunity

This often is created in the absence of, or weaknesses in, internal controls. Common internal controls include approvals, reconciliations, segregation of duties, access controls and reviews. When some individuals identify an opportunity, and upon their assessment of the risk of being caught as being low, they decide to abuse their position of trust. Examples include an individual who notices that certain bank accounts are not being reconciled timely or appropriately and concludes that inappropriate transactions using those accounts will escape detection. Similar conclusions may be drawn from poor intrusion detection controls, a lack of oversight over transactions below a certain monetary threshold or insufficient segregation of duties.

The International Standards for the Professional Practice of Internal Auditing (the *Standards*) state that "the internal audit activity should assist the organization by identifying and evaluating exposures to risk and contributing to the improvement of risk management and control systems" (Standard 2110). Clearly, fraud risks are related to this mandate and internal auditors accomplish this when they document and test the effectiveness of controls, which are essential activities to reduce the likelihood that weak controls will create opportunities for fraud.

Justification

This occurs when an individual develops a rationale for their fraudulent activities and considers the act acceptable. Some fraudsters conclude that since they were overlooked for a promotion they believe they deserve, that they will "make things right" by stealing from the organization. A similar conclusion may be drawn from reductions in employee benefits, feelings of being underpaid, perceptions of poor management practices, favoritism, and other workplace human relations issues. Sometimes an individual considers the funds taken as merely being borrowed and argues that they will return them at a later date.

The likelihood that employees will commit fraud and rationalize its acceptability increase with poor management practices, unclear expectations, favoritism, and the subjective granting of workplace rewards and perks. Auditors should evaluate management's competence, consistency, objectivity, documentation, and transparency to identify vulnerabilities and fraud risks.

The Other Factors

While the Fraud Triangle is a useful tool to categorize the drivers of fraudulent activities, most users of the model fail to consider a very important aspect of fraudulent activities and the people who commit them: Their competence, character, and arrogance (Figure 57.1).

Competence

Individuals with a deep understanding of the controls in their work areas may also have a deep understanding of the ways that those controls can be circumvented.

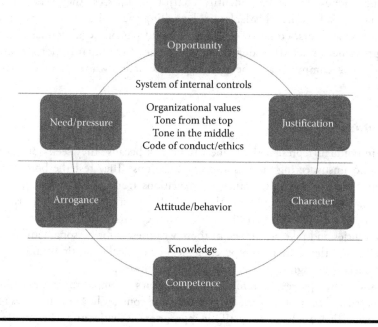

Figure 57.1   The Fraud Hexagon.

It is very important for management to understand the exposure that this creates and make sure that oversight is not replaced simply by trust, as many fraudsters abuse the trust bestowed on them to commit their crimes.

Character

Individuals bring to organizations elements of their upbringing, cultures, and ethical and moral beliefs. These ingredients are the foundation of people's attitudes, which become the key factors determining their behaviors and ultimately, their character. When these elements are placed along a moral continuum, the result is that people are essentially Honest, Dishonest or Situational/Potential, as relates to fraud.

Honest

Honest individuals always do the right thing and as such represent the lowest fraud risk. When an excruciating or unexpected financial need arises, they work over-time, hold two or more jobs, cut back on their expenses and seek help from friends, family or others to bridge the gap. They sacrifice to meet their financial obligations and adapt accordingly. They are driven by high moral values and address social and political setbacks as learning opportunities and challenges to overcome.

When honest individuals identify control weaknesses, they tend to notify their managers, become whistleblowers by calling the ethics hotline or confide in the internal auditors, compliance officer, ombudsperson, legal counsel, or other appropriate personnel. They don't take advantage of the organization's weakness. Instead, they communicate their finding to someone who can take corrective action.

Dishonest

These individuals represent the highest fraud risk because they seek opportunities to defraud unsuspecting victims and organizations. They test the boundaries to determine management's tolerance for deviations from company policy and are constantly in search of loopholes. They typically question authority and rules, lie, and should not be placed in positions where they control company assets. They seek vulnerabilities and take advantage of those weaknesses for personal gain. In some extreme cases, they suffer from psychological or clinical conditions and may seek power, success, recognition, and grandeur by all means.

Dishonest employees ignore the organization's attempts to create a positive, productive, and controlled work environment and constantly search for ways to beat the system. They are likely to justify inappropriate activities and when confronted may state that "everyone does it."

Situational/Potential

These employees are generally honest, disciplined, and committed employees and they make conscious efforts to comply with the organization's policies and procedures. Although they have the best intentions at heart, to varying degrees they are also susceptible to break the rules. When the organization's culture condones deviations from the stated policy, they may follow their peers in those practices. They seek and need reminders, reassurance, guidance, and follow-up to ensure their continued awareness and compliance. When management fails to document, provide training and sanction unethical practices, fraud risks grow rapidly and while these employees may follow the explicit organizational rules, they may disregard the spirit of the law.

Due to the possibility of succumbing to temptation, these individuals benefit from effective controls, a strong tone at the top, visible leadership, clearly documented policies, and frequent audits. These individuals represent the largest percentage of an organization's population. As a result, organizational policies, operating procedures and internal controls should take a risk-based approach to fraud and consider this portion of the workforce as a potential fraud risk pool.

Arrogance

Arrogance involves egotism, overconfidence, self-importance, condescension, the lack of conscience, an attitude of superiority, entitlement, or greed by individuals who believe the organization's policies and procedures do not apply to them. Furthermore, arrogant individuals disregard the consequences to victims, so they often also lack empathy.

This extreme egotism can result in the individual not having any feeling of guilt for what is about to be done and the impact it may have on the many stakeholders organizations are accountable to.

Antifraud Programs and the Fraud Triangle

Internal auditors should assist management in the development of effective antifraud programs. To reduce fraud risks, these programs should contain the necessary elements to deter, prevent, detect, and investigate fraud. Deterrence is achieved when senior management and the board clearly, consistently, and formally state their expectations for ethical behavior, when management institutes effective controls, employees become aware of the many activities carried out to make committing fraud fruitless, and employees develop a perception that the costs of fraudulent activities outweigh any potential benefits.

Actions that set the right tone include filing a police report and lawsuit against fraudsters that then becomes a public record, to demanding restitution, adoption of a no-tolerance policy, training and having a visible and capable internal audit function that employs data analytics tools. The knowledge of observant managers familiar with fraud red flags and an active internal audit team, act like the highway patrol on the side of the road whose mere presence results in drivers adhering to the speed limit.

If deterrence fails to thwart fraudulent activities, preventive controls should mitigate the fraud risks present by stopping any attempts to act inappropriately. In the oft chance that the individual succeeds and commits the fraud, detective controls should provide prompt notification to the control owners so corrective action can take place promptly through an investigation and remediation. Since these practices can reduce the likelihood that Situational/Potentials act dishonestly, internal auditors should include fraud risk factors while developing audit programs to verify the existence and effectiveness of related controls.

Fraud-related controls should exist to prevent the hiring of dishonest individuals. To reduce the likelihood of hiring dishonest people, organizations should conduct effective pre-employment background checks, verify credentials, check references, and review civil and criminal records. Where allowed, many organizations conduct competency, personality and psychological tests, and make sure that all interviews are thorough. Behavioral interview questions are quite effective to determine if the individual meets the technical, interpersonal, and manageability qualities desired. These controls can significantly reduce the risk that potential fraudsters are hired.

Knowing that Situational/Potentials may succumb to temptation and commit fraud due to financial pressures, organizations often implement Employee Assistance Programs (EAPs) as an employee benefit. These programs are typically staffed with counselors who can provide assistance to employees experiencing marital, financial, substance-abuse, emotional, or medical hardship. Through early intervention and consultations with experts, employees may be able to address and cope with challenging situations that if left unchecked could escalate into damaging and inappropriate activities.

Effective management, conflict resolution, cross-cultural team building, and similar workplace training can help managers and employees alike work in a professional, congenial, and results-oriented environment. Respectful workplaces are less likely to lead to situations where employees see reprisals as necessary or justified to correct workplace wrongs. Furthermore, these practices create a support environment where employees look out for each other, feel empowered to call the ethics hotline when concerns surface and collectively create a positive environment that respects and follows the organization's policies and procedures.

Logically, organizations should actively seek to hire the maximum number of honest individuals as possible. Recruiting, selection, and employee retention policies should reflect this objective and should be included in Human Resources audits. This can also be achieved by identifying individuals with ethically-spotless records, having stringent employee selection processes, and making sure that questionable practices are dealt with promptly, fairly, and consistently. Also important to note that honest individuals are likely to leave their organizations when they feel their moral compass is compromised and their values no longer match their employer's, so auditors should review exit interview notes and survey results for indicators of festering problems.

Implications for Internal Auditors

Internal auditors can play a crucial role helping their organizations lower their vulnerability to fraud. Reviews of the organization's employment practices, tone throughout the organization, reliability of the system of internal controls and assessing employees' understanding of the word and the spirit of the law in policies and procedures, can help identify early warning signals of fraud risks.

Internal auditors can assist management in the identification of control weaknesses and unmanaged risks. By working collaboratively with senior management and the board, internal auditors can help the organization establish a strong control environment that will keep fraud at bay and reduce the likelihood of having to use the Fraud Hexagon to determine why a fraud was committed.

Summary

1. The Fraud Triangle can be expanded to cover six attributes that contribute to fraud, thus creating a Hexagon: Opportunity, Need/Pressure, Justification, Arrogance, Character, Competence.
2. Internal auditors should help their organization assess the potential for fraud and incorporate fraud detection procedures in their audit programs.
3. Character is a key determinant of the potential for fraud, so hiring techniques within the organization should also include procedures to assess the character of job candidates.

Chapter 58

GANTT Charts

Gantt Charts are a form of bar chart that shows the activities of a project's schedule. They show the activities that need to be performed on the vertical (*Y*-axis), and the duration of each activity on the horizontal (*X*-axis). They can be enhanced by also showing the sequence of activities on the schedule.

To prepare a Gantt chart:

1. Identify and list the key activities of the project. The level of detail of these activities, and the number of activities identified for charting may vary based on the project manager's preferences and needs. The items can be initially defined using a work breakdown structure (WBS).
2. Determine the start and end dates for each activity identified
3. Determine the dependency that exists among the activities. This consists of identifying which activities must be completed before others can begin. It also involves identifying which activities can be started simultaneously, or can be delayed, without negatively impacting the projects' timeline. The preferred approach is to use the earliest start time for all activities, where each activity is scheduled to begin immediately after its prerequisites (or predecessor activities) have been completed.

Gantt charts are created electronically using tools like Microsoft Project, Workzone, Sharepoint, Pentalogic, and Ganttpro, so internal auditors should familiarize themselves with the exact steps required to create the diagram. In addition to the ease to create, electronic Gantt charts also make it easy to make schedule changes, add new activities, and adjust the duration of existing activities.

A common challenge when preparing Gantt Charts is defining the duration of an activity. Due to the vagaries of life, most things have an optimistic, pessimistic, and most-likely scenario. So, when entering the duration of an activity, it is useful to use a probabilistic approach to set the expected duration.

$$Te = \frac{(To + 4Tm + Tp)}{6}$$

where:

Te = Expected Time
To = Optimistic Time
Tm = Most Likely Time
Tp = Pessimistic Time

When reviewing the Gantt Chart as part of project management activities, some software applications use a color-coding, shading, or numerical indicator to show the percentage of completion for each activity. This is a very useful feature to track progress.

The Critical Path is useful to identify the activities on the longest trajectory, and the earliest and latest that each activity can start and finish without making the project longer. Items on the Critical Path have no float, which means they cannot be delayed without delaying the entire project. For this reason, project managers should pay particularly close attention to the activities on the Critical Path because any delays on those activities will delay the completion of the work, unless changes can be introduced later. Some of the ways to recover is by re-scheduling future activities, delaying activities with float (i.e., those that can be delayed without making the project longer), securing additional resources, or reducing the scope of work.

Summary

1. Gantt Charts show activities/tasks, timelines, milestones, and can also show the Critical Path and activities with or without float. This information is vital for effective project management and reducing the likelihood that a project will deliver its work late.
2. By using the earliest start approach, the project can maximize float time or slack, which is the amount of time that an activity can be delayed without delaying the entire project's completion date.
3. Internal auditors can use Gantt Charts to improve their project management efforts, identify dependencies, manage timelines and milestones, and assign tasks to minimize downtime.

Chapter 59

Governance, Risk Management, and Compliance (GRC)

GRC refers to the integration of corporate governance, risk management, and compliance principles, structures, and practices. It provides a comprehensive mechanism to develop and sustain the elements that have been identified as essential for long term value preservation and enhancement, while addressing the needs of multiple stakeholders.

The principles of GRC are aligned with the IIA professional standards and should be referred to in the context of a common language established within the organization. However, many organizations are subject to a mix-match of GRC elements and varying degrees of success with their implementation. There is often a lack of knowledge about the concepts, practices, and expectations that GRC should contain and the GRC infrastructure is sometimes deficient because senior management, the board, vendors, consultants, and regulators may approach the topic from different perspectives. These different frames of reference can create confusion, allow gaps in oversight to exist, and in general reduce the effectiveness of the GRC program.

The continuing emphasis on internal controls, fraud risk, management of third-party providers, supply chain, financial reporting, public policy initiatives, environmental concerns, energy needs, and financial services regulations may require new or modified GRC processes.

In general, governance refers to the responsibility of the board and senior management centered on creating organizational expectations and transparency so that its constituents follow established policies and procedures. A properly developed and functioning governance strategy implements systems to record and monitor business activities, takes appropriate steps to make sure there is compliance with agreed policies, and provides corrective actions when the rules have been ignored or misunderstood.

Risk management is the process organizations use to set their risk appetite, identify potential risks, and prioritize the responses to risk based on the organization's business objectives. These responses can include avoid, share, transfer, mitigate, accept, or embrace.

Compliance is the process that documents requirements and verifies adherence with these expectations through monitoring activities. These requirements can be external or internal.

While internal auditors have historically emphasized financial and compliance requirements, the focus expanded to include risk management and corporate governance in the early and mid 2000s. This broader focus was attributed to a large extent to the collapse of companies like Enron, WorldCom, and Arthur Andersen, followed by Lehman Brothers, Wachovia, Countrywide, Bear Stearns, and Merrill Lynch, among others, where the problems that precipitated those failures was poor risk management and inadequate corporate governance.

GRC is concerned with the activities of the Board of Directors and senior management, as they integrate elements of strategy development, risk assessment and risk management, internal, and external auditing, legal counsel, compliance activities, information technology, and security, ethics, human resources, and corporate culture. The CEO plays a key role mobilizing the related functions to make sure they work collaboratively. These efforts must be supported by every executive in the organization.

Whistleblowing programs, engaged audit committees, and anti-retaliation policies also play an important role in making sure the organization's practices are congruent with expectations of good practice. Overall, GRC's value lies in the organization's ability to make sound decisions because it has the right principles in place to drive the business.

The following actions are essential to make GRC's purpose a reality:

- Proper board oversight
- Senior management setting and exemplifying the correct tone at the top
- Supervisors encouraging follow-through on those principles and promoting a healthy tone in the middle
- Effective risk assessment and management practices
- Active compliance and monitoring
- Clear ethics standards
- Effective and consistent investigation of inappropriate conduct

By adopting these actions, organizations will be well-positioned to benefit from the true purpose of GRC.

Summary

1. GRC refers to the collection of overlapping elements related to corporate governance, culture, leadership and management of people, processes, and technology.
2. Internal auditors can help their clients eliminate the silos that often limit the effectiveness of GRC initiatives.
3. A strategic partnership among all related functions is essential for the success of GRC programs.

Chapter 60

GTAG

As technology evolves and impacts the work of internal auditors and their clients, it continues to require the publication of guides to address IT management, security, and IT controls. The Institute of Internal Auditors (IIA) has released multiple Global Technology Audit Guides (GTAGs) to help in this regard.

GTAG-1—Information Technology Risk and Controls: This guide provides an overview of IT risks and controls in non-technical terms. It helps internal auditors become more knowledgeable about the risks, controls, and governance issues affecting IT so they can communicate effectively with the audit committee, senior management, IT management. It also presents frameworks for assessing IT risks and controls.

GTAG-2—Change and Patch Management Controls: Critical for Organizational Success: It covers IT change and patch management issues in a language that allows CAEs to confidently build their knowledge of these topics and communicate effectively with the board, senior management, and IT management. It focuses on the management of the enhancements, updates, fixes and patches to production systems, including application code revisions, system upgrades (e.g., applications, operating systems, databases) and infrastructure changes (e.g., servers, cabling, routers, firewalls). It also includes the related controls, such as segregation of duties between the preparer, tester, implementer and approver, and monitoring controls that will reduce the risk of errors and fraud.

GTAG-3—Continuous Auditing: Coordinating Continuous Auditing and Monitoring to Provide Continuous Assurance: It provides technology-centric guidance to successfully implement a continuous auditing approach. It addresses the key terms and techniques for continuous auditing, ongoing control assessment, ongoing risk assessment, continuous monitoring, and assurance. It also identifies areas where continuous auditing can be applied by the internal audit activity, in addition to the challenges and opportunities related to continuous auditing.

GTAG-4—Management of IT Auditing: This guide focuses on IT auditing and the latest developments in the IT environment that allows CAEs to better manage their IT audit work. The emphasis is on determining where IT audit resources are needed, how to accurately evaluate IT-related risks, and how to effectively execute IT audit work. GTAG 4 also discusses the skill sets IT audit resources should have to be effective in their roles and the general criteria for assessing the maturity of the IT audit work performed.

GTAG-5—Auditing Privacy Risks: This GTAG was replaced by the Practice Guide: Auditing Privacy Risks. It provides guidance on how to protect data and comply with applicable data privacy and security laws and regulations from countries around the world. The numerous incidents of security breaches involving the loss or unintended disclosure of personal information highlights the magnitude of related risks. This guide provides internal auditors with key information for meeting the expectations from the board, management, employees, customers, vendors, outsource providers, business partners, regulators, and other stakeholders.

GTAG-6—Managing and Auditing IT Vulnerabilities: This GTAG was deleted from the IPPF. Some of its concepts are combined with the 2nd edition of GTAG 4.

GTAG-7—Information Technology Outsourcing: This guide addresses companies' increasing practice of outsourcing portions of their IT processes so they can focus on their core business. While some companies use a single IT service provider, others use multi-sourcing to achieve an optimal balance of providers. This guide helps to determine the extent of auditor involvement when IT is partially or fully outsourced in their organizations. IT addresses the contracting of IT outsourcing services to an external service provider, the different types of IT outsourcing, the life cycle of outsourcing, and how internal auditors can approach risk related to IT outsourcing activities. GTAG 7 also addresses IT control activities in an IT outsourcing environment; the involvement of IT auditors during key stages of the outsourcing life cycle; the knowledge and experience that IT auditors should have to effectively consider the related risks; the roles and expectations when IT control activities are transitioned to an IT provider; and the role of internal auditors during negotiation, renegotiation, repatriation, and renewal of outsourcing contracts.

GTAG-8—Auditing Application Controls: This GTAG focuses on how to evaluate application controls that ensure the integrity, accuracy, confidentiality, and completeness of the organization's data and systems. This is particularly important given the large sums of money spent annually implementing new or upgrading business application systems. This guide provides a list of key application controls, a sample audit plan, a list of application control review tools as guidance on how to determine if the application controls are designed appropriately and operating effectively.

GTAG-9—Identity and Access Management: This guide helps internal auditors understand how to evaluate the development of their organizations' identity and access management as a way to manage who has access to what information over time. This process impacts regulatory compliance and the protection of data from misuse, abuse, or loss, so this GTAG explains the key concepts and techniques, shows how to analyze and monitor these processes, and provides a checklist for identity and access management review.

GTAG-10—Business Continuity Management (BCM): Natural or man-made disasters can strike at any time and organizations should have a mechanism in place to ensure business continuity. This guide helps internal auditors communicate business continuity risk awareness and support management in the development and maintenance of a BCM program to address disruptive events. This GTAG includes guidance on how to verify that business application systems are protected, and that disaster recovery planning for the continuity of the organization's critical IT infrastructure is in place and ready for implementation in the event of a disaster.

GTAG-11—Developing the IT Audit Plan: This GTAG provides guidance to develop an appropriate IT audit plan, which is a one of the weaknesses affecting many internal audit departments. Rather than merely reviewing what internal auditors know and outsourcing to other companies what they don't, letting them decide what and how to perform those reviews. This guide helps CAEs formalize the annual IT audit plan, define the role and methodology that risk assessments play in determining the IT audit universe, understand the IT environment, and understand the organization and how IT supports it.

GTAG-12—Auditing IT Projects: IT projects represent a large investment, and a critical risk to many organizations, whether the project is conducted in-house or performed by third-party providers. This guide helps internal auditors get involved in reviewing IT projects effectively by understanding the different types of projects and their characteristics, identifying key project management risks, how internal audit can actively and effectively participate in the review of IT projects while retaining its requisite independence, key components of IT projects to consider when building an audit approach, and a suggested list of questions to use during project assessments.

GTAG-13—Fraud Prevention and Detection in an Automated World: Technology is an enabler of faster and cheaper operational processing, but also an avenue for fraudsters to perpetrate their crimes. Internal auditors can use technology to prevent and detect these abuses by using technology to implement real-time fraud prevention and detection programs. This guide focuses on IT-related fraud risks, risk assessments, and ways to use technology so it helps auditors address fraud risks in an automated environment.

This GTAG includes a detailed process to audit an organization's fraud prevention program, data analysis techniques for detecting fraud, and a template to perform a technology fraud risk assessment.

GTAG-14—Auditing User-developed Applications: Workers in organizations build user-developed applications (UDAs) to extract, manipulate, summarize, and analyze data without assistance from IT, but this also exposes them to risks that IT once controlled. This guide helps internal auditors scope an audit of UDAs, assess the risks affecting data integrity, availability and confidentiality causes by UDAs, provides key elements that should be considered when performing audits of UDAs, and clarifies the role of internal auditors as advisors to management on how to develop an effective UDA control framework. This guide includes a sample UDA process flow, an audit program and worksheets to help internal auditors prepare for organize and perform an audit.

GTAG-15—Information Security Governance: This guide provides a process to help develop an audit of the organization's information security governance (ISG) program. This GTAG defines governance in information security, helps auditors formulate the best questions to ask and which documents are essential, and describes the internal auditors' role in ISG. A key objective of auditing ISG is verifying that the organization's actions set the right infrastructure, it delivers the expected behaviors and practices, and executes information security in ways that protect the collection, use, retention, and disposal of information in daily business processing.

GTAG-16—Data Analysis Technologies: This guide shows internal auditors how to incorporate data analysis through adequate planning, why data analysis is significant to organizations, how to provide assurance more efficiently with the use of data analysis technologies, become familiar with the challenges and risks that are faced when implementing data analysis technologies, and an overview of how to recognize opportunities, trends, and advantages of making use of data analysis technologies. It also includes an example of the application of data analytics in a procurement function to show how move beyond traditional manual auditing.

GTAG-17—Auditing IT Governance: This guide covers the elements of governance needed to ensure IT supports the strategies and objectives of the organization and how to verify they are in place and working effectively. It describes the components of effective governance and performance frameworks (e.g., balanced scorecards, maturity models, and quality systems). It includes sample controls that address IT governance risks and are essential to develop an appropriate scope, define audit objectives, prepare comprehensive audit programs, evaluate risks and controls, and perform effective verification, testing, and reporting.

GTAG (no number)—Auditing Smart Devices: An Internal Auditor's Guide to Understanding and Auditing Smart Devices: This guide helps internal auditors identify the risks related to smart devices and ways to provide assurance that the controls and governance mechanism in place are adequate to mitigate those risks. Organizations and their workers have embraced smart devices, but there is a need to balance the risks and opportunities that these devices create. This GTAG provides insights that allow internal auditors to better understand the technology behind smart devices.

GTAG (no number)—Assessing Cybersecurity Risk: Roles of the Three Lines of Defense: This guide reviews the role of internal audit in cybersecurity by discussing threats, emerging risks, and ways to assess management's response capabilities. All three lines of defense are confronted by cyber threats affecting computers, networks, programs, applications, portable devices, data, and social media.

GTAG (no number)—Understanding and Auditing Big Data. This guide helps internal auditors understand and review the consolidation and consumption of large volumes of structured and unstructured data, unique analytics techniques, and the delivery of reports. It provides guidance to effectively evaluate, assess risks, and advise management during the planning and implementation of big data programs to design plans that include the necessary controls to ensure the success of the program from a strategic, operational, and security perspective. This GTAG includes concepts to help internal auditors identify the different components of a big data program, including strategic objectives, success criteria, governance, and operational processes, technology, tools, and other resources. It also helps to understand how to align internal audit activities in support of the organization's big data initiatives. Lastly, it also includes a framework of key risks, challenges, and examples of controls that should be considered when planning audits of big data.

Summary

1. The IIA has published almost twenty Global Technology Audit Guides (GTAGs) to provide additional guidance for internal auditors.
2. These GTAGs cover risks, controls, change and patch management, continuous auditing, privacy, outsourcing, access, business continuity management, IT projects, fraud, information and cyber security, data analysis, IT governance, big data, and auditing smart devices.
3. Internal auditors can use the GTAGs to improve their review of information technology and information security topics.

Chapter 61

Histograms

Histograms show the distribution of a continuous variable in a diagram similar to a bar graph. They show the distribution of values over a range. The terms used to describe the patterns (or shapes) of histograms are as follows: Symmetric, skewed left, skewed right, bimodal, or multimodal.

Histograms can be useful when analyzing data to better understand its distribution or "fluidity." Examples include number of calls received in a call center, requests for technical support, customers requesting service, cars going through a toll plaza or airplanes landing or taking off from an airport over a time period (e.g., workday). One of the benefits of this analysis is that the internal auditor can compare the information on the histogram with other attributes like the number of people working during the time period, or the number of errors based on the time period when they occurred. This way low-staffing situations causing delays or errors can be pinpointed, or errors caused by particular operators who may lack necessary training. This information can enhance root cause analysis significantly.

The following are the steps to prepare a histogram:

1. Calculate the range (maximum—minimum value)
2. Divide the range of values into a series of intervals
3. Count how many values fall into each interval. Make sure each interval (or bin) is consecutive and adjacent (not overlapping). They are generally of equal size.
4. Create a rectangle over each interval (bin) where the height represents the frequency (how many items) are in each interval.

Histograms are similar to bar charts and are sometimes confused with them. However, bar charts use categorical data and have gaps between the rectangles. Histograms, on the other hand, use continuous data and consequently there are no gaps between the rectangles.

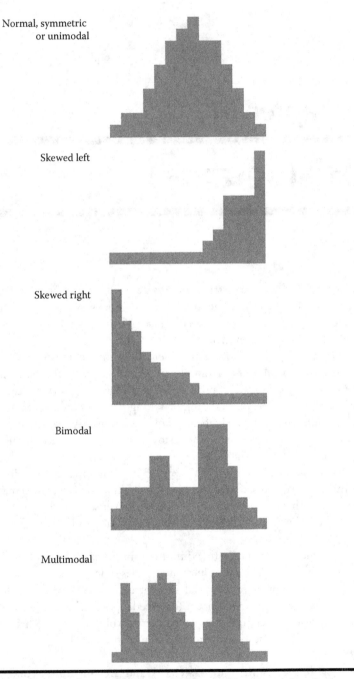

Figure 61.1 Histogram shapes. (*Operational Auditing: Principles and Techniques for a Changing World* by Hernan Murdock.)

Summary

1. Histograms can be used for root cause analysis and is one of the essential quality control tools.
2. Internal auditors can use histograms to better understand the distribution of continuous data, and when paired with other variables and information can help to pinpoint anomalies.
3. Since histograms are a visual tool, it facilitates the analysis of the data, encourages discussion with process owners, and can convey important points more easily than text-heavy approaches.

Chapter 62

IT Application and General Computer Controls (GCC)

Today's computer systems are seen less as collateral to the organization's success but rather as essential to the achievement of the business' goals and objectives. However, poor controls within the IT infrastructure may negatively affect the reliability of application controls across many systems causing issues that affect multiple stakeholders. Key IT infrastructure areas need to be reviewed to ensure appropriate levels of controls are in place and working as intended. In general, IT general controls are encompassing controls designed to cover the entire organizations' IT infrastructure, as opposed to specific applications. They help ensure confidentiality, integrity and availability.

Two important types of controls that must be reviewed are business application controls and IT general controls (also often referred to as IT infrastructure controls). An organization cannot rely on application controls without having assurance that the IT general controls are also effective (Table 62.1).

Business applications are the responsibility of business process owners and focus on transactions (e.g., input, process, outputs). The objectives for these types of applications are data accuracy, completeness, and validity of information.

Business application systems support areas familiar to most business internal auditors, such as: Accounts Payable (AP), Accounts Receivable (AR), Customer Resource Management systems (CRM), Enterprise Resource Planning systems (ERP), the General Ledger (GL), Groupware (e.g., Lotus Notes/Electronic Workpapers), Human

Table 62.1   IT General and Business Process Controls

IT general controls	Access controls
	Segregation of duties
	Contingency planning
	Security management
	Configuration management
Business process application controls	Business process controls
	Interfaces
	Data management systems

Source: Adapted from the *Federal Information System Controls Audit Manual (FISCAM).*

Resources (HR), Payroll, Inventory Systems, Material Requirement Planning (MRP) systems, and end user computing (e.g., Spreadsheets).

General computer controls (GCCs) are the responsibility of IT management and focus on the hardware, software, networks and data within them. Control objectives include confidentiality, integrity, and availability. The systems covered under GCCs are not always readily familiar to business auditors, but they are often used by, or are impacted by, these systems. Examples include database management systems (DBMS), operating system software, system administration, utility software, job scheduling systems, security software, firewalls, and intrusion detection systems.

In terms of general business process risks and controls, an effective approach is to consider them in terms of completeness, accuracy, validity, confidentiality, and availability of the systems and the data. The first three relate to and can be summarized as referring to integrity. Without those five attributes, computer systems would not be able to provide the support the business needs. To address those risk categories, there are several controls that ensure the proper functioning of the systems and mitigation of risks:

Completeness Controls

They provide reasonable assurance that all transactions that occurred are entered into the system, are accepted for processing, are processed only once by the system, and are properly included in output. Common completeness controls are batch totals, sequence checking, matching, duplicate checking, reconciliations, control totals and exception reporting.

Accuracy Controls

They provide reasonable assurance that transactions are recorded properly and timely (in the proper period), with the correct amounts, and data are processed accurately producing reliable results and accurate output. Accuracy controls include edit checks (e.g., validation, reasonableness checks, dependency checks, existence checks, format checks, mathematical accuracy, range checks), batch totals, and check digit verification.

Validity Controls

They provide reasonable assurance that all recorded transactions occurred, that they relate to the organization, and were approved properly according to management's authorization. A transaction is valid when it has been authorized and when the master data relating to that transaction is reliable. In the case of a vendor payment, it includes the name of the vendor, the bank name and account, the amount, and other details from the vendor master file. Validity controls include the verification of authenticity, such as one-for-one checking and matching.

Confidentiality Controls

They provide reasonable assurance that application data and reports, and other output are protected against unauthorized access. Confidentiality controls include restricted physical and logical access to sensitive business process applications, data files, transactions, outputs and requisite segregation of duties. It also includes restricted access to data reporting and extraction tools.

Availability Controls

They provide reasonable assurance that application data and reports and other relevant business information are readily available to users when needed. Availability controls are typically addressed in application controls such as contingency planning.

In general, the overarching question is Are there appropriate controls in place to prevent or detect, and correct errors in the processing of application transactions? If we follow a process approach (data input, processing and output), we can trace the flow of information and apply the concept of risks and controls to them.

Input

The goal is to ensure the accuracy of data entering an application. A single input control is usually not enough to ensure the accuracy of data being entered, instead, what is needed is a combination of input controls. For example, to ensure completeness and accuracy of input, data field edit checks and format checks are put in place. These work by checking individual fields to validate the correct entry of data. This often includes checks to confirm they contain appropriate alphabetic or numeric entries.

For completeness, a control may consist of checking to make sure all necessary fields have appropriate information entered. For example, the invoice number field is complete and does not contain any blanks.

The duplicate check is designed to prevent (or determine) if an entry has been made multiple times. A common example relates to the problem of paying an invoice multiple times, so with a duplicate check an invoice cannot be entered twice in the system for payment.

File or database matching is done to make sure that the data entered is matched to an existing record in a file or database. To illustrate this condition, consider a user who enters a vendor master number resulting in that vendor's master record being retrieved. Note that this check will only validate that the vendor master exists for the entered vendor number, but it might be the vendor number for the wrong vendor.

The key verification or duplicate entry check works by having the information entered twice, either by the same person or by two different people. If both entries are the same there is assurance that the information was entered correctly. For example, consider a scenario where changes to an employee's weekly pay amount are entered twice to make sure it is entered correctly. While this is an effective control, it is not used frequently due to the associated expense.

The limit or range check is used to make sure that data entered falls within predetermined values considered acceptable. For example, invoice values must be between $10 and $5,000. Invoices outside the predetermined values are rejected.

The purpose of logical relationship checks is to make sure that contents of two or more fields are related logically. For example, in a file recording information related to life insurance policy claims, the date of death is after the date of birth.

Mathematical Accuracy checks verify the accuracy of calculations. For example, the amount due on an invoice is based on the quantity and price.

Reasonableness checks are somewhat similar to logical and range checks, but they operate on a slightly different premise. Reasonableness checks examine the data entered to determine if it falls within a predetermined "reasonable" range of values. For example, at an electric utility, such check could be applied to customers' monthly electric utility usage when it exceeds the average monthly usage by 100 percent. Such transactions are highlighted for follow-up to determine if the transaction is correct or if the amount entered contained an error.

Validity checks verify that the data entered satisfy a predetermined criterion. For example, in the case of employee benefits files, a field designating a person's gender must be "F" or "M." All other values are rejected.

One to one (1:1) checking operate by making sure that individual documents agree with a detailed listing of documents processed in the application. For example, in an Accounts Payable unit, users verify that each invoice processed is correct by matching each hardcopy invoice with the electronic invoice within the application.

Data Entry Overrides allow managers (or other selected few individuals) to override or bypass data validation and editing checks in a limited number of acceptable circumstances. For example, a data entry clerk in the sales or marketing department tries, but is not permitted, to enter a lower price for a product on a customer's order. This clerk is not allowed to override that field level check, but the manager could be. Note: A good practice is to make sure that all overrides are automatically logged, as in some business areas it is a common prelude to abuse or fraud.

Processing

The objective of processing controls is to make sure that only authorized transactions are accepted by the application system, they are accurately processed with valid business rules, are processed completely, are available for authorized users in accordance with business requirements, and are processed effectively and efficiently.

Some of the controls internal auditors should be aware of are as follows:

Duplicate Processing controls determine if the entry has already been processed. For example, in a payroll processing unit, weekly hours worked being processed is rejected because it has already been paid.

Exception Reporting generate exception reports upon situations that appear to be incorrect. This may occur in an Accounts Payable (AP) unit when an invoice is due to be paid for product that was never received by the organization.

Edit Checks provide assurance during processing activities to verify the accuracy and completeness of the data. Editing checks, which were also mentioned in the input controls section, can also function as processing controls if they operate during the processing phase of the application flow. For example, as data passes from one program to another, fields are checked to confirm accurate and complete data exists.

File Reconciliations or Run-to-Run Balancing reconcile file totals from start-to-finish and run-to-run to ensure records were not lost along the way. This control can be generated and reconciled automatically by the application. It can also be used to reconcile data flow between application phases to ensure that data is not lost during processing. This run-to-run balancing check could be applied in a production environment whereby Thursday's start-of-day file totals are the same as Wednesday's end-of-day file totals.

Limits for System Calculations are validations that calculate values to make sure they do not exceed a predetermined limit. For example, in a manufacturing environment the system calculates monthly inventory reorder quantities and flags amounts that exceed an annual inventory usage quantity.

Programmed Balancing Controls operate by validating that all of the information entered was processed correctly by balancing the number of records or control totals at the end of each stage of processing. In an AP unit, the same numbers of invoices entered were paid and the total dollar amount paid is equal to the sum of the invoice dollar values entered.

Programmed Procedures consist of programmed code to satisfy the intended business objectives of the application. Consider for example an AP application system that contains automated controls to pay vendor invoices based on a three-way match of the following items: (1) Invoice (e.g., quantity, price), (2) Purchase order (e.g., quantity, price), and (3) Goods Received (e.g., quantity, date received)

Reasonableness Verification are applied during each phase of processing. The processed values are compared with predetermined values considered "reasonable" to validate the accuracy of the processing. This is similar to the reasonableness check in the input section. For example, a customer's monthly electric utility usage exceeds the average monthly usage by 100 percent. The transaction is highlighted for follow-up to validate the accuracy of the value calculated.

Output

Output controls are used to provide reasonable assurance that transaction data is complete, accurate, valid, and confidential. They also help to make sure that the correct and timely distribution of output is produced. Output can be in the form of hardcopy printouts, information for online viewing, updates for files and databases, or as interfaces to other systems.

Output should be delivered to the appropriate authorized end user, it should be restricted from unauthorized access, and there should be policies providing guidance related to backup schedules for output data and record retention.

Some of the controls include:

Balancing and reconciliation of output, which should be done back to control totals, general ledger or other reliable information to verify their accuracy.

Output error handling consisting of written procedures for handling output errors. This should include the name of responsible individuals who resolve the errors.

Controls related to sensitive and critical documents to make sure they are stored securely, retained for an appropriate amount of time, and disposed or destroyed appropriately. These controls need to apply to both hardcopy and electronic records and may require the involvement of legal counsel to make sure record retention policies and guidelines comply with legal, tax, regulatory and other government requirements.

The disposal of output should address the secure removal of hardware (e.g., desktops, laptops, tablets, hard drives, phones), electronic information (e.g., erasure) and hardcopies (e.g., shredding). When disposal is performed by a third party, the vendor should be bonded and the processes checked to make sure it is reliable.

With regards to interfaces, internal auditors generally verify that all input is processed completely by checking data validation and reconciliation from the receiving system perspective. Often this involves checking the timeliness, accuracy, and completeness of the information between applications and other feeder and receiving systems. These interface controls are typically automated, but could also be performed manually, triggered by a set schedule or driven by specific events.

Spreadsheets

Spreadsheets are widely used and very common tools that organizations depend on. They are prone to input errors, such as wrong data, inaccurate referencing to other cells or mistakes made while cutting and pasting information. There may also be logic errors caused by inappropriate formulas created or the wrong use of macros. Since some spreadsheets depend on data from other software applications, it can also succumb to interface errors. Other errors include the wrong definition of cell ranges, inaccurately referenced cells or improperly linked spreadsheets and workbooks.

Many organizations have created an inventory of key spreadsheets that support significant financial or operational processes. This effort began for most companies as a result of the Sarbanes–Oxley Act of 2002, which focuses on the internal controls over financial reporting. Since many organizations rely on spreadsheets as part of their financial reporting cycle, spreadsheets were included in the scope for review. Two common spreadsheet controls relate to access (e.g., passwords and server controls) and version (e.g., naming conventions and retention of previous versions) controls.

Logical Security Controls

They focus on the confidentiality, integrity, and availability of systems and data. Related controls include authentication controls to prevent user accounts from being compromised and access to files restricted to appropriate users. Patches and system updates should be applied promptly and anti-virus software should be installed and up-to-date. Sensitive data should be encrypted.*

---

* This section provides an overview of IT/IS basic risks and controls. This topic is quite extensive. A one-stop, fairly comprehensive review of this subject is provided in the Federal Information System Controls Audit Manual (FISCAM) available at https://www.gao.gov/assets/80/77142.pdf.

Sample Tests

1. Compare password controls to make sure their length, complexity, and expiration protocols are consistent with organizational requirements and best practices.
2. Verify that sensitive information is not shared inappropriately.
3. Examine the process to apply patches and updates to operating systems, databases and applications to make sure they are applied timely to address known vulnerabilities.
4. Verify that anti-virus settings are up-to-date and they are scanning drives regularly.
5. Verify that sensitive data is encrypted when at rest (e.g., in hard drives) or in motion (e.g., during transmission from network to network or across the internet).
6. Perform security scans to identify services that may be vulnerable.
7. Verify that user system activity is identifiable.
8. Verify that user access requests, changes, and removals are documented and approved prior to execution.
9. Verify that the access of terminated users is removed promptly.
10. Verify that access rights are assigned based on the users' job duties and role, and updated promptly when those duties change. This includes administrator-level accounts.
11. Verify that remote access occurs using only secure protocols.
12. Perform a walkthrough to verify that physical security and environmental controls protect the data center, server rooms, network closets, and other controlled areas from unauthorized access, theft, damage or environmental hazards (e.g., excessive heat, fire, humidity) through appropriate fire suppression systems, smoke detectors, water sensors, and other devices.
13. Verify protection from power surges, that uninterruptable power supply (UPS) and backup power generators are available in the event of power disruptions, that their configuration will provide continuous computer service, and the duration of power generation in the event of prolonged outages.
14. Determine if an up-to-date business continuity and disaster recovery plan (BC/DR) is in place and if testing includes a plan review (i.e., document review), tabletop exercises (i.e., step-by-step walkthrough of plan activities) and simulation (e.g., using recovery sites, backup systems, alternate site deployment to restart systems and business functions, and running scenarios).
15. Examine visitor and maintenance logs of controlled areas.

Summary

1. IT Application and General Controls are essential to protect the organization's computer systems, networks, and related technologies. Internal auditors

are expected to review the hardware, software, networks, and other aspects of the organization's information technology and security.

2. Controls protect data input, processing and output to ensure availability, reliability, confidentiality, and integrity. They also protect hardware from theft and damage.

3. Business continuity and disaster recovery plans reduce the likelihood that events will disrupt operating activities.

Chapter 63

Information Systems Audit and Controls Association (ISACA)

While the Institute of Internal Auditors (IIA) represents the largest membership association of internal auditors, there are other specialized organizations with a strong reputation that provide thought leadership, promote best practices, and offer recognized certification credentials that internal auditors may also join. One such organization is the Information Systems Audit and Controls Association (ISACA). Founded in 1969, it was established to bring together Information Technology (IT) auditors. ISACA currently has more than 100,000 members in over 180 countries. It is a global association with more than 190 chapters in more than 75 countries.

ISACA identified the need for a control framework tailored for the special needs of IT and in 1996 published the Control Objectives for Information and Related Technologies (COBIT) framework. ISACA provides continuing education and offers several IT certifications:

CISA: Certified Information Systems Auditor. The CISA designation is a globally recognized certification for information systems audit control, assurance, and security professionals. It is arguably the most recognizable certification for IT auditors, focusing on the assessment of vulnerabilities, reporting on compliance, and IT controls within organizations.

CISM: Certified Information Security Manager. The CISM certification focuses on information security management. It is designed for individuals who manage, design, oversee, and assess an organization's information security.

CGEIT: Certified in the Governance of Enterprise IT. This certification focuses on enterprise IT governance principles and practices.

CRISC: Certified in Risk and Information Systems Control. Achieving the CRISC certification requires an understanding of the impact of IT risk and how it relates to organizations.*

Summary

1. The Information Systems Audit and Controls Association (ISACA) provides guidance and thought leadership on IT risks and controls.
2. There are several certifications that internal auditors often find useful to advance their knowledge and careers, including CISA, CISM, CGEIT, and CRISC
3. ISACA created COBIT, which provides a widely used framework for IT governance and management.

---

* Detailed information about the Information Systems Audit and Control Association (ISACA), their publications, certification, and membership, visit www.isaca.org/pages/default.aspx.

Chapter 64

Institute of Internal Auditors (IIA)

The Institute of Internal Auditors (IIA) was established in 1941 and serves as the professional association setting the practices, advocating for, and largest educator of internal auditors worldwide. Its mission is to provide leadership:

- Advocating and promoting the value of internal auditing
- Setting performance standards and related guidance, and developing best practices for internal auditors
- Providing professional education and development
- Managing certification programs
- Conducting research on internal auditing, governance, risk, control and compliance-related topics, and disseminating the results to practitioners and stakeholders
- Serving as a link, bringing together internal auditors worldwide to share information, practices, and experiences

The IIA sets the definition of internal auditing, the Code of Ethics (COE) guidance for practitioners, the *Standards* defining its practice, and manages several certifications.

The IIA defines internal auditing as follows:

> Internal auditing is an independent, objective assurance and consulting activity designed to add value and improve an organization's operations. It helps an organization accomplish its objectives by bringing a systematic, disciplined approach to evaluate and improve the effectiveness of risk management, control, and governance processes.

The COE has four principles that internal auditors are expected to uphold:

1. Integrity: The integrity of internal auditors establishes trust and thus provides the basis for reliance on their judgment. Internal auditors must perform their work with honesty, diligence, and responsibility, observe the law, and make disclosures as legally expected of them. They should abstain from knowingly be a party to any illegal act, or engage in actions that will discredit the profession.
2. Objectivity: Internal auditors must exhibit the highest level of professional objectivity in gathering, evaluating, and communicating information about the activities and processes being examined. They must make a balanced assessment of all the relevant circumstances and should not be unduly influenced by their own interests or by others in forming judgments. Internal auditors must not participate in activities or relationships, or accept anything, that may limit, or appear to limit, their unbiased assessments. They must disclose all material facts known to them, including those that if not disclosed, may distort the reporting of activities being examined.
3. Confidentiality: Internal auditors must respect the value and ownership of information they receive and must not disclose information without appropriate authority unless there is a legal or professional obligation to do so. Consequently, internal auditors must be prudent in the protection and use of information obtained while performing their duties and must not use information for any personal gain or in any other manner that would be unlawful or to the detriment of the legitimate and ethical objectives of the organization
4. Competency: Internal auditors apply the knowledge, skills, and experience needed in the performance of internal audit services. Therefore, they must engage only in those services for which they have the requisite skills, knowledge, and experience. Internal audits must be performed in accordance with the *Standards* and continually improve their proficiency, effectiveness, and the quality of their work.

To do this, the IIA provides internal auditors with mandatory and recommended guidance.

Mandatory Guidance

- Core Principles for the Professional Practice of Internal Auditing
  - Demonstrate integrity, competence, and due professional care
  - Be objective and independent, therefore free from undue influence
  - Align with the strategies, objectives, and risks of the organization
  - Be appropriately positioned, resourced, and communicate effectively

- Demonstrate quality and promote self and organizational improvement
- Provide risk-based assurance
- Be insightful, proactive, and future-focused
■ The Definition of Internal Auditing
■ The COE
■ The International Standards for the Professional Practice of Internal Auditing (*Standards*)

Recommended Guidance

■ Implementation guidance to assist internal auditors in applying the *Standards*
■ Supplemental guidance (i.e., Practice Guides), which provide detailed processes and procedures

Certifications

The IIA provides several certifications for internal auditors. Each certification program has its own unique and specific exam and education eligibility requirements that a candidate must meet. While the CIA is a broad certification, the others are specialized.

CIA: Certified Internal Auditor (CIA). The premier designation for the profession

CGAP: Certified Government Auditing Professional. Focuses on public sector auditors and the unique characteristics of their work, including budget constraints, political and public pressures.

CFSA: Certified Financial Services Auditor. Specializes in auditors working in banking, lending, and investing service organizations, including insurance companies, security and commodity services, credit agencies, and financial services regulatory agencies.

CCSA: Certification in Control Self-Assessment. This certification focuses on control self-assessment fundamentals, processes, and related topics such as risk, controls, and business objectives.

CRMA: Certification in Risk Management Assurance. This certification emphasizes the key elements to provide advice and assurance on risk management to audit committees and executive management.

CPEA: Certified Professional Environmental Auditor. This credential demonstrates the holder's understanding of the changing environmental, health & safety regulatory environment.

CPSA: Certified Process Safety Auditor. This certification demonstrates the individuals' understanding of process safety elements and regulations for all industries with processes that involve explosive materials.

Internal Audit Foundation

The IIA Foundation, formerly known as the IIA Research Foundation (IIARF), provides research, knowledge, and insight into the profession to help practitioners, students, academics, and others advance in their careers and become trusted advisors, thought leaders, and change agents. It provides and facilitates research, supports students, and academics through grants, awards, and an Audit Career Center. It also has a bookstore that publishes and sells an extensive collection of books, guides, research reports, and similar materials.

In addition to the *Standards*, Guidance, COE, and other related materials, the IIA also provides direction, certification, and qualified individuals who can assist organizations comply with Standard 1300-Quality Assurance and Improvement Program. Other services provided include the Chief Audit Executive Resources Center, compensation studies, IA (previously Internal Auditor) magazine, and Pulse of Internal Audit publications.*

Summary

1. The Institute of Internal Auditors (IIA) provides guidance and thought leadership on internal auditing methodology.
2. There are several certifications that internal auditors often find useful to advance their knowledge and careers: CIA, CGAP, CFSA, CCSA, CRMA, CPEA, and CPSA.
3. The IIA publishes IA magazine and books through the IIA Foundation, runs a bookstore, and several programs on internal audit leadership.

---

* For additional information regarding the Institue of Internal Auditors (IIA), certification, its services and publications, see https://na.theiia.org/Pages/IIAHome.aspx.

Chapter 65

Interviewing

A key aspect of internal auditing is learning how business programs and processes are designed and operating. The process of learning about the area being reviewed is essential for the internal auditor to know what needs to be examined. Interviews are a widely used, and very useful tool to help internal auditors acquire that knowledge.

Interviewing is often done 1-on-1 between an auditor and an audit client. I prefer to think about interviews as "chatting with the client" rather than an interview, which can appear overly formal, one-directional (one person asks the questions, the other answers them), and even threatening to some. While it doesn't rise to the same level as an interrogation, which are reserved for fraud investigations and similar forensic activities, an interview can cause auditees to become unnecessarily nervous.

By embracing an approach reminiscent of conversing with the client, the internal auditor can build a more relaxed environment to learn, get accurate information, and be better prepared to conduct the review.

Interview preparation often entails making a list of questions to guide the discussion and to make sure that important points are addressed during the meeting. While preparing such a list is very helpful, internal auditors should be careful not to adhere too rigidly to the list. Internal auditors should be flexible during the interview and adapt as necessary. The need to "go off script" may occur due to unexpected answers or the way the interviewee responds. If the interviewee appears overly nervous, deflects to avoid answering the question, or provides inconsistent answers, the internal auditor should probe further to gain clarity and obtain complete and accurate information.

Prefacing

A common challenge new auditors experience is the difficulty of interviewing clients with expertise in their work area when the auditor is not as familiar with the intricacies of the area being reviewed. In those cases, prefacing the question could be an effective technique to demonstrate that the auditor is qualified and informed, and the question has a purpose. For example, a typical early-stage question is "Does your department have procedures documentation?" This serves multiple purposes, including finding out if they have them (because they should), and as a prelude to another question, "When were they last reviewed and re-certified?" Or "Great, may I have a copy?" But if the first question is "Do you have procedures documentation?" The responder may mentally start wondering how productive the meeting will be, if the internal auditor has prepared for the meeting and the audit, and how could someone so seemingly unprepared review, question, critique, and write audit reports that could get me in trouble with the boss?

So, prefacing can help. In the scenario above, a better question might be "There are units we have audited before without up-to-date procedures documentation and it became a problem for them when a key employee left. As they tried to train the replacement, they found it was very difficult because they had no procedures documentation. May I take a look at your procedures documentation?"

Open vs. Close-Ended Questions

There are many factors that determine the effectiveness of questions, including content, tone, and delivery (e.g., sequence). Another very important element is format (open vs. closed). Closed questions are generally phrased so the responder gives a "yes" or "no" answer, but it could also be a fact, name, location, address, date, or another specific answer. They are generally simple and straightforward, and they don't encourage elaboration or detailed answers. In fact, they discourage detail.

> How many people have access to the cash room?
> Did you perform cycle counts last month?
> Do you have a key fob token?
> Are the doors to the computer room locked?

An examination of the questions shows that for each of them the answer could be one or a few words. While some people will still give detailed answers whether you want them to or not regardless of the way the question is asked, others will stick to the question and not be as forthcoming. When working with someone who is reluctant to talk, a closed-ended question will result in a brief answer.

Another potential shortcoming of closed questions is that they could allow the person to tell an untruth by guessing what the correct, or expected, answer is.

Closed questions are not bad, they just need to be understood and used appropriately. They are appropriate when all that is needed is a specific fact, when due to time constraints you need to move things along, or you want to corroborate a piece of information. If the person is monopolizing the conversation or drifting into unrelated topics, asking a closed question can change the meeting dynamics politely, so the person is re-directed to the topic you need to discuss without telling them outright that what they are discussing is irrelevant, which could be interpreted as offensive, rude, and disrespectful.

In general, the use of closed questions should be driven by your intent, not by accident.

Open questions elicit a more detailed response. It encourages the person answering the question to elaborate and provide detailed information. Compare the following questions to the ones above.

Who are the people with access to the cash room?
Could you please walk me through the cycle-counting procedures?
How many people use the key fob token?
How do you prevent unauthorized individuals from accessing the computer room?

These questions are better because they encourage the person to give an answer that goes beyond a simple "yes" or "no." If only a limited number of people should have access, then when the audit client mentions multiple names the auditor would discover that more people than necessary have access, but also who those additional people are. If cycle-counting is being performed, it is more informative to understand *how* they do them, rather than *whether* they do them. It is fairly easy for someone to say they lock the doors at 5:00 PM, but that is only part of a broader objective of securing facilities during and after business hours.

A simple way to rephrase closed questions is to start them with the Five Ws: who, what, when, where, why:

Who is (or was or did) ...
What is (or was or did) ...
When is (or was or did) ...
Where is (or was or did) ...
Why is (or was or did) ...
Another effective question is "Please describe ..."

Don't Give Them the Answer

Internal auditors should be careful not to offer the auditee an answer when asking a question. In effect, it leads the responder and could result in getting faulty answers. For example:

Don't ask: Who has access to the cash room, Brian and Jeff?
Better to ask: Who are the workers with access to the cash room?

Don't ask: Is access restricted to the warehouse after 5:00 PM?
Better to ask: What are the times that the warehouse is accessible?

Asking questions poorly, like the "don't ask" examples shown above, will likely result in unwanted responses because it suggests to the client what the expected or desirable answer is, and what the auditor believes, expects, or knows. It can also tell the other person what the auditor doesn't know, so in the first question above, if Brian and Jeff have access, but also a third person who the auditors don't know (or shouldn't know about in their mind) then the person can control the disclosure of that information and potentially confirm the incomplete information.

A similar dynamic can occur if asking about a control activity like a reconciliation. Do you perform bank reconciliations? The person is likely to answer "yes," even though they do them in three's, right before the quarterly financial statement review. The question should probe about the reconciliations being performed monthly and if reconciling items are addressed immediately as well.

Summary

1. When the objective is to get details, open-ended questions are better. Close questions are useful to obtain or confirm a specific fact, figure, date, name, and location.
2. Think of interviews as conversations with audit clients, but conduct the interview strategically and logically, asking well-placed questions, managing the time effectively, and always showing respect and interest.
3. Internal auditors should know why they ask their questions, remember the importance of body language and allow the audit client ample time to elaborate on their answers.

Chapter 66

Key Performance Indicators (KPI) and Key Risk Indicators (KRI)

Information drives modern organizations. It is imperative that metrics be put in place that give management objective information about the progress made toward the achievement of organizational goals and objectives. Consequently, having quantitative and qualitative data goes a long way toward providing proper oversight and timely correction regarding performance.

Key Performance Indicators are measurable values that show how effectively an organization is achieving key objectives. They are metrics that evaluate the success of an organization, program, or process. They facilitate management by providing a scorecard showing how well the strategy and the related goals are being achieved. With this information the organization can manage, control and make sure it is achieving the desired results. Examples include sales, number of employees, number of product shipments, number of interviews, sales calls, and meetings held. With this information, management and employees can gauge their efforts toward various goals.

Key Risk Indicators are also metrics and constitute a subset of KPIs. For example, while sales matter a great deal to organizations, getting paid on the amount of those sales is critical. Any organization that fails to collect on its Accounts Receivable (AR) will encounter serious financial hardship. So, while sales are very good KPIs, AR delinquent balances and AR write-offs are essential KRIs to determine how successful those sales really were. Similarly, the number of product shipments is a very good KPI, but what if those shipments are incomplete, made to incorrect addresses, or are shipped late and miss the due-date agreed upon with the client? So, shipment accuracy, completeness, and timeliness are necessary KRIs to obtain better visibility into the effectiveness of that process.

KPIs and KRIs require data to be collected, evaluated, assessed, and shared. So poor data quality is a problem that needs to be examined and addressed. Likewise, narrowly collecting and analyzing the data, without sharing the information with others who can take corrective action or otherwise benefit from the information needs to be addressed.

Organizations don't need many KPIs or KRIs. As the name suggests, only the key ones are required. Therefore, the organization should carefully select, report, and manage those chosen. The selection of KPIs begins with the business objectives and focus not only on what the goals are, but on how (i.e., discrete steps) those goals take the organization to its destination. Consistent with the definition of "key," it is best to limit the number to less than 10, preferably 5 or 6. A dashboard can be treated similarly to the one on automobiles, where the dashboard is used to monitor the major activities and functions at a glance using the instrument panel.

The presentation of the data is also very important. Long text with embedded figures is not the most effective way of handling KPIs and KRIs. Tables are better, but key figures could be hidden and escape scrutiny when they are embedded in large tables. So increasingly organizations develop dashboards that provide progress reports using visual tools to present the information. Dashboards are often displayed on a webpage that is linked to a database, so the reports can be updated constantly. In a manufacturing organization a dashboard will focus on productivity metrics, like number of parts made and the number of errors or failed quality inspections per day. In a human resources unit, a dashboard may show the number of full and part-time employees, number of open positions, number of interviews conducted, cost per recruit, and turnover figures.

Line Charts, Pie Charts, and Bar Charts are typically very helpful, especially when they are accompanied by color and other visual cues that highlight anomalies and show patterns and proximity to concerning boundaries. This snapshot view using visual presentation of data allows the organization to:

- Measure efficiencies and inefficiencies
- Identify and correct negative trends
- Align strategies and organizational goals
- Save time compared to running multiple reports
- Have visibility of all major programs, processes, and units immediately

Metrics can improve the quality of risk oversight, enhanced by having a dynamic risk assessment that feeds timely information into the risk management program—but they depend on data. Boards are increasing their emphasis on risk and looking beyond financial risks. They are also providing oversight over strategic, legal and regulatory compliance, IT, logical and physical security (including privacy), and fraud risks. After all, primary oversight over risks rests with the board. Given the multitude of data points, KRIs can be very valuable helping to identify the metrics of importance.

The construction of KPIs should always begin with a clear understanding of the desired business goals, outcomes, and results. However, simply stating the goal and measuring sales (the "what"), for example, may yield limited results. Instead, appropriate metrics may include details about progress (the "how"). For example: sales cycle, lead generation, and repeat business.

These metrics can then be supplemented with boundaries, so limits can be placed to indicate thresholds. In that case:

- *Sales cycle* may be measured against a goal to reduce the sales cycle by 50 percent (i.e., sell faster!)
- *Lead generation* may have a goal of generating 50 percent more leads (i.e., larger pool of potential buyers!)
- *Repeat business* could have a goal of having existing customers buy an additional 25 percent or more.

In effect, knowing what you want to accomplish and monitoring the key steps to get you there.

Wishing the data is not enough. We need to get it, so the next step is to find the source of the data and also determine how frequently to generate these figures. In some organizations the dashboard can be updated daily or weekly. Some with ready access to real time data can generate dashboards at any time. Others with more manual processes may have two, three or four-week cycles. The challenge is that the longer the interval between updates, the likelihood of deviation, and their magnitude increases because by the time the report is produced, some of the KPIs/KRIs could have drifted substantially.

When setting the goals to measure progress, it is important to make sure these are realistic. Otherwise, the goals are potentially unachievable, or those providing the information may falsify the information in their efforts to conceal their failure. This was one of the contributing issues at the Veteran Affairs (VA) Hospital in Phoenix, AZ, where at least 35 veterans died while waiting for care. Even after the delays turned into a scandal, a scheduling employee at the Phoenix VA Health Care System shared that she was the keeper of a "secret list" of veterans who were forced to wait for months to receive medical care. She also accused others of altering records after the scandal broke to try to hide the deaths of at least seven veterans awaiting care.*

---

* For additional information about the Veterans Affairs (VA) Hospital scandal, see www.nbcnews. com/storyline/va-hospital-scandal and www.usatoday.com/story/news/usanow/2014/06/23/ phoenix-va-whistleblower/11297069/.

Finally, a comparison point is helpful to assess progress on each KPI/KRI. This can be the previous year, quarter, week, or month. Having owners for each KPI/KRI is also helpful so if deviations from expected results emerge, accountabilities are established and it is clear who should be contacted to research, explain, and resolve these deviations.

Summary

1. Metrics should be developed carefully, by those who know the organization well, and select those indicators that will provide hindsight, insight, and foresight.
2. KPIs measure production and outputs. KRIs measure the underlying risks and the deviations of key attributes that impact the achievement of business objectives.
3. KPIs and KRIs require data, so the organization needs sufficient, usable, reliable, and timely data that is distributed to individuals who are responsible for the achievement of objectives and can correct deviations timely.

Chapter 67

Lean Six Sigma

Six Sigma was developed at Motorola in the 1980s. It is a strategic business initiative designed to identify sources of error and determine how best to eliminate them. It has a long history based on process improvement and has influenced, and been influenced, by tools and techniques from Total Quality Management (TQM), Total Quality Control (TQC), Continuous Quality Improvement (CQI), and others. It leverages the principles found in programs like four Ps (People/Partners, Process, Problem Solving and Performance), PDCA (Plan, Do, Check, Act) and five S (Sort, Straighten, Shine, Standardize, Sustain). The benefits of Six Sigma are to minimize errors, eliminate hidden inventory, free up floor space by eliminating clutter, improve the flow of materials, reduce walk and transportation time, and eliminate unnecessary items for reuse somewhere else.

It uses management tools and methodologies to reduce variation, errors, and increase speed. It is a business process that allows companies to drastically improve their bottom line by designing and monitoring everyday business activities in ways that minimize waste and resources while increasing satisfaction. The main objective is to identify and eliminate inconsistencies, errors, and defects by emphasizing consistent performance and producing within specifications.

The primary goal is to perform near perfection. Based on statistical analysis of variability, Six Sigma aims for an error rate of 3.4 defects per million opportunities (DPMO). Average error rate in typical organizations is between two and three sigma. See Figure 67.1.

A key feature of Lean Six Sigma is that time and resources are dedicated to what is critical to quality—those attributes most important to the customer so there is as little variation in expectations as possible. The resulting operational stability ensures consistency, predictable processes that deliver, and improve, what the customer wants.

Sigma	PPM out of Specification	% out of Specification	Comparative Position
1σ	690,000	69	Out of Business
2σ	308,537	30.8537	Non Competitive
3σ	66,807	6.6807	Under Industry Average
4σ	6,210	0.621	Industry Average
5σ	233	0.0233	Best in Industry
6σ	3.4	0.00034	World Leader

Figure 67.1 Six Sigma levels and related error rates.

The most common Six Sigma methodology is known by the acronym DMAIC:

D: Define the current process and high-level project goals.

M: Measure key aspects of the current process and collect relevant data.

A: Analyze the data to verify cause-and-effect relationships. Determine what the relationships are and attempt to ensure that all factors have been considered.

I: Improve and optimize the process based on data analysis.

C: Control the process to ensure that any deviations from the target are corrected before they result in defects. Set up pilot runs to establish process capability, move to production, set control mechanisms, and continuously monitor the process.

In addition to the use of statistical methods, it creates an infrastructure of qualified individuals who are trained, certified, and become experts in the tools and methodology. When implemented as a strategic initiative, the goal is for everyone to receive at least basic training. The roles within Six Sigma are shown on Table 67.1.

The Impact on the Work Environment

While Lean Six Sigma relies heavily on statistical analysis to calculate operational capacity and error rates, there is also a work environment impact that generally receives little attention. In many organizations employees describe their work environments as being in a constant state of firefighting. They are constantly in a reactive mode, fixing problems, reworking transactions, appeasing customers, and using mostly intuition to make decisions because there are limited or unreliable data.

With Six Sigma, work environments are transformed and are more structured, metrics-driven, proactive, use reliable data for ongoing monitoring, and in general

Table 67.1   Roles in Six Sigma

Role	Description
White belt	Recipients of basic Six Sigma training.
Yellow belt	Similar to staff in internal audit. They support Six Sigma projects and work closely with Green Belts.
Green belt	Similar to seniors in internal audit. They apply and implement Six Sigma tools and principles, and work under the guidance of Black Belts.
Black belt	Similar to managers in internal audit. They apply the methodology to projects and focus on project management. Typically requires two successful projects as Green Belt and passing an exam.
Master black belt	Six Sigma coaches that ensure the consistent application of Six Sigma, manage education, training, development, and promotion of the program.
Process owners	Individuals responsible for a process, who define and monitor its performance.
Executive management	CEO and others in senior management who set up the vision for Six Sigma. They empower other role holders providing authority, resources, and freedom to make necessary improvements.

provide better customer service. Some key questions to evaluate the process under review include:

- Who are the customers and what are their requirements?
- What are the performance metrics of the process? Why were these selected? How precise is the measurement system?
- How is the process performed? Which tasks are value/non-value adding and what is the ratio between them?
- Is the process in control? (i.e., yielding predictable and error-free results or subject to variation)
- What causes variability in the process?
- How are the operating results affecting customers, vendors, and the organization financially?
- Are suppliers a source of variability? If yes, who are they and what is the organization doing to eliminate this variability (and waste)?
- What are the key input variables affecting the average and standard deviation of performance measures?
- What is being done to continuously improve the process?

Six Sigma focuses on eliminating mistakes, rework, and waste. It recognizes that improved quality is a means to an end. The goal is to make customers happy and increase the bottom line. In non-profit environments, it can significantly improve the delivery of services while reducing costs and cycle times. These goals are compatible with the objectives that internal auditors pursue during the course of their work.

Summary

1. Six Sigma principles are applicable in industrial (e.g., manufacturing) and service (e.g., payment, customer service, transaction processing) environments. Its goals are to improve the quality and reduce errors, improve operational speed, eliminate waste, and reduce total costs.
2. Internal auditors can use Lean Six Sigma to perform more in-depth analyses of the activities audited, identify the root causes of issues and make more impactful recommendations.
3. Management should support and allocate resources, establish the infrastructure (i.e., people, process and policy), select projects, apply metrics and follow-up, provide training, and involve customers and suppliers. This involvement will improve the organization's internal controls and will yield results similar to those achieved from having a control self-assessment (CSA) mechanism.

Chapter 68

Mentoring/Coaching

Internal auditing is a complex field of work that is undergoing many and significant changes. Internal audit managers and directors work diligently to make sure their staff has the needed skills to perform their duties and develop leadership, communication, and negotiation skills. Similarly, internal auditors are tasked with managing their careers, so they remain relevant in the short and longer terms. Given this complex environment, it is not surprising that mentoring and coaching have emerged as essential tools to help auditors grow professionally.

With coaching, the learner is supported to achieve specific professional (or personal) goals through training and guidance. In a corporate environment, it is common for coaching to have a duration of a year or less. Mentoring is similar to coaching, but it generally focuses more on developing the individual, rather than training the person for a particular job or task. Mentoring also has a deeper relationship component where the mentor guides the protégé over one or more years and the development is multi-faceted focusing on work, career, and professional development.

Coaching and mentoring can be done formally or informally. Either program has resulted in the personal, academic, and professional advancement of many people and is known to have transformed many individuals' futures. Its origins can be traced back to apprenticeship programs and remain useful today given the many changes impacting business and personal dynamics.

Coaching is usually geared to helping new hires transition into the department. It can accelerate the assimilation process, ease stress, and minimize errors. By making the integration process smoother and faster, engagement levels will be enhanced and this should reduce turnover.

Formal coaches should be selected carefully, focusing on those that have a natural interest in teaching, who have a friendly and easy-going personality to make the learning process enjoyable, and the flexibility to respond to their partners' needs without protesting. Informal coaches emerge spontaneously, and the natural affiliation provides similar benefits to the coach and apprentice.

Mentoring programs can be formal and run within the internal audit department if it is large enough to support it. Ideally mentors would not be the current or future manager of the protégé because the manager-subordinate relationship can sometimes limit the candor and long-term plans that will be developed. While there is no precise number to consider a department "large enough" to sustain its own formal mentoring program, one with fewer than 40 employees will probably face difficulties having enough people that can serve as mentors, for enough proteges, who are not currently, or won't later become their immediate manager. But one can still be arranged, often with the help of other division heads or with the support of the Human Resources department, which is often the one that establishes and sustains company-wide mentoring programs.

As individuals advance in their careers and reach higher levels within the organization's hierarchy, they often enter executive coaching programs. The Executive Coach Academy defines executive coaching as "a facilitative one-to-one, mutually designed relationship between a professional coach and a key contributor who has a powerful position in the organization. The coaching is contracted for the benefit of a client who is accountable for highly complex decisions with wide scope of impact on the organization and industry. The focus of the coaching is usually on organizational performance or development, but it may also serve a personal component as well."* Executive coaching arrangements tend to be customized company-sponsored programs for high-ranking and high-potential employees that are collaborative, pragmatic, strategic, and consider the leadership and psychological ingredients for success for the individual. The relationship generally involves the executive, the person's boss, the human resources manager and the executive coach.

While most people think about a one-to-one relationship (i.e., one mentor to one protégé), it is possible to have multiple mentors. This can be beneficial because more than one mentor will widen the knowledge of the individual as different mentors may have different strengths. For example, an internal auditor could have a mentor where the relationship focuses primarily on personal attributes like public speaking, leadership, and community involvement. However, another may focus on career advancement within internal audit.

Concerns over succession planning and knowledge transfer due to the mass retirement of baby boomers are forcing many organizations to implement coaching and mentoring programs. This is a very powerful supplement to merely documenting people's knowledge in procedures documents and flowcharts. By implementing a mentoring program, less-experienced workers would have access to an expert who can give feedback, and answer questions they may not know where to find answers to. Also, more experienced individuals can transfer their knowledge and experience to younger workers and help them take over the unit when the mentors retire.

---

* See www.executivecoachacademy.com/definitions.html.

A less common dynamic that internal auditors should consider as well is reverse mentoring. While the typical relationship involves the more experienced, and typically older employee providing guidance to a younger employee, the opposite approach can also be used. With the increase in digital innovations, internet and technological applications, and social media, in some cases new and younger employees have become mentors to their otherwise more experienced counterparts. Millennials are generally more familiar with these technologies than senior employees in the organization, so they can help them understand, use, and embrace these tools and trends. In this upside-down arrangement younger employees will benefit from gaining a better understanding of the bigger picture, institutional history, and context, while more senior employees can learn about social, demographic and technological developments that are impacting the workplace and internal audit clients.

New and experienced internal auditors need guidance, support, inspiration, and an example to follow. It makes the journey more enjoyable. It helps to avoid mistakes by having someone whose expertise and experience can help to clarify options and issues. Coaching and mentoring programs may not guarantee success for everyone involved, but it has been proven beneficial to many for hundreds of years, and it could enhance the work environment in your internal audit department now too.

Summary

1. Coaching arrangements typically last 1 year or less and generally focus on job requirements.
2. Mentoring arrangements typically last 1 year or more, and generally focus on career development and personal growth.
3. Mentoring and coaching programs are beneficial to mentors and proteges, because both can learn from each other, develop interpersonal skills, build stronger relationships, and enhance communication.

Chapter 69

Objectives

Internal auditors focus on three key types of objectives: 1. The Audit Objectives, 2. Business Objectives, and 3. Control Objectives.

Audit Objectives

These are the objectives set for conducting an audit. The objectives could be set by changing laws, regulations, concerns, or specific requests. Internal auditors could be asked to review a program or process to verify that it is complying with certain applicable regulations. A process owner could ask the auditors to investigate an abnormal increase in employee turnover or allegations of embezzlement.

Business Objectives

Organizations pursue a mission and vision, set strategies for the future, and establish business objectives to track their progress. These objectives could relate to growth projections, market share, product diversification, geographic expansion, customer satisfaction, retention rates, or system up time.

Typical categories include growth, profitability, productivity, employee retention, liquidity and financing, change enablement, innovation, and return on investment and assets.

Control Objectives

Control objectives are the aim, reason, or purpose why controls should be implemented. They refer to risks that the controls are supposed to mitigate and form the basis for the evaluation of their existence and performance.

They are a series of statements made by an organization that address risks, and these risks need to be effectively mitigated through policies, procedures, and related activities that are in place within the organization's control environment.

Control objectives relate to the reliability of financial and operational reporting, timely feedback and reporting on the achievement of operational and strategic goals, and compliance with laws, regulations, and other requirements. In terms of a computer system, a control objective may relate to its stability, reliability and security and read as follows: "Controls provide reasonable assurance that critical network devices and system are operating as designed, administered by qualified personnel, secure and equipped to protect the organization's network infrastructure from external vulnerabilities."*

Since risks jeopardize the achievement of objectives, business objectives and control objectives are closely linked.

Summary

1. Internal auditors should be clear when they start an engagement, during their internal communications with fellow auditors, and when working with audit clients to clearly define what objectives are being discussed.
2. While each of the three types of objectives is related, they serve different purposes. All three must be present and agreed upon to improve the quality of audit engagements. Having a common language facilitates communication among stakeholders.
3. Linking strategy, objectives, risks and controls is an effective way to ensure alignment between these key elements and assemble a value chain for internal audit work.

---

* See https://socreports.com/glossary/83-control-objectives-example-control-objectives-for-soc-1-ssae-16-reporting-ssae16org.html.

Chapter 70

Pareto Chart

A Pareto Chart is a two-axis chart that contains both bars and a line graph; the individual values are represented by bars in descending order while the cumulative total (percentage) is represented by a line. The left vertical axis is the frequency of occurrence (e.g., errors, cost). The right vertical axis is the cumulative percentage of the total number of occurrences (e.g., errors, cost).

Pareto Charts are related to the 80/20 rule, which states that for many events close to 80 percent of the effects are caused by 20 percent of the causes. The concentration of sources is important because it helps to prioritize issues and focus on the solutions that provide the largest value for money. The Pareto chart highlights the most important factors. In quality control, it could represent the most common

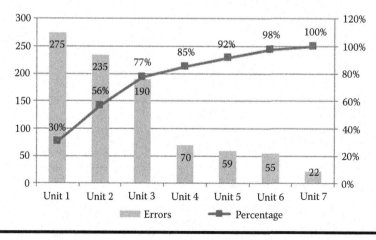

Figure 70.1 Sample Pareto chart.

sources of defects, the highest occurring type of defect, or the most frequent reasons for customer dissatisfaction.

Pareto charts can be generated in software applications like Microsoft Excel, Tableau, specialized statistical software tools, and quality charts generators (Figure 70.1).

Summary

1. Internal auditors can use Pareto Charts to assess the most frequently occurring defects by category.
2. By focusing on the 20 percent of causes, process owners can resolve close to 80 percent of the effects.
3. As a visual tool, it is an effective tool to convey information more quickly than text-heavy alternatives.

Chapter 71

Persuasion

Persuasion is an important aspect of internal auditing that doesn't receive enough attention or coverage. Internal auditing is done for a reason: identify opportunities for improvement within organizations. If the internal auditor identifies opportunities for improvement, but is unable to convince the relevant stakeholders to take action, how effective is that? From an output perspective, the auditor could be producing many reports, maybe even voluminous ones. But from an outcome perspective, that same auditor could be considered ineffective due to the inability to get the right reaction from the board and management.

The Difference Is Persuasion

Audit testing is generally done to answer some key questions: Are we achieving our mission and objectives? Are the right risks identified and mitigated appropriately? Are controls doing what they are supposed to do? The testing done answers those questions. If all is satisfactory, then there isn't much more that needs to be done. But if the pursuit of the mission and objectives, or the dynamics surrounding risks and controls can be improved upon, then findings should contain the necessary details, presented clearly and succinctly, for the recommendation to be convincing and compel action to make the necessary corrections.

Persuasion is accomplished by appealing to:

Reason: Derived from the Greek, Logos. People generally think they are logical and reasonable.
Character: Derived from the Greek word Ethos: Character of the presenter who must be trustworthy, honest, intelligent, and credible.

Emotion: Derived from the Greek, Pathos: Express feelings on a subject, get an emotional reaction, or both.

Internal auditors generally appeal, and are mostly receptive, to the top two: Reason and Character. But they should not underestimate the power of appealing to the third, emotion. In fact, the recent efforts within the profession to improve the image of internal auditors, to be more collaborative, to build better relationships with audit clients and to create an atmosphere where internal auditors are respected more, and feared less, requires an attention to emotion.

Many audit clients are apprehensive of internal auditors. They also fear the consequences of audit findings, so they say as little as possible, and provide as little information as possible.

When trying to mobilize the organization, internal auditors are encouraged to consider not only the rationale for their work, the methodology followed and the quantitative and qualitative benefits of recommendations. They should also burnish their reputation as subject matter experts in the field of governance, risk management, and compliance. But internal auditors should also spruce up the image of being friendly, approachable, if not likeable. This does not mean that internal auditors should get into a personality contest, or attempt to be more photogenic. It means that selling a finding should also involve describing the human impact and how poor human resource and management practices affect employees, customers, and vendors emotionally. Consider the difference when framing process inefficiencies in human terms while speaking with audit clients:

- How can I help you get home at 5 p.m. rather than 8 p.m. by eliminating the corrections you have to make?
- How can I help you stop customers from calling you and complaining about delays and errors made?
- What are the issues that are causing you and your colleagues stress?

Another important element is making sure the communication is at the right level of knowledge of the recipients. While it is likely that at the management level most report readers will be familiar with the subject being discussed, that may not be the case at the board level. Assessing the reader's depth of knowledge may indicate that the language, acronyms and terminology may need to be addressed through footnotes, endnotes, a glossary, spelling-out of acronyms, replacing technical terms with layman's language, and so on. See Figure 71.1, where the letters A, B, C, …, F represent the individuals receiving the communication.

Internal auditors also refer often to the main driving force for their work: determine if the organization is achieving its objectives, and if controls are effective mitigating risks. But when writing audit reports, quite often the focus is on the failed controls, without explaining the link between the failed controls, the exposure to the risks occurring, and the threat to the achievement of the

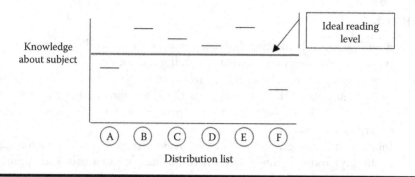

Figure 71.1   Reader's level of knowledge.

Objectives	Risks												Controls				Audit program steps
Objective	Risks	S	O	R	C	IT	F	Prob.	Imp.	Vel	Pers.	Control	P/D	A/M	X/D/W/M/Q	Audit step
O1	R11											C111				AS1 (C111, C112, C113, C121)
												C112				
												C113				
	R12											C121				AS2 (C122, C123)
												C122				
												C123				
												C124				AS3 (C124)
	R13											-				
	-											C141				

Figure 71.2   The link between a failed control and the impact on business objectives.

organization's objectives and possibly, the mission itself. That story should be told, and that story can be extracted from the risk and control matrix as shown in Figure 71.2, where the link between a failed control and the impact on business objectives is evident.

When it comes to recommendations, it should not just be a matter of doing something so the findings don't recur, but it should also be a matter of working together to make sure things are done once and done right. Otherwise, if the root cause is not found, the audit client will still have to deal with the problems sooner or later. Keeping the customer happy is a good way to avoid unhappy conversations with the boss.

These are some examples of the emotional side of findings and recommendations and getting employees on board is the first step in them telling you what is broken and what needs to be fixed. After all, quite often employees know what is not working and they also know what is needed to fix those things. We just need them to see the value in our visit, the benefits to collaborating and the benefits of the recommendations.

Summary

1. A key aspect of effective internal auditing is persuading the client to communicate openly about what is working and what is not.
2. When issues emerge, internal auditors must be able to effectively persuade audit clients about the importance of the issue, and the need to take corrective action. If the audit client is not persuaded to act, the purpose of the engagement comes into question.
3. Internal auditors generally focus on reason (e.g., logic), character (e.g., credibility) and emotion in that order, but should use a balanced approach whenever possible.

Chapter 72

Planning

Planning is one of the most important activities in internal auditing. Unfortunately, too many internal auditors rush through the planning phase so they can get the testing started, not realizing that poor planning results in poor execution.

The planning phase often begins with the notification to the client that the audit is imminent. This notification is sometimes made after the annual plan is formalized. In other instances, it is announced a few weeks in advance of the expected fieldwork, with several activities occurring 8 weeks, 7 weeks, 6 weeks before the fieldwork, and so on.

It is important to note that this milestone-driven countdown is typical of most audits, but some are performed as surprised audits. Surprise audits are common in environments where there is cash collected, controlled substances are used or dispensed, and in organizations where there are branch or franchise locations.

The engagement letter often constitutes the initial notification to the client. This letter often outlines the reason for the audit, when the opening meeting will take place, who constitutes the audit team, a high-level overview of the audit process, when the closing meeting is expected to occur, and the delivery of the product: the final report.

Another important document produced during the planning phase is the planning memo. This is produced for use within the internal audit function, and it often includes critical background information, the names of key client personnel, the audit program, the budget (monetary and time) and the names of the audit staff members committed to the engagement.

Preliminary meetings provide a great mechanism to collect critical information as the internal auditors prepare for the audit. Internal auditors should approach these meetings with the goal of collecting key information, become more informed about the program or processes' activities, key systems, documents and data in use, nuances about the area in scope and seek client input.

Auditor Essentials

Although internal auditors are encouraged to ask lots of questions, they should review as much available information before the meeting as possible. If organizational charts, operating and financial reports, policies and procedures, and budgets are available, these documents should be obtained and reviewed prior to the meeting so the questions asked can be more meaningful.

Summary

1. Failing to plan is planning to fail.
2. Approximately a third of the engagement's budget should be allocated and spent in planning activities.
3. The start of the planning may vary by organization and type of engagement. Internal auditors should gauge the effectiveness of their lead time and planning phase length to make sure they are not delaying fieldwork, or rushing through planning, as these changes generally result in more inefficient fieldwork testing.

Chapter 73

Poka-yoke

Internal audit clients are often worried that mistakes made during their daily activities will result in audit report findings. In fact, many audit report findings are not due to fraud or outright negligent behavior, but the result of mistakes people make. What we sometimes don't examine sufficiently, or explain to our clients, is that processes should be built to operate error-free in the first place. Even when controls detect errors, customers report gaffes, or sheer luck saves the day, these events often cause rework. Reportable or not, these events create opportunities to add value to our clients.

Poka-yoke is a Japanese term meaning mistake-proofing. It is a methodology that focuses on eliminating defects in products and services by preventing or drawing attention to human errors that can occur.

The technique can be used as follows in service environments:

Spreadsheets
> Color-code and password-protect cells so data can only be entered on predetermined fields. Also use validation checks, such as range and format checks, to identify typing errors during data entry. Batch and hash totals can also be used to count how many items, records, documents, or the sum of a chosen field. With this information, the manual entries can be compared to the source to verify that nothing is missing or is entered more than once.

Reconciliations and Templates
> Use formulas with check totals that indicate through color changes when the totals agree or disagree.

Data Entry
> Require operators to re-enter certain figures to make sure data entry is accurate.

Expense Reports
Program the system to automatically display a child (i.e., pop-up) window when the amount of the expense is above an established threshold, or in relation to predetermined categories such as mileage, meals, airfare, hotel costs or other/miscellaneous.

Entry-Logs
For manual or semi-automated entry logs, set the requirement that all or some of the information be selected from a pull-down menu (e.g., employees, students), and the rest be typed rather than hand-written. This eliminates penmanship issues, which is a limitation of sign-in sheets where the information provided cannot be deciphered on the entry-exit log. In addition, by increasing automation data entry requirements can be enhanced so essential information cannot be left blank.

In industrial environments, poka-yoke is often used as follows:

Orientation
Parts in an assembly won't fit if placed incorrectly.

Sequence
The process must be performed in a predetermined sequence so steps cannot be missed or done in a different order.

Weights
Inaccurate weight forces the machine to stop before further work can be performed.

Location, Size, Count
Requires the presence, absence, or different size of components to proceed

Machine or System Check
The machine stops operating when out of specification

While the term poka-yoke may be new, all of us has benefited from the application of its principles. The evidence is virtually everywhere around us.

Power plugs
Typically, they can only be plugged in one way because they don't fit into the power outlet otherwise.

Cables
USB and Ethernet cables can only be plugged in one way and they typically have a small latch to keep the cable from being pulled out of the device accidentally.

Garage and elevator doors
They have sensors to prevent them from closing accidentally when an object is in the door's path, which can cause injury or damages.

Microwave machines
  The motor in the microwave oven stops working when the door is opened.
Automobiles
  The driver cannot start the engine or change the gears from Park to Drive unless the brake pedal is pressed.

Principles

When applying poka-yoke in your observations, analysis, and recommendations, you should follow these principles:

- Simple and Intuitive: The procedure should be easy to figure out and use
- Inexpensive: Consider the cost-benefit involved
- Fail-Safe: Make sure to consider various scenarios so the mechanism or approach works every time
- Mandatory: Every user should be required to follow the procedure

Poka-yoke or mistake-proofing is done so errors don't happen in processes in the first place. But it also reduces training time, the number of rejects and warranty claims, the need for inspection and quality control later, and lowers user and worker frustration by preventing avoidable mistakes.

Audit clients appreciate recommendations that improve the work environment and increase efficiencies and overall effectiveness. Poka-yoke does that and its principles can be used in service and industrial environments alike. This will result in more meaningful discussions with your clients, improve client relations, and demonstrate that as internal auditors we are not only trying to find mistakes but also helping the organization avoid them.

While detecting problems is good, preventing them is much better.

Summary

1. Poka-yoke is a technique to mistake-proof processes, so instead of focusing on finding errors the focus is on preventing them.
2. This technique can be applied to industrial and service environments, resulting in lower production and inspection costs, increased customer satisfaction, less rework, and fewer returns.
3. Poka-yoke works well with the principles of quality assurance (rather than quality control) and its use by internal auditors would add value to their clients as a way to prevent issues, rather than detecting them later.

Chapter 74

Policies and Procedures

Organizations have been encouraged for decades to document their expectations by publishing policy documents that outline high-level guidelines for proper conduct. These should be complimented by procedures documents that give employees and other interested parties specific information about the way the work should be performed. Unfortunately, too many organizations lack one or both. Sometimes these documents don't exist at all, and sometimes they exist, but their quality could be improved upon.

The absence of policy documents can result in confusion or lack of accountability, as expectations are not clearly defined. The lack of procedures documents often result in inconsistent performance, finger-pointing, and lack of accountability as well. But why aren't these documents prepared? There are several arguments made to justify the reluctance to produce procedures documents, including:

- Those performing the work are already familiar with the work and know how to do their jobs.
- The work environment changes too often so by the time the documentation is prepared, it would be outdated.
- Employees are too busy with their daily activities and cannot take on this task.

The reality is that organizations can ill-afford not having detailed policy and procedures documents. These documents are not merely intended to appease auditors but instead provide some specific benefits to the organizations. They:

- Specify performance expectations that can make feedback sessions (e.g., performance evaluations) more productive
- Facilitate onboarding and employee training activities
- Strengthen business continuity plans

■ Clarify responsibilities so finger-pointing is minimized if required activities are not performed as expected

Standard audit procedures dictate that internal auditors ask auditees for the policy and procedures documents for the areas under review. This is done to help the auditor become acquainted with the area being audited and understand the expectations of business managers. It is also a quick diagnostic about the maturity of the area as indicated in the Carnegie Mellon Capability Maturity Model (CMM). In it, programs, processes and controls can be assessed on a 5-point scale similar to the one shown below (Table 74.1):

The evaluation criteria used must fit the organization, its size, industry, maturity, and culture. So internal auditors should decide which audit techniques they want to use when evaluating controls. For example:

■ At the lowest level are techniques that only identify errors
■ At the next level are techniques that identify the control weakness that can lead to the errors
■ At the highest level are techniques that identify the root cause of the control weakness*

When internal auditors ask for these documents the response allows them to make an assessment about that program or process: If absent or outdated, the risk exists that work will be performed inconsistently between one operator and another, that upon staff turnover essential knowledge will be lost, that newly hired employees will experience an unpredictable onboarding process, and that when questions arise answers will be given from memory rather than using an authoritative source.

When organizations have difficulty producing or maintaining detailed and up-to-date procedures documents the cause is typically either a severe staff shortage or ownership of these documents has not been established.

If the problem is caused by severe staff shortages, management should evaluate its operational resources because with severe staff shortages it won't be long before quality, speed, accuracy, and customer satisfaction deteriorates and turnover increases.

If the problem is caused by the lack of ownership, the organization can use a centralized or decentralized approach to solve it.

Centralized

Under the centralized approach, a dedicated unit is created that takes ownership of the process and documents; they document or facilitate the preparation of these

---

* See *Best Practices: Evaluating the Corporate Culture* by James Roth, IIA Research Foundation, 2010, p. 2.

Table 74.1 Capability Maturity Model

Level	Rating	Characteristics	Related to Policies and Procedures (P&Ps)
1	Initial/Ad-hoc	Random, unpredictable, and inconsistent conditions or practices prevail.	P&Ps consist of handwritten or loosely typed noted that describe the way the work is performed in a very basic way.
2	Informal and repeatable	Conditions and practices follow a pattern that is discernible and provide some predictability.	P&Ps are typed and sufficiently detailed to gain a general understanding of how the work is supposed to be performed.
3	Formal or documented	Conditions and practices have been formally documented and represent the way the work is performed.	P&Ps have been formally documented, professionally-looking, reviewed, and approved for all key units, programs, and processes. Operating units use templates to capture relevant elements consistently.
4	Managed	Conditions and practices are evaluated periodically against documented expectations. Deviations are noted and corrected appropriately within a reasonable amount of time. Improvements are done based on the monitoring of KPIs.	P&Ps form the basis for the work performed and metrics (e.g., KPIs) are in place to verify adherence with the expectations set forth in these documents. Minimum requirements have been set for P&Ps providing consistency across various programs, processes, and operating units.
5	Optimized	Conditions and practices undergo periodic or constant review in search of ways to improve its characteristics, throughput, efficiency, and effectiveness. Best practices are applied to methods and metrics.	P&Ps are reviewed within reasonable and pre-determined cycles to make sure they represent the work being performed. Their format and presentation are detailed, consist of computer screenshots, when applicable, are centralized and reviewed for relevance with regard to the objectives of the programs and processes they represent.

documents, keep them in their custody, reference and archive them, manage version control, and obtain re-certification annually to make sure that as procedures change in the field, that the documents are updated.

Decentralized

A de-centralized approach is also useful, whereby individuals in their corresponding units prepare, maintain, and update these documents. The key is to establish ownership of these procedures documents and make it a part of someone's job responsibilities. This way, follow-through is expected and the owners are rewarded during their annual performance evaluation process for doing it, or are reprimanded when they fail to do so.

Summary

1. Policy and procedures documents play a key role ensuring expectations are documented and serve as a basis for reviewing compliance with those expectations.
2. More than having these documents, they should be sufficiently detailed, easily available for use, and up-to-date so they can be used as training documents.
3. Clear ownership for their preparation and maintenance is essential.

Chapter 75

Professional Skepticism

Professional skepticism is a key component of an auditor's duty of care that applies throughout the engagement. It is an attitude that includes a questioning mind and a critical assessment of the appropriateness and sufficiency of audit evidence. It requires being alert to conditions that may indicate possible misstatement due to error or fraud, and a critical assessment of audit evidence.

Jeanette Franzel, Board Member of the PCAOB, in a speech delivered at the American Accounting Association (AAA) Annual Meeting* stated that for external auditors, professional skepticism is required as "due professional care is to be exercised in the planning and performance of the audit and the preparation of the report" according to AU § 230.01. and "due professional care requires the auditor to exercise professional skepticism" as stated in AS 13.7; AU § 230.07, § 316.13.

These requirements are similar to the IIA Standards, which state that "internal auditors must possess the knowledge, skills, and other competencies needed to perform their individual responsibilities" (Standard 1210—Proficiency) and "internal auditors must have sufficient knowledge to evaluate the risk of fraud and the manner in which it is managed by the organization but are not expected to have the expertise of a person whose primary responsibility is detecting and investigating fraud" (Standard 1210.A2). Similar guidance is provided regarding IT risks and controls in Standard 1210.A3, and this is not only at a point in time or a static requirement, but rather, internal auditors "must enhance their knowledge, skills, and other competencies through continuing professional development" (Standard 1230).

---

* The presentation made by Jeanette M. Franzel, Board member of the PCAOB at the American Accounting Association (AAA) annual meeting held August 5, 2013 is available here https://pcaobus.org/News/Speech/Documents/08052013_Presentation.pdf.

Auditors use their knowledge, skills, and abilities to diligently perform, in good faith and with integrity, the gathering and objective evaluation of evidence.

The scandals at Enron, WorldCom, Waste Management, Tyco, Parmalat, Stanford International Bank, Madoff, and many of the dealings that caused the 2008 financial collapse, among others, have raised questions about whether auditors have been sufficiently skeptical in recent times. Concerns of some regulators and other stakeholders have been highlighted in the media and continue to feed the audit debate.

Professional skepticism is fundamental to the role and performance of internal auditors and it is a key aspect of audit quality. It has three elements:

1. Attributes: This refers to the knowledge, skill and overall ability of the auditor.
2. Mindset: This relates to the integrity and good faith of the auditor who does not assume honesty or dishonesty on the part of the audit client, yet recognizes the possibility of fraud, misstatement or misrepresentation of important facts. Internal auditors should not be satisfied with less than persuasive evidence assuming that management and employees are honest.
3. Action: This element refers to the importance of performing a risk assessment, planning the engagement based on the risks involved, the need for engagement supervision, and the diligent gathering and evaluation of audit evidence.

Internal auditing best practices make it clear that objectivity and professional skepticism are a key attribute of the capabilities of internal audit firms and their staff. This is also essential when applying the requisite judgment in selecting the audit procedures, choosing the sampling (or 100 percent testing) methodology, evaluating results, formulating conclusions, and the overall conduct of the audit work.

Among the auditable areas and topics that require internal auditor skepticism are as follows:

■ Gaining an understanding of the methods and assumptions used to determine fair value estimates for assets and financial instruments
■ Evaluating the procedures over asset impairment, work in process, and percentage of completion calculations
■ Examining variance and sensitivity analyses
■ Reviewing management assumptions for calculating inventory reserves.
■ Reviewing production figures and system reports

Note that these procedures require more robust procedures than merely enquiry.

While planning and conducting fieldwork, internal auditors should schedule procedures and conduct testing commensurate with the related risks and key controls, not make their decision based on evidence that is easier to obtain. The focus should be on the evidence that is more relevant and reliable, getting enough of it (i.e. sufficiency) and use corroborating evidence rather than simply using, or giving undue weight to confirming evidence.

Although internal auditors are reminded to foster positive relationship with their clients, they should not allow the fear of conflicts with management, the desire for high post-audit satisfaction ratings, or maintaining a long-term audit client to cloud their thinking. Neither should deadlines, the desire to keep audit costs low or pressure to remain within budget limit the rigor of their work. Third party internal audit service providers should adhere to rigorous testing procedures commensurate with the circumstances, even though they may desire to cross-sell, or up-sell services to their audit clients.

Internal audit managers should encourage the audit team to confidently, yet professionally, challenge management representations, and be actively involved in planning, directing, and reviewing the work of the audit team. All involved should also leverage their knowledge and experience during the planning, fieldwork, and reporting phases.

Summary

1. Professional skepticism is a key component of effective internal audits and a key ingredient of audit quality.
2. Internal auditors should not assume that audit clients are honest or dishonest, but rather verify through appropriate audit procedures the veracity of the information provided and examined.
3. Care is required because time and cost constraints, familiarity with the client, stress, and the amount of experience may affect the degree of skepticism applied. Internal auditors should remain vigilant and appropriately skeptical while performing their duties.

Chapter 76

Project Management

The Project Management Body of Knowledge (PMBOK) from the Project Management Institute (PMI) divides projects into five phases. They are as follows:

1. Initiating. The project is authorized, funded, and defined. This phase occurs on the organizational level, above the project. The organization defines a business need the project is meant to satisfy.
2. Planning. The project manager (PM) develops a project management plan, which defines how the project will be carried out, who will do the work, how long it will take, and how much it will cost. The project management plan must be approved by the project sponsor to become official, and changes must be re-approved based on the change management processes and protocol established.
3. Execution. The project team works on producing the project's deliverables.
4. Monitoring and Controlling. The PM makes sure the work is performed according to the plan, and tracks deviations. The PM also monitors the scope, communications, vendor relations, and other matters necessary to ensure the project is performed according to plan.
5. Closing. The project must be officially closed, final details determined, and vendors released.

Although the term 'phase' implies that they are carried out in chronological order, in practice they can sometimes be performed out of order. For example, when project changes occur during execution, the PM could proceed back to the planning phase. During reporting, internal auditors should verify the accuracy of all statements, results, and conclusions derived during fieldwork.

Initiating: This phase includes the initial work necessary to create and authorize the project. For business projects it includes developing a project charter to make

Project Management Phases	Internal Audit Phases	Key Internal Audit Activities
Initiating, Planning	Planning	Send announcement or engagement memo to the audit client, prepare a planning memo for the audit team, define scope and objectives, prepare risk assessment and audit program, define timeline, prepare communications plan, and status reporting contents and deadlines.
Executing	Fieldwork	Perform tests, discuss issues with audit client
Monitoring	Administration	Review workpapers, provide status updates to stakeholders, perform variance analysis of the budget.
Closing	Reporting	Publish draft report, gather management responses, distribute final report, closeout workpapers, and send audit client survey.

the project official and authorize the PM. The charter generally includes the scope, budget, and a list of primary stakeholders. Internal auditors use the engagement letter to announce the project, and inform the audit client who are the members of the audit team, who the in-charge auditor is, the timeline of the audit, and the audit reports as main deliverables. Internal auditors also have a standing charter that defines the overall scope, authority, risk-based approach, types of audits, and special projects allowed, the independence and objectivity of the internal audit function, and the types of deliverables to be expected.

Planning: The success of the project usually depends on the amount of planning done. During planning, the PM should document success factors (e.g., schedule, budget and key deliverables), scope definition (especially if it was fine-tuned from the initiating phase), and timeline and deadlines for key deliverables. Also, the cost to perform each task and the roll-up or cumulative cost of all the tasks into an overall budget. Planning also entails identifying the project team, defining the members' roles and responsibilities. Another important aspect of project planning is defining, or confirming, the quality standards for the deliverables and the control metrics that will be used for tracking performance. Procedures should be defined during planning to address change requests.

Execution: During this phase most of the project work gets done. The PM directs, manages, and monitors the project work, while the project team carries it out. Deliverables are produced and delivered. The PM must also prepare regular status updates and should include cost, schedule, progress toward achievement of deliverables, and future activities and projections. Another key activity is providing stakeholder communications. Each stakeholder should receive communications and status updates based on their needs and requirements. This can be done via reports, face-to-face meetings, or calls. Audit findings should be presented and discussed with audit clients during the execution phase to make sure there are no misunderstandings, to give the audit client an opportunity to communicate the matter up the chain of command, and to begin preparing an action plan.

Monitoring and Controlling: This occurs simultaneously as the execution phase. The PM should monitor and control the project to make sure that the deliverables are produced and delivered on time, on budget, and with high quality. Two key metrics involve assessing the budget in relation to the actual status on the project schedule and cost.

Closing: This is often ignored because the work is done, or mostly done, the deadline has come or passed, the deliverables have been submitted and team members are being re-assigned or have already left the project. In internal auditing this involves issuing the audit reports but may also include sending a post-audit questionnaire to the audit client, closing out the workpapers, capturing lessons learned, and holding post-audit feedback meetings with staff members.

Triple Constraints

An important aspect of project management is the Triple Constraints, which posit that all projects are subject to constraints impacting scope, budget (or cost, or resources) and timeline (or schedule). These three elements form a triangle with quality as a constant, hence placed in the middle (Figure 76.1).

Scope: Projects are expected to provide deliverables that are defined by the scope. They must meet the agreed-upon scope.

Figure 76.1 The triple constraints of project management.

346 ■ *Auditor Essentials*

Budget: Projects must be delivered within cost
Schedule: Projects must be delivered on time
Quality: Projects must meet quality requirements

The Triple Constraints also suggests that the three elements must remain in equilibrium. An increase in the scope will result in an increase in the cost or a delay in the timeline. A reduction in the available resources will require a reduction in the scope or increase in time (i.e., delay in completing the project). A shortening of the time available will cause costs to increase or require a scope reduction. These dynamics will hold true if there is an expectation that the work will be done with high quality.

Scope increases can occur as a major enhancement to the previously agreed-upon scope, or in small increments, often called scope creep. This scope creep is typically due to undefined requirements during the planning phase or by small increases in the scope during fieldwork, as auditors add seemingly innocuous additional procedures and activities to the project without re-balancing the cost and timeline.

The expression "Which two do you want, fast, cheap or good?" is worth remembering because projects tend to be constrained by these elements. PMs rarely have the budget to complete their projects on time with high quality. As a result, they are weighing one constraint against another as they manage stakeholder expectations to reach the best outcome.

Summary

1. Internal audits are typically defined as having a planning, fieldwork, and reporting phase. In addition, monitoring, and controlling activities are performed to ensure adherence with good auditing practices.
2. Project management is essential for the completion of audit and consulting projects that achieve the stated objectives within the scope defined, the resources provided, and the expected timeline.
3. In-charge auditors typically serve as PMs and should balance their technical audit skills with project administration, leadership, negotiation, and time management skills.

Chapter 77

Quality Assurance and Improvement Programs (QAIP)

While conducting an audit I was confronted by an audit client who asked "who audits you?" I believe in teachable moments, so I treated this exchange like one. I told him that I understood his concern and unease at being questioned about his work, how he did it, and the results. I explained the purpose of internal audit as a service unit verifying compliance but also helping the business identify areas for improvement. Then I proceeded to explain to him how internal auditors are required to follow policies and procedures like other employees and are subject to internal and external quality control reviews. I also explained to him that in my first internal audit job, one of our annual assignments was to travel to our foreign offices and review the work of our auditors stationed there. The encounter ended well, and we proceeded with the work on what turned out to be a very productive audit, after he asked me to tell him what it was like in various Latin American countries.

Internal auditors are required to implement a Quality Assurance and Improvement Program (QAIP) covering all aspects of the internal audit activity (Standard 1300). The program's goals are to make sure internal auditors' work is done in conformance with the *Standards*, and make sure internal auditors are acting according to the requirements of the Code of Ethics. Another very important goal is to evaluate the efficiency and effectiveness of the internal audit activity and identify opportunities for improvement. Lastly, getting feedback from customers is a good way to receive valuable input on how to improve performance, which along the way will also improve communications.

There are two types or components to the QAIP:

Internal

Requires ongoing monitoring of the work and periodic assessments by others within the organization who are familiar with the work of the internal auditors. This is often accomplished through the review of all, or a sample of, auditor workpapers and client surveys.

The review of workpapers focuses on whether the documentation for auditor engagements is clear, complete, referenced and self-contained (i.e., speaks for itself). Since internal audit departments should have policies and procedures (Standard 2040) delineating what should be in the workpapers and how they should be prepared and referenced, this internal review verifies that the auditors working on projects are meeting these requirements.

External

External assessments must be conducted at least once every 5 years by a qualified, independent assessor, or assessment team from outside the organization. This review is more comprehensive and typically includes the review of workpapers as performed during the internal assessment, but also include interviews with the organization's audit committee, audit clients, internal auditors, a review of the department's audit plan and budget, and training practices.

Surveys

Surveys are a common way to perform the periodic assessments and obtain feedback from audit clients within the organization. These surveys are sent at the completion of audit or consulting engagement. The survey should be sent to the person that the auditors interacted most closely with. This way the response will relate to the first-hand experiences encountered, rather than hear-say. If due to the organization's protocol it is sent to someone else, care should be applied to the results since they may not reflect the experience accurately. In fact, in some organizations they have two versions of the questionnaire, one for the individuals the auditors worked closely with, and another for senior management focusing on higher-level dynamics and audit results.

The moment of distribution of the survey varies. Typically, it is sent two weeks after the final report is published. In some organizations it is handed out during the Exit Meeting, but since the reports have not been published yet, that may be somewhat premature, especially since a common survey question is to ask about the quality of the audit report, whether it addressed client needs, and if it was published promptly after fieldwork.

Some internal audit units experience a low response rate. This may occur due to "survey fatigue," which occurs when organizations conduct what employees consider too many surveys, so they abstain from participation. But it may also occur because audit clients don't think the survey is important, used, or beneficial. In my experience, response rates increase when audit clients understand that these surveys are used to improve the quality of the services that internal audit provides by linking it to performance evaluations, to training, development, and audit planning practices.

It also helps to improve response rates when internal auditors contact audit clients to enquire about unexpected results like very low scores and negative comments. By having a manager contact the audit client to get more detailed information, it will become clearer to the organization that their responses are taken seriously; they are reviewed thoroughly and acted upon.

Another reason for low response rates tends to be questionnaires that are too long or confusing. In general, internal auditors should strive for short questionnaires with 15 questions or less. The questions can be closed ended or open ended.

Closed-ended questions are those where respondents have a few options to choose from or are asked for a specific piece of information. Closed-ended questions usually consist of "Yes" or "No" options or a series of options showing the degree of agreement or disagreement with a statement, like "Totally Agree," "Somewhat Agree," "Neutral," "Somewhat Disagree," or "Totally Disagree." It is a good idea to have a "Not Applicable" option as well.

When using closed-ended questions, it may be useful to add a field for comments next to each statement as it helps to give respondents an opportunity to elaborate, especially when they provide a low score.

Open-ended questions are those where respondents are given the opportunity to comment and write their opinions. When using open-ended questions, instead of asking to rate the statement on a scale (e.g., Strongly Disagree to Strongly Agree), the respondent can be asked to describe their experiences with auditor interactions, the auditors' level of technical proficiency, the timeliness or usefulness of status updates, and so on.

Over the years many internal auditors have shared with me the concern that auditees will use the survey to "get back at the auditors," in other words, retaliate by giving them low scores if there are multiple, or significant findings in their audit reports. In my experience there has not been a direct correlation between the number or severity of findings and the rating on the surveys. The auditors could do a great job, have multiple findings, work well with audit clients, jointly develop effective and much-needed recommendations, and get very good survey results. Internal auditors could do a poor job relating to the audit client, yet despite few findings on the audit report, receive, deservedly, low survey results.

Consider a case where internal auditors do a poor job working with the client, and publish a report that doesn't highlight areas for improvement, yet the client knows that internal audit is a service organization and should have highlighted areas for improvement that they are clearly aware of, and in desperate need of assistance with. They could be justified in rating the internal auditors poorly because they expected much but received little.

The Global Internal Audit Common Body of Knowledge (CBOK) project by the IIARF shows that only 9 percent of respondents said their audit departments were using exit surveys in 2010. But the number is rising, because by 2015, 50 percent were doing so.

The process of developing and conducting exit surveys should be the client's experience with the audit process, and less with the audit results, even though some questions may be useful as well. The following are some suggested themes and questions to consider when conducting exit surveys:

Overall Satisfaction
- The audit was beneficial and added value to my operation
- The audit was conducted in an efficient and timely manner
- My department's concerns and perspective were adequately considered during the audit
- Audit duration was appropriate

Communication
- The audit process, duration, objectives, and scope were communicated clearly to me
- The audit leader kept me informed about the audit process
- Update meetings were helpful to me
- Audit findings were communicated clearly, accurately, and promptly

Scope of Audit Work
- The auditors focused on areas that are important to our department
- The auditors considered my suggestions and concerns during the audit

Professional Proficiency
- The audit team maintained a professional approach during the audit
- The disruption of daily activities was minimized as much as possible
- The auditors were knowledgeable about my unit/processes
- The auditors understand my business
- Audit findings were accurate

Audit Outcomes
- The audit work will assist me achieve our business objectives
- The audit will help us improve our risk management activities
- The audit will help us improve our work environment

Reporting
- The conclusions were reasonable and based on a sound understanding of our business processes and activities

- Audit recommendations will improve operational controls in our department
- Audit recommendations were valuable to my operation
- The audit report was clear
- The audit report was concise
- The final report was issued timely

It is also useful to consider having a general statement at the end for respondents to provide information that was not asked in the questionnaire. The following are some examples:

- What aspects of the audit were most beneficial to you?
- What aspects of the audit were the least beneficial to you?
- Was there anything that you would recommend about the audit, and the auditors you worked with, to improve the process?
- Was there anything about the audit and consulting services that you liked?
- How might the internal audit activity better add value to you?

Internal auditors and their clients expect survey results to be used. The information collected should be used to improve the process and auditor performance. In many organizations the results are another ingredient going into the auditors' individual and the entire departments' performance evaluation.

Many auditors are concerned that their performance evaluation could be negatively affected by unhappy customers, and that is a reasonable concern. The evaluation process should not lead internal auditors to lose their objectivity and suppress or downgrade audit findings in hopes of getting better feedback. On the other hand, auditors should not act as if customer service didn't matter, and they only need to find something, so they can get the report underway. A balanced approach is imperative and internal audit management should make sure the performance evaluation is fair and balanced.

Summary

1. The Quality Assurance and Improvement Program (QAIP) provides valuable information to evaluate the quality of the work of internal auditors.
2. A QAIP has two components: Internal assessments performed on an ongoing basis, focusing primarily on workpaper quality and audit execution. External assessments are performed by parties outside the organization who review workpapers, interview key stakeholders, review the audit plan, the department's budget, and training program.
3. The results of the QAIP should be communicated to internal auditors and used to improve the quality of the unit's training and development activities.

Chapter 78

Questionnaires/Surveys

Surveys can be used to collect information from many individuals while performing a variety of audit and consulting engagements. Operational audits can benefit from the information about workplace practices and makes it possible to compare, contrast, and benchmark information. Surveys are also effective for reviewing intangible topics such as the ethical environment, the corporate culture, and entity-level controls, which require an examination of soft controls like integrity, values, accountability, leadership, openness, empowerment, and competence. These soft controls and other control environment elements are complex and arguably some of the most difficult to assess.

COSO's Internal Control—Integrated Framework (IC-IF) draws attention to the vital role that the control environment and entity-level controls play in establishing and preserving a strong internal control environment. Internal auditors are expected to evaluate the organization's tone at the top, management's operating style, and risk management philosophy. While reviewing these subjects often pose unique challenges, with data internal auditors can make appropriate recommendations to improve the organization's governance and promote appropriate ethics and values within the organization.

Surveys should be conducted like projects so good planning and preparation reduce the likelihood that key steps will be missed and avoid wasting time and money. To conduct surveys effectively, the following stages are critical:

1. Set Objectives: A successful survey begins with the establishment of clear objectives that define what will be accomplished. This will provide guidance for information collection and establish the baseline for everything from the resources needed to the amount of time the survey will last until completion. Conversely, when objectives are not clear, surveys lack focus, ask confusing, vague or unrelated questions, and in the worst-case scenario become a costly waste of time and money. Always ask, what exactly do we want to find out?

2. Design the survey: This is a good time to apply the maxim "An ounce of prevention is worth a pound of cure." The following questions are essential to design a survey effectively:
   – How many people should be polled to feel comfortable acting on their responses?
   – Who will be included and who will be excluded from the survey?
   – How is the data going to be collected and tabulated?
   – What will be done with the data after getting it?
   – What resources (e.g., money, time, skills, tools) are available to pursue the objectives?
   – Do we have the support from senior management to do this?
   – What can go wrong and what needs to go right?
3. Prepare the questionnaire. Make sure to use clear and simple language. Match what information you are seeking against the amount of time available to find out. You should not conduct a larger-than-necessary survey asking myriad questions because the response rate and the quality of data will decrease with longer questionnaires. Close-ended questions are easier to tabulate and analyze, but open-ended questions should be considered too because they provide insightful feedback from survey participants.
4. Administer the survey. While running the survey look out for unusual and unexpected situations developing and be receptive to informal feedback from participants. Treat the survey with a sense of urgency, giving reasonable but short deadlines for completion. Have a high-ranking officer in the organization write the cover letter or announcement, and have a process in place to send reminder notices. Use blanket reminders if anonymity is more important than response rate; otherwise, you can target your reminders.
5. Manage and analyze survey data. This involves collecting, tabulating, and reviewing the data. When conducting a survey, you are likely to notice that data starts coming in shortly after the questionnaire is distributed, and the number of responses decreases over time. This is another reason not to give participants too much time. If they don't complete it immediately, many of them will not do it later. As the completed questionnaires start coming in you can start to enter the information in your spreadsheet or database. If you are using an online survey application, it will likely have basic data analysis built-in and you can download the data, so there is no need to manually enter information into a spreadsheet. Either way, look at the data early on as it will help you identify issues with the data if there are any and decide how they should be addressed. Don't be intimidated by statistics because you are likely to find out what you need by using simple calculations. Just remember to ask these two key questions during the analysis. 1. What is the overall score for each question and 2. What is the score among {subgroup}. The results can be plotted on graphs and charts.

6. Report the results. The last step is reporting the results, which also includes making presentations of the methodology, results, analysis, and conclusions. Reports often include charts, tables, and graphs and most use colors liberally. The objective is to communicate the results clearly and concisely.

Tips for Designing Effective Surveys

1. Avoid lengthy questionnaires, keep the questions simple, and the response options logical.
2. Avoid jargon, abbreviations, very technical, colloquial, or slang terms.
3. Plan and design appropriately so the survey can be repeated in the future to compare results and perform trend analysis.
4. Avoid negative questions such as "Did the auditor in-charge fail to give you timely status updates?"
5. Avoid confusion with Agree/Disagree items. For example: "Employees should not be required to work excessive overtime or travel on weekends."
6. Decide carefully when to use closed or open-ended questions.
7. Phrase your question clearly when asking open-ended questions.
8. Learn the characteristics of the survey's targeted respondents, so the response categories make sense to them.
9. Questions that rely on time periods should be specific and defined clearly, ideally instructing respondents what units of time to use.
10. Run the questionnaire with the endorsement of senior management
11. Analyze the data without overcomplicating the process with excessive statistics.
12. Whenever possible, share the information with employees so they know that you valued their input and that something was done with the results. They will be far more willing to complete the next survey you send to them.

Surveys make it possible for internal auditors to collect large amounts of data. When used as a complement to other sources of evidence, the result is better and more authoritative evidence to evaluate objective and subjective topics.

Summary

1. Surveys allow internal auditors to collect objective information to better assess objective and subjective topics, like the corporate culture, ethics, leadership style, and workplace politics.
2. Surveys are typically conducted online, but they can also be conducted orally (by phone or face-to-face) and they can be conducted in group settings too.
3. Repeating the survey over time allows internal auditors to compare results, perform trend analysis, and evaluate changes within the organization.

Chapter 79

RACI Chart

Effective communications, teamwork, accountability, follow-through and supervision are key ingredients in the effective work of programs, processes, and projects. Unfortunately, many organizations suffer under the weight of problematic dynamics that limit the opportunities for success caused by confusion, finger-pointing, misunderstandings, and other group dysfunctions. These issues can be lessened by using a tool that clarifies ownership, collaboration, and delegation so everyone involved knows what is expected of them.

An effective process is characterized by clarity related to what tasks will be performed, who will do them, who will provide assistance, who will be informed about what is being done, and who accepts the results and determines they are acceptable. This facilitates coordination, delegation, accountability, communication, supervision and typical related controls like segregation of duties, and reviews and approvals.

The RACI Chart or Diagram is a very useful tool to help processes operate effectively. RACI is an acronym derived from the four roles and responsibilities that various parties play in a program or process. It describes the participants' roles in completing tasks and it is especially useful in clarifying roles and responsibilities because it identifies who does what. The roles identified in a RACI Diagram are Responsible, Accountable (or Approver), Consulted, and Informed and it can apply to individuals or departments, but the more specific the parties mentioned are, the less likely it is that there will be confusion.

Responsible

This refers to those individuals responsible for performing the task and making sure the work is done. Naturally, for every task identified there needs to be at least one participant assigned as Responsible who makes sure that the task is performed according to specifications and as required by the approver. Others may assist or lend support, but they work as resources allocated to those responsible and this arrangement keeps accountabilities in place.

The participant role Responsible on the RACI Diagram indicates "who" and is noted with the letter R.

Accountable (also Approver)

This identifies the individual that approves the completed activity. Since a review is required before an approval, this individual is accountable for making sure the activity is satisfactory and meets performance standards. In many instances, this person could also be the one who delegates the work. There must be only one accountable person specified for each task.

The role Accountable provides information about who approves the activity after it is completed and is noted with the letter A.

Consulted

This role describes those whose knowledge and expertise is important for the task to be completed effectively. Those consulted are sometimes referred to as subject matter experts (SMEs) and there is a two-way communication between those responsible and those consulted. This role is similar to a support role, helping through their expertise to enable the completion of tasks or deliverables.

Consulted assist the people responsible and is shown with the letter C.

Informed

This role refers to those who should be kept up to date about the activities being performed, the progress made on them, or their completion. Sometimes the communication occurs only when the task is completed, but that should be agreed upon. It consists of one-way communications.

This role is shown with the letter I.

Sometimes the person that is Accountable for a task is also the person Responsible for completing it. When this happens, it is indicated in the matrix in one of two ways:

1. The task or deliverable has a role Accountable on it, but no role Responsible for its completion. In this case Responsible is implied.
2. The task or deliverable has a role of R/A: Responsible/Approver. This is the preferred approach due to its clarity.

Every task should have at least one R, and one A or R/A—someone has to do it, and someone has to be accountable for it being done correctly. Additionally, everyone listed in the RACI Diagram should agree with the roles being assigned to them and have the necessary skills and resources to get the work done.

Since the list of participants on the top row of the RACI Diagram is often taken from the organization's chart, some may find it useful to also indicate who is not involved in the sequence of activities. So, by specifying who does not participate, it can make it clear that those resources are relieved from any involvement in the project or process, and are therefore free to engage in other activities. If this dimension is added to the RACI Diagram, it can be indicated using the letter O (for Omitted), thus resulting in an RACIO Diagram.

How to Construct a RACI Chart

The matrix is typically created with a vertical axis (left-hand column) listing of tasks or activities. The items on the list can consist of the key activates from a Gantt Chart, Work Breakdown Structure (WBS) or other list of activities or deliverables for a process or project. The horizontal axis on the top row shows the parties involved; it can be individuals, teams, or relevant units from an organizational chart, but I prefer individual's names whenever possible to be specific and ensure clarity.

At the intersecting point the corresponding letter is entered based on the role each person plays in the accomplishment of the activities noted. The following is an illustration of a RACI Diagram used in the preparation for and delivery of an in-house training program (Table 79.1).

In addition to the benefits it provides during planning for the effective execution of project and process activities, a RACI chart can be a very helpful tool as

Table 79.1 Sample RACI Chart for Departmental Training

Tasks	Sam	John	Sandy (Manager)	Vendor
Perform needs assessment	R	C	A	
Review existing training	R	C	A	
Develop course	C	C	A	R
Handle logistics	A	R	I	C
Deliver course	C	C	A	R
Evaluate course	I	R	A	
Debrief	C	C	R/A	C

an add-on to procedures documents. Since in many organizations the procedures documents show what needs to be done, but sometimes don't show who is expected to perform those activities, finger-pointing and missed steps become the norm. In those cases, a RACI chart added to the procedures documents will often solve the problem.

Similarly, RACI charts can also serve as a great supplement to risk and control matrices by showing not only what risks and controls pertain to the area in scope, but also the roles of various individuals as they relate to the performance of the control activities. In fact, the procedures documents can identify the key activities and controls, and by adding the RACI roles provide a more comprehensive view of these elements.

Since the RACI Diagram does not include due dates or details about how to communicate with those labeled "I," other tools may serve as companions. Gantt Charts can be useful when necessary to show task start, end, and duration. A Communications Matrix may be useful as well to indicate how communication should be provided to those that should be Informed, how often, using what media (e.g., meeting, phone, video conference, report), who should be copied, and where the corresponding document or notes should be stored.

Summary

1. RACI Diagrams help organizations correct a lack of accountability.
2. RACI diagrams show for each key activity in a process or project, who is responsible for performing the activity, who is accountable (or approver) to make sure it is done according to established specifications, who should be consulted and who should be informed during the work or upon completion.
3. A RACI Diagram can be added to a Risk and Control Matrix, and can be accompanied by a Communications Matrix to add additional details, like which activities are controls, when communications should occur, and using which media.

Chapter 80

Recommendations

Internal auditors review the activities of the organization to identify conditions and practices that are below expectations and that limit the organization's ability to achieve its objectives. When these opportunities for improvement are identified, we can refer to the IIA Standards for guidance. Standard 2210—Governance states:

The internal audit activity must assess and make appropriate recommendations to improve the organization's governance processes for:

- Making strategic and operational decisions.
- Overseeing risk management and control.
- Promoting appropriate ethics and values within the organization.
- Ensuring effective organizational performance management and accountability.
- Communicating risk and control information to appropriate areas of the organization.
- Coordinating the activities of, and communicating information among, the board, external and internal auditors, other assurance providers, and management.

When communicating with audit clients, internal auditors'

final communication of engagement results must include applicable conclusions, as well as applicable recommendations and/or action plans. Where appropriate, the internal auditors' opinion should be provided. An opinion must take into account the expectations of senior management, the board, and other stakeholders and must be supported by sufficient, reliable, relevant, and useful information.

(Standard 2410.A1)

Engagement recommendations are based on the auditors' observations and conclusions. They consist of actions that are expected to correct existing issues or improve operations. Recommendations may suggest approaches to correcting or improving conditions and performance, and should help management achieve desired objectives. Recommendations can be general or specific. For example, under some circumstances an internal auditor may recommend a general course of action and specific suggestions for implementation. In other cases, the internal auditor may suggest further investigation or study to determine what is the best course of action.

Recommendations should be developed carefully, giving consideration to the costs of their implementation in relation to the expected benefits.

A challenge some internal auditors encounter is deciding what the best recommendation is, especially since many are not experts in the program or process they are reviewing. While planning for every engagement is expected, many auditors may not become "experts" before or during the audit. This does not preclude their ability to perform the review, but it could limit their ability to develop exceptional recommendations. Given these dynamics, the following are some scenarios and suggested approaches.

1. If the internal auditor has expertise in the subject matter, which could have been gained by previously working in that area or having performed similar reviews in the past, the internal auditor may be able to provide valuable recommendations based on that in-depth knowledge.
2. If the internal auditor lacks sufficient expertise, but has access to a robust database of related topics and/or subject matter experts in the field (within the internal audit department or otherwise), such database or SME could be contacted for guidance and assistance.
3. If the internal auditor lacks both the expertise and available resources, the internal auditor can discuss the matter with the client and work collaboratively to determine what is an appropriate course of action.

Internal auditors should consider engaging the client and working collaboratively as suggested in Step 3 regardless of the amount of expertise the auditor possesses. In fact, even if the auditor has the expertise, the decision to make the recommendation is best managed as follows:

1. If the audit client is unfamiliar with the subject matter or otherwise unable to decide what remediation is appropriate, the auditor should provide the recommendation.
2. If the audit client has the familiarity and knowledge of the subject matter and can formulate a reasonable corrective action, the internal auditor should describe and discuss the criteria used, the condition noted, the cause triggering the issue, and the effect and consequences the issue is causing. Then ask the audit client to provide some thoughts on how best to address the matter.

Engaging the audit client in the formulation of the recommendation has multiple benefits. Audit clients are responsible for the objectives, risks, controls, and resources assigned to programs and processes. As such, they should "act like owners" and correct issues affecting those programs and processes. When the auditor provides all the answers (i.e., recommendations too), audit clients may treat the recommendation as a mandate, therefore limiting their ownership of the issue and commitment for the corrective action. They may also embrace the mindset of "I'm doing this because the auditor told me to," rather than taking ownership of the problem and the solution to it. This approach, when repeated, also results in creating or promoting a sense of dependency whereby the audit client, rather than fixing the issues related to their areas of responsibility, rely on others (in this case the auditor) to provide them with the problem and its solution.

Everyone working in organizations should take ownership for their work area and the results of their efforts. They should also create and promote a culture of fixing problems when they occur. Internal auditors should help create this type of initiative, ownership, accountability, creativity, and resourcefulness within the units audited whenever possible. Giving recommendations without healthy discussions with process owners may reduce the likelihood of this work environment taking root.

Summary

1. Internal auditors can add value by providing recommendations to their audit clients. This way, auditors are not only communicating issues, but also possible solutions to the issues.
2. It is recommended that internal auditors work collaboratively with audit clients in the formulation of recommendations for corrective action. This practice increases ownership by audit clients.
3. Recommendations should balance the cost of implementing the corrective action in relation to the benefits expected from it. This practice is consistent with a risk-based approach and reduces bureaucracy, excess paperwork, and unnecessary work.

Chapter 81

Reporting

The IIA Standards indicate that internal auditors must communicate the results of their work. Reporting is the third phase after planning and fieldwork, and typically results in the publication of a draft report approximately 2 weeks after the end of fieldwork, and the publication of a final report 2 weeks after that. Some organizations issue the draft report at the time of the exit meeting, but that represents a small percentage of internal audit departments. Some auditors take longer than 2 weeks after fieldwork to release their reports, which is problematic because delays publishing reports diminish the internal audit unit's image.

While the IIA Standards do not prescribe a format for the audit report, they state that they must include applicable conclusions, applicable recommendations, or action plans. Reports may also include an opinion and typically include a background, scope, and objectives section to provide context for the readers.

Reports should be clear and avoid jargon and overly-complex and technical language that readers may find confusing. Sometimes technical language cannot be avoided. In those cases, complex terms should be replaced if possible, or explained when used. Internal auditors can also use footers, endnotes, or a glossary.

In many organizations, audit reports are fifteen pages or less, focusing on the key issues that need to be communicated, while avoiding lengthy elaborations and excessive wordiness because readers have limited time. An executive summary also helps by providing a one or two-page synopsis of the most important audit findings.

To be helpful, audit reports should balance what is said with how it is said. Tone matters, so using a positive tone helps to minimize the potential for negative feelings surrounding what is for many an already stressful situation. Grammar and logical flow also matter as they make the document easier to read and readers can focus on the information contained without the distraction of typographical or grammatical errors.

Observations should be presented in descending order of importance. If the report is organized in sub-sections, each of them should have its findings presented in descending order.

Accuracy is extremely important as errors will negatively impact the credibility of the internal audit team. Audit reports should be factually correct, so all of the information should be documented and referenced in the workpapers.

The audit report is written to share and communicate the results of the audit, but also should be written persuasively to convince the reader of the significant of the findings. Reports should compel management to take corrective action.

Audit clients may offer to correct an issue during fieldwork and ask that in return it not be mentioned in the report. Internal auditors cannot do this. Since the item was discovered during the audit, it is reportable. However, in this situation internal auditors should give the client credit for their prompt response resolving the issue and indicate in the report that it was corrected during fieldwork. It is important for auditors to work with audit clients to not only address the identified issues but the root cause of the issues themselves.

Internal auditors should also acknowledge satisfactory performance in audit reports. This practice is fair to audit clients and will also help to improve the image of internal auditors, whose reports are exception-based focusing on issues, but sometimes not mentioning the positive dynamics that internal auditors witness during their reviews. It is important to balance the acknowledgment of satisfactory performance with the severity of the findings presented in the report. If the issues are serious, acknowledging positive events could detract from the severity and tone that the report should present, and it may appear gratuitous.

The percentage of the audit that should be allocated to writing the audit report varies. It depends on the complexity of the engagement, the number of findings, and the writing ability of the writer. It may also be impacted by the quality of the workpapers and the ease and ability of the report writer to verify the information during the writing process. Confusing or incomplete workpapers, and poorly referenced documents often delay the report-writing process.

Internal auditors should discuss audit findings with the main audit contact during fieldwork to get agreement about the issues. By discussing these observations and issuing findings throughout the audit, exit meetings are generally more productive and shorter. A similar benefit is obtained during the report-writing process, because that earlier agreement serves to expedite the acceptance of the draft and the release of the final report.

Accelerating the Publication of Audit Reports

Sometimes internal auditors have difficulties publishing reports promptly. This can be caused by having multiple layers of internal auditors in the chain of command reviewing the audit reports before they are published. While it is important to have several individuals check the completeness, accuracy, and tone of the report, too may reviewers operating in sequence can delay the process.

Some organizations have removed some of the layers of review for standardized, recurring and somewhat simple engagement reports to accelerate the reporting process. Others have simplified the process by replacing text-heavy, long-sentence reports, with templates that can be completed with bulleted items and short sentences. Some publish their audit reports using Microsoft PowerPoint.

Other organizations conduct cluster reviews, where rather than having several reviewers examine the report one after the other, most or all the reviewers gather and review the report simultaneously. This parallel processing reduces the back-and-forth that the traditional and iterative review process produces, and all review notes are received and addressed once.

Management should respond to draft reports promptly, so the final report can be issued. The response to the draft report generally consists of management's agreement with the findings and the submission of an action plan that includes the detail of the corrective action, the date when this action will be implemented and the title and/or name of the person who is responsible for doing it. When this urgency does not occur naturally in the organization, it may be necessary to make this a policy requirement instituted by senior management and/or the audit committee of the board. By setting expectations before the audit begins, delays can be avoided later.

Audit reports are the product of internal auditors and in most cases the only thing that audit clients see. As such, it should be done professionally, accurately, and delivered promptly.

Summary

1. Audit reports should be written accurately, objectively, clearly, concisely, constructively, the information presented should be complete, and the reports should be published promptly.
2. Reports should be written persuasively, with an appropriate tone that balances what is said with how it is said.
3. Findings should be discussed with the audit client during fieldwork to verify their accuracy and for the client to begin preparing a management response. This approach typically reduces delays so final audit reports can be published promptly.

Chapter 82

Risk

While regulatory risks are always front-of-mind for internal auditors, it is also important to consider the cost of compliance failures. Fines, penalties, and the loss of operating licenses remain key concerns, but increasingly organizations are subject to lawsuits that can result in large financial impacts and reputational damage. Some of these lawsuits are due to failures to implement effective privacy controls or respond promptly and appropriately to operational breakdowns thus precipitating crises.

Some of the risks of concern in today's digital economy include:

Privacy and data protection. The protection of information that could result in identity theft, fraud or the loss of wealth-generating proprietary assets, such as know-how, patents, and other forms of intellectual property. This personal and proprietary information is highly valuable, and it is also subject to regulatory risks so internal auditors should include privacy in their risk assessments and test the related controls over personal and corporate information. Testing should include encryption and penetration testing to assess the organization's preparedness.

Cloud computing. Organizations are increasing the use of cloud services to benefit from the versatility, higher employee productivity, and low cost that these services represent. However, storing corporate data in unsecure apps can compromise security and expose sensitive information. Storing data, files, and passwords without controls like encryption or lack of multi-factor authentication to access the service can result in the loss of intellectual property, compliance violations that trigger regulatory action, malware infections, breach of contract with customers, and revenue and market share loss.

Service provider risks. Many organizations have outsourced non-critical services to third party providers, so they can focus on their core business. This action can lower operating costs and allow management to focus on key business functions. However, using service providers can result in some risks caused by the fact that the hiring organization does not control the processes at the service provider and as such are not privy to the operational and transaction risks that exist. There are also risks to the confidentiality of the information being stored or transmitted, the business continuity plans, or lack thereof, and the potential for business disruption caused by adverse events affecting the outsource provider. Disruptions at a service provider can carry a high financial and reputational cost but may also trigger regulatory issues if reports are not filed, or if data is compromised.

Social media. The organization should have a policy in place, assigned staffing with adequate funding to carry out its duties, and provide appropriate training on acceptable content, privacy protection and issue resolution. Access controls are also essential to limit the ability to act as the representative of the organization in social media, and training (or at least expressing expectations through policies and memos) to employees of the proper use of social media. In addition, internal auditors should examine the strategy in place to benefit from social media and the alignment between strategy and operating practices. This includes channel selection, consistency of messaging and standardization, and activity monitoring. Examples include the number of comments that mention the organization, comparison and benchmarking to competitors, issues resolved successfully, customer satisfaction and comparison to other customer service channels, amount of sales and number of customers originating through social media channels, retention rates and repeat customer purchases.

Supply chain. Many organizations have diversified their supply chain to lower costs. While companies improve the acquisition of products, supply chains can also cause risks due to customer demands for faster response times, hiring and retaining skilled workers, over-concentration of suppliers, quality management, natural or environmental threats, counterfeit products, poor quality, and business interruption due to supply chain disruption.

Knowledge. The uniqueness of business activities can be a competitive advantage, but an aging workforce, especially as these individuals retire, can create a difficult situation for companies to avoid business disruptions. Technological changes, reengineering, and business changes also contribute to the challenges of obtaining, retaining, and upgrading the skills of workers. Without the requisite knowledge, business disruption is likely to occur, impacting customer sales, market share, and even compliance with complex business requirements.

Competition. Most companies have faced competition from domestic and international organizations. In some cases, the location of the competitor is irrelevant due to the use of the internet, which has allowed even small and new companies to become major market disruptors. Organizations must address

the new types, and intensity of competitive pressures, understanding that these pressures can cause substantial financial effects including insolvency.
Regardless of the type of risk, organizations should consider using a two-layer approach to protect the organization and its assets.

Governance. This consists of the structures, roles, and responsibilities needed to manage risks at the entity, business unit, and program levels.
Process. These focus on identifying the location and manner that risks may be triggered affecting operations, systems, and third parties.

When the organization's risk assessment includes an international dimension, a unique range of new considerations are needed as new risks are created or existing ones are amplified. Examples include political, foreign currency, taxation, linguistic, cultural, communications, accounting, legal, and economic risks.

The impact can be substantial. Since legal cultures vary, it generally impacts how contracts are written and enforced, insolvency laws, protection of property rights, anti-corruption laws and practices, data privacy, employee relations, workplace conditions and practices, and the treatment of creditors. In some countries, bureaucracy can complicate, delay and even restrict import, export, licensing, and other matters. Protectionist trade policies and practices can result in tariffs, quotas on imports and exports, exchange rate manipulation, and even the adoption of restrictions under the guise that they are due to safety concerns. Economic practices may result in capital controls, limiting the flow of money or assets, whose severity could restrict cross-border payments, the purchase of needed supplies or equipment, the exchange of currencies, and the repatriation of profits.

Environmental regulations, practices, and issues can also affect international organizations through changing regulations, customer preferences, and social dynamics. These dynamics can require adherence with unclear, complex and expensive procedures to meet environmental standards.

Given the diversity of topics affecting domestic and international organizations, it is important to obtain relevant and timely information on regulatory matters. All organizations must understand and monitor the regulatory risks they are exposed to, and how they affect the achievement of business objectives, because they need to respond timely and appropriately to any changes. This type of risk intelligence can be obtained by leveraging internal or external expertise. Prompt action helps to contain revenue loss and protect the organization's reputation, customer and vendor confidence.

One of the main objectives of risk management is to protect assets and stakeholders of the organization from harm. This harm can occur in the form of financial loss, poor reputation, bodily injury, contamination, and other outcomes.

Another important objective of risk management is to take advantage of opportunities.

Businesses tend to focus on the "inbound" harm that an organization could suffer, but the organization itself could also cause harm to others. This harm by the company could result in contamination, bodily injury to customers or bystanders, structural damage to structures, loss of personal information, among others.

Internal auditors should audit the risk management process, its objectives, and practices. The content of management's risk reports, and the determination of their completeness and accuracy, are generally considered the responsibility of management. However, the absence of important risks, and faulty methodologies that yield concerning results may warrant auditor comments as well.

Strategic risks have played a prominent role in internal auditors' and risk managers' lexicon over the past few years. It reflects a growing realization that organizations should not expect to succeed in the long term if they are only managing for the short term. Sustainability has also become part of the driving force as stakeholders demand responsible actions by organizations, so they remain a going concern, and can continue to contribute to the stakeholders that depend on them. This of course goes far beyond shareholders, who wish to maximize their financial returns, but also the employees whose livelihoods depend on these organizations, providers whose business futures are close intertwined, and the local, state/provincial and federal/national taxing authorities that depend on them for tax revenue.

When considering strategic, operational, financial, compliance, IT or other types of risks that can impact the achievement of objectives, it is important to balance:

Internal: What can occur within the organization
External: What can occur outside the organization
Present/Immediate: What can happen within the next year
Future/Emerging: What can happen more than a year into the future

Having a broad perspective to the identification and subsequent assessment and management of risks will undoubtedly bring up scenarios impacting people (e.g., what they do, where they are, how qualified, motivated and ethical they are), processes (e.g., how sensibly they are structured, how clear are the expectations and instructions for performing the work, how well products or services are produced), technology (e.g., how reliable and secure are the systems, how easy to use and helpful making it easy to enter, calculate, and create useful output).

With these elements in mind, The Sarasota County COSO Strategic Risk Framework provides an apt illustration of 25 strategic risks and related dynamics that should be considered during such assessment of organizational risks.

1. Managers reinforce the need for ethical decision-making.
2. Executives reinforce the need for ethical decision-making.
3. In doing the work, people follow pertinent laws, regulations, and policies.
4. People use appropriately the county resources entrusted to them.
5. People in the departments do not accept personal gifts or other things of value from anyone with whom they do business.

6. People are free of outside interests that conflict with the duties and responsibilities of their jobs.
7. The job training employees receive improves customer service/outcomes.
8. The organization orients new employees to their jobs.
9. People understand the desired outcomes most important fulfilling their mission and objectives.
10. People routinely accomplish those outcomes most important to their mission and objectives.
11. People have a healthy work environment.
12. People have a safe work environment.
13. People are safe from potential physical harm.
14. People are safe from potential emotional harm.
15. If there is a major computer systems failure, the organization could resume effective operations with minimum disruption.
16. The organization could continue effective operations if it had to evacuate the facilities for 2–3 days.
17. The organization's practices minimize the chance an employee could be accused of improper behavior.
18. Cash and other valuables entrusted to the organization are physically protected from theft or harm.
19. The organization's irreplaceable records are physically protected from theft or harm.
20. Access to confidential information is restricted.
21. People communicate across organizational boundaries.
22. Access to key business records and confidential information is monitored routinely.
23. Supervisors are notified routinely when significant issues or concerns arise.
24. Managers are responsive to tissues brought to their attention.
25. Executives are responsive to issues brought to their attention.*

Internal auditors' objective is to determine if the risk management program provides reasonable assurance that risks are being managed within desirable ranges enabling the organization to achieve its objectives. These risks relate to uncertainty that can cause potential harm, like the impact of natural disasters, man-made hazards, losses due to theft or embezzlement, the unintended disclosure of confidential information or the loss of key personnel. Risk management is also concerned with opportunities, such as technological advances, competitor insolvency, the ability to hire high-potential and talent individuals or entering an emerging market or sector.

---

* The list was adapted from the Sarasota County COSO Focus Points / Strategic Risks / Elements of High Performance, from the book *Best Practices: Evaluating Corporate Culture* by James Roth.

It behooves auditors to keep a broad perspective, be imaginative, introduce quantitative and qualitative elements to their work, and work collaboratively with management to make sure risk is managed, or embraced, appropriately.

Summary

1. Risks are events that can affect the organization's ability to achieve its objectives. Some events are negative, others represent opportunities.
2. Internal auditors should help the organization identify, assess, and manage strategic, operational, reporting, compliance, IT, fraud, and other risks to the organization.
3. Risks should be examined in terms of their likelihood and impact, how long their effects could linger harming the organization, and how quickly these risks could materialize and impact the organization. In addition, risks should be assessed based on their historical and current existence, as well as their future potential.

Chapter 83

Risk-Control Matrix

The Risk-Control Matrix (sometimes also referred to as the Risks and Controls Matrix and RCM) is a tool used to primarily document business objectives, risks, and controls. It provides a centralized repository of this information so internal auditors can better understand the link between these three components.

Internal auditors must be focused during their reviews, prioritize what to audit, and concentrate on what matters most to the business. Since there are often insufficient resources to cover the entire audit plan, internal auditors can no longer conduct sprawling or unclear audits looking under every rock hoping to find something somewhere.

An audit is a complex undertaking that requires examining documents, speaking with employees, observing business practices, and evaluating controls in business programs and processes. Given these dynamics, this document organizes what needs to be understood and provides a clear roadmap for effective testing.

Key criteria for risk and control matrices include:

1. The *objectives* of the activity under review. If you don't know what auditees are supposed to accomplish, what are you auditing? You need to know the criteria under review to determine if the program or process is achieving its purpose.
2. The *risks* jeopardizing the achievement of the objectives. Modern internal auditing is risk-based, which means we need to know what are the biggest factors and events that could prevent business objectives from being met.
3. The *controls* that manage or mitigate the business risks assessed. Well-designed programs and processes should include controls to manage risks.
4. The *audit steps* to be performed to evaluate the design and operating effectiveness of internal controls.

How to Prepare a Risk and Control Matrix

Objectives

The first step is to document the objectives of the unit, program, or process under review. If management has not documented the objectives, or if these have not been communicated and linked to employees' performance evaluations, that is a design weakness that should be discussed with business management. After all, if employees don't know what they're supposed to do, what exactly are they doing every day? How could we assess efficiency and effectiveness without the required parameters?

Risks

Next, we need to list the risks that threaten the achievement of business objectives. Quite often this step is not exhaustive enough or is performed by individuals with limited knowledge of the process being assessed. The most important problem this creates is that if a risk has not been identified, it won't be measured or analyzed either, so brainstorming, partnering with process owners and fellow auditors, and using prefabricated lists of common risks will help.

After listing the risks, we should categorize them. Common categories include Compliance, Operational, Financial Reporting, non-Financial Reporting, Strategic, Information Technology, Information Security, and Fraud.

Risks are often measured using a 3-point scale of High–Medium–Low. Using these measures, the Impact of the risk, if it were to materialize, and the likelihood of the risk occurring, is rated. A more precise assessment is possible by using a 5-point scale like this one:

Impact	Likelihood
1. Insignificant	1. Rare
2. Minor	2. Unlikely
3. Moderate	3. Possible
4. Major	4. Likely
5. Catastrophic	5. Almost certain

A key limitation of only using adjectives as measures is that they are subjective. As such, one person's "Minor" risk could be someone else's "Moderate" risk, and so on. While this difference of opinion will always exist, the prevalence and magnitude of the differences generally increases when the risk assessment process is predominantly subjective. To improve on this, impact ratings can be expanded to provide more detailed descriptions based on explicit ranges, facts, or events for each. This may involve monetary amounts, the degree of disruption to the organization, bodily injury to workers and others, security, health and safety, social, economic, reputational and environmental impacts. A similar process can be followed with Likelihood, where estimated probability ranges provide greater clarity.

Controls

Next, we need to document the controls that business management has put in place to mitigate the risks and protect company assets. For each risk, we should list the corresponding control(s) that mitigate them. Each control is also categorized based on its characteristics. For example:

Type:	Preventive: Prevents a risk from occurring Detective: Detects when a risk event occurred
Automation:	Manual: Performed by an individual Automated: Performed by a computer application or other machine Combination: Semi-automated
Frequency:	Annual, Semi-annual, Quarterly, Monthly, Weekly, Daily, Multiple Times a Day, or With Every Transaction

It is important to list the name and position of the owner for each control, especially those controls that mitigate high risks. The risk owner is the individual with the knowledge, resources, and authority to be responsible for the management and monitoring of the risk identified. This person is also responsible for the implementation of responses, so by identifying the risk owner, the specific activities taken to perform the control activity, and the mechanism that tells the risk owner if the control has failed (e.g., reports, metrics), accountability for control oversight is clearer.

An important step now is to examine the design of the program or process and ask questions like:

- Are there significant risks lacking at least one mitigating control?
- Are there highly-rated risks with too few controls?
- Are there low-rated risks with too many controls?
- Are controls mostly detective?
- Are controls mostly manual?

Audit Steps

The next step is to prepare to test control effectiveness.

Internal auditors should use a risk-based, top–down approach to testing and focus on those controls related to important risks, and whose failure would significantly jeopardize the achievement of business objectives. The focus is placed on those controls that cover or mitigate more than one risk, support an entire process, are among the organization's entity-level controls, or contain analytic elements to provide broader coverage of the underlying transactions and activities.

Additional considerations are the potential for fraud, inefficiency, abuse, and waste that could have a significant impact on the business. The range of scope is smaller than financial statement materiality as defined by external auditors, and although I agree with John Wooden that "little things make big things happen," as internal auditors we must use our judgment to test judiciously and know why we test what we test.

Testing procedures can include any or a combination of: Inspection, observation, confirmation, reperformance, recalculation, and analytical procedures.

As internal auditors gather and analyze the results of the testing, it is important to compare the inherent risk (i.e., before the control is considered), to the residual risk (i.e., after the control has been assessed). This will provide valuable insights into the quality of the control structure and the reliability that can be placed on it.

A risk and control matrix may look as shown on Figure 83.1, but organizations generally add additional information to meet their unique needs, like the risk and control owners, residual risk, a SOX control identifier, and other types of risk categories instead of the SORCItF (Strategic, Operational, Reporting, Compliance, IT, Fraud) such as CAMELS (Capital Adequacy, Asset Quality, Management, Earnings, Liquidity, Sensitivity to Market Risk—used in financial services), PESTLE (Political, Economic, Social, Technological, Legal, Environmental—as general risk categories), HACCP (Hazard Analysis and Critical Control Points—food safety), and CVE (cybersecurity vulnerabilities)*.

The Risk and Control Matrix is your roadmap during planning, an indispensable aide when preparing your work program, a prioritization tool when deciding

Objectives	Risks											Controls				Audit Program Steps
Objective	Risks	S	O	R	C	IT	F	Prob.	Imp.	Vel	Pers.	Control	P/D	A/M	X/D/W/M/Q	Audit Step
O1	R11											C111				AS1 (C111, C112, C113, C121)
												C112				
												C113				
	R12											C121				AS2 (C122, C123)
												C122				
												C123				
												C124				AS3 (C124)
	R13											-				
	-											C141				

Figure 83.1   Risk and control matrix.

---

* CAMELS: Capital adequacy, Asset quality, Management, Earnings, Liquidity, and Sensitivity. PESTLE: Political, Economic, Social, Technological, Legal, Environmental. HACCP: Hazard Analysis, Critical Control Point. CVE: Common Vulnerabilities and Exposures.

what to test, and in general the most important workpaper to determine what is relevant and useful during every engagement. By sorting the risks based on significance and impact, every audit step will be purposeful and will enable internal auditors to only review important controls. The RCM helps facilitate the decision process to make sure internal auditors are focused on what matters most to the business.

Summary

1. The Risk and Controls Matrix (RCM) gathers information related to the business objectives, risks, controls, and audit steps pertaining to the area being audited.
2. The RCM helps auditors focus on what matters most to the organization. By collecting and analyzing the information in the RCM, internal auditors are better prepared to conduct risk-based audits.
3. The RCM provides a mechanism to identify design deficiencies, and relate operating deficiencies to the corresponding controls, risks, and business objectives.

Chapter 84

Risk-Based Auditing

Risk-based auditing has become a key characteristic of modern internal auditing. For decades traditional internal auditing practices focused on testing controls to determine whether these were present and functioning, but increasingly a key question was asked: Why are we testing these controls? This question was sometimes answered with: Because it is there, because it is mentioned in the policies and procedures, or because the manager/process owner indicated that it is a control they perform within the process being audited.

The fact is that testing a control because it is there is not a sufficiently compelling reason. Some of the limitations of that rationale are that some controls exist because those involved in the process have always performed that activity, or they were told to perform that activity. A control's usefulness depends on its ability to mitigate a risk adequately so its resulting potential impact and/or likelihood lies within the acceptable risk appetite.

Internal auditors should examine controls and consider them in relation to the risks those controls are supposed to mitigate. With regard to these risks, they only matter to the extent that they could limit the entity's ability to achieve its objectives. In other words, the driver of every internal audit should be the entity's objectives and the risks that threaten the achievement of the objectives. Controls, then, are valuable to the extent that they mitigate those worrisome risks. Risk-based auditing consists of understanding these three components: (1) focusing on prioritizing the objectives, (2) reviewing the objectives in relation to risks, and (3) ranking the mitigating controls so only the key ones are tested.

Another important aspect of risk-based auditing is deciding, based on an examination of the process' design and information provided by relevant management, if there are too many controls for low-rated risks. When that is the case, internal auditors are encouraged to discuss the imbalance with management and right-size the situation by eliminating unnecessary controls or modifying the process so controls are better aligned with business needs.

Traditional auditing often consisted of controls-based auditing and auditors whose focus was disproportionately centered on compliance reviews should be aware of the risk of testing controls by rote. Many compliance audits are mandated by regulators, and they sometimes provide checklists and specify which procedures to perform and how. While internal auditors may not have any say into what and how these reviews are performed, this practice should not carry onto traditional internal auditing.

A risk-based audit approach makes it possible for internal auditors to prioritize activities in the internal audit universe, which consists of the entire range of auditable activities relevant to the organization and that the internal audit function must provide assurance on.

Testing controls merely because they are there or because auditors have always tested them is outdated and represents a controls-based approach to auditing. A risk-based approach is more effective, economical, aligns better with business needs, and allows internal auditors to prioritize their work so their limited resources can be used to audit what matters most.

Summary

1. Modern internal auditing is risk-based. Controls are tested to the extent that they mitigate high risks. As such, controls are a means to an end, not an end onto itself.
2. Risks should be tested in descending order; higher risks, and their related controls, first.
3. Compliance auditing may resemble controls-based auditing due to the prescribed nature of these reviews, and are sometimes mandated to use checklists and perform specific audit tests without deviation or consideration of the underlying risks. This practice should be minimized while performing internal audits, and replaced with a risk-based approach that evaluates the underlying risks to the program or process.

Chapter 85

Root-Cause Analysis

Internal auditors are expected to go beyond merely listing issues and symptoms noticed during their reviews, and through research identify the source of the issues noted. The misplaced focus on symptoms leads to the focus on the wrong culprit, and the issuance of vague and ineffective recommendations that come short of truly helping internal audit clients. The result is that problems persist or recur. Root-cause analysis (RCA) is a problem-solving technique to identify the source of defects, and by correcting issues at the source, help organizations, programs, and processes achieve their objectives.

The expectation that internal auditors will perform RCA and get to the heart of the problems identified has been around for decades, yet it remains an elusive goal for many. There are multiple reasons why this occurs.

1. Lack of knowledge of how to perform RCA.
2. A deeply-ingrained poor habit. This habit is often acquired as a result of performing compliance or financial audits over a long time. This occurs because these types of audits typically don't require an in-depth examination of the source of problems since they have a different set of primary objectives when compared to operational reviews. Compliance audits are generally binary in the sense that when performing tests, the result is either "yes" or "no," "pass" or "fail," "it was done" or "it wasn't done." With regards to financial audits, the overarching questions are whether transactions were posted in such a way that financial statement assertions are achieved and there are no material concerns related to the financial reports. How does this affect corrective actions? Since compliance is not negotiable, if "they" didn't do it, they need to do it. And financial audits? There are specific rules regarding the posting of financial transactions, so the dynamics are generally similar to compliance audits—if "they" didn't post the transactions appropriately, they need to do

it. The dynamics surrounding operational audits and consulting engagements are different because the internal auditor must evaluate the manner in which the work is done, determine why issues occur, and what is the best corrective action given the circumstances. As much as the testing is seldom binary, the solution is seldom singular.

3. Limited time. This absence of time available in the budget for RCA is due to an overly-extensive audit program. The problem with overly ambitious work programs is that they don't provide enough flexibility to "do the deep dive" when issues are identified.

It is important to remember that a fundamental goal of every process should be to process error free and on time.

There are three typical causes of issues:

■ Physical causes: Something broke or failed to operate properly
■ Human causes: Someone did the wrong thing, or someone didn't do something
■ Organizational causes: Structures, systems, policies, or processes are faulty

Internal auditors should systematically examine situations, identify the contributing causes, select the best corrective action(s) and present the results convincingly during internal audits and consulting projects.

The following seven steps provide a useful methodology to perform RCA:

1. Define the problem clearly.
2. Collect and analyze data: Gather data related to the program or process, and through the analysis of these data, determine the nature of the anomaly. Over the years I have found the following questions useful when performing this analysis and searching for the source of issues:
    - Is data already in existence or does it have to be collected?
    - Is there evidence proving the existence of a problem?
    - Is it possible to examine 100 percent of the transactions?
    - Are there concentrations, outliers, or patterns (e.g., trends)?
    - How long has the problem existed?
    - What appears to have triggered or caused the problem?
    - What processes are affected, and which systems are involved?
    - Is there an association between the anomaly and certain individuals, vendors, customers, products, services, work shifts, or locations?
3. Identify possible causes. More than noting the manifestation of the problem, the objective is to determine what appears to be causing the problem. Brainstorming possibilities and scenarios is particularly useful at this point to balance the need for patience and urgency. Some useful questions include:
    - What events led to the problem and allowed the problem to occur?
    - Who caused, or is causing, the problem?

4. Identify the root cause(s). This step involves asking, and answering, more than who, what, when, where, and how. The key goal is to determine "why."
   - Why does the causal factor exist?
   - What is the real reason the problem occurred?
   - Use data, if possible, to verify the accuracy of the assessment
   - Work with process owners and operators
   - Consider the people, process, and technology involved

5. Recommend and implement solutions. This step requires creativity to determine what can be done to eliminate the problem. It is very important to take the time to examine alternatives to select the best option. Here, the internal auditor should avoid jumping to conclusions and be careful not to too casually select the first, and easiest solution that comes to mind as it might be insufficient or inadequate given the circumstances involved. Resource constraints and politics often limit the solution to the best relative solution given the circumstances. This also includes taking cost/benefit considerations in mind. The solution should cost less than the cost of the problem; otherwise, it is not worth fixing. Note however, that this cost/benefit assessment should factor in short and long term, tangible and intangible, reputation and moral costs, in addition to the precedent the decision may set as a determinant of future behaviors. Communication and adopting a participatory solution style is highly recommended. I like this approach because it involves the audit client promoting ownership on their part. People usually support what they helped to create. It also helps to build the unit's capacity to search for the solution to their own problems—this could be greatly useful later if other issues emerge; it is best for the unit involved not to wait until the auditor's arrival to begin the search for solutions. Some useful questions follow:
   - What can be done to eliminate the problem?
   - How will the solution be implemented?
   - Who will be responsible for implementation?
   - What are the costs of this solution?
   - What are the risks of this solution?
   - How will performance be monitored to know if the problem recurs?
   - The three outcomes approach is useful too:
   - Resolve it—find an adequate solution
   - Solve it—find the optimal/best solution
   - Dissolve it—find a solution that changes everything, so the problem cannot recur

Some of the tools used for RCA include:

   - Cause and Effect Diagram, Fishbone Diagram, Ishikawa Diagram
   - 5 Whys
   - Is Is-Not

  – Pareto Diagram
  – Scatter Diagram

When performing RCA the internal auditor should link events, consequences, and corrective actions. I have found this conceptual chain very useful because it makes it easier to understand the cause-effect-solution triplet. It also serves as a useful presentation approach when discussing the matter with process owners, operators, and other stakeholders. This helps to define the problem in terms of the business impact and articulating the reason the board and management should take corrective action, thus making for more persuasive arguments.

Summary

1. RCA is an indispensable component of modern internal auditing. It makes the audit process more effective, because problems are corrected at the source so they don't recur.
2. RCA requires extra time and effort, but it is worthwhile because it allows internal auditors to provide a more value-added result than merely tackling symptoms. There are several tools that are useful for RCA.
3. Sometimes internal auditors limit their ability to perform RCA by preparing work programs that are so extensive and ambitious that there is little or no time available to research problems when they occur.

Chapter 86

Rotation Programs

As business processes become more complex, information more widely dispersed, and the risk environment more complicated, the need for internal auditors to adapt to this new environment becomes imperative. To manage this change, internal auditors must continuously educate themselves, and enhance their skills on new technologies and competencies that are required now and in the future. This is the only way to add value to the organization—develop a broad set of skills and diversify the staffing mix by giving internal auditors hands-on experience in different roles within the organization.

Having a highly competent staff is imperative to the internal audit function because as organizations change, and the role of internal auditor evolves, new skills and competencies are required that exceed the traditional accounting-focused skills of the past. Internal auditors need the knowledge that allows them to do work that is better aligned with the review of business objectives and risks, which are increasingly driven by technology, operational change, the use of outsourcing, relentless competition, demands for higher quality, and supply chain expansion. Rotation programs can be very helpful to accelerate the learning process and provide greater opportunities to perform high-quality risk-based audits, while enhancing the career opportunities of internal auditors.

Rotation programs are a career development initiative used to rotate employees' assigned jobs around the organization. Employers practice this technique for many reasons. They are designed to promote flexibility of employees and to keep employees interested into staying with the organization employing them.

There are different types of rotation programs involving internal audit. Some allow non-auditors to rotate in and spend time in the internal audit department, and then return to their regularly assigned, or another job, at the completion of their rotation. Internal auditors may also rotate out to another job assignment for a period of time before returning to their audit role. Another type are one-of exchanges where a non-auditor works with an audit team for one assignment.

Benefits and Challenges

These programs present many benefits. They encourage employee learning and make employees more versatile by gaining a broader understanding of the business. This allows them to be better prepared to be promoted to management or to be placed throughout the company. It also enhances motivation because it reduces boredom while increasing the knowledge about the company, other jobs, and the possibility of promotions. It may also result in candidates who want to join the internal audit department permanently at some later date.

Rotation programs can become a training mechanism for future leaders, whose exposure and work in internal audit exposes them to the concepts, methodologies, and practices of risk management, corporate governance, compliance, and the administrative requirements for effective management.

There are some challenges, however. Having non-auditors perform audits requires having an efficient and effective training program that is sometimes supplemented by coaching and extensive feedback. Although those rotating within internal audit may not have internal audit skills, per se, they often bring extensive business knowledge, are highly motivated, and have high potential, so they serve as subject matter experts (SMEs) in other ways, while bringing in new perspectives to the audit process.

Rotation programs differ from full-blown transfers, as the individual is not considered a permanent member of the department but is expected instead to be only there temporarily. In general, typical rotation programs have assignment durations from 6 months to 3 years.

In some internal audit departments, rotation programs are so ingrained in their staffing structure that there is an expectation for 100 percent turnover within 5–8 years. In other organizations, the rotation "out and into the business" is for all auditors except for a core group of managers who are professional or career auditors and are retained to ensure consistency, continuity, competence, and institutional knowledge.

Some individuals express concern that a rotation program will compromise internal audit independence and objectivity. While this could occur, it can be prevented by following the *Standards*:

> Internal auditors must refrain from assessing specific operations for which they were previously responsible. Objectivity is presumed to be impaired if an internal auditor provides assurance services for an activity for which the internal auditor had responsibility within the previous year. Standard 1130.A1

The internal audit activity may provide assurance services where it had previously performed consulting services, provided the nature of the consulting did not impair objectivity and provided individual objectivity is managed when assigning resources to the engagement. Standard 1130.A3

Internal auditors may provide consulting services relating to operations for which they had previous responsibilities. Standard 1130.C1

If internal auditors have potential impairments to independence or objectivity relating to proposed consulting services, disclosure must be made to the engagement client prior to accepting the engagement. Standard 1130.C2

So as long as the rotating individual observes the 1-year cooling off period, discloses any conflicts of interest, and only serves in a resource and SME capacity where conflicts may jeopardize the quality of the engagement, the rotation program should work with minimal downsides.

Regardless of the methodology used, rotation programs should increase the knowledge of internal auditors while providing opportunities for career advancement.

Summary

1. Rotation programs provide a mechanism to transfer knowledge into and out of internal audit. Business SMEs bring their skills into internal audit, while auditors take their governance, risk, and compliance skills into the business.
2. Rotation programs enhance the career opportunities of internal auditors within the organization.
3. Success depends on having an effective onboarding and training program in place to facilitate the assimilation of new internal auditors.

Chapter 87

Sampling

In statistics, quality assurance, and survey methodology, sampling is the selection of a subset (a sample) of individuals or transactions from within a population to estimate characteristics of the whole population. Two advantages of sampling are that the cost is lower and data collection is faster than measuring the entire population. Because there is rarely enough time or resources to examine everyone or everything in a population, the goal becomes finding a representative sample (or subset) of that population.

Each observation measures one or more properties that are of interest to internal auditors. This may include the accuracy, completeness, review, and approval of each item. In internal audit, sampling is widely used for gathering information about a population, verifying that certain conditions or practices are employed, and the items meet the governing specifications.

Sampling includes several stages:

1. Defining the population of interest: Before the population can be identified, the auditor needs to know what the objective of the engagement or the test procedure is. Objectives vary, and could include finding out why inventory shrinkage is so high, why it is taking so long to collect on Accounts Receivable, why there are errors committed while processing Accounts Payable, or where Fixed Assets are because they appear to be lost. The objective could be to test whether a control is present and functioning, like bank reconciliations or segregation of duties. The objective could be to assess a risk, like a concern that employees on mandatory vacation are still accessing their electronic records remotely, or that someone who was terminated could still be receiving payroll payments.

    What defines a population can consist of various items, like all the payments made during the fiscal year, the payments received from customers

during a 3-month period, or the employees paid through payroll during a 2-year period. It could also consist of physical items, like fixed assets purchased at a location, the inventory in a warehouse or the reconciliation forms for a specific bank account.
2. Specifying a sampling method for selecting items: Sampling methods can be probability or non-probability.

Statistical or probability:

Items have an equal chance of being selected and the characteristics of the sample represent the overall population (are representative). Therefore, the results can be extrapolated (or generalized) to the entire population with a calculated degree of confidence.
- Random: Each item in the population has an equal chance of being selected
- Systematic or interval: Arrange the population items in some order (e.g., numerical, sequential) and then select items at regular intervals (e.g., every *n*th item) from a random start
- Stratified: Organize the population into categories (e.g., geography, month), then sample from each category (i.e., strata)

Non-Probability or non-statistical:

- Convenience: Select items from the population that are convenient, willing, able, and easily available to participate in the study. Examples include attendees at a conference, students at a university, or employees on-site during the review.
- Judgmental: Items are selected because they are believed to be appropriate for the test (e.g., senior managers because they are familiar with the organization's strategic planning process)
3. Determining the sample size: The sample size helps the auditor achieve the attribute of sufficiency and feeling confident that enough items were evaluated to draw a conclusion. The larger the sample size (assuming it was done appropriately), the higher the precision achieved because the sample will approximate the population itself. A sample that is too small may lead to inaccurate results, and one that is too large may waste time and money. Unfortunately, resource limitations often limit internal audit's ability to test large sample sizes.

With statistical sampling, the auditor will generally attempt a 95 percent confidence level. To determine the sample size needed to achieve this confidence level, the auditor will typically use a sampling calculator. This tool can be obtained from many sources on the internet, or from desktop applications like Microsoft Excel, ACL, and IDEA. If the sample is not statistical, or the exact confidence level is not sought, a rule of thumb or convention typically applies. Table 87.1 shows the relationship between the frequency with which

Table 87.1 Sample Sizes

Frequency of Transaction and Control (Population)	Sample Size
Annual (1)	1
Semi-annual (2)	1
Quarterly (4)	2
Monthly (12)	3
Bi-weekly (24)	5
Weekly (52)	5–15
Daily (365)	20–40
Multiple times a day or with every transaction	25–60

Table 87.2 Required Sample Sizes

| Population | Sampling Error | | |
	5%	3%	1%
50	44	48	50
100	79	92	99
200	132	169	196
1,000	278	521	907
5,000	357	894	3,311
10,000	370	982	4,950
50,000	381	1,066	8,195
100,000	383	1,077	8,926

a manual control is performed, and the sample size. Sample size should be determined based on the complexity of the control, the level of competence needed to perform the control, the frequency of operation of the control and the importance of the control.

Table 87.2 shows the required sample sizes based on the population size and the desired accuracy level at 95 percent confidence level.

If the control is automated, internal auditors can perform one test per condition because the computer system will process similar transactions equally. This is often referred to as "a test of one."

4. Implementing the sampling plan: Internal auditors select the corresponding items based on the sampling methodology and size chosen. The actual items might consist of electronic records, hardcopy documents, or other items for review.
5. Testing and documentation: Internal auditors perform the test procedures and document the results.

Summary

1. When sampling, internal auditors should first define the objective of the engagement and the purpose of the test, the population of interest, the type of sample that will best address the purpose of the test and the sample size that will provide enough evidence to rely on the results.
2. Sampling can be statistical (e.g., random, interval or stratified) or non-statistical (e.g., convenience, judgmental).
3. Sample sizes vary based on the population size, the rating of the risk, the number of times the control is performed, and the type of control.

Chapter 88

Sarbanes–Oxley Act

The Sarbanes–Oxley Act of 2002, which is often referred to as SOX or S-OX, is a law passed in the United States in response to the corporate and accounting scandals primarily involving Enron and WorldCom, but also influenced by the problems at Adelphia, Tyco, Qwest Communications, Global Crossing, ImClone, Waste Management, Computer Associates, Xerox, and other companies. These scandals cost investors billions of dollars when the share prices of the companies involved collapsed. Furthermore, it damaged public confidence in the US securities markets, thus creating the need for quick and decisive action.

Although all of the large external audit firms were impacted, Arthur Andersen, which signed off on Enron's and WorldCom's books, was convicted of obstruction of justice related to those scandals. As a result, the firm was prohibited from auditing public companies which put the firm out of business.

The name Sarbanes–Oxley refers to the names of the two congressmen, Senator Paul Sarbanes (D-MD) and Representative Michael Oxley (R-OH), who co-sponsored the act. SOX contains eleven sections covering responsibilities of a public company's board of directors, creates the Public Company Accounting Oversight Board (PCAOB), mandates the review of internal control over financial reporting (ICFR), adds criminal penalties for certain misconduct, and requires the Securities and Exchange Commission (SEC) to create regulations to define how public corporations are to comply with the law.

The PCAOB is subject to oversight by the Securities and Exchange Commission (SEC) and is responsible for establishing related auditing practices, quality control requirements, ethical expectations, and auditor independence standards.

Titles/Contents

1. The PCAOB: This section creates the PCAOB, which registers and provides oversight of public accounting firms, it defines the procedures for financial statement audits, inspects and conducts quality control reviews of external audit firms, investigates and disciplines public accounting firms and their associates, and enforces compliance with the provisions of SOX.

2. Auditor independence: This section establishes standards for external auditor independence to limit conflicts of interest, like forbidding a public accounting firm from providing any audit service to an issuer if the company's CEO, CFO, CAO (Chief Accounting Officer), or controller was previously employed by the auditor and participated in any capacity in the audit of the company during the preceding year. It also addresses new auditor approval requirements, by requiring the preapproval by the company's audit committee. This title also includes provisions for audit partner rotation every 5 years, and auditor reporting requirements to audit committees. It restricts external audit firms from providing certain non-audit services for the same clients. For example, internal audit services, bookkeeping, financial systems design and implementation, legal services unrelated to the audit, management functions, or human resources.

3. Corporate responsibility: Title III mandates the establishment of a mechanism to receive and treat complains, and handle whistleblower allegations. It establishes independence requirements for members of the audit committee. It requires the company's Chief Executive Officer and Chief Financial Officer certify and approve the integrity of their company's financial reports quarterly. It forbids the improper influence on audits and provides a claw-back provision for the forfeiture of CEO and CFO bonuses if there was material noncompliance resulting in a restatement of the financial statements.

4. Enhanced financial disclosures: This title requires an assessment of internal controls for assuring the accuracy of financial reports (i.e., internal controls over financial reporting—ICFR) and related disclosures. It describes reporting requirements for financial transactions, including off-balance-sheet transactions, pro-forma figures, and stock transactions by corporate officers and principal stockholders. It also requires timely reporting of material changes in financial conditions, a code of ethics for senior financial officers, and the presence of a financial expert on the audit committee

5. Analyst conflicts of interest: It includes measures to help restore investor confidence in the reporting done by securities analysts. It defines the codes of conduct for these analysts and requires them to disclosure knowable conflicts of interest.

6. Commission resources and authority: It provides funding for the SEC and presents the SEC's authority to censure or bar securities professionals from practicing. It defines conditions under which a person can be barred from practicing as a broker or dealer, and the qualifications of associated persons.

7. Studies and reports: It instructs the Government Accountability Office (GAO) and the SEC to perform various studies and report their findings related to the effects of the consolidation of public accounting firms, the role of credit rating agencies in the operation of financial markets, violators and their securities violations, enforcement actions, and the role of investment banks in the manipulation of earnings and hiding of the true financial conditions of affected firms leading to the financial breakdowns that occurred.

8. Corporate and criminal fraud accountability: This title describes specific criminal penalties for altering or destroying financial records, debts that are not dischargeable if incurred in violation of securities fraud laws, statute of limitations for securities fraud, review of Federal Sentencing Guidelines for obstruction of justice, and extensive criminal fraud, criminal penalties for defrauding shareholders and protection for employees of publicly traded companies who provide evidence of fraud.

9. White-collar crime penalty enhancements: It increases the criminal penalties for committing or conspiring to commit white-collar crimes, provides penalties for mail and wire fraud, violations of the Employee Retirement Income Security Act of 1974 (ERISA), and declares the failure to certify corporate financial reports a criminal offense.

10. Corporate tax returns: It states that the CEO should sign the company tax return.

11. Corporate fraud accountability: This title declares corporate fraud and records tampering as criminal offenses and provides specific penalties for those offenses. It allows the SEC to temporarily freeze payments (e.g., compensation) that have been deemed "large" or "unusual" if the beneficiary of the payment is a party being investigated. It also provides fines or imprisonment for anyone who retaliates against anyone for providing information relating to the commission or possible commission of a federal offense.*

The Sarbanes–Oxley Act was written primarily for boards of directors, financial managers at publicly traded companies, external auditors, investors, and regulators. Internal auditors play an important but somewhat tangential role in that they assist and support the efforts of these parties making sure that the provisions of the Act are complied with. Additionally, because the intent of the Act is to improve financial reporting, corporate governance, risk management and related controls, internal auditors find that it supports areas of common interest.

The most popular provision of Sarbanes–Oxley involving internal auditors is the work related to Section 404: Management Assessment of Internal Controls. This section states the responsibility of management for establishing and maintaining an adequate internal control structure and procedures for financial reporting; and contain an assessment of the effectiveness of the internal control structure and

---

* For the full text of the Sarbanes Oxley Act of 2002, see www.sec.gov/about/laws/soa2002.pdf.

procedures of the issuer for financial reporting. As such, internal auditors work with the external auditors to identify the risks and test the ICFR.

Although Sarbanes–Oxley was passed in 2002, compliance requirements, especially for Section 404, were staggered so there were large and accelerated filers (i.e., the largest companies trading in the stock exchange), who were required to comply first, followed by midsize and smaller firms. Early on, the requirements to comply with Section 404 were substantial. The act requires public companies to assess the effectiveness of their ICFR. This means documenting the process, identifying and assessing risks, identifying related controls, deciding how to test these controls, and report on the results. Guidance was issued in the form of Auditing Standard No. 2. This process was considered burdensome for large filers so in consideration of the feedback received, the data showing that the costs were excessive, that too many resources were being devoted for compliance rather than other business activities, and the knowledge that smaller filers would need to comply with Section 404 soon, Auditing Standard No. 5 (AS 5) was released. This update in many ways simplified the process by highlighting the importance of focusing on key risks and controls. AS 5 states in regard to deficiencies.

> The auditor must evaluate the severity of each control deficiency that comes to his or her attention to determine whether the deficiencies, individually or in combination, are material weaknesses as of the date of management's assessment. In planning and performing the audit, however, the auditor is not required to search for deficiencies that, individually or in combination, are less severe than a material weakness.[*]

These key controls over financial reporting are those specifically designed to address risks related to financial reporting. They are designed to provide reasonable assurance that the company's financial statements are reliable and prepared in accordance with Generally Acceptable Accounting Practices (GAAP). These controls require the maintenance of detailed and accurate records so financial statements can be prepared reflecting the transactions and dispositions of the assets of the company. Additionally, income and expenses of the company should only be made in accordance with proper authorization, and prevent or detect timely unauthorized purchase, use or disposal of company assets that could have a material effect on the financial statements.

During the early years of SOX implementation, internal auditors in their support role, sometimes devoted 100 percent of their budget to helping their organizations comply with the law. This occurred due to companies' resource and expertise limitations, and the general lack of familiarity with formal internal control frameworks. This situation was also created because many companies had never documented their internal controls and needed to make significant improvements to them during the initial implementation of section 404.

---

[*] See https://pcaobus.org/Standards/Auditing/pages/auditing_standard_5.aspx.

This percentage has been decreasing since then, and now it is common for internal audit departments to devote 30 percent or less of their budget to SOX work. In some organizations it is zero, because a SOX unit has been created with its own budget and staff to test these controls. Because financial reporting occurs quarterly in the form of the 10-Q reports, and annually, in the form of the 10-Ks, testing is done year-round. Additionally, since an objective of SOX 404 testing is to correct any issues found before year end, testing is often concentrated on the first two quarters of the year so that if there are any problems, enough transactions are generated, and re-testing can be performed to demonstrate effective remediation before the 10-Ks are produced.

While corporations have been dealing with the Sarbanes–Oxley Act for more than 15 years, many do not have a well-managed and optimized process in place and still experience significant annual resource requirements to meet the law's provisions. According to Protiviti's 2016 Sarbanes–Oxley Compliance Survey company's internal costs of compliance are over $1 million a year, and for companies with more than $20 billion in revenues, the figure is over $2 million. Many companies reported that the number of hours spent on SOX compliance increased by over 10 percent that year. The 2017 Sarbanes Oxley Compliance Survey found similar results and highlighted the fact that the number of controls has also increased partly because revenue recognition, cyber security, and PCAOB guidance for audit firms has resulted in more work being required by control owners. Nevertheless, SOX continues to be viewed as having a positive effect on companies' ICFR and overall governance.*

Since SOX remains and will continue to be required of publicly traded companies, updating documentation and re-evaluating and testing controls is no simple task, so companies should continuously pursue opportunities to optimize their approach and improve their processes to make them as efficient as possible. The following are some areas for improvement for many filers:

- Improve collaboration among all three lines of defense
- Increase automation throughout the control identification, testing, documentation, and remediation process
- Apply data analytics to test controls

Deficiencies

According to the PCAOB Auditing Standard No. 5,† "the severity of a deficiency depends on whether there is a reasonable possibility that the company's controls

---

* Protiviti's 2016 and 2017 Sarbanes–Oxley Compliance Surveys are available at www.protiviti. com/US-en/insights/sox-compliance-survey.
† For a the full text of the PCAOB Auditing Standard No. 5 visit https://pcaobus.org/Standards/ Auditing/pages/auditing_standard_5.aspx.

will fail to prevent or detect a misstatement of an account balance or disclosure; and the magnitude of the potential misstatement resulting from the deficiency or deficiencies.

The severity of a deficiency does not depend on whether a misstatement actually has occurred but rather on whether there is a reasonable possibility that the company's controls will fail to prevent or detect a misstatement."

There are three types of deficiencies related to Section 404 compliance:

1. Material Weakness (MW). This is a deficiency, or a combination of deficiencies, in internal control over financial reporting, such that there is a reasonable possibility that a material misstatement of the company's annual or interim financial statements will not be prevented or detected on a timely basis.
2. Significant Deficiency (SD): This is a deficiency, or a combination of deficiencies, in internal control over financial reporting that is less severe than an MD, yet important enough to merit attention by those responsible for oversight of the company's financial reporting.
3. Deficiency (D): A deficiency exists when the design or operation of a control does not allow management or employees, in the normal course of performing their assigned functions, to prevent or detect misstatements on a timely basis.

For many new internal auditors, SOX testing is one of the first assignments they get. This is done because SOX testing can be very effective as a training exercise providing what some characterize as teaching them simple blocking and tackling techniques—the fundamental skills necessary to the work as an internal auditor. This hands-on training exposes them to audit terminology and primarily involves sampling, document review, and documentation of test results.

Although the Sarbanes–Oxley Act has been praised by some and blamed by others as being too costly to comply with, and creating an overly burdensome regulatory environment in the financial markets, it improved the public and investors' confidence in the veracity of financial statements.

Summary

1. The Sarbanes Oxley Act of 2002 (SOX) was passed to address the massive financial breakdowns of companies like WorldCom and Enron, that cost investors billions of dollars. It was enacted to restore confidence in the financial markets and the financial statements used to evaluate the financial position of publicly traded companies. It addresses topics related to the role of the board of directors and the audit committee, oversight over public accounting firms, the review of internal controls over financial reporting, the

role of financial analysts, and accountability for criminal offenses, among others.

2. It has eleven titles (or sections), with most of internal auditors' efforts dedicated to supporting the external auditors' work related to Section 404. Issues identified can be rated a Material Weakness, a Significant Deficiency, or a Deficiency.

3. Many internal auditors are assigned testing procedures related to SOX compliance reviews early in their careers because they provide an effective introduction to risk assessment, testing, and documentation.

Chapter 89

Scatter Diagram

Internal auditors can use scatter diagrams to analyze pairs of numerical data and show the relationship between two variables. Other names used are scatter plot and *X–Y* Graph, where one variable is plotted on the horizontal axis, while the other is plotted on the *y*-axis. If the variables are correlated, the points will fall along a line or a curve.

Whereas many auditors examine error rates, delays, merchandise returns, warranty claims and accident rates as individual metrics to determine their magnitude and direction (i.e., flat, increasing, decreasing), there are other analyses that could be of interest too. For example, is there a correlation between the accident rate and the number of hours worked per shift? Does it increase and if so, at what rate? Is there any relationship between the number of merchandise returns or the number of items shipped to the wrong address as the delivery date promised to customers decreases?

Scatter diagrams can help find the answer to these questions. When analyzing the plotted data, the objective is to determine if a correlation exists between two variables. There is a correlation if a change in one value causes a change in another value. The relationship between the two variables has two key elements: Direction and Intensity.

Direction: If the two variables increase with each other, there is a positive correlation between them. If one variable decreases, while the other increases, there is a negative correlation between them.

Intensity: This term relates to the strength of the relationship (i.e., correlation coefficient). The stronger the relationship, the higher the correlation between the two. Correlation coefficients range from +1: Highly Positive Correlation, to −1: Highly Negative Correlation. When examining the plotted data, the closer the data points resemble a straight line, the stronger the linear correlation between them (there could also be a positive or negative non-linear correlation, often in the

Table 89.1 Range of Correlation Coefficients and Their Interpretation

Correlation Coefficient	Meaning
0.0–0.3	Little to no correlation
0.3–0.5	Low correlation
0.5–0.7	Moderate correlation
0.7–0.9	High correlation
0.9–1.0	Very high correlation

shape of a logarithmic curve). If a line is not clearly noticeable, statistical analysis will indicate whether there is reasonable certainty that a relationship exists. If the statistics show that no relationship exists, the pattern could have occurred by random.

Table 89.1 shows the range of correlation coefficients and interpretation.

Correlation analysis using Scatter Diagrams can help identify the root cause of a problem by examining the behavior of two variables. It is important to keep in mind that even if the scatter diagram shows a relationship, and even a very high correlation, auditors should not assume that one variable caused the other: Correlation is different from causation. Two variables could be correlated, but one may not necessarily cause the other. They could be influenced by a third variable, but the information is still useful. For example, the correlation could form the basis for estimating the future values of the variables involved.

Let's consider the relationship between the volume of transactions processed and the number of errors made. Most individuals will agree that as the number of transactions processed increases, the number of errors will, or is very likely, to also increase. This happens because the increased volume causes processors to make data entry and calculation mistakes. While this outcome is expected intuitively, the auditor may want to know how strong the correlation is, and how steep the slope is. In one case there could be only a slight increase in the error rate when the volume increases, while in another the error rate could increase substantially when the volume rises. By using growth projections (e.g., from the organization's strategic plan) and projecting the processing unit's results into the future, the internal auditor could have a very productive discussion with the manager of the processing unit to implement measures designed to prevent, or at least minimize, what would otherwise be an increasing operational problem. Scalability can be a difficult topic to discuss with process owners, but data makes this conversation more objective and productive, and less hypothetical.

In general auditors should think creatively how to use scatter diagrams to discover root causes and support their findings with information about the relationship between multiple variables. This can enable them to provide management with useful forward-looking assistance when making decisions.

Summary

1. Scatter Diagrams show the relationship between two variables, which can be useful to identify patterns among the data.
2. Internal auditors can use Scatter Diagrams to help them find the root cause of problems and the scalability of processes being examined.
3. By understanding the direction and intensity of the correlation between two variables, internal auditors can have more meaningful discussions with process owners about process quality.

Chapter 90

SIPOC Diagrams

An essential step early in the internal audit cycle is gaining familiarity with the process that will be reviewed. Two challenges faced with virtually every audit are the limited knowledge of the stakeholders involved and inadequate understanding of the process itself. Drawing flowcharts with swimming lanes often help ameliorate these issues because these diagrams show the activities performed and the identities of those performing the activities. However, even flowcharts often fail to incorporate other critical components, such as the essential contributors to the process and key supplies for effective product and service delivery.

As internal auditors apply risk-based auditing techniques to their reviews and increase their focus on the needs of customers to achieve organizational aims, it is essential to gain a panoramic understanding of the process. This must be done effectively during the Planning Phase, or the entire review could result in poor outcomes. A SIPOC Diagram can be very helpful in that regard because it identifies the participants, summarizes the process, and lists the inputs and outputs produced. A SIPOC diagram is a tool every internal audit team should consider using to identify the relevant elements of a process before fieldwork begins.

SIPOC is an acronym that stands for suppliers, inputs, process, outputs, and customers. These items form the columns of the matrix and preparing the diagram is very easy. It can be done using flipchart paper, standard notepad paper, directly on a computer using word processing or presentation software, or Post-it notes.

- Suppliers: List the organizations, departments, or individuals that provide the inputs required by the process.
- Inputs: List the objects, materials, or data that enter the process.
- Process: Draw a high-level, four to nine-step, map of the process.
- Outputs: List the outputs the process produces.
- Customers: Identify the customers that will receive the process outputs.

The SIPOC Diagram is particularly useful when defining the scope of the review because it can give internal auditors a high-level overview of the process. All of the elements captured in the SIPOC Diagram are important to understand what the internal auditors are going to review. Failing to do so can result in a poorly-defined scope during planning, or limit the team's ability to understand the process during fieldwork effectively.

SIPOC Diagrams can also help perform a stakeholder analysis, so the key participants in the process are identified. It will help avoid the exasperating situation encountered when deep into the audit cycle someone asks: "Did you talk to so-and-so about this?" Or "Did you know that if X is unavailable, Y performs that task?" The interactions among the stakeholders involved can help define risk exposures, the size of the operation and related audit coverage needed, and customer requirements. Some stakeholders share in the benefits a company creates, while others bear the risks that are generated as a result of the organization's activities. Internal auditors should be aware of both.

The following are some key questions internal auditors should ask before every engagement, and the SIPOC Diagram can help answer them:

■ Who supplies the inputs the process requires?
■ What is supplied and what material or informational inputs enter the process?
■ How critical are these inputs to the effective functioning of the program or process?
■ What does a high-level breakdown (or flowchart) of the process look like?
■ What does the program or process produce?
■ Who are the customers of the process?
■ What are the requirements of the customers?

In addition to these questions, further analysis of each of the components can provide valuable assessment information too. For example, the location of the suppliers can provide some insights into the length of the supply chain, the risk of foreign currency conversion, and political risk. Suppliers and customers may be internal or external to the organization that performs the process, so all of this is vital information that can inform the auditor about the size, spread, and complexity of the network. Inputs and outputs may be materials, services, data, or information, so gaining an understanding about these, can help define the role IT plays during integrated audits.

The SIPOC Diagram is a very simple yet very useful and powerful tool. The time spent preparing it will greatly enhance the value obtained from every internal audit. Good outcomes are the result of effective planning, and SIPOC Diagrams are a great tool to help in that regard.

Summary

1. SIPOC Diagrams can help internal auditors plan their engagements more effectively. They capture the list of Suppliers, Inputs, the Process, Outputs, and Customers.
2. These diagrams are an effective complement to flowcharts, narratives, and stakeholder analysis.
3. SIPIC Diagrams can also help to relate IT elements into the planning, and improve the quality of integrated audits.

Chapter 91

Soft Skills

Internal auditors need strong technical skills to perform their daily work, but results will be limited if they lack soft skills. It is no longer enough to be a functional expert. CAEs recognize this and acknowledge that practitioners with soft skills have a higher probability of overcoming any technical deficiency. Bill Taylor, in his acclaimed Harvard Business Review article *Hire for Attitude, Train for Skill* states that over the years, as he has studied high-impact organizations they have adopted a range of strategies and business models and "they all agree on one core 'people' proposition: They hire for attitude and train for skill. They believe that one of the biggest challenges they face is to fill their ranks with executives and front-line employees whose personal values are in sync with the values that make the organization tick. As a result, they believe that character counts for more than credentials."

Referring to Southwest Airlines, which has embraced this philosophy since its inception, he states "the company evaluates talent based on the proposition that who you are as a person counts for as much as what you know at any point in time—and subjects prospective employees to a barrage of character tests before they join the organization. Over the years, Southwest has elevated to something of a science the practice of identifying its star performers, understanding what makes them tick, and devising interviews, group exercises, and other techniques to probe for those same attributes in new employees."

Knowing the subject at hand is important, but if the individual has a poor attitude, is abrasive, condescending, cuts-off clients mid-sentence, appears uninterested in the client's problems, does not deliver on schedule, or lacks motivation and energy, all of that technical knowledge will be for naught.

So, what are some of the key skills that CAE's want? According to the IIARF's publication *The Top 7 Skills CAEs Want: Building the Right Mix of Talent for Your Organization*, personal skills are in high demand, with specific mention of analytical/critical thinking and communication skills. The remaining five skills are accounting, risk management assurance, information technology, industry-specific knowledge, and data mining and analytics.

The report states that "analytical/critical thinking and communication are personal skills that bring together all the other components of an audit practitioner's competency set. They give the internal auditor the ability to apply technical knowledge and then communicate what has been applied to stakeholders." The CAE at Arab Tunisian Bank states that critical thinking is the most important skill his bank is looking for. "It is important to know how to think and analyze Analytics and critical thinking are harder behavioral skills to learn. Given that, he believes CAEs should consider screening for these personal skills when evaluating candidates at all staff levels—junior to the most senior—in part because today's junior staff will become tomorrow's senior leaders in the internal audit function or the organization."

Written communication skills are especially important because being able to summarize the results of an audit or consulting project is critical for success. Tomáš Pivoňka, the CAE at CEZ, a large electricity company in the Czech Republic stated "Audit summary is an art. If staff have weak writing skills, CAEs spend a great deal of time with draft reports that need additional rewrites and changes before they are presented to the client. Writing skills can be harder to assess and develop than technical skills. They require a different mix of classroom teaching, on-the-job experience, and coaching to improve."

On a broader level, as the profession moves toward an increasingly higher proportion of risk-based auditing and more advisory or consultative work geared toward being a trusted advisor to management, CAEs will need practitioners with greater critical thinking and communications skills. "The need for a 'general' auditor who is just checking for regulatory compliance or working off a checklist will decrease," suggests Tania Stegemann, executive audit manager at CIMIC Group Limited, an international contracting company located in Melbourne, Australia.

Robert Half, in collaboration with the IIA published the paper *Succeeding as a 21st Century Internal Auditor: 7 Attributes of Highly Effective Internal Auditors*, which identifies teamwork, communications, relationship building, diversity and partnering as five of the seven attributes (the other two being: continuous learning and integrity). In the paper, other important attributes include natural inquisitiveness, persuasiveness, change management proficiency, a service orientation, an ability to recognize and respond to diverse thinking styles, learning styles and cultural qualities; and a global mindset. Other important dimensions are:

1. Presenting (public speaking)
2. Developing board committee relations (beyond audit committee) and developing outside contacts/networking
3. Persuasion: Using/mastering new technology and applications
4. Negotiation: Dealing with confrontation

In fact, Larry Harrington, CAE at Raytheon and former global chairman of The IIA stated "Soft skills are the new hard skills" in the article 7 Attributes of Highly Effective Internal Auditors. Soft skills are often harder to teach than to hire for. Therefore, behavioral interviewing, other forms of assessment (e.g., personality traits, communication styles) should be considered as supplements to the existing technical skills training offered. When hiring, internal audit departments should look at diverse academic backgrounds and experiences to find internal auditors who can deliver value, engage in collaborative auditing approaches, and build relationships with audit clients.

David Richards, former CAE of FirstEnergy and former president of The IIA shared during the MIS Leadership Institute that there are ten key attributes of successful internal auditors:

1. Relationship Building: Developing and maintaining win/win relationships and partnerships. This will result in positive image building, deeper knowledge of the organization, gaining support and influence on actions, and greater acceptance while working with organizational management and employees.
2. Team Building: Working co-operatively and productively with others to achieve results. This provides better working relationships, cooperation, greater involvement and commitment, and more innovative recommendations.
3. Communication: Clearly conveying and receiving messages to meet the needs of all. This may involve listening, interpreting, formulating, and delivering verbal, non-verbal, written, and/or electronic messages. Effective communications result in a better understanding of the direction and the type of communication that should be taken when sharing information with others, it clarifies priorities of what to communicate, and ensures the tone is appropriate for the audience.
4. Innovation: Using original and creative thinking to make improvements and/or develop and initiate new approaches. The benefits include enhanced processes, new ideas, and recommendations for improvement, thinking "outside the box," and a willingness to take risk.
5. Leadership: Positively influencing people and events in a leadership role. The results include keeping people informed, promoting team effectiveness, advocating for the group, communicating a compelling vision, and leading strategically.
6. Strategic Thinking: Taking a broad scale, long-term view, assessing options, and implications, structuring plans to lead to improvements. The benefits include a better understanding of organization strategies, aligning actions with the organization's mission and goals, applying a longer-term perspective, articulating a strategy, understanding external impacts on the vision, organizational awareness, more influence with greater impact, self-management, problem-solving, and judgment that is aligned with the organization's direction.

7. Organizational Awareness: Understands the structure and culture of the organization. This will lead to a better understanding of the relation of the unit to overall results, knowledge of who is who in the organization, an ability to identify key business functions, and gain an awareness of the overall organizational culture.

8. Impact and Influence: Persuading, convincing, or influencing. This makes it easier to gain acceptance of internal audit's recommendations, the ability to influence needed changes, find partners to support and bring about needed changes.

9. Self-Management: Reflecting on past experiences to manage and continually improve own performance. The results include recognizing opportunities for improvement, remaining positive and addressing difficulties, taking responsibility, learning from mistakes and successes, and seeking input from others.

10. Problem-Solving and Judgment: The ability to assess options and implications, in order to identify a solution. This leads to being able to break down problems, seeing relationships in processes, seeing multiple relationships (i.e., connection to other relationships and dependencies), and making complex plans or analyses.

Soft skills are vital in today's service economy and team-focused environment. To succeed in this environment, internal auditors, like most professionals, should be agile, adaptable, and creative at solving problems.

Other key soft skills include:

1. Strong Work Ethic: Being motivated and dedicated to getting the job done. Also being conscientious and doing the best work possible.

2. Problem-Solving Skills: Being resourceful and creative when solving problems. Taking ownership of problems.

3. Positive Attitude: Being optimistic and upbeat.

4. Flexibility/Adaptability: Being able to adapt to new situations and challenges, embracing change, and being open to new ideas.

5. Good Communication Skills: Being verbally articulate and a good listener. Being able to make your case while building bridges with colleagues and customers.

6. Time Management Abilities: Being able to prioritize tasks and work on different projects simultaneously. Using time wisely.

7. Acting as a Team Player: Working effectively in teams. Being cooperative and taking a leadership role when appropriate.

8. Self-Confidence: Believing in one's abilities to get the job done. Projecting a sense of calm while inspiring others. Having the courage to ask questions and contributing ideas.

9. Accept and Learn from Criticism: Being able to handle criticism, being coachable, and open to learning while growing as a professional.
10. Working Well Under Pressure: Being able to handle stress and work effectively when working under pressure due to deadlines or crises.

Summary

1. Soft skills are vital for success in today's service-oriented economy and enhance the value of technical skills.
2. Internal audit recruiters and practitioners are increasingly searching for individuals with the personality, resourcefulness, team player, and communication skills that help build bridges with audit clients.
3. Soft skills become increasingly important in the career advancement of internal auditors as they move from individual contributors to managers and leaders.

Chapter 92

Standards

The International Standards for the Professional Practice of Internal Auditing (*Standards*) provide a framework for performing internal audits. The *Standards* are mandatory and consist of requirements for the professional practice of internal auditing and for evaluating the effectiveness of its performance. The requirements are internationally applicable at the organizational and individual levels.

The mandatory elements of the IPPF are as follows:

- Core Principles for the Professional Practice of Internal Auditing
- Definition of Internal Auditing
- Code of Ethics
- International Standards for the Professional Practice of Internal Auditing

The Core Principles

The Core Principles set forth the guidelines to determine if an internal audit function is effective. For an internal audit function to be considered effective, all Principles should be present and operating effectively. Internal auditors can demonstrate achievement of the Core Principles differently from organization to organization, due to the diversity of sizes, industries, resources and priorities of internal audit functions. However, failure to achieve any of the Core Principles implies that an internal audit activity was not as effective as it could be in achieving its mission. According to the Institute of Internal Auditors (IIA's) Core Principles*, internal auditors must:

---

* The IIA Core Principles are available at https://na.theiia.org/standards-guidance/mandatory-guidance/Pages/Core-Principles-for-the-Professional-Practice-of-Internal-Auditing.aspx.

- Demonstrate integrity.
- Demonstrate competence and due professional care.
- Be objective and free from undue influence through independence.
- Align with the strategies, objectives, and risks of the organization.
- Be appropriately positioned and adequately resourced.
- Demonstrate quality and continuous improvement.
- Communicate effectively.
- Provide risk-based assurance.
- Be insightful, proactive, and future-focused.
- Promote organizational improvement.

The Definition of Internal Auditing

The Definition of Internal Auditing states the purpose, nature, and scope of internal auditing. It reads:

> Internal auditing is an independent, objective assurance and consulting activity designed to add value and improve an organization's operations. It helps an organization accomplish its objectives by bringing a systematic, disciplined approach to evaluate and improve the effectiveness of risk management, control, and governance processes.*

The Code of Ethics

The Code of Ethics states the principles and expectations governing the behavior of individuals and organizations that conduct internal auditing. It consists of the minimum requirements for the appropriate behavioral expectations and not specific activities. The purpose of The Code of Ethics is to promote an ethical culture in the profession and it goes beyond the Definition of Internal Auditing to include two essential components:

1. Principles that are relevant to the profession and practice of internal auditing.
2. Rules of Conduct that describe the behavior expected of internal auditors.

Internal auditors are expected to abide by the following principles:

1. Integrity: The integrity of internal auditors creates trust and the basis for relying on their judgment.
2. Objectivity: Internal auditors demonstrate the highest level of professional objectivity in collecting, examining, and communicating the results of their

---

* The Definition of Internal Auditing is available at https://na.theiia.org/standards-guidance/mandatory-guidance/Pages/Definition-of-Internal-Auditing.aspx.

activities and the processes examined. They make a balanced evaluation of all the relevant conditions and are not unduly influenced by their own interests or others when forming their judgments.

3. Confidentiality: Internal auditors respect the importance of information received and do not disclose it without appropriate authority unless they are compelled by a legal or professional obligation to do so.

4. Competency: Internal auditors obtain and apply the knowledge, skills, and experience needed to perform internal audit services.*

The Mission of Internal Audit:

The mission of internal audit is "to enhance and protect organizational value by providing risk-based and objective assurance, advice, and insight."†

Standards & Guidance—International Professional Practices Framework (IPPF)

The International Professional Practices Framework (IPPF) is the framework that organizes the guidance issued by The IIA—the governing body of internal auditors. It includes both mandatory and recommended guidance for all internal auditors. They also include Interpretations, which clarify terms or concepts within the statements and a Glossary of terms. It is necessary to consider both the statements and their interpretations to understand and apply the *Standards* correctly. The *Standards* use terms that have been given specific meanings as noted in the Glossary, which is also part of the *Standards*.

Recommended elements of the IPPF are Implementation Guidance, which assist internal auditors in applying the *Standards*, and Supplemental Guidance, which provide detailed guidance for conducting internal audit activities. Supplemental Guidance include Practice Guides, Global Technology Audit Guides (GTAGs), and Guides to the Assessment of IT Risks (GAIT).

Summary

1. The IIA is the standards-setter for internal auditors, providing guidance on the practice of internal auditing, the Code of Ethics, and other principles, some mandatory, others recommended.

---

* The IIA Code of Ethics is available at https://na.theiia.org/standards-guidance/mandatory-guidance/Pages/Code-of-Ethics.aspx.
† The Mission of Internal Auditing is available at https://na.theiia.org/standards-guidance/Pages/Mission-of-Internal-Audit.aspx.

2. The mission of internal auditors is to enhance and protect organizational value, and provide risk-based assurance, advice, and insight objectively.

3. By acting objectively, independently, with integrity, and applying a sound methodology that helps the organization achieve its objectives, internal auditors will increase their credibility, become trusted advisors, and add value to their clients.

Chapter 93

Testing

This is one of the most common activities internal auditors engage in and is often considered one of the main activities of the Fieldwork phase of internal audits. There are many elements involved in Fieldwork testing: test planning, test performance/execution, analysis, and summary of results, formulating a conclusion, and communicating the results of the testing. However, we can generalize the testing activity as fulfilling a very important purpose: verifying that the controls management believes are in place, are in fact present, and that those controls present are working as intended to mitigate relevant risks. So, testing is done to verify that progress is being made toward the achievement of stated objectives, that risks are not occurring, and controls are working as expected.

Before engaging in any kind of testing, internal auditors are highly encouraged to invest in the preparation of a Risk and Controls Matrix (RCM). This matrix will provide a panoramic view of the business objectives, relevant risks, and controls related to the program or process being reviewed based on the scope of the audit. With this knowledge, internal auditors can develop the necessary tests.

Test of Design

Internal auditors test the design of internal controls to determine whether, if they are operated as required by individuals having the necessary authority and competence to perform the control effectively, they meet the organization's control objectives and can effectively prevent or detect errors or fraud. When done for financial audits, the result of nonperforming controls is that they could result in material misstatements in the financial statements.

Tests of design effectiveness may include a combination of inquiry of appropriate personnel, observation of the organization's operations, and the review of relevant documents. Walkthroughs that include these procedures are generally sufficient and may include a one-transaction test to verify the application of controls in the process under review.

Test of Performance

This involves testing transactions to determine the operating effectiveness of a control. The objective is to determine whether the control is operating as designed and whether the person performing the control has the necessary authority and competence to perform the control effectively.

The test of performance of the controls (i.e., operating effectiveness) include a mix of inquiry of appropriate personnel, observation of operations, inspection of documents, and re-performance of the control. It may also involve a variety of decisions, including the following:

- Can we test 100 percent of the transactions in the population?
- If we can't test 100 percent, what is the best sampling methodology (e.g., Statistical, Nonstatistical, Judgmental) to use?
- If Nonstatistical, what is the sample size?

For many tests, the procedures include verifying:

- The mathematical accuracy of transactions.
- That transactions were posted accurately and timely in the corresponding financial and operational systems.
- That activities were appropriate for their business purpose.
- That configurations (e.g., physical and logical settings), are in place to protect people, and safeguard materials and other assets.

Testing instructions typically include the following:

- Compare: Determine the similarity, or dissimilarity between two or more items.
- Obtain: Get or secure an item for inspection.
- Confirm: Determine the correctness of something.
- Trace: Follow a transaction from the source document to its destination (e.g., the journal or ledger). This procedure is often performed to verify that records are complete. In other words, determine if the transactions at the source are not lost along the way but instead are recorded as required at their destination.
- Vouch: This involves following a transaction backwards from the destination to its source. This procedure is often performed to verify that records exist (i.e., are real) and verify that the events at the source occurred.

- Reconcile: Harmonize accounts or records to make sure they agree and are consistent.
- Observe: Watch conditions or activities carefully.
- Count: Determine the total number of items.
- Tour: Walk within or around to explore conditions. This may also involve verifying the existence and condition of assets and physical facilities.
- Verify: Make sure or demonstrate the accuracy or validity of something.
- Agree: Determine if two or more items are consistent with an established expectation or criteria.
- Recalculate: Calculate again using the same or different data to verify the accuracy of a previous document, fact or figure.
- Foot: Add the numbers in a single column and calculate the sum to verify if that figure is correct.
- Cross-foot: Add the sum of the totals in various columns to verify that it agrees to a grand total. In a spreadsheet or report, this entails making sure the total for all the rows, equals the total for all the columns.

Testing results are usually recorded on check sheets, which capture pertinent information related to the transactions tested. Sufficient information should be recorded in the workpapers so the tester can repeat the work done in the future or another reasonable and qualified individual can 1. Understand what was done and why, and 2. Reproduce the work performed.

When documenting testing activities, internal auditors should remember to document:

- The population and sampling selected and used
- The source of the information used
- The procedures performed
- Enough details (e.g., demographic information) to identify the transactions tested
- The results obtained
- The conclusion based on the results
- The name of the tester and the date(s) when the testing was performed
- The name of the reviewer/approver

IT Testing

In an IT environment, there are several objectives and attributes that are typically included in the review. Some of the goals are to determine if the business application controls (both automated and manual) are satisfactory to provide reasonable assurance that errors in the operation of the application will be prevented, or detected and corrected in a timely manner. Also, to validate that information assets are adequately protected, determine if the application is in compliance with relevant laws, regulations and organization policies, and to validate that the application controls provide assurance over the confidentiality, integrity, and availability of system information.

Completeness

Completeness controls provide reasonable assurance that all transactions are entered into the system, accepted for processing, processed once and only once by the system, and properly included in output. Common completeness controls are batch totals, sequence checking, matching, duplicate checking, reconciliations, control totals, and exception reporting.

Accuracy

Accuracy controls provide reasonable assurance that transactions are properly recorded timely with the correct amounts, and data is processed accurately by applications producing reliable output. Accuracy control techniques include edit checks (e.g., validation, reasonableness checks, dependency checks, existence checks, format checks, mathematical accuracy, range checks), batch totals, and check digit verification.

Validity

Validity controls provide reasonable assurance that all recorded transactions occurred (are real) and were properly approved in accordance with management's authorization. A transaction is valid when it has been authorized and when the master data relating to that transaction is reliable, like the name, bank account, and other details from the vendor master file. Examples of validity controls include transaction authentication, one-for-one checking, and matching.

Since computer systems are being purchased and enhanced continually, internal auditors are tasked with finding out if they satisfy the business needs of the organization's employees and managers, customers, vendors, and other relevant stakeholders. Some key objectives are to determine if the controls are still appropriate to protect assets and provide adequate audit trails, and in terms of system development, verify that change management processes are handled appropriately, that testing is appropriate, and security is satisfactory. In addition, internal auditors need to determine if access to system information is provided only to authorized individuals based on a "need to know" basis.

Summary

1. Testing is one of the most important tasks internal auditors perform, because it consists of verifying that the structures and controls are in place and working effectively.
2. Internal auditors often check the mathematical accuracy of transactions, their timely posting, that activities are appropriate, and that configurations are in place to protect people and assets.
3. Transaction testing typically includes comparing, confirming, tracing, vouching, reconciling, observing, counting, verifying, recalculating, footing, and cross-footing amounts. IT testing often includes verifying the completeness, accuracy, and the validity of transactions, in addition to the protection of assets, effective system development and change management processes, information security, and access controls.

Chapter 94

Three Lines of Defense

The Three Lines of Defense Model provides a framework to clarify the involvement and alignment of multiple assurance providers within organizations. Over the years, it has become increasingly common to have multiple risk and control professionals working side by side to help their organizations manage risk and increase the likelihood of achieving their strategic and operational goals.

Coordination with other assurance units is essential to make sure the organization benefits from the best level of overall assurance. In fact, Standard 2050-Coordination and Reliance states that the head of internal audit should share information, coordinate activities, and consider relying upon the work of other internal and external assurance service providers to ensure proper coverage and minimize duplication of effort.

These assurance providers include risk management, compliance, quality control, fraud investigators, internal and external auditors, inspectors, and regulators. Each group has its own perspective and skillset, but they operate within different areas of the organization, report into different sections of management and are accountable to diverse stakeholders. So, it is not enough to have these units within the corporate umbrella, they must have clear roles, coordinate their duties effectively, and make concerted efforts to minimize overlap and avoid gaps in coverage.

While the model is simple, it has profound implications for helping organizations achieve reasonable assurance over their risk management and compliance functions. Together they support the organization's governance framework and play a pivotal role in it.

The first line of defense consists of management controls. These are the controls embedded in everyday programs and processes, and are typically performed during the normal course of business. These controls are owned and overseen at the program and transaction levels by operational managers.

The second line of defense consists of the various risk, control, and compliance functions set up by management. These are functions that help build and monitor risks and controls at the first line of defense level within the organization. These units report to senior management, but in some cases may also report to the governing body (e.g., board of directors, board of trustees). It includes risk management, corporate and regulatory compliance, quality control, IT and physical security, health and safety, and financial reporting control functions.

While the second line of defense is important for the establishment and operation of effective internal controls, it cannot provide truly independent analysis and assurance to its governing body because it reports directly to management. However, they support and monitor adherence with management policies, so through training and by providing guidance on risk management processes, they alert management to emerging issues, and help to develop effective business practices.

The following list shows the key responsibilities of the Second Line of Defense:

- Support management policies
- Identify current and emerging issues
- Help to develop processes and controls
- Identify shifts in the risk appetite
- Facilitate, guide, and train others on risk management processes
- Monitor the adequacy and effectiveness of internal controls
- Monitor the remediation of identified deficiencies

The third line of defense consists of the internal audit function as an independent and objective assurance provider. The goal of internal audit is to provide assurance regarding the effectiveness of governance, risk management, and internal controls. It also includes the evaluation of the effectiveness of the first and second lines of defense.

The following list shows the key responsibilities of the Third Line of Defense:

- Evaluate the activities that support the achievement of strategic objectives
- Examine the efficiency, effectiveness, and economy of operations
- Verify the safeguarding of assets
- Assess the reliability and integrity of financial and operational reporting processes
- Verify compliance with applicable laws, regulations, and other obligations
- Assess the organization's internal control environment
- Audit important functions, programs, units, processes, and systems of the organization
- Evaluate the effectiveness of the first and second lines of defense

All organizations, regardless of their size, location, industry, or complexity, should have some form of the three lines of defense. While it is best when each line is separate and operates with clearly defined roles, some organizations find it advantageous to combine some of these lines of defense. When this is done, internal audit also performs compliance and risk management activities, for example. In these cases, internal audit should communicate the implications of this action to the board and senior management.

Regulators, external auditors, and other external parties are outside the organization's structure, yet they play an important role supporting the organization's corporate governance, risk management, and control activities. They set requirements and review compliance by the three lines of defense with those requirements through audits and reviews. While they are not considered a line of defense on their own, they act as one, providing assurance to shareholders and other stakeholders. Their work is limited however by the fact that each has a limited oversight scope (Figure 94.1).

The Three Lines of Defense Model is a very useful framework to raise awareness among management and employees, who sometimes misunderstand the roles and responsibilities of the various parties involved. The model shows that everyone in the organization plays a role in terms of managing risks and controls. It includes the governing body because as the highest authority, it has final oversight over the activities of the organization. It is also accountable to the owners or shareholders and in many cases also to its employees. The model also includes senior management, since it has the authority and responsibility of setting structures and expectations, providing needed resources, establishing the scope of work, and overseeing the activities of organizational activities.

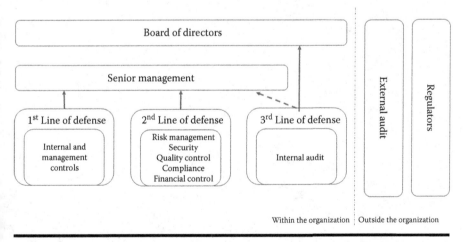

Figure 94.1 The Three Lines of Defense Model. (Adapted from The Three Lines of Defense in Effective Risk Management and Control, IIA Position Paper, January 2013.)

The comprehensive nature of the framework helps employees understand the role they and others related to the organization play, setting and achieving risk management and control objectives.

Summary

1. The first line of defense consists of management controls embedded in everyday programs and processes. The second line of defense is comprised of the various risk, control, and compliance functions set up by management. The third line of defense is internal audit.
2. The Three Lines of Defense Model delineates the responsibilities that various parties have for overseeing the organization's risk, control, and compliance activities, while reporting to the board of directors and senior management. The Model also shows regulators and external auditors as involved in providing assurance to the owners, the board, and management.
3. The Three Lines of Defense Model can be used to raise awareness and encourage collaboration among the various groups overseeing the organization's risk management and control activities.

Chapter 95

Time Management

Internal auditors typically work on projects, which are endeavors with a defined scope or deliverable, a budget and a timeline for completion. As such, internal auditors are often under pressure to finish their assignments by the due date. At the same time, internal auditors like virtually all professionals today are faced with an increasing list of demands on their available time. So, how can internal auditors increase their chances of meeting deadlines?

Time management consists of planning and consciously controlling the amount of time spent on various activities. The goal is to increase efficiency, effectiveness and overall productivity by working smarter so more gets done, in less time, with lower stress levels.

The first step in effective time management is to reframe the thought process away from outputs and toward outcomes. Some people are tremendously busy, but they are not necessarily effective. Dividing one's attention into myriad activities may actually result in achieving less.

The following are some of the actions that will help improve your time management and get more done.

- List and rate the tasks you are working on. They should be rated high, medium, or low based on their importance and urgency.
- Work on the tasks with the highest priority, so prioritize your To Do list.
- After addressing the urgent tasks, work on the important but not urgent ones so they don't become crises later. This allows you to focus on preventative tasks going forward.
- Spend enough time planning and scheduling so you don't find yourself finishing tasks at the last minute, or asking for a deadline extension.
- Determine how much time you spend on each, or at least the majority, of your tasks by preparing a time diary.

- If you are constantly interrupted, try to find quiet time.
- Set goals and check your progress toward them.
- Add some contingency time to your schedule to address unexpected events.
- Confirm your priorities with your manager periodically, especially when new tasks are delegated to you.

Common time management mistakes include the following:

- Not keeping a to-do list: Just being busy is not enough.
- Failing to set goals: Helps you to focus on what is important.
- Not prioritizing tasks: It results in valuable time spent on contradictory tasks.
- Failing to manage distractions: Your time is taken over by others.
- Scheduling ineffectively: Poor sequencing keeps you running in circles.
- Procrastination: Extensive delays keeps you from making progress.
- Taking on more than can be handled: Causes frustration and stress, which rob you of valuable energy.
- Focusing on busy (output) and not enough on outcomes: It is better to work smarter, not necessarily harder.
- Multitasking: Constantly moving from one task to another is often inefficient and requires stopping and starting, which can impact the quality of your work.
- Not taking breaks: You need to renew your energy to maintain work–life balance.

Defining Goals

One of the first requirements to start managing time effectively is to set goals. They define the desired destination, and with that information, you can start to figure out what needs to be done and in what order. The lack of clearly defined goals and a plan to achieve them often results in time spent dealing with confusion and resolving inconsistent priorities.

People often pay little attention to setting goals because it requires time and effort, but they forget that the time and energy spent in the beginning will save time, effort, and energy, and reduce stress and frustration later.

Prioritizing Activities

It is very important to prioritize what must be done. Without setting priorities, someone may work very hard but probably won't achieve the desired results because the time and energy will be spent working on things that are not strategically important (i.e., your goals).

While many people prepare "to-do" lists, these are usually just a list of things lacking any order, priority, sequence, deadline, or reason. The items on to-do lists should be ranked and ideally completed in descending order: Most urgent, then most important. Most people have a tendency to work on the easiest first, but this could be counterproductive if most of the time is spent on urgent but unimportant tasks that leave little or no time for the truly important. Having a deadline with items on the to-do list usually helps to make sure they are appropriately prioritized as well.

Managing Interruptions

The next step is to minimize interruptions. With the constant demand on everyone's time, most people have little time to work without distractions and interruptions on their to-do lists. Most internal auditors must handle meetings, phone calls, information requests, questions from audit clients, making sure the documentation for past, present and future audits is completed, and many more demands on their time.

Some auditors and managers must be available immediately for others, so interruptions are to be expected and part of the job. Try to minimize it, and if possible, schedule time to address questions and time to work without interruptions. It also helps to create a log of interruptions, so the person, date, time, and type of interruptions are visible. Then you can assess whether the interruption was necessary and urgent. This information can be useful to manage others and situations, so they are minimized in the future.

Procrastination

This is a common downfall of many projects, to-do lists, and employees' credibility. The first step is to recognize the problem and then the need to address it. Reminders, personal rewards, working with a trusted partner, limiting the time spent on social media, scheduling time to read and respond to e-mail instead of reading e-mail at all times throughout the day (if possible), and being decisive helps to avoid procrastination.

Some people procrastinate, or can't finish what they start, because they are perfectionists. While we should thrive to do everything with the highest quality possible, the expression "don't let the perfect be the enemy of the good" is also important to keep in mind.

Scheduling

After defining your goals and the corresponding priorities, the next step is to create a schedule to keep you on track and gage progress. Having a schedule can also reduce stress and keep important activities from becoming last-minute crises.

Preparing a schedule involves understanding the dynamics that define how long activities take and how much time you have available to dedicate to the work that needs to be done. This should include time to address interruptions, build in contingency time to deal with the unexpected. A schedule makes it possible to control the time available, and the demands on that time, better, resulting in more control, balance, and less stress.

When preparing a schedule, try to be realistic, allocate time to required tasks, add contingency time, don't take on more than can be handled reasonably, and allocate some time to personal renewal, rest, and hobbies so there is work–life balance. Ignoring time for renewal often leads to burnout, which undercuts any efforts to achieve your goals.*

Summary

1. Time management is an essential skill that helps internal auditors keep their assignments under control, stress to a minimum, and make continuous progress toward the achievement of goals.
2. Internal auditors must strategize their tasks, create a realistic schedule, and work smarter toward the achievement of the things that are the highest priority.
3. Common mistakes include failing to set goals, not keeping a prioritized to-do list, poor scheduling, being interrupted too much, procrastination, too much multitasking and failing to take time off.

---

* Additional suggestions and tools to improve your time management skills are available from Mind Tools, at https://www.mindtools.com/pages/article/newHTE_00.htm.

Chapter 96

Tone at the Top

The Tone at the Top refers to management's leadership, commitment and enforcement of openness, integrity, honesty, fairness, and ethical behavior in the organization. It also refers to the ethical atmosphere that is created, and sustained, by an organization's leaders. It plays a pivotal role in the control environment of the organization and is set and reinforced by all levels of management. From there, it cascades throughout the organization affecting all employees.

This process begins with the definition and institutionalization of the expected behaviors within the organization. Management should clearly communicate its ethics, values, and expectations throughout the area they manage, starting at the top and extending throughout the entire organization. These values and expectations can be communicated formally through codes of conduct, policies, staff meetings, memos, e-mails or informally during their daily activities. These elements play an important role in shaping and building the organizational culture.

Congruence between words and actions is pivotal to ensure consistency and prevent the dilution or distortion of the tone set at the top. Management, at all levels, should lead by example. Similarly, if senior manager's words and actions are similar, it is more likely that employees will hold and practice the same values. The concept of Tone *at* the Top may then be complemented with the concept of Tone *from* the Top.

This process begins when employees are hired and should be part of the onboarding process. In some organizations, onboarding is well-organized, going beyond the signing of a myriad forms, and including sessions covering the organization's history, values, leadership style, expectations for proper conduct, recourse if unacceptable behaviors are witnessed in the organization, avenues for socialization with colleagues, and promotion and career advancement practices.

Another important element related to the tone at the top is the creation and support of mechanisms to train employees. Some industries require mandatory training, such as ethics, sexual harassment, and safety classes. Other topics that support the creation of a strong tone within organizations include team building, conflict resolution, communications, and leadership training. These subjects increase employees' capacity to work effectively in pursuit of the organization's mission, vision, and values.

- Teamwork: It enhances the bond among employees, who will be better equipped to support each other, promote positive peer pressure, treat each other with mutual respect, and acquire a sense of belonging.
- Conflict Resolution: This training prepares employees to handle incidents responsibly and in accordance with expectations.
- Critical Thinking and Problem Solving: While these programs typically focus on ways to think in a disciplined way, analyze problems, foster creativity, and implement innovative ideas in a practical way, what is sometimes overlooked is that this type of training also promotes transparency, fact-based decision-making, planning, and accountability. All of these attributes are essential for a healthy organizational culture.
- Communication: Effective verbal and written communications are essential to promote better relationships and reduce barriers among employees, and with vendors, suppliers, and other stakeholders. This will help reduce confusion, misunderstandings, and other operational issues.
- Leadership and Management: Organizations perpetuate the existing culture, or transform it if necessary, through the actions of their leaders. Leadership training helps organizations identify, develop, and place capable leaders in positions where they can influence their organizations positively. Developing leadership capacity is essential for the organization's cultural sustainability and the protection of the proper tone and culture.

Organizations should provide employees who witness unethical behaviors a mechanism to report such behavior. This typically includes an ethics or whistleblowing hotline. Management should explain to employees that they have an obligation to report unethical behavior and should reassure them so they feel safe from retaliation while doing so.

The tone set within an organization will have a cascading effect on its employees. If the tone promotes ethics, integrity, and fair treatment of others, employees will be more likely to support and replicate these same values. However, if the organization's leaders do not appear interested in ethics, focusing exclusively on revenues, profits and market share (i.e., the bottom line), employees will be more likely to commit fraud because they will assume that ethical conduct is not a priority within the organization. Employees follow their leaders, so if these leaders pay scant attention to, discuss, measure, promote, or support ethical conduct, employees won't either.

Given the number of financial shenanigans who have destroyed organizations, wiped out stockholder investments and squandered taxpayer resources, it is essential that leaders send the message that success is measured as much by what is achieved as by how it is achieved. In the extreme cases, management's focus, rewards and lack of disciplinary measures could result in fraud being seen as acceptable as long as it makes the organization profitable.

Summary

1. Tone at the Top describes the behavioral, performance, and ethical expectations set at the highest levels of the organization. The board and senior management set the tone at the top of the organization.
2. The term Tone *from* the Top is important and while the difference appears to be subtle, it is significant because it implies that the tone set at the tone cascades downward throughout the entire organization without dilution, distortion, or gaps. In some organizations the messages and example set at the tone are not replicated equally throughout the enterprise.
3. Internal auditors are often tasked with reviewing the Tone at the Top in their organizations, because it impacts many aspects of the control environment and the performance of internal controls.

Chapter 97

Training and Development

Internal Auditors operate in an increasingly complex and challenging environment. Business dynamics are changing constantly impacting the regulatory, IT, operational, and financial environments. If in the past auditors could go into auto-pilot mode after getting their credentials that is certainly not the case anymore. They must keep up to date with the changes affecting their companies, industries, and in many cases the entire economy, so they understand what the performance standards are, and they can look for current and emerging risks, and make useful recommendations. Internal auditors must keep up to date so they can review what matters most to their clients.

A well-developed training and development program is essential for internal auditors to keep up. It should include a combination of technical and soft skills, but also include topics that are relevant to their industry as well as the practices of their organizations. In many ways, the technical and soft skills will address the general knowledge, skills, and competencies internal auditors should possess to be competent in their role and show proficiency and due professional care. These are the things that all auditors should know based on their title and role in the function.

For staff auditors the focus might be on interviewing, testing, and documentation techniques. Senior auditors, who are starting to act in an in-charge capacity, need to add client communications, time management, and report writing techniques. When entering management ranks, internal auditors need to strengthen their client relationship, project management, risk assessment and management, budgeting, and staff selection skills. Directors find that leadership, strategic planning, multi-year annual plan development, and partnership management skills are key. This doesn't mean that each of the items mentioned above fit neatly into each job title/role, because leadership skills, for example, can be developed starting at the staff level.

The development of these core skills and competencies are then applied in specific industries and organizations, so the need for industry-specific training becomes apparent. There is a context to the place and manner that internal auditing is performed. All auditors should know about inventory management, how physical and cycle counts are performed and some of the common failure points related to ordering, receiving, warehousing, retrieving materials for use, and disposing unneeded ones as excess-and-obsolete (E&O). But this training, and the nuances about it, are not as pressing to auditors in the insurance industry as they are for those working in the manufacturing or retail sectors.

Essential Skills

The Global Internal Audit Common Body of Knowledge (CBOK) report indicates that the 7 skills CAEs want are as follows:

Personal Skills:
1. Analytical/critical thinking
2. Communication

Technical Skills
3. Accounting
4. Risk management assurance
5. Information technology (general)
6. Industry-specific knowledge
7. Data mining and analytics

Other skills mentioned include:

- Business acumen
- Fraud auditing
- Finance
- Forensics and investigations
- Cybersecurity and privacy
- Legal knowledge
- Quality controls (e.g., Six Sigma, ISO)

Successful internal auditors act in dual capacities: one as an internal auditor and the other as a partner to the organization, looking at the business and its programs, processes, and activities searching for opportunities to improve operating practices. So, when doing their work, internal auditors need to critically examine what the organization wants to accomplish. This could mean, using their critical thinking skills to challenge policies and practices not supporting business objectives. This also means doing more than merely checking off items from their checklists while testing controls for compliance. Internal auditors need to address issues, find viable solutions, and communicate clearly and persuasively.

360-Degree Program

In addition to the feedback from customers and the team leader, internal audit departments should consider implementing a 360-degree review process. These provide a holistic and comprehensive review mechanism by gathering feedback from an employee's manager, peers, and direct reports. Sometimes external consultants or vendors (e.g., co-source providers) who work regularly with the employee are included too.

By increasing the number of participants in the review process, a better understanding of the person's strengths and weaknesses can be gained. It provides a rounded view, especially since many internal auditors work on projects away from the daily eyesight of the immediate manager. In some organizations auditors don't work exclusively with one manager; instead, they work for multiple managers as they are assigned to different projects, so one manager would not have a full appreciation for the person's performance over the entire review period.

The following are some essential elements to make the 360-degree review process work well:

1. The culture must be conducive to it. Many organizations enjoy subpar results and eventually discontinue the program because they lack a work environment of fair, objective, and honest feedback. When this happens, the 360-degree review process is tainted by retaliation or the fear of it. In some cases, employees are afraid to provide honest feedback about their managers or use the process to damage the reputation of others. Any of these cultural defects will derail the program.
2. It must be forward-looking. Like all performance evaluation programs, it should look to the past sufficiently to get an understanding of past performance, but it must also focus on how skills and competencies can be enhanced. By having a development component that addresses future needs and performance, the program will be more effective and valuable to the employee whose performance is being reviewed.
3. It should be comprehensive. The review should not be limited to technical skills, but should also include leadership, communication, teamwork, decision-making, problem-resolution, time management, effectiveness, and collaboration.

A 360-degree employee assessment is useful to the department, managers, and staff. Managers benefit from getting feedback from a variety of sources, which helps them improve and provides valuable input, so they can also support their staff. The staff benefits because they are eager to do a better job, advance in their careers, and want feedback to do this. The department benefits because 360s promote a culture of getting and receiving feedback, and continuously improving how the work gets done. This will result in a stronger and more engaged internal audit unit.

Summary

1. Internal auditors should acquire a variety of technical and soft skills to maximize their contribution to their clients and their career advancement opportunities. Technical skill subjects that internal auditors should train on include accounting, risk management, IT, cybersecurity, fraud auditing, data mining, and analytics. Soft skills training subjects include critical thinking and communication.
2. In general, as internal auditors move up in their careers, the balance tends to shift from technical skills to soft skills.
3. 360-degree programs are an effective mechanism to provide performance feedback and highlight training and development needs. For these programs to be effective, the organizational culture must support honest feedback without the fear of retaliation, they must be forward-looking and comprehensive.

Chapter 98

Trusted Advisors

Too many internal auditors have the unfortunate distinction of being called the corporate cops. What's worst, this moniker extends to all auditors in the minds of some business managers and employees. Being called the corporate cop is neither glamourous nor desirable. In fact, the internal auditing profession has been trying to change this image for years and has provided an alternative image, which for many is also a goal: To become trusted advisors. But what is a trusted advisor? What does a trusted advisor do? What behaviors are necessary to become a trusted advisor?

A trusted advisor is the person a client turns to when an issue arises, often when there is urgency like in times of crisis or change. But often this will also extend to times when an important decision has to be made and the decision-maker needs someone with the knowledge, track record, reputation, level-headedness, creditability, and dependability to provide good, honest advice. This is the characteristic of a deep and trusting relationship.

But getting to this point, to be recognized as a trusted advisor, doesn't happen overnight. Relationships mature and in their early stages they are characterized by the internal auditor being able to perform a needed task or act as a subject matter expert. Being able to perform compliance or financial reviews with competence and speed are examples of this.

Over time, audit clients notice that the auditor has capabilities not directly related to the original area of expertise but can also solve and provide valuable insights related to more general business issues. An example might include auditors being able to address topics related to IT concepts, systems development, project management, and process efficiencies.

The next level in this maturity progression is when internal auditors might be consulted on broader strategy issues. The internal auditor is more than a technically proficient problem-solving professional but is also able to put issues in

Characteristics of relationship levels				
	Focus is on:	Energy spent on:	Client receives:	Indicators of success:
Service-based	Answers, expertise, input	Explaining	Information	Timely, high quality
Needs-based	Business problem	Problem-Solving	Solutions	Problems resolved
Relationship-based	Client organization	Providing insights	Ideas	Repeat business
Trust-based	Client as individual	Understanding the client	Safe haven for hard issues	Varied (e.g. creative pricing)

(Left margin labels: "Auditors act like technicians" spanning Service-based and Needs-based rows; "Auditors act like advisors" spanning Relationship-based and Trust-based rows.)

Figure 98.1   Types of relationships. (Adapted from *The Trusted Advisor* by David Maister.)

organizational context and can provide perspective to them. The internal auditor can also offer advice proactively so that more than auditing projects after they have begun, they can recommend best practices so they meet expectations and deliver on time, within budget and with high quality.

When internal auditors are trusted advisors, they provide a safe harbor for the board and management to discuss and explore. This attribute involves the integration of content expertise, organizational awareness and strong interpersonal skills. At this point, internal auditors are a sounding board before decisions are being made to gain the auditors' perspective on complex topics, opinions on emerging threats, and the precedent that decisions might have among the multiple stakeholders the organization is accountable to (Figure 98.1).

How to Become a Trusted Advisor

The process of becoming a trusted advisor takes time and consistency. Some of the actions that helps deepen the relationship are as follows:

Be positive and show interest. Some internal auditors have promoted an image of being the "no" people. Management and employees, and even some board members may become familiar with the internal auditor objecting too often, too readily, and without evidence, to business initiatives, goals, and objectives. Internal auditors must show they are interested and on-board with the organization's goal to add value to its stakeholders, take appropriate and well-thought out risks, and promote change where change is needed, not just perpetuating the status quo.

Follow through. A quick way to lose credibility is to promise, or over-promise, and under-deliver. If you want to become a trusted advisor, don't make promises you can't keep. Trusted advisors say what they mean and mean what they say: Trusted advisors "give it to their clients straight" and avoid being unnecessarily vague.

Keep in touch with the client via e-mail, by phone, and in person. Trusted advisors keep in touch to show their genuine interest in the client. A problem I have heard many people share with me is that they only hear from the auditor when the auditor needs something, or the communication is about an ongoing or future audit. An increasingly common practice in many internal audit departments is for managers to be given relationship-building responsibilities with key management contacts. This requires meeting with the client once a quarter or every six months to "check in." During these meetings, the agenda consists of discussing dynamics in their unit, upcoming changes and initiatives, concerns, and other matters that the internal auditors can assist with from a risk and controls perspective.

Give them something. More than keeping in touch to say hello, trusted advisors also give freely. They share information, updates, news, and other developments that they believe the client might be interested in and might find useful. The typical auditor–client relationship is characterized by a series of requests from the auditor (e.g., for documents, data, meetings), who then sends a report showing all the mistakes found and requesting, once again, the client to agree to the report and provide corrective actions. If requests are all the client gets, the relationship is lopsided.

Be respectful. Trusted advisors impress their clients with their knowledge without embarrassing them over what they should, but don't know. Most managers and employees are proud of their jobs and don't appreciate someone going into their office and shaming them.

Ask mindful questions, mindfully. Trusted advisors ask Probing (open-ended), Clarifying (double-check), Process (relevant to the program or process' mission and objectives) and Empathetic (show they care), questions. They also apply the 80/20 Rule: They ask good questions using 20 percent of the time, and allow the client to describe, explain, elaborate using 80 percent of the time. We learn when we listen.

Be helpful. Internal auditors' future is linked with the organization's future. A key aspect of effective internal auditing is understanding the mission, vision, objectives (strategic, operational and otherwise), the risks that get in the way of achieving these objectives, and assessing and recommending controls and other mechanisms that prevent risks from derailing the organization's success. So, the goal is to be helpful and support those efforts. Empty preferences (criteria), out-of-context findings (condition), unresearched causes of problems (cause), unquantifiable issues (effects) and unrealistic corrective actions (recommendations) are seldom helpful. Just saying that you are right because you can show that something is broken is not necessarily helpful.

Explain and help them understand. Finding anomalies is a good start, but it is important to show the client the relevance of the issue, how it was discovered, its implications, how big an issue it is, how long it has been occurring, what is causing it, and some thoughts on how it might be fixed. By explaining the who, what, when, where, and why of issues, clients will understand better why control breakdowns and other vulnerabilities matter to them.

Be understanding. Trusted advisors try to understand their client's situation and the context of the situation they are dealing with. They also realize that by being empathetic and understanding how the client feels about their challenges they can connect emotionally and support the relationship.

Summary

1. Internal auditors should work diligently to reframe the image away from the corporate cop and toward being a trusted advisor. This change takes time, consistency, and depth.
2. Trusted advisors go beyond listing issues and problems. They are fair, listen carefully, and provide useful, appropriate, timely, and relevant suggestions for improvement.
3. Becoming a trusted advisor requires building a strong relationship, characterized by honesty, good communications, understanding of business dynamics and challenges, and a common purpose: create and preserve stakeholder value.

Chapter 99

Whistleblowing Programs

Whistleblowing is defined as the act of revealing inappropriate activities to parties within or outside the organization with the purpose of alerting individuals who are able to take corrective action. It is preferable for whistleblowing to occur within the organization so management can remediate the issue without the negative effects caused by public disclosure, such as financial distress, reputation damage, and a drop in the organization's stock value due to negative publicity. Whistleblowing programs should provide a mechanism for individuals, employees, contractors, and others, to discreetly and anonymously, if they so choose, disclose their concerns without the fear of reprisals. This makes it possible for anyone to help the organization stay on track.

It is important for organizations to implement whistleblowing programs and make sure they are credible and effective. It is also a good practice for organizations to make this mechanism known to individuals inside and outside the organization (e.g., customers, suppliers) in the event these parties know of inappropriate actions. Advertising can include business cards, posters in common areas, mention in the company's newsletter, a post and link on the company's intranet and Internet, a note in company contracts and purchase orders, and reminders during staff meetings and during the annual Code of Ethics and Conflict of Interest recertification processes.

The Sarbanes–Oxley Act of 2002 Section 301.4 states that "each audit committee shall establish procedures for A. The receipt, retention, and treatment of complaints received by the issuer regarding accounting, internal accounting controls, or auditing matters; and B. The confidential, anonymous submission by employees of the issuer of concerns regarding questionable accounting or auditing matters." To provide protection for whistleblowers, Section 806 states that "no company, officer, employee, contractor, subcontractor or agent of such company may discharge, demote, suspend, threaten, harass, or in any other manner discriminate against an employee in terms of conditions of employment because the individual provided information or assisted in an investigation regarding any conduct reasonably believed to be violation of SEC regulations.* Other protections exist for whistleblowers like the Whistleblower Protection Act of 2017† and the targeted Department of Veterans Affairs Accountability and Whistleblower Protection Act of 2017".‡ Organizations are encouraged to institute their own administrative whistleblowing and protection policy as well.

The purpose of the policy is to encourage all employees to disclose any questionable accounting, internal controls, health and safety, or fraudulent activities that may adversely impact the organization, its customers, shareholders, employees, investors, or the public at large. A key factor defining the potential success of the program is to minimize the fear of retaliation. If employees fear they will suffer retaliation, harassment, alienation, intimidation, discrimination, job loss, stress, or emotional hardship, they will not be honest about issues and avoid calling the ethics hotline to report problems within the organization.

The policy should set procedures for employees, contractors, and other interested parties to report their concerns on a confidential and anonymous basis. It should also delineate an investigative process for handling all allegations, including an escalation protocol in case the situation requires emergency provisions. The policy should also state that frivolous or malicious allegations are not permitted to prevent cruel or spiteful acts.

Outsourcing the Whistleblowing Program

While some organizations handle whistleblower hotlines internally, outsourcing the program to an organization that specializes in these hotlines is highly recommended. Due to the prevalence of these programs, and advances in telecommunication mechanisms, it is possible to find vendors who can provide around-the-clock coverage in multiple languages, using case management portals at a reasonable cost. Pricing schemes exist based on a per-incident or flat fee that make these programs affordable to small and large organizations alike.

Having an outside provider handle the whistleblower hotline also provides an additional level of anonymity that whistleblowers may appreciate. With a third-party provider, there is less worry that the responder may recognize the caller's voice or have other connections or interests in the organization.

---

* To read the full text of Sarbanes–Oxley Act of 2002, Section 806 providing protection for whistleblowers, see www.sarbanes-oxley-act.biz/SarbanesOxleySection806.htm.
† For the full text of Dr. Chris Kirkpatrick Whistleblower Protection Act see www.congress.gov/bill/115th-congress/senate-bill/585/text.
‡ For more details regarding the Department of Veterans Affairs Accountability and Whistleblower Protection Act of 2017 see www.congress.gov/bill/115th-congress/senate-bill/1094.

Auditing Whistleblowing Programs

Like any important program, process or control, whistleblowing hotlines should be audited. The following are key steps that should be considered when auditing these programs:

1. Review the program's protocol to make sure it provides clear and specific guidance on what to do and whom to contact in response to a variety of scenarios. The protocol should also include escalation provisions to address emergency situations.

2. Examine allegation files to verify that information is collected consistently and as fully as possible, so investigations are not impaired. Auditors should also verify that the whistleblowers' identities were protected and that a key, code or case number, rather than the whistleblowers' names were used during the investigation and reporting.

3. Review the composition of the oversight board, if there is one, and the investigative team, to make sure it is multi-functional. Key members should include senior officers from the legal, accounting/finance, human resources, and internal audit units. The oversight board and response team should meet frequently and be prepared to take quick and decisive action in the event of questionable activities.

4. Verify the autonomy of the program to make sure the program is independent. By having a direct reporting line to the board, and having the board oversee the whistleblowing program, a single individual should not be able to reduce the budget or impair investigations through direct means or the threat of cutbacks. This type of interference would impair the program's effectiveness, independence, and objectivity. Additionally, there should be a direct reporting line to the audit committee, or other high-level oversight function.

5. Review performance reports to make sure these are accurate, useful, produced timely, and shared narrowly. The oversight board (or audit committee) should agree on the content and frequency of reports, which should include at a minimum the number of allegations received, the number of substantiated allegations, a ranking of the impact of these allegations to the organization, and turnaround times from notification to investigation, and from investigation to resolution.

6. Review the program's budget to make sure investigations can be handled promptly by qualified individuals. Funding should be enough to hire competent staff to handle whistleblowers' communications and to conduct professional investigations.

7. Review the employee manual and code of ethics (or code of conduct) to make sure the whistleblower program is referenced in these policy documents. This will add to the program's legitimacy and make it a permanent component of the organization's corporate governance infrastructure. It should be clear that retaliation is forbidden.

8. Verify access to the program by making sure the phone and fax numbers, e-mail address, and website links are correct, operational 24 h a day and 7 days a week and staffed by qualified individuals.

9. Confirm the qualifications of the case management staff so it is not treated as a simple data entry job. Staffers doing intake should have the ability to handle stressful situations, communicate with whistleblowers professionally, be discreet and in general have superior customer service skills to collect sufficient and actionable information whenever possible so fair and thorough investigations can be conducted. The investigative team should be highly qualified, cross functional in their backgrounds, and have high integrity.

10. Survey employees to obtain their opinions about the program. The organization's culture resides in the perceptions and opinions of employees, not in the words, or documents management issues. The objective of surveys is to determine if employees are aware of the program, believe in its usefulness, feel safe from retaliation, and believe that the organization is committed to integrity, transparency, fairness, and compliance. If employees are unaware of the program's existence, doubt that reporting anomalies will result in corrective action, or fear retaliation, the effectiveness of the whistleblowing program would be in doubt.

There are many questions that can be asked in the ethics survey. The following are some examples:

a. Management demonstrates the importance of integrity and ethical behavior to employees

b. Management sometimes overrides policies, procedures, workplace rules or otherwise takes shortcuts that are contrary to the organization's policy

c. I know where to find the Code of Ethics and Business Conduct Guide.

d. I know who to contact if I have questions about the Code of Ethics and Business Conduct Guide.

e. I am familiar with the Ethics Hotline and other options to report potential ethical issues.

f. If I suspected someone was violating the Code of Ethics I would contact the Ethics Hotline or one of the other options to report the suspected violation.

g. If I reported a possible violation, I believe it would be investigated and resolved appropriately.

h. If I reported a possible violation, I would not fear retaliation.

i. I never feel pressured by co-workers or managers to compromise ethical standards.*

---

* For additional examples of questions that can be asked while conducting a survey of ethics or the ethics hotline, see *Best Practices: Evaluating the Corporate Culture* by James Roth, IIA Research Foundation, 2010, and *Internal Auditing: Assurance & Consulting Services* by Kurt Reding, et al., 2015.

Table 99.1   Eleven Key Steps for Auditing the Whistleblowing Hotline

1. Review the protocol
2. Examine allegation files
3. Review the composition of the oversight board
4. Verify the autonomy of the program
5. Review performance reviews
6. Review the program's budget
7. Review policy documents
8. Verify access
9. Confirm qualifications of staff
10. Survey employees
11. Verify advertising

11. Verify advertising of the program is in place in high-traffic areas (e.g., online on the company's Internet site, break rooms). Details about the program can also be advertised using business cards, magnets, mouse pads, mugs, key chains, and the company's newsletter.

Employee's opinions are essential to the success of whistleblower programs, because if employees are unaware of it, or refuse to use it, the program is a failure (Table 99.1).*

Summary

1. For the whistleblowing program to be effective, employees must know about it, believe that it is an effective mechanism to alert someone who can act to correct what is perceived as a problem within the organization, and believe that the benefits outweigh the cost of possible retaliation.
2. Internal auditors should audit their organizations' whistleblowing program to make sure it is working effectively.
3. Surveys are an essential procedure to determine if employees believe the whistleblowing program is credible and effective.

---

* For a more detailed description of the implementation and audit of whistleblowing programs see Early Warning System, by Hernan Murdock in *Internal Auditor*, August 2003, p. 57–61.

Chapter 100

Workpapers

Internal auditors must document relevant information related to the planning, fieldwork, reporting, and administration of their engagements. Workpapers are the collection of engagement documents and records supporting the work done. They capture the information obtained, the analyses made, and support the results and conclusions of the engagement. They can consist of client-provided documents (e.g., invoices, purchase orders, reports), auditor-generated documents (e.g., re-calculated figures, narratives, flowcharts, pictures) or items provided by third-parties (e.g., confirmations, statements, reports, receipts).

The exact nature, number, design, and content of workpapers will vary based on the type of engagement the internal auditors work on, but there should be some general characteristics and procedures followed when preparing these documents. The *Standards* indicate that "Internal auditors must develop and document a plan for each engagement, including the engagement's objectives, scope, timing, and resource allocations." (Standard 2200), "Internal auditors must develop and document work programs that achieve the engagement objectives." (Standard 2240), "Work programs must include the procedures for identifying, analyzing, evaluating, and documenting information during the engagement. The work program must be approved prior to its implementation, and any adjustments approved promptly." (Standard 2240.A1), and "Internal auditors must document sufficient, reliable, relevant, and useful information to support the engagement results and conclusions" (Standard 2330). Practice Advisory 2330–1 indicates that audit workpapers generally:

- Aid in the planning, performance, and review of engagements.
- Provide the principal support for engagement results.
- Document whether engagement objectives were achieved.
- Support the accuracy and completeness of the work performed.

- Provide a basis for the internal audit activity's Quality Assurance and Improvement Program (QAIP).
- Facilitate third-party reviews.

Audit workpapers link the agreed scope of work, the audit program, and the audit report. Therefore, internal audit departments should provide specific guidance in their policies and procedures regarding what to use and include, how to document, who should prepare and who should review, when these documents should be prepared, and where they should be stored.

The workpapers from previous years' audits or consulting engagements are helpful during the planning phase because they provide information about the amount of time and effort it took to perform the work for the previous review(s). That way, they help to gauge how much time should be allocated for the current audit. Similarly, fieldwork documents, exit meeting notes and audit reports, show auditors what work was done and how results and conclusions were formulated.

Workpapers are also helpful as a training tool and help in the professional development of auditors. Engagement supervisors are required to review the work done by the audit team and provide review notes that result in clearer, more accurate documents, and to ensure the integrity of audit reports. By using these documents and the related review notes as coaching and training notes, audit supervisors can provide valuable feedback to improve the quality of the work done.

Format

It is best if internal audit departments develop templates for their auditors to use. This would ensure workpapers have a similar look-and-feel and there is consistency in their appearance. The uniformity of appearance will make it easier for subsequent teams to review prior workpapers, to train auditors on how to prepare them, and for reviewers to do so as part of the unit's quality control program. There is no right or wrong format for completing workpapers as long as the evidence is captured fully.

Key Elements

Workpapers should have a consistent format, and while they may be prepared manually or electronically, they can vary in terms of their type, format, length, and contents. Narratives, flowcharts, memos, test grids, meeting notes, audit program steps, pictures, and reports will look differently in terms of their actual contents and appearance, but some key elements should always be present.

- Name of the client.
- The period covered.

- The date when the workpaper was prepared.
- Purpose of the workpaper or procedure.
- Source of the data or information (e.g., system name), or name and title of the individual providing the documentation.
- Scope explaining the type and extent of information used and procedures performed.
- Results based on the outcome of the testing performed. All exceptions should be documented clearly and thoroughly, and referenced to other related workpapers and documents. This referencing should extend to the audit report as well.
- Conclusion reached when judgment is applied to the results obtained. Quite often it is a determination of whether the risk is adequately managed, and the control is working as intended.
- Legends explaining the contents of the workpaper, headings, and testing performed.
- Tickmarks or check marks showing that the requisite operations, tasks or audit steps were completed, and an explanation of the symbols used showing the results. They often indicate if the particular item (in the case of transaction testing) met the criterium it was tested against, did not meet the requirements, was found to not meet the requirement but the condition was not reportable, or the item is not applicable. Some auditors like to use a separate tickmark for each exception. The definition of all tickmarks should be included on each audit workpaper or centrally describing the work done.

Internal audit teams and departments may want to consider developing some standardized sets of tickmarks, providing at least a substantial baseline for their naming, description, and usage. This would facilitate the cross-training and assignment of auditors to different audit teams. Care should be exercised not to create an extremely confusing set of tickmarks that cause confusion, complicate the review process unnecessarily, or could result in reporting errors.

- Authorship and Sign-Off: Each workpaper should indicate the name and title of the preparer and the reviewer, as well as the dates showing the corresponding sign-off as evidence of completion and accountability.
- Reference and cross-reference to supporting or related documents and the audit program.

Characteristics

Workpapers should be neat, easy to read, and easy to review. Complex or unusual terminology should be explained (e.g., in the paragraph where it is mentioned, using parenthesis next to the item, footers, endnotes, or a glossary), acronyms should be explained, and jargon explained. It is often a good idea to explain system names, what systems do, and why they are important to the narrative, flowchart, walkthrough, or finding/observation.

Workpaper preparers must remember that while these documents capture the procedures followed and the results and conclusions reached, they are not written for the writer, they are written for the reader.

Workpapers should be complete, accurate, well-organized, relevant, and concise.

Completeness: Workpapers must "stand on their own," which means that workpapers must be self-explanatory so a reasonable and prudent individual upon review of the workpapers would understand what was done, why it was done, what the results were, who did the work, and who reviewed it. If a workpaper is separated from the file, the reader should be able to determine the purpose, work performed, results obtained, and the justification for the conclusion reached. There should be no need for the reader of workpapers to have to call the preparer or reviewer for clarification. By standing on their own, well-prepared workpapers would ensure reproducibility. Reproducibility means that the analysis described in the workpaper can be duplicated by the same internal auditor or someone else working independently reaching the same results.

Workpapers should also leave no questions unanswered. All open points, incomplete notes or other evidence of unfinished work should be addressed before the audit is completed, and preferably as an ongoing practice while the audit is underway.

Accuracy: Well-developed workpapers contain all needed computations and related information that is accurate and correct. Errors will cast doubt on the procedures performed and the results obtained. To verify accuracy, computations should include tick marks, validation checks (e.g., range and format checks), cross-reference computation data to source documents, and use batch and hash totals to make sure errors are detected and corrected before workpapers are finalized. Auditors should also differentiate factual statements from opinions when applicable.

All information should be technically correct and where necessary cross-referenced to other working papers. If there are soft copies, they should be referenced appropriately so the documentation shows how all files can be accessed.

Organization: Workpapers should be arranged logically using a numbering system for referencing the documentation. In electronic workpaper systems, the workpapers should be saved, uploaded, and linked in their designated location for search, retrieval, and overall organization. Their individual layout should be neat, consistent, and logical too, so an individual unfamiliar with the audit can find needed documents, and understand the purpose and procedures followed for each of them. Cross-referencing should link the risk matrix to the testing procedures, to audit findings, and to the audit report. This way an individual reviewing the audit documentation can trace from the purpose to the results, or vouch from the report to the purpose.

Relevance: The audit objective should determine why audit procedures are performed, and the workpapers should explain how each of them is relevant in meeting the applicable objective. Workpapers are deemed appropriate if they support the achievement of the audit objectives.

Concise: Notes should be concise and unnecessary pages removed because they will limit the efficiency of workpaper reviews. Workpapers should give information clearly and be brief but comprehensive. Ultimately, the quality of the documentation will be compromised if there are extraneous, redundant, unnecessary and overly-verbose elements in audit workpapers.

Required Characteristics of Workpapers

- Completeness
- Accuracy
- Organization
- Relevance
- Conciseness

Additionally, having a consistent appearance will make their preparation and review faster, and reduce administrative time and effort. Establishing standard workpaper templates, styles and expectations will improve the quality of the audit documentation and reflect positively on the professionalism of the unit. Standardizing the methodology is essential to ensure a consistent approach to all audits. This will make it easier for auditors when assigned to different teams under various supervisors, provide a means for easier review and quality control under the QAIP, and make sure that essential information is not overlooked.

Software

Workpapers should be arranged in a way that replicate the typical audit cycle. Table 100.1 provides a general workpaper index.

Table 100.1 Workpaper Index

Section	Typical Contents
Planning	Planning memo, audit memo, budget, schedule, ICQ
Fieldwork	Narratives, flowcharts, walkthroughs, policies, and procedures, rules, regulations, contracts, service-level agreements (SLAs), prior audit report, exit meeting notes, findings templates
Reporting	Draft report, final report, management responses
Administration	Progress/variance reports, evaluations

Another important feature common to most software applications is the ability to prepare risk assessments, assign tasks, track time, capture workpaper notes, and track the creation and resolution of audit findings. By centralizing this information, internal audit management can reduce administrative time substantially.

Summary

1. Workpapers is the term used to describe any document related to an internal audit engagement. It includes risk matrices, flowcharts, narratives, test sheets, invoices, purchase orders, reports, receipts, and pictures.
2. Workpapers should be complete, accurate, well-organized, relevant, concise, and clear.
3. Internal auditors should prepare workpapers that stand on their own, which means they should be self-explanatory.

Conclusion

Successful internal auditors master technical and soft skills. They are familiar with the regulatory, financial reporting, and sector-specific requirements of the organizations they serve, and they also have strong communication and interpersonal skills to work effectively with their colleagues, business partners, senior management, and other stakeholders. They can "think risk" and anticipate outcomes based on their analysis of available evidence, and the application of their experience, sound judgment, and critical thinking skills. They know that deep knowledge is of limited value if it cannot be used for timely and effective decision-making. Effective internal auditors know that information is valuable to the extent that it can enable positive change.

How internal auditors present themselves, and the way they create context around business topics will make a substantial difference in the results achieved. Good ideas presented poorly are likely to be rejected more readily than poor ideas that are presented well. Internal auditors who can't present important information effectively will likely be overlooked.

The delivery of crisp, timely, accurate, clear, and unbiased insights, consistently, is essential to becoming a trusted advisor. By telling clients something they don't know internal auditors build their credibility as knowledge leaders, risk experts, and control specialists. When they also become efficiency and effectiveness authorities, they will enhance their reputation as business partners.

This book covered 100 essential topics to build the credibility needed to become a go-to advisor and a reliable resource within the organization. These Auditor Essentials are a foundation upon which to build your brand as an internal auditor. As you continue your journey, I invite you to keep on learning and honing your skills on these 100 essential concepts, tips, tools, and techniques.

Other Books by the Author

Operational Auditing: Principles and Techniques for a Changing World
Ten Key Techniques to Improve Team Productivity
Using Surveys in Internal Audits

Further Reading

Auditing Standard No. 5. (2007). An audit of internal control over financial reporting that is integrated with an audit of financial statements. Public Company Accounting Oversight Board (PCAOB). November.

Auditing Standard No. 13. (2010). The auditor's responses to the risks of material misstatement. Public Company Accounting Oversight Board (PCAOB). December.

Bluetow, B, and Marks, J. (2010). The other whistleblower. *Internal Auditor.* April 2010 (pp. 25–27).

Bowel, T., and Kemp, G. (2010). *Critical Thinking: A Concise Guide.* Routledge, New York.

Brookfield, S. (2012). *Teaching for Critical Thinking.* Wiley, San Francisco, CA.

Brown, A. S. (2005). The charter: Selling your project. Paper presented at PMI® global congress 2005—North America, Toronto, Ontario, Canada. Project Management Institute, Newtown Square, PA.

Chambers, R., and McDonald, P. 7 attributes of highly effective internal auditors: Succeeding as a 21st century internal auditor. Robert Half and the Institute of Internal Auditors.

Chartered Institute of Internal Auditors (2017). Working papers: Top tips.

COSO (2017). Enterprise risk management: Integrating with strategy and performance—Executive summary. Committee of Sponsoring Organizations of the Treadway Commission. June 2017.

Covey, S. (2004). *Seven Habits of Highly Effective People.* Free Press, New York.

Deloitte. (2018). Continuous monitoring and continuous auditing: From idea to implementation. Retrieved on 1/15/2018 from https://www2.deloitte.com/us/en/pages/audit/articles/continuous-monitoring-continuous-auditing.html.

Durtschi, C., Hillison, W., and Pacini, C. (2004). The effective use of Benford's law to assist in detecting fraud in accounting data. *Journal of Forensic Accounting,* 1524–5586(V), 17–34.

Franzel, J. M. (2013). Auditor objectivity and skepticism. Presentation at the American Accounting Association Annual Meeting. Delivered on August 5, 2013 in Anaheim, CA. Retrieved 2/7/18 from https://pcaobus.org/News/Speech/Documents/08052013_Presentation.pdf.

Goleman, D. (1995). *Emotional Intelligence.* Bantam Books, New York.

Goleman, D. (1998). *Working with Emotional Intelligence.* Bantam Books, New York.

Governance Insights Center. (2017). PwC 2017 annual corporate directors survey. Retrieved from https://www.pwc.com/us/en/governance-insights-center/annual-corporate-directors-survey/assets/pwc-2017-annual-corporate--directors--survey.pdf on February 6, 2018.

Harry, M., and Schoeder, R. (2005). *Six Sigma: The Breakthrough Management Strategy Revolutionizing the World's Top Corporations.* Currency, New York.

Kallet, M. (2014). *Think Smarter: Critical Thinking to Improve Problem-Solving and Decision-Making Skills.* John Wiley, Hoboken, NJ.

Kreitner, R., and Kinicki A. (2004). *Organizational Behavior,* 6th ed. McGraw-Irwin, New York.

Murdock, H. (2016). *Operational Auditing: Principles and Techniques for a Changing World.* CRC Publications, Boca Raton, FL.

Murdock, H. (2011). *Ten Key Techniques to Improve Team Productivity.* IIA Research Foundation, Altamonte Springs, FL.

Murdock, H. (2008). The three dimensions of fraud: Auditors should understand the needs, opportunities, and justifications that lead individuals to commit fraudulent acts. *Internal Auditor*. August (Vol. LXV:IV, pp. 81–83).

Murdock, H. (2009). *Using Surveys in Internal Audits*. IIA Research Foundation, Altamonte Springs, FL.

Nance, J. (2004). *Conquering Deception*. Irvin-Benham, Kansas City, MO.

Roth, J. (2010). *Best Practices: Evaluating the Corporate Culture*. IIA Research Foundation, Altamonte Springs, FL.

The Institute of Internal Auditors. (2004). *The Role of Internal Auditing in Enterprise-wide Risk Management*. The Institute of Internal Auditors, Position Statement. The Institute of Internal Auditors, Altamonte Springs, FL.

The Institute of Internal Auditors (2013). The three lines of defense in effective risk management and control: IIA position paper. January 2013. The Institute of Internal Auditors, Altamonte Springs, FL.

U.S. Government Accountability Office (GAO). (2011) Government auditing standards (yellow book). https://www.gao.gov/assets/590/587281.pdf.

Mahoney, D. (2018). The evolving role of corporate audit committees: Implications of recent SEC actions. The CPA Journal. Retrieved on 2/16/18 from http://archives.cpajournal.com/1999/0899/features/F34899.HTM.

Maister, D. (2000). *The Trusted Advisor*. Simon & Schuster, New York.

Marzano, R., and Kendall, J. (2008). *Designing & Assessing Educational Objectives*. Corwin Press, Thousand Oaks, CA.

Reding, K. (2007). *Internal Auditing: Assurance and Consulting Services*. The IIA Research Foundation, Altamonte Springs, FL.

Rittenberg, L. (2013). *COSO Internal Control—Integrated Framework: Turning Principles into Positive Actin*. The Institute of Internal Auditors Research Foundation (IIARF), Altamonte Springs, FL.

Rose, J. (2015). The top 7 skills CAEs want: Building the right mix of talent for your organization. The Institute of Internal Auditors, Altamonte Springs, FL.

Roth, J. (2010). *Best Practices: Evaluating Corporate Culture*. The IIA Research Foundation, Altamonte Springs, FL.

Taylor, B. (2011). Hire for attitude, train for skill. *Harvard Business Review*. Retrieved from https://hbr.org/2011/02/hire-for-attitude-train-for-sk on 1/31/18.

Index

Printed in the United States
by Baker & Taylor Publisher Services